Essay

ESSENTIALS

WITH READINGS

Essay ESSENTIALS
WITH READINGS

Sarah Norton
CENTENNIAL COLLEGE

Brian Green
NIAGARA COLLEGE

HARCOURT
BRACE
CANADA

Harcourt Brace & Company, Canada

Toronto Montreal Fort Worth New York Orlando
Philadelphia San Diego London Sydney Tokyo

Canadian Cataloguing in Publication Data

Norton, Sarah
  Essay essentials with readings
Includes bibliographical references and index.
ISBN 0–7747–3582–1

1. Report writing.   2. Essays.   I. Green, Brian.   II. Title.
PE1471.N68 1997   808'.042   C97-930294–3

Director of Product Development: Heather McWhinney
Acquisitions Editor: Kelly V. Cochrane
Projects Manager: Liz Radojkovic
Developmental Editor: Su Mei Ku
Director of Publishing Services: Jean Davies
Editorial Manager: Marcel Chiera
Supervising Editor: Semareh Al-Hillal
Production Editor: Louisa Schulz
Production Manager: Sue-Ann Becker
Production Co-ordinator: Sheila Barry
Copy Editor: Riça Night
Cover Design: Sonya V. Thursby/Opus House
Interior Design: Robert Garbutt Productions
Typesetting and Assembly: Carolyn Hutchings
Printing and Binding: Webcom Limited

This book was printed in Canada

3 4 5   01 00 99 98

About the Authors

A native of Vancouver, B.C., Sarah Norton completed her graduate degree in English at the University of Wisconsin before joining Centennial College. She has worked as a teacher and administrator in the Ontario college system for more than twenty-six years. She is co-author, with Brian Green, of *The Bare Essentials* and *Essay Essentials*, Second Edition, and is co-editor, with Nell Waldman, of *Canadian Content*.

Brian Green graduated from the University of Guelph with an Honours B.A. in English. In 1971 he joined Niagara College, where he has taught a variety of subjects including English, broadcast journalism, history, and computer studies. In addition to his co-authorship with Sarah Norton, he is the author of *Broadcast News Essentials*.

Preface

Preface

Essay Essentials with Readings is a self-contained, comprehensive text designed for Canadian college students taking an introductory course in essay writing. Based on the second edition of *Essay Essentials*, this book features twelve new readings that exemplify a combination of rhetorical modes. The additional essays vary in reading difficulty and address a diverse range of topics that appeal to a broad spectrum of student interests. Like its predecessors, *Essay Essentials with Readings* presents instruction, exercises, and practical assignments designed to teach and reinforce good writing skills. The new readings have been carefully chosen for their value as good prose models, for their ability to provoke thought and discussion, and for their potential to stimulate writing that requires students to integrate what they have learned about essay development.

Units One through Five focus on selecting, adapting, and researching a subject appropriate to a particular audience; on planning, organizing, and developing an essay; on revising, formatting, and proofreading. We acknowledge that these are not discrete "steps" in the composition process: when they don't occur almost simultaneously, they overlap. Nevertheless, we believe students can learn to write effectively only if they can identify and practise "stages" in the writing process, and the information in the first five units is organized to that end.

Units Six through Ten are presented as discrete sections, to be introduced in any order the instructor chooses. The chapters within these units, however, are interdependent. Competency in dealing with material in the latter chapters often depends on mastery of subject matter contained in earlier ones. For the convenience of students working through these units on their own, answers to most exercises are given in Appendix C. An asterisk beside an exercise number indicates that an answer for that exercise is provided in the back of the book. Answers to the mastery tests, together with suggested answers to some of the exercises in the first five units, are provided in the Instructor's Manual.

Acknowledgements

We wish to thank our colleagues across Canada whose responses to our publisher's surveys prompted us to develop this text. Special thanks go to John Robert Colombo and Michael Park, whose essays were written for this book, and to Greg Darling, whose electronic research continually unearths eccentric bits of information on which many of our humorous exercises are based.

A Note from the Publisher

Thank you for selecting *Essay Essentials with Readings*, by Sarah Norton and Brian Green. The authors and publisher have devoted considerable time to the careful development of this book. We appreciate your recognition of this effort and accomplishment.

We want to hear what you think about *Essay Essentials with Readings*. Please take a few minutes to fill out the stamped reply card at the back of the book. Your comments and suggestions will be valuable to us as we prepare new editions and other books.

Contents

UNIT TEN　　**THE FINISHING TOUCHES**

APPENDICES

READINGS

What This Book Can Do for You

Let's face it: not many people enjoy writing essays. Can you imagine anyone including "essay writing" in a list of hobbies or favourite leisure time activities, or putting "career as an essayist" high on a list of vocational goals? So, you may be wondering, what does learning to write essays have to do with me and my future?

You may not be inclined to write for fun, but someday, in a manner of speaking, you will write for profit. The kinds of writing you will learn in this book are the kinds of writing you'll be expected to do in your job. If your résumé shows you've graduated from college or university, your prospective employer will assume that you are able to communicate in writing, frequently, correctly, and as a representative who will not mar the company's image. Are you ready for that? For some people, it's a frightening fact. What's even more alarming, judgements about your ability to perform your job will be based, to a large extent, on your skills as a communicator.

You won't need to be a Margaret Atwood or a Pierre Berton to succeed as an engineer, nurse, fashion consultant, or graphic artist. But in any job that requires communication beyond diagrams, charts, sketches, or mock-ups, you will be expected to be able to present your ideas in well-organized, readable prose that is clearly and correctly written. Whether your output is an interoffice memo, an accident report, a sales presentation, a patient history, or a legal brief, writing is the record of your activity—the evidence of the job you're doing and how well you're doing it. Ask any graduate who is currently working in your career field; ask any employer. College and university training personnel at all levels and in all disciplines are told again and again, "Teach students to communicate clearly." Over the past two decades, the most frequent lament of faculty at colleges and universities has been that entry level students lack basic communication skills, while those ready to graduate have not fully mastered them.

Before you can attempt the specialized kinds of communication that will be required of you in your career, you need to learn how to present your ideas clearly and correctly. In this book, you will learn to organize your thoughts, to develop your ideas in coherent paragraphs, and to express yourself clearly, concisely, and correctly. Adapting these essay-writing skills to the specific types and formats of written communication required on your job will be a fairly simple task. Learning to write well in the first place, however, is not easy for most people. It requires patience, concentration, and practice. The *ability* to write well is within the grasp of any college or university student; what's usually lacking is *motivation*. You can learn to write well if you're willing to work hard at it. We've designed this text so that you can master the theory of good writing and practise it confidently, producing effective essays in college and creditable communications in your career or profession.

Most composition texts claim that if you follow the authors' instructions carefully and do all the exercises faithfully, writing will become easy. This text makes no such claim. Nearly 200 years ago, Richard Brinsley Sheridan warned, "Easy writing's cursed hard reading." What will get easier as you work your way through this book is your readers' ability to read, understand, remember, and perhaps enjoy what you've written. But that, you're smart enough to know, is everything any writer can hope for.

If you learn how to avoid frustrating or misleading your reader, how to keep your subject development on track, and how to include your significant information or arguments in a clearly organized, non-boring way, you'll probably be writing on the job for thirty to forty years, maybe even longer. Isn't it worth spending a term or two to learn how to communicate your ideas clearly and convincingly?

The Process of Writing

This text explains and illustrates two approaches to the process of writing: top-down and bottom-up. The **top-down approach** assumes that you know what you want to say before you begin to write. You identify your subject and main points, establish your preview statement (the statement that orients your readers to the content of the paper), and plan your topic sentences (those sentences that identify the content of each paragraph).

The **bottom-up approach** is founded on the belief that, like most writers, you do not know what you want to say until you begin to write; you discover your meaning through the act of writing. With this approach, you rely on prewriting strategies such as brainstorming and freewriting to "get into" the process of writing.

You will probably need to use both approaches. In some circumstances, you will discover your subject through writing; at other times, use of strategies will help you to express clearly what you already know. You should experiment with both approaches so that you can comfortably use the one that is more appropriate for a particular writing task.

What Your Readers Expect

Whichever approach you use, your goal is to make your finished essay easy for your readers to read and to understand. To achieve that goal, you must meet your readers' expectations.

Readers have five unconscious expectations when they begin to read a piece of extended prose. They expect:

1. To see paragraphs;
2. To have the first sentence of a paragraph orient them to the content of the paragraph by identifying its topic;
3. To see paragraph units that are coherent and unified, with each one exploring a single topic;
4. To have the paragraphs connect to each other according to some logical pattern that shows external as well as internal coherence;
5. To be introduced, very early, to the content of the whole, preferably through the writer's preview of the main points that are to be covered.

You should keep in mind, as you write, that your readers' overriding motive will be to obtain information quickly and easily, without unnecessary backtracking. A well-organized paper, with well-developed paragraphs, results in shorter reading time and in higher recall of the content. Your readers will rely on you to make efficient reading possible.

According to researchers, your readers will read with more ease and remember more of what they read if you include a preview statement to introduce them to the content and organization of the piece, and if you begin each paragraph with a topic sentence to identify the subject of that paragraph. If you do not organize and develop your paper and its paragraphs in a clearly identifiable way, your readers will impose their own organization on the paper. The result will be longer reading time, or difficulty in understanding and remembering the content, or, worse, the assumption that a paragraph or even the whole paper has a meaning other than the one you intended. Writers can help readers to read efficiently if they follow the old adage: "Tell them what you're going to tell them; tell them; then tell them what you've told them."

How to Begin

We have all listened to people who ramble on and on in conversation and never seem to get to the point. Perhaps these speakers have no point to make or are hoping one will turn up as they speak. For their unfortunate listeners, the experience is both tiresome and frustrating. Readers react similarly to poor writing. An essay—or any other form of written communication—that has no point and that rambles on will turn them off.

How can you avoid boring, confusing, or annoying your readers?

First, you need to have something to say and a reason for saying it. In other words, you need to do some thinking before you begin to write. Very few people can write an essay straight through from start to finish without spending a considerable amount of time thinking and planning. Some prewriting will help you to develop the structure more easily; freewriting and brainstorming (Chapter 3 will explain these) are useful to stimulate thinking.

Second, once you've determined what it is you want to say, you need to arrange your main points in the most effective order possible. If you organize your ideas carefully, you won't ramble. Writing an essay is like building a house. If you have a clear plan or blueprint, you can construct the house without the frustration of having to tear down misplaced walls or convert windows to doors. You are less likely to need to double back or even to start all over again from the beginning. A good plan saves time.

As a general rule, the more time you spend on prewriting and planning, the less time you'll need to spend on writing and revising. Careful up-front planning will enable you to produce papers that your readers will find clear and understandable.

The Parts of an Essay

An essay, like most other forms of oral and written communication, has a beginning, a middle, and an end.

The beginning, or **introduction,** tells your readers the point, the purpose, and the scope of your paper. If your introduction is well crafted, its preview statement will tell your readers what main points will be discussed in the paragraphs that follow. Your introduction is to your readers what a highway sign is to travellers: it tells them where they're going and what main points of interest are to be found on the way.

The middle, or **body,** of an essay consists of several paragraphs that discuss in detail the points that are identified or previewed in the introduction. In a short essay, three, four, or more paragraphs will each focus on a separate main point.

Each paragraph should consist of two essential components: the **topic sentence,** which identifies the issue or subject to be examined in that paragraph; and the development, or **support,** of the topic sentence, which sets forth in additional sentences the detailed information the reader needs in order to understand the topic clearly. The topic sentence of each body paragraph connects to the preview statement, and the development of each paragraph supports and explains its topic sentence.

The end, or **conclusion,** of the essay is a brief final paragraph. After the main points of your paper have been introduced and developed, you summarize them to reinforce them for your readers. You then say goodbye with a memorable statement that will give your readers something to think about after they have finished reading your essay.

Bertrand Russell's short essay "What I Have Lived For" is a good example of a well-structured essay. The introduction contains a clear preview statement. Each paragraph of the body consists of a clearly identifiable topic sentence and development sufficient to explain it. The conclusion is brief, pointed, and memorable.

What I Have Lived For
Bertrand Russell

Preview Statement
INTRODUCTION

Three passions, simple but overwhelmingly strong, have governed my life: the longing for love, the search for knowledge, and unbearable pity for the suffering of mankind. These passions, like great winds, have blown me hither and thither, in a wayward course, over a deep ocean of anguish, reaching to the very verge of despair.

Topic Sentence

I have sought love, first, because it brings ecstasy—ecstasy so great that I would often have sacrificed all the rest of life for a few hours of this joy. I have sought it, next, because it relieves loneliness—that terrible loneliness in which one shivering consciousness looks over the rim of the world into the cold unfathomable lifeless abyss. I have sought it, finally, because in the union of love I have seen, in a mystic miniature, the prefiguring vision of the heaven that saints and poets have imagined. This is what I sought, and though it might seem too good for human life, this is what—at last—I have found.

BODY

With equal passion I have sought knowledge. I have wished to understand the hearts of men. I have wished to know why the stars shine. And I have tried to apprehend the Pythagorean power by which number holds sway above the flux. A little of this, but not much, I have achieved.

Topic Sentence

Topic Sentence

Love and knowledge, so far as they were possible, led upward toward the heavens. But always pity brought me back to earth. Echoes of cries of pain reverberate in my heart. Children in famine, victims tortured by oppressors, helpless old people a hated burden to their sons, and the whole world of loneliness, poverty, and pain make a mockery of what human life should be. I long to alleviate the evil, but I cannot, and I too suffer.

CONCLUSION

This has been my life. I have found it worth living, and would gladly live it again if the chance were offered me.

Bertrand Russell, "What I Have Lived For," from *The Autobiography of Bertrand Russell*, Routledge. Bertrand Russell Peace Foundation. Reprinted by permission.

Planning the Essay

CHAPTER 1

Your Audience and You

Before you begin to write anything—an essay, a report, a letter to a friend, or even a shopping list—you must have not only something to write about (your subject) but also someone to write for (your audience). Writing is communication, and for communication to take place, you (the writer) must be able to make your ideas or message clear to your readers. If no one reads your piece, communication does not take place and your writing is just another exercise, a practice for the real thing.

Addressing Your Readers

It is vital that you keep your intended readers in mind at all times—when you plan, write, and revise your paper. Think of every piece of writing as if it were a letter. Letter writers always have their readers in mind; usually someone specific is addressed. As an essay writer, you can do the same thing. Think of your essay as a letter to specific people. Are your readers going to be interested in what you have to say? Is your information sufficiently new, different, thought-provoking, amusing, convincing, or instructive to make your readers stay with you to the end?

> Before you begin to plan an essay, write at the top of the page the specific audience for whom your message is intended.

Naturally, your instructor is going to be reading your early (and your late) assignments, but, for your first draft, you should write at the top of the page the name of someone other than your instructor whom you might expect to be interested in your subject. Be creative; write the name of your supervisor, the prime minister, the editor of your local newspaper, a potential employer, a friend, an enemy, or even yourself. Keeping this reader in mind will help you plan, develop, and write your assignments in a tone and style appropriate to your message.

Spend a little time thinking about your subject in relation to your audience. Consider carefully these three questions when you are deciding what to include in your essay:

1. What do my readers know about my subject?
2. What is my readers' attitude towards my subject?
3. What are my readers' needs in regard to my subject?

Readers' Knowledge

The first question will help guide your choice of the amount and type of information you include. Are you writing for novices or for people with a fairly detailed knowledge of your subject? Do you have to cover the background and all the basics, or can you take it for granted that your readers are familiar with them? You don't want to bore your readers by telling them things they already know; but if you fail to provide information necessary to their understanding of your message, you'll turn them off or lose them entirely.

Readers' Attitudes

The second question helps you determine your approach to your subject. Will your readers be sympathetic to your point of view? If so, your aim will be to reinforce their agreement. You will want to state your opinion up front, to show you're on their side and to enlist their sympathy early. On the other hand, if they can be expected to resist your arguments, you might be wise to provide reasoning and support for your ideas before revealing your point of view. Gentle persuasion is usually more effective than confrontation—in writing and in life.

Readers' Needs

The third question helps you decide whether to persuade or instruct; whether to compare, or classify, or describe, or analyze. Which type of essay will best give your readers what they need to know about your subject? The answers to this question will determine whether you should be fairly general or quite specific in your comments. Is it your intention to add to or reinforce your readers' general knowledge, or is your information to be applied in specific situations?

Reflecting Yourself

Once you are clear about who your readers are, what they know, and what they need to know, you should spend a little time considering your own role in the communication process. Any time you speak or write, you present yourself in a particular way to the people who hear or read what you have to say. We all play a variety of roles. We choose a role, often unconsciously, that we hope will suit the expectations of a particular audience. These roles are not false or hypocritical; they are simply facets of our personality that we try to match to the needs of each communication encounter. Choosing and maintaining an appropriate role is essential in successful communication.

Each day, for example, you meet a variety of people. Some of them you know well—parents, siblings, friends, classmates, teachers, co-workers, supervisors. Others you know only casually—the cashier in a restaurant, a police officer at a radar trap, an enumerator for an upcoming election, a check-out person in a grocery store. With each of these people, whether the contact is casual or intense, you consciously or unconsciously adjust your language in order to communicate well. If you speak to your spouse as you might to your dog, you'll be sleeping on the couch. If you speak to a salesperson as you would to a love interest, you'll get arrested.

Consider these three questions when you are deciding what role would be most appropriate in a particular communication situation:

1. What is my purpose in writing?
2. What is my attitude towards my subject?
3. What are my readers' expectations of me in this communication?

Your Purpose

The most common purposes of writing are to inform, to persuade, and to entertain. Your purpose will depend largely on the needs and expectations of your readers. It will influence your choice of supporting details to develop your points and will affect your tone. How you say something often has more impact on your audience than what you say.

Your Attitude

The second question requires you to clarify your attitude towards the subject of your paper. You've already considered what your readers' attitudes are likely to be; now it's important to determine whether your own attitude coincides or is in conflict. You might be positive or negative about a subject, depending on your purpose in writing and on your relationship with your readers. Your attitude towards your subject, like your purpose in writing, will influence your tone and the kinds of supporting evidence you will use to develop your points.

Your Role

The third question is designed to help you match your role to what your audience is likely to expect from you. What would your readers expect from someone in your position who is writing on your particular subject? Are you able and willing to meet these expectations? Taking the time to think through your relationship with your readers will help you make appropriate choices for your point of view, your support statements for your ideas, and your level of language.

Levels of Language

There are many **levels of language** in spoken English. They range from almost unintelligible mutters and groans; through colloquial slang and professional jargon; right up to the formal, correct English used in the law courts, in the speech from the throne, and on other formal occasions. A parallel range is possible in written English: from graffiti up to the formal report.

The key to finding the proper level for your message is to consider not only the subject but also the receiver. Sometimes compromises must be made, as when you send one message to a wide variety of receivers. In general, you aim at the highest level of receiver and trust that the others will understand. Thus, wedding invitations, even those to the bridegroom's buddies, are usually stylized and formal.

No one has to tell you what level of language to use when you communicate with your friends at lunch or after school; that level has been clearly established over many years. In other circumstances, however, it's not clear what level you should be using, and at such times a careful consideration of the needs and preferences of your receiver is necessary. If your sociology teacher wants you to write papers in a formal style, and you want to get good marks, you will have to write formally. Likewise, because employers generally favour formal letters of application over casual ones, if you want to get a job you will have to write your letter in a formal style. A more relaxed and personal style may be appropriate for a talk given to your class. Letters to friends and conversations with parents are still less formal, although they probably retain a degree of correctness not found in your conversations with your friends (or enemies).

There are no hard-and-fast divisions of language into levels; nevertheless, to help you choose the style most appropriate to the message and the receiver you are considering, we have outlined the basic characteristics of colloquial, general, and formal language in the table below.

	COLLOQUIAL	GENERAL	FORMAL
Vocabulary	casual, everyday; usually concrete; some slang, colloquial expressions, contractions	the language of educated persons; nonspecialized; balance of abstract and concrete; readily understood	often abstract; technical; specialized; no contractions or colloquialisms
Sentence and Paragraph Structure	sentences short, simple; some sentence fragments; paragraphs short	complete sentences of varying length; paragraphs vary, but often short	all sentences complete; sentences usually long, complex; paragraphs fully developed, often at length
Tone	conversational, casual; sounds like ordinary speech	varies to suit message and purpose of writer	impersonal, serious, often instructional
Typical Uses	personal letters, some fiction, some newspapers, much advertising	most of what we read: newspapers, magazines, novels, business correspondence	legal documents, some textbooks, academic writing, scientific reports

No one level is "better" than another. Each has its place and function. Your message, your audience, and your purpose in writing are the factors that determine which level of usage is appropriate.

Read the following selections and consider each writer's purpose in writing, the audience for whom the message is intended, and how the writer's choice of language is appropriate to the readers, the subject, and the writer's purpose.

Colloquial

I love baseball the way some people love candy, but even I don't understand all the rules. I'd like to tell you about a rule that I do understand but, from what I've seen and heard at the ball park, not many other people have figured out. That's the balk rule.

The reason for the rule is so that a runner at first base can't be tricked unfairly by the pitcher. Let's say you've made it to first base. Your next goal is to get to second base. OK, I'm the pitcher and I've got two jobs. First, I've got to try to get the next batter out, and second, I've got to make sure you don't get to second base. Without the balk rule, I could wind up and make all the motions as if I were going to throw a pitch and then, at the last second, whip the ball over to the first baseman. Bingo! You're out because you've taken a lead away from the base towards second to get a head start. If I were allowed to do this, you'd never take a lead away from the base, would you? You'd stick right on the bag and wait until there was a safe hit before taking off for second. That would take a lot of the exciting plays out of the game. Plays like steals, advancing to third on a single, and the hit-and-run would be out the window.

The only way to keep a balance between your being able to make it to second and my being able to get you out is to make sure I can't trick you like that. The balk rule says that I have to come to a complete stop before throwing the ball. After that pause, I have to throw to the plate or to first base, but I must move clearly one way or the other. In other words, I can't make a motion towards the plate, even with my knee or foot, and then throw to first. This protects you from being fooled by me and allows you to take a reasonable lead.

Who is the intended audience? These paragraphs are intended for general readers, but not people who are seeking a definitive and legal description of the baseball rule. The writer assumes some knowledge of and interest in the subject, but not much expertise.

What is the author's role? The author is seeking to inform readers, but not by coming across as a teacher or an expert. This sort of information is discussed among friends. One can imagine the writer and the audience sharing a relaxed and informal conversation about their favourite game.

How does the language work? The use of contractions and colloquialisms ("out the window," "OK," "taking off") and especially the use of the first and second persons ("you," the baserunner, and "I," the pitcher) clearly make this an informal and friendly communication. Short sentences and many instances of conversational style ("a lot," "your being able to make it to second") add to the informal tone.

General

A good business letter is one that gets results. The best way to get results is to develop a letter that, in its appearance, style, and content, conveys information efficiently. To perform this function, a business letter should be concise, clear, and courteous.

The business letter must be concise. Little introduction or preliminary chat is necessary. Get to the point, make the point, and leave it. It is safe to assume that your letter is being read by a very busy person with all kinds of paper to deal with. Such a person does not want to spend very much time with a newsy letter about your ski trip or medical problem. Hone and refine your message until the words and sentences you have used are precise. This takes time for revision and rereading but is a necessary part of writing a good letter. A short business letter that makes its point quickly has much more impact on a reader than a long-winded, rambling exercise in creative writing. This does not mean that there is no place for style or even, on occasion, humour in the business letter. While it conveys a message in its contents, the letter also provides the reader with an impression of you, its author: the medium is part of the message.

The business letter must be clear. You should have a very firm idea of what you want to say, and you should let the reader know it. Use the structure of the letter—paragraphs, topic sentences, introduction, and conclusion—to guide the reader point by point from your introduction, through your reasoning, to your conclusion. Paragraph often, to break up the page and to lend an air of organization to the letter. Use an accepted business-letter format: there are several, and they can be found in any book of business English. Reread what you have written from the point of view of someone who is seeing it for the first time, and be sure that all explanations are adequate and all necessary information is provided (including reference numbers, dates, and other identification). A clear message, clearly delivered, is the essence of business communication.

The business letter must be courteous. Sarcasm and insults are ineffective and can often work against you. If you are sure you are right, point that out as politely as possible, explain why you are right, and outline what the reader is expected to do about it. Always put yourself in the place of the person to whom you are writing. What sort of letter would you respond to? How effective would sarcasm and threats be in making you fulfil a request? Another form of courtesy is taking care in your writing and typing of the business letter. Grammatical and spelling errors (even if you call them typing errors) tell a reader that you don't think enough of him or her to be careful. Such mistakes can lower the reader's opinion of you faster than anything you say, no matter how idiotic. There are excuses for ignorance; there are no excuses for sloppiness.

The business letter is your custom-made representative. It speaks for you and is a permanent record of your message. It can pay big dividends on the time you invest in giving it a concise message, a clear structure, and a courteous tone.

Who is the intended audience? Readers of this essay will be seeking specific information about business-letter style. They will, therefore, have some knowledge about the subject and high-school-graduate levels of reading and writing ability.

What is the author's role? The author is providing information from an expert point of view but in a friendly way. The use of humour and casual language makes the instruction easy to take. A persuasive element in the essay makes it warmer and gentler than straightforward instruction would be.

How does the language work? There are no contractions or slang, as might be found in colloquial writing, but the vocabulary and writing style are easily understood by general readers. The use of the second person and direct address ("If you are sure you are right, point that out as politely as possible, . . .") adds to the personal nature of the language. Questions addressed to the readers in order to assist persuasion also make the tone more conversational than formal, without ever becoming colloquial. This message is designed to appeal to the widest possible audience.

Formal

Scorched Earth
David E. Loper

"The earth speaks of its internal movements through the silent voice of the magnetic needle." So wrote the Norwegian astronomer Christopher Hansteen in 1819, in eloquent summary of his conclusion that the slow wandering of magnetic north—the north of compass needles—is actually a reflection of movements deep below the surface. Hansteen was not the first to make such a proposal. In 1635 the English cartographer Henry Gillibrand had published a chart showing that the direction of magnetic north, as measured at London, had changed by seven degrees in the preceding fifty-five years. Edmond Halley, of comet fame, presciently suggested in 1692 that such changes were caused by the slow rotation of a vast magnetized body deep within the earth. The annual change in the direction of magnetic north is now duly recorded on the legend of nearly every topographic map published by the U.S. Geological Survey.

But the voice of the magnetic needle was muffled until recently; through the nineteenth century and much of the twentieth a static view of the earth held sway. The planet's interior was seen as motionless and changeless except for a slow loss of heat and, by some accounts, the contraction of the cooling globe. Mountains had been uplifted by the contraction like wrinkles on a drying apple, but the continents as a whole, and the thousands of miles of rock below them, stayed put.

Twenty-five years ago that static image of the earth was replaced by the dynamic view of plate tectonics: the idea that the surface of the earth is made up of rigid plates, sixty miles thick on average, that are constantly shifting and jostling. Fittingly, the plate-tectonic revolution was triggered by new studies of the earth's magnetism. Magnetically polarized grains in cooling lava or compacting sedimentary rock record the direction of the magnetic field, just as a compass needle does. As the rock solidifies, the direction of the field freezes in. Layered deposits of volcanic or sedimentary rock thus yield vertical records of the magnetic field, which show that at intervals ranging from tens of thousands to millions of years the field reverses its direction, as if a giant bar magnet within the earth were sporadically flipping back and forth.

The Sciences, September/October 1990, 23. Reprinted by permission. Individual subscriptions are $21 per year in the U.S. Write to: The Sciences, 2 East 63rd Street, NY, NY 10021.

Who is the intended audience? The readers of this paragraph must be knowledgeable about and interested in the subject of geology. They must also be literate and well read. It is expected that this audience will be capable of studying and digesting abstract ideas without requiring the support of concrete examples.

What is the author's role? The author's purpose is to inform; the author's role is that of distant expert. The information is presented from the point of view of one who is extremely knowledgeable, and the tone and content assume that the readers are less well informed . . . students, perhaps.

How does the language work? The vocabulary is abstract and academic. The sentences are long and complex. There are no contractions, no colloquialisms, no references to first or second persons. Sentences are bookish in tone. The style distances the readers from the writer and ensures that their connection is purely in the realm of ideas; there is no attempt at personal or friendly contact.

EXERCISE 1.1

Read the excerpts below, and discuss the intended audience, the author's role, and the appropriateness of the language.

1.   Have faith. Keep in mind those bizarre recipes where you mix unlikely stuff—a peanut butter–chicken stew, for instance—and end up with something great.

   In the case of this inspired comedy [*The Freshman*], the plot is a dignified bonkers combination of *The Graduate*, *The Sting*, *The Godfather* and *The Producers:* A naive young man comes to New York City to go to film school, gets suckered by a cheap crook, then gets introduced to a mobster you wouldn't believe.

   Actually, you might believe him since it's Brando, parodying his own *Godfather* role so closely that other characters keep starting to tell him, "Say, you look just like . . ." before henchmen shut them up. When someone asks Brando if he is making a promise, he pauses—anyone else forgotten what great comic timing he has?—and slowly replies in his raspy Don Corleone voice: "Every word I say, by definition, is a promise."

(from *People Weekly*, July 30, 1990, 11)

Who is the intended audience? _____

_____

_____

_____

_____

What is the author's role? _____

_____

_____

_____

_____

_____

How does the language work? _____

_____

_____

_____

_____

2.   I have always disliked being a man. The whole idea of manhood in America is pitiful, in my opinion. This version of masculinity is a little like having to wear an ill-fitting coat for one's entire life (by contrast, I imagine femininity to be an oppressive sense of nakedness). Even the expression "Be a man!" strikes me as insulting and abusive. It means: Be stupid, be unfeeling, obedient, soldierly and stop thinking. Man means "manly"—how can one think about men without considering the terrible ambition of manliness? And yet it is part of every man's life. It is a hideous and crippling lie; it not only insists on difference and connives at superiority, it is also by its very nature destructive—emotionally damaging and socially harmful.

_____

(from Paul Theroux, "Being a Man," in *Sunrise with Seamonsters*. London: Hamish Hamilton, 1985, 309)

Who is the intended audience? _____

_____

_____

_____

_____

What is the author's role? _____

_____

_____

_____

_____

How does the language work? _____

_____

_____

_____

_____

3.   "Ignorance corrupts. Absolute ignorance corrupts absolutely." This paraphrase of a famous remark tells us something about the seeds of prejudice. Without ignorance, racism and discriminatory persecution would not be possible. Enlightened attitudes could not support the unfounded maltreatment of another human being. Nonetheless, ignorance is not a passive void waiting to be filled; it is an active rejection of civilizing insights. What causes this stubborn resistance to common sense? Some influences might be a deeply embedded traditional opinion, a deep-seated fear of change and growth, or a personal rigidity that cannot assimilate different or opposing views.

Who is the intended audience? _____

_____

_____

_____

_____

What is the author's role? _____

_____

_____

_____

_____

How does the language work? _____

_____

_____

_____

_____

4.   A study of history reminds one that mankind has its ups and downs and during the ups has accomplished many brave and beautiful things, exerted stupendous endeavors, explored and conquered oceans and wildernesses, achieved marvels of beauty in the creative arts and marvels of science and social progress, loved liberty with a passion that throughout history has led men to fight and die for it over and over again, pursued knowledge, exercised reason, enjoyed laughter and pleasures, played games with zest, shown courage, heroism, altruism, honor and decency; experienced love, known comfort, contentment, and, occasionally, happiness. All these qualities have been part of human experience and if they have not had as important notice as the negatives nor exerted as wide and persistent an influence as the evils we do, they nevertheless deserve attention, for they currently are all but forgotten.

_____

(from Barbara Tuchman, "Mankind's Better Moments," from a Thomas Jefferson lecture delivered in Washington. Copyright Autumn 1980.)

Who is the intended audience? _____

_____

_____

_____

_____

What is the author's role? _____

_____

_____

_____

_____

How does the language work? _____

_____

_____

_____

_____

_____

_____

_____

Why do I eat so much? Is it just a bad habit, or was I born to eat continually? These are questions I often ask myself as I sit in front of the TV and munch my way through a giant bowl of popcorn, a family-size chocolate bar, and a one-litre bottle of pop. Twenty minutes later, I kick myself because I've consumed all the food and I'm no closer to answering my questions. Maybe by looking at some of the psychological explanations for overeating I can find some answers — perhaps even some help.

"If you eat all your carrots, Mommy will take you shopping." I was served promises like this many times in my childhood. My parents believed in the reward system: a child will eat, even is she is not hungry, just to get a treat. The reward theory comes from the behavioural school of psychology. I eat; therefore, I get. I do not eat; therefore, I do not get. Breaking the cycle is difficult when you have been trained for years to participate in this game. I overeat now because I think that by doing so I will get a reward: I will feel good. I need to change the reward system so that I get a prize for not eating.

Or I could try to solve my overeating problem by looking at it from a humanistic point of view. I am free to choose between a trim, fit body and that double cheeseburger. It's all up to me. So why don't I go for a walk instead of gobbling down a triple fudge sundae? I am free to make the choice, aren't I? I guess it comes down to a question of will power. I need to find the will to control my appetite.

But what if there is no hope for me at all? According to the biopsychologists, I was born with the tendency to eat too much, and there is nothing I can do about it short of changing my gene pool. I have inherited my overeating habit, and I had better get used to it. Thanks a lot, Mom and Dad.

Well, there you have it. I'm more confused now than ever, and I still haven't found an answer to my problem. One group of psychologists tells me I can stop overeating, and another tells me I can't. Maybe I should start my own school, the "I'm going nuts" school of human behaviour. Ummm, nuts....

_____

Lisa Temple, in-class assignment, Centennial College, 1996.

Who is the intended audience? _____

_____

_____

_____

_____

What is the author's role? _____

_____

_____

_____

_____

How does the language work? _____

_____

_____

_____

Role Playing

Now let's try an exercise in **role playing**—communicating effectively with an audience by adjusting your role (and your language) to suit your purpose, your message, and your audience.

EXERCISE 1.2

Imagine, in each of the following situations, that you must deal with four different audiences face to face. Before you begin, analyze each audience in terms of knowledge, attitudes, and needs; then clarify your own purpose in communicating your message, your attitude towards your subject, and your audience's expectations of you.

1. You wrote your end-of-term essay, the major assignment in your English course, on your home computer, a Compaq. When you tried to print out your final copy, the computer said it could not read the floppy disk on which you had stored your essay. You went to a friend's house, but her computer, an IBM clone, could not read the disk either. Now desperate, you took the disk to FutureTech Computers, where you originally bought it, and asked them to retrieve your essay. They were unable to do so, but offered to replace the defective disk free of charge. Your essay, on which you had been working for more than a month, was lost. Explain this tragedy to

   the English instructor, who is expecting the essay today
   the head office of FutureTech Computers
   a friend who is thinking of buying a computer at FutureTech
   a friend who knows nothing about computers.

2. At 8:30 this morning, you got a phone call from your friend Jaron, who was calling from a police station. He had been arrested because, according to the arresting officer, he had 37 unpaid parking tickets outstanding.

He claims he's innocent; he's never had a parking ticket. He has called to ask you to come down and bail him out. If you do so, you will be late, possibly very late, for work. Jaron refuses to call his parents for help. Tell this story to

> your parents
> your boss
> a friend
> Jaron's parents.

3. You recently bought a pair of silk pants from Bottom Drawers Pants Company. They ripped in the crotch the first time you bent over. You were doing the lambada with a very attractive partner and were deeply embarrassed. Before you could recover your composure, the owner of the club asked you to leave immediately. Tell your story to

> Bottom Drawers
> a friend
> the owner of the club
> a tailor.

4. You recently saw a film in which a married man has an affair with an unmarried woman. He refuses to leave his wife and family; consequently, she decides to marry her old boyfriend in revenge. You enjoyed the film, but your date didn't. Describe the plot of the film, inventing any details you need, to

> a close friend of the same sex
> your eight-year-old sister
> a priest or other member of the clergy
> a marriage counsellor.

5. You are short of money—so short you can't even buy gas for your car. If you can't get gas money, you will be late for work, and your boss is already annoyed because you've been late twice this week already. Ask for money from

> your parents
> a friend
> someone who owes you money
> your boss.

6. Turn one of the twenty role-playing situations above into a written assignment.

When you have a clear fix on your intended reader and on your own purpose and role in writing, it's time to turn to the first step in the actual writing of your essay: choosing a suitable subject for your paper.

CHAPTER 2

Selecting a Subject

Most of the time you devote to producing an essay should be spent on the planning stage. If you take the time to analyze your audience, to find a good subject, and to identify interesting main points to make about that subject, you will find that the mechanics of writing will fall into place much more easily than if you go through the motions of writing an essay only because it's been assigned. After you have considered your readers' background, needs, and expectations, the next step is to choose a satisfactory subject to write about.

Even when you are assigned a topic for an essay, you need to examine it, focus it, and consider different ways of approaching it. Depending on your knowledge of the topic and the readers you are writing for, the range of specific subjects for any broad topic is almost endless. For example, given the broad topic "Microcomputers," here are some of the approaches you might choose from.

> How to buy a microcomputer
> The IBM PC and the Apple Mac: a comparison
> Graphics on the Amiga
> The advantages of Warp vs. Windows 95
> Why I love my laptop

Your first task, then, is to choose a satisfactory subject, one that satisfies the basic principles of the **4-S test:**

A satisfactory subject is *significant, single, specific,* and *supportable.*

If it passes the 4-S test, your subject is the basis of a good essay.

Make Your Subject *Significant*

Your subject and your approach to that subject must be significant and meaningful both to you and to your readers. The subject you choose must be worthy of the time and attention you expect your readers to give to your paper. Can you imagine the subject "How to buy movie tickets" or "Why I hate pants with button flies," for example, as being significant for most readers?

EXERCISE 2.1

From the list below, choose those subjects that would be significant to a typical reader. Revise the others to make them significant, if possible. If not, suggest another, related subject that is significant.

1. Tips for travelling with small children
2. How to choose shoelaces
3. Using the Reference Library
4. How CDs have changed the world's listening habits
5. Page-turning techniques
6. The perfect vacation spot
7. How to find "r" on the computer keyboard
8. Television is a threat to Canadian independence
9. Colour television versus black-and-white
10. Why you should write on one side of the page only

Make Your Subject *Single*

Don't try to crowd too much into one paper. Naturally, different assignments in school and projects on the job will have varying requirements of length and scope, but be careful that your subject is not actually two or three related subjects masquerading as one. If you attempt to write about a multiple subject, your readers will get a superficial and possibly confusing overview instead of the interesting and satisfying detail they expect to find in a well-planned paper. A subject such as "The problem of league expansion in hockey and other sports" includes too much to be dealt with satisfactorily in one essay. You'd need to write a book to give your readers new and significant information on such a broad topic. In an essay, you and your readers will both benefit if you try something like "The problems of league expansion in the NHL" or "Why Halifax can't get an NHL franchise."

EXERCISE 2.2

From the list below, choose the subjects that are single and could be satisfactorily explored in a short essay. Revise the others to make them single.

1. Causes of inflation in Canada and South America
2. Pub night at different colleges
3. The instant replay in sports
4. How to change a tire and adjust the timing
5. Abortion and capital punishment
6. The importance of accuracy in newspaper and television reporting
7. Methods of preventing the spread of AIDS
8. Causes of injury in industry and professional sports
9. Nursing and engineering: rewarding careers
10. Vacationing on the islands of Corsica, Corfu, and Manitoulin

Make Your Subject *Specific*

Given a choice between a broad, general topic and a narrow, specific one, you should always choose the specific one. Again, assignments and projects will vary in length and scope, but remember that your readers want to be both informed and interested in what you have to say. Most readers find concrete, specific details more interesting than broad generalizations.

It would be difficult to say anything very detailed about a huge subject like "The roles of women in history," for example. But with some research, you could write an interesting paper on "The roles of women in medieval England" or "Famous women pilots." You can narrow a broad subject and make it more specific by applying one or more *limiting factors* to it. Try thinking of your subject in terms of a specific *kind*, or *time*, or *place*, or *number*, or *person* associated with it. By applying this technique to the last potential subject above, you might come up with "Amelia Earhart's last flight."

EXERCISE 2.3

In the list below, identify the subjects that are specific and could be explained satisfactorily in a short essay. Revise the others to make them specific by applying one or more of the limiting factors to each one.

1. The two main problems confronting the federal government
2. Summer employment
3. Modern heroes
4. Enjoying winter weather
5. Drug abuse
6. The effects of government cutbacks on low-income families
7. The problems of urban living
8. How to repair your home appliances
9. Planning your wedding
10. Female aggression

Make Your Subject *Supportable*

You must know something about your subject (preferably more than your readers know), or you must be able to find out about it. Remember, your readers want information that is new, interesting, and thought-provoking—not obvious observations familiar to everyone. You should be able to include *specific examples, facts, figures, quotations, anecdotes,* and other *supporting details.* (Think again about a reader whose name might be at the top of your page. What kind of supporting information will interest or persuade that person?) Supporting information can be gathered from your own experience, from the experience of other people, or from both. If you don't know enough about your topic to write anything but the obvious, be prepared to do some research.

EXERCISE 2.4

From the subjects given below, choose those that are clearly supportable in a short essay. Revise the others to make them supportable.

1. The principles of cold fusion
2. My career as a student
3. Movie review: *October*
4. Corporate mergers in the 1990s
5. The Chinese secret service
6. Religion in Canada
7. Space travel in the year 2100
8. Bass fishing techniques
9. Art through the ages
10. The hazards of working in a fast-food outlet

EXERCISE 2.5

Indicate with check marks (√) whether each subject below passes the 4-S test by being *sig*nificant, *si*ngle, *sp*ecific, and *sup*portable. Revise each unsatisfactory subject (fewer than four check marks) to make it a satisfactory subject for a short essay.

The 4-S Test

SUBJECT	SIG	SI	SP	SUP	REVISION
1. The Canadian climate	__	__	__	__	_____
2. Computers	__	__	__	__	_____
3. Whitewater rafting	__	__	__	__	_____
4. Insomnia and other stress-related disorders	__	__	__	__	_____
5. Blue: a nice colour	__	__	__	__	_____
6. Calgary in 200 years	__	__	__	__	_____
7. Dressing for an interview	__	__	__	__	_____
8. Canadian sports figures	__	__	__	__	_____
9. Architecture	__	__	__	__	_____
10. Life in the Andromeda galaxy	__	__	__	__	_____

Now that you've learned how to select an appropriate subject, it's time to move on to the next stage: identifying solid main points to support that subject.

CHAPTER 3

Managing the Main Points

While you were selecting subjects and testing them against the four principles presented in Chapter 2, you were thinking about some of the things you might say about each. **Main points** are the two or three or four most important things you have to say about your subject. Selecting them carefully is a vitally important part of the essay-writing process.

If you begin to write as soon as you have chosen a subject, and you march merrily down the page explaining everything that comes to mind, you will have to go back and revise your "thought flow" several times, writing draft after draft until your ideas take shape and are clear in your mind, let alone on the page. But if, before you begin to write, you take time to select strong main points and to decide on the best order in which to present them, you will be able to get the essence of your essay down on paper in just one or two drafts instead of three or more. A second or third draft will be necessary to refine the content and polish the writing, of course, but you will have a finished product in two or three drafts instead of needing five or six, or nine, or. . . .

Generating Main Points: The Bottom-Up Approach

If you are feeling a little intimidated by your task and unsure about how to present your subject, some prewriting activities can be helpful. Writers use several methods to stimulate thinking and prepare for a productive first draft. Two techniques are especially effective: freewriting and brainstorming. Either will get your creative juices flowing; we recommend that you try both, to see which works best for you in particular situations. Understand that these techniques are used when you already have the necessary material in your head. Either you are writing from personal experience or you've done some research. (You'll learn about research in Unit Five.) Freewriting and brainstorming are designed to get your ideas on the page in any order, shape, or form. Don't worry about making a mess. You can clean it up later.

Freewriting

Freewriting does what its name implies. It sets you free to write down your ideas by removing whatever may be inhibiting your thought flow: worries about grammar, spelling, punctuation, sentence structure, sequence, or word choice, for example. We are not suggesting that you abandon these important considerations forever. Just forget about them for a while, until you get some ideas down on the page. Here's how to go about freewriting:

1. Write your subject at the top of the page. Ideally, it will have passed the 4-S test, but if you're really stuck, you can begin with just a word or a phrase.
2. Start writing. Don't worry about sentence structure. Ramble as much as you like. If you wander away from your subject, circle back and get on track. The important thing to remember is to keep writing. Don't pause for breath or thought or hand-cramp. If you are at a loss for words, repeat over and over the last phrase you've written, until something new comes to mind. (Don't worry, it will!)
3. Keep up this pace for a specified length of time. Start with two minutes and work up to four minutes, six minutes, or longer if necessary. You will be surprised how much paper you can cover in a limited time.
4. Put onto the page whatever comes into your mind. Forget about elegant phrasing, proper paragraphing, effective transitions, and the like. Don't stop. Don't pause to analyze your ideas or to evaluate them. This technique is designed to get thoughts into words as quickly as possible without self-consciousness. Don't edit what you're writing.
5. After your time is up, stop and stretch. Then take a look at the ideas and expressions you have discovered. Underline anything, even a single word, that is related to your subject. Much of your freewriting will be irrelevant nonsense that can be discarded. But what you have underlined will be useful in the next step—identifying the main points that you will focus on in explaining your subject.
6. Turn the fragments, words, and sentences that you have underlined into clear, understandable points. If you don't end up with at least a dozen points, continue freewriting for another few minutes and see what new points you can discover.

7. On a separate sheet of paper, list the points you have identified. Study the relationships among these points and cluster them under three or four main headings. These are your main points. Now you can move on to the next step: testing each main point to be sure it is satisfactory for your essay.

Here is an example of the freewriting technique. The subject was left open for students to choose. This student had recently bought a car and chose to write about how he selected his dream car.

Choosing My Car

I knew I wanted a sports car but I didn't know which one to get so I went out and compared a bunch of them so I could make the best buy. I compared the Corvette and the Porsche 944 and the Jaguar Vandenplatz. I liked the Corvette's speed because it was the fastest 0 to 100 in 6 seconds and has a really sexy body styling. The wheels they put on it are also really neat looking and add performance.

The Jag was really luxurious but I felt old when I drove it even though it has a good top end and moves pretty quick, not as quick as the other two. The interior is almost too nice and I felt I wouldn't be able to relax in the car and for sure I would never invite any of my friends to ride in it because they're such slobs. You should see my girlfriend's car it's a complete mess with candy wrappers and coffee cups all over the floor and dog hair from her German Shepherd thick all over the upholstery. Anyway, I would never let her in my car if I bought the Vandenplatz. It was sure the quietest of the three, but I kind of like the roar of a well tuned exhaust.

The Porsche was my favourite and it was the one I bought even though it cost more than the Corvette and didn't perform quite as well because it's a heavier car. It made it from 0 to 100 in 6.6 seconds and cornered better than the 'Vet but its braking is a shade slower. I've got the stats at home and can't remember all of them right now but I'll put them in the final essay. Neither of them were as quiet or luxurious as the Jag, but as I already said, I decided against the Jag for other reasons. Maybe when I'm old I'll get one of them for tooling along to the country club or something. Anyway, the Porsche isn't as sexy looking as the Corvette but everyone recognizes a Porsche and it really gets attention. Of the three, I'd guess the Corvette was most common. There are lots of Corvettes on the road.

I really like the Jag's looks, but most people think it's an old person's car.

Lucky for me I didn't have to worry about cost. Since my grandfather was buying it for me for graduating from college, I didn't really care, but since this is supposed to be a comparison, I'd say the Corvette was the better deal since it cost about $3000 less and gets better mileage and costs less to repair. But not having to worry about money I bought the one I wanted—the Porsche.

After completing this ten-minute freewriting exercise, the student underlined all the points he considered both significant and related to his subject. He then clustered them into four main points:

1. Performance: 'Vet faster, better brakes
   Porsche better handling
   Jag quieter
2. Styling: 'Vet very sexy, great tires
   Porsche I don't think is as nice, but better image
   Porsche really gets attention
   Jag has old image
3. Comfort: Jag is best
4. Cost: 'Vet costs less and is more economical

After thinking about these main points for a while, the student realized that one of his selections, the Jaguar, weakened the comparison, because it had been eliminated almost from the beginning. Dropping the Jaguar, he fleshed out the other two entries and developed a useful blueprint for a comparison paper. His last move before writing the first draft was to eliminate the category "styling," because it was highly subjective while the other criteria could be judged factually. After two preliminary drafts and the addition of the facts and statistics that he had at home, the student submitted "Car Wars," the essay on pp. 180–81.

EXERCISE 3.1

Choose a subject, or work with an assigned subject. Generate some ideas using the freewriting method.

Brainstorming

In **brainstorming,** you generate ideas by asking all the questions you can think of about a specific subject: who? what? when? where? why? how? You storm your brain for quick, spontaneous answers and for ideas connected to those answers. The best brainstorming strategy is a direct assault on a specific subject. Here's how to proceed.

1. Write your topic at the top of the page. Again, you'll save time if you've checked that your subject passes the 4-S test.
2. Ask all the questions you can think of about your subject, and record your answers in a list. Each point in the list might be only a word or a phrase. Work quickly. Don't slow yourself down by worrying about grammar or sentence structure or repetition. As in freewriting, working against the clock (allowing yourself two, four, six, or more minutes) can bring surprising results. Many of the points won't be usable in the final list; worry about that later.

3. Once you have generated a dozen or more answers to your questions, relax for a moment, then go down the list carefully. Underline the answers that seem most clearly related to your subject. Ignore any phrases that are unclear or off-topic. If you don't end up with at least three or four points that are meaningful to you, brainstorm again for a few minutes to generate more ideas.

4. Take your three or four most significant points and rephrase them in clear, comprehensible form on a clean sheet of paper. Now you're ready to move on to the next step: testing your points to ensure they are suitable for use in your essay.

The following example demonstrates how brainstorming can be used to overcome the most frustrating inertia. The subject was "The value of a college English course." As you might expect, the class groaned when the subject was assigned, but quick brainstorming produced some unique and interesting approaches to the topic. Through brainstorming, one student found he believed his career opportunities would improve if he learned how to communicate better. The time limit given for this exercise was four minutes.

The Value of a College English Course

- I have to take it
- I should like it but I don't
- People want me to take it
- I speak better
- People listen
- Speaking is important
- Speaking's easier than writing
- Writing is like speaking really
- Bosses will hire you if you can write
- You can get a job
- You can write a letter of application
- I have to write in my job
- I have to write to my boss
- I have to write to other departments
- I have to write to my customers
- I'm embarrassed I can't write well
- Nobody respects a poor speaker
- Nobody respects a poor writer
- Writing helps you think
- Writing helps you speak
- Think of the reports I have to do
- It's better to know how to do a good one
- I need to write to get promoted

This student's initial resistance gave way to some significant points. The phrases or sentences in his list were in no special order; in fact, he circled around and doubled back to the essential features of the relationship between writing and speaking and between good communication and job opportunities. After he underlined the points he felt were most important, he noticed that several points said almost the same thing. These he put together into one revised phrase. Here is his list of revised points.

College English is useful because

- **it improves speaking skills and thinking skills**
- **you will get hired**
- **you will communicate better on the job**
- **you will get promoted.**

Now it's your turn. Try your hand at the exercise below.

EXERCISE 3.2

Choose a subject, or work with an assigned subject. Brainstorm for five minutes; then underline your three or four best ideas.

Generating Main Points: The Top-Down Approach

Another way to find suitable main points is to ask yourself some specific questions about the proposed subject of your essay. The top-down approach is more highly structured than the bottom-up approach, but top-down has the advantage of producing clearly identifiable main points with few or no off-topic responses.

The list of questions on p. 34 serves as a kind of filter. Apply each question to your subject until you find a question that produces answers that are solid main points. Applying each of these questions to your subject is especially helpful if you're stuck for ideas.

Notice that a particular question produces a particular kind of essay. When you come to Unit Four, you'll see how the various kinds of essays can be developed to satisfy the needs of your audience as well as your purpose in writing.

THE ANSWERS TO THESE QUESTIONS

WILL PRODUCE THESE KINDS OF ESSAYS:

1. How is your subject *made* or *done*?
2. How does your subject work?

} *Process*

THE ANSWERS TO THESE QUESTIONS	WILL PRODUCE THESE KINDS OF ESSAYS:
3. What are the main *kinds* of your subject?	
4. What are the component *parts* of your subject?	*Classification/ Division*
5. What are the significant *features* or *characteristics* of your subject?	
6. What are the main *functions* of your subject?	
7. What are the *causes* of your subject?	*Cause and Effect*
8. What are the *effects* or *consequences* of your subject?	
9. What are the *similarities* and/or *differences* between your subject and X?	*Comparison and Contrast*
10. What are the main *advantages/disadvantages* of your subject?	*Persuasion*
11. What are the reasons *in favour of/against* your subject?	
12. What does your subject *look, feel, sound, smell,* and/or *taste* like?	*Description*
13. How did your subject *happen*?	*Narration*

By applying these questions to your subject, you will find at least one question to which you can give answers appropriate to your purpose. Your answers will be the main points of your essay. As an example, we've chosen the subject "Great rock bands." The subject passes the 4-S test: it is single, specific, supportable, and (we think) significant to our readers. Now let's apply the questions, to find our main points.

1. How is a great rock band made?
   Some ideas come to mind, but since great bands usually just "happen" rather than being deliberately put together, the answers to the question are going to be vague or, at best, not supportable with much detail.
2. How does a great rock band work?
   They all work differently, so we would have to answer the question separately for each band. No way.
3. What are the main kinds or types of great rock bands?
   This question presents possibilities. We could manage this one by distinguishing heavy metal bands, personality bands, dance bands, post-punk anarcho-machinist bands, and many more. We can put a star beside this question as the best possibility so far.
4. What are the main parts of a great rock band?
   This question produces answers (drums, keyboards, strings), but since great bands and terrible bands can have exactly the same instruments and personnel, it won't provide any useful information.

5. What are the significant features or characteristics of a great rock band?

   Bingo. We can begin to answer this question because, while bands are all different, we have some clear ideas about what characteristics make a *great* band: performance, determination, appeal, and adaptability, just to name a few. But let's try the rest of the questions, to make sure there isn't a better one.

6. What are the main functions of a great rock band?

   To entertain. The answer is so obvious that the question is useless.

7. What are the causes of a great rock band?

   This question doesn't produce any usable answers.

8. What are the effects or consequences of a great rock band?

   We could say something about a great band's effects on its fans, but specific answers to this question are hard to devise.

9. What are the similarities and/or differences between great rock bands and . . . what? lousy rock bands? great marching bands? great rock single performers?

   We can't think of a comparison that would be significant for our readers.

10. What are the advantages (or disadvantages) of a great rock band?

    Doesn't make sense.

11. What are the reasons in favour of (or against) great rock bands?

    Doesn't make sense.

12. What does a great rock band look, feel, and sound like?

    We could certainly describe how a particular great rock band looks and sounds, but every great rock band sounds different, and we can't describe them all.

13. How did a great rock band happen?

    We could tell how one particular band came about, but that wouldn't be very enlightening about great rock bands in general.

We found two questions that work for our subject. Now we can choose the question we have more to say about, or the one that is more appropriate to our intended audience and writing purpose, and begin developing the answers that will become our main points.

We chose question 5 and found three answers that would serve as good main points: "The main characteristics of a great rock band are popular appeal, exciting stage performance, and ability to adapt." (To see how the essay worked out, turn to "Rock of Ages" on pp. 157–58.)

Generating main points is not a difficult process, but it can be time consuming. Don't rush; take the necessary time. This is a crucial stage in the writing process. To sharpen your skills, look at the sample subjects given here, the questions that might be applied to them, and the main points that could result. Study these samples until you're sure you understand how to find suitable main points for any subject. As you read these subjects and main points, imagine the essay that might result; you'll find the essay taking shape very easily in your mind.

SUBJECT	SELECTED QUESTION	MAIN POINTS
Hockey violence	What are the reasons in favour of violence in hockey?	• releases aggression • keeps players alert • attracts fans
Law enforcement officers	What are the main functions of law enforcement officers?	• preventing crime • apprehending criminals • enforcing the law • acting as role model
Dog ownership	What are the main disadvantages of dog ownership?	• damage to property • drain on nerves • drain on finances • damage to relationships
Job interviews	How do you make a negative impression in a job interview?	• be late • be inappropriately dressed • be ignorant about the company • complain about former employers
Essay topics	What are the characteristics of a satisfactory essay topic?	• single • significant • specific • supportable

EXERCISE 3.3

For each of the subjects listed below, apply the questions on p. 33–34. Select the question that produces the answers you like best, and list three or four of those answers as main points.

SUBJECT	SELECTED QUESTION	MAIN POINTS
1. Passing midterm tests	_____	_____
	_____	_____
	_____	_____
	_____	_____

SUBJECT	SELECTED QUESTION	MAIN POINTS
2. Teacher strikes	_____	_____
	_____	_____
	_____	_____
3. Blue jeans	_____	_____
	_____	_____
	_____	_____
4. The federal deficit	_____	_____
	_____	_____
	_____	_____
5. Living away from home	_____	_____
	_____	_____
	_____	_____
6. Automated telephone answering systems	_____	_____
	_____	_____
	_____	_____
7. TV sitcoms	_____	_____
	_____	_____
	_____	_____
	_____	_____
8. Quebec independence	_____	_____
	_____	_____
	_____	_____
9. Pizza	_____	_____
	_____	_____
	_____	_____
10. Canadian Football League	_____	_____
	_____	_____
	_____	_____
	_____	_____
	_____	_____

EXERCISE 3.4

Choose five subjects of your own that you think would be suitable for a short essay. Remember that satisfactory subjects are single, significant, supportable, and specific. For each of your five subjects, list at least three main points. Use the questions on p. 34 to help you identify main points.

SUBJECT	SELECTED QUESTION	MAIN POINTS
1.	_____	_____
		_____
		_____
2.	_____	_____
		_____
		_____
3.	_____	_____
		_____
		_____
4.	_____	_____
		_____
		_____
5.	_____	_____
		_____
		_____

Testing Your Main Points

Now that you've practised identifying main points using freewriting, brainstorming, and the questioning approach, the next step is to examine the points you've come up with, to make sure each is going to work as a major component in your essay. Some may be too minor to bother with; some may overlap in meaning; some may even be unrelated to your subject. Here's how to test your main points to be sure they are satisfactory.

Whether you've arrived at your main points through freewriting, brainstorming, or questioning, the test is the same:

> Main points must be
> *significant, distinct,* and *relevant.*

Are Your Main Points Significant?

Each main point should be worth writing and reading about. If you can't write at least one interesting and informative paragraph about a point, it is probably not significant enough to bother with. To waste your readers' time with trivial matters gains you only irritated readers. In the following example, one of the main points does not have the same "weight" or importance as the others. It should be eliminated or replaced.

Reasons for attending college
- to learn career skills
- to improve one's general knowledge of the world
- to enjoy pub nights
- to participate in student government

Are Your Main Points Distinct?

Each of the main points you choose must be different from all the others; there must be no overlap in meaning. Check to be sure you haven't given two different labels to what is really only one aspect of your subject. Eliminate or replace any main points that duplicate other points or that can easily be covered under another point. Here's an example of a list that contains a redundant main point.

Advantages of cycling
- improves fitness
- stimulates enjoyment of surroundings
- keeps one in shape
- doesn't damage the environment

Are Your Main Points Relevant?

The main points you choose must be clearly and directly related to your subject. They all must be aspects of that subject and must add to the development of your readers' information on the subject. In this example, the third main point listed is inappropriate because it does not relate to the stated topic. It must be eliminated.

The miseries of winter

- numbing cold
- layers of uncomfortable clothes
- Christmas presents
- dangerous driving conditions

EXERCISE 3.5

Circle the unsatisfactory main point in each group.

1. How to catch a cold
   - associate closely with infected friends
   - get wet and remain in damp clothing
   - take Aspirin and drink plenty of liquids
   - make sure you are tired and run down

2. Levels of education
   - high school
   - primary school
   - preschool
   - college
   - secondary school

3. Why I drive a Ford
   - stylish body design
   - plenty of power
   - comparatively good value
   - substandard fit and finish
   - high acceleration and top speed

4. Causes of college failure
   - lack of preparation in high school
   - poor study habits
   - irregular attendance
   - card playing

5. Effects of cigarette smoking
   - smelly clothing
   - emphysema
   - heart disease
   - lung cancer

6. Major world religions
   - Roman Catholicism
   - Islam
   - Judaism
   - Christianity
   - Buddhism
   - Hinduism

7. How to choose a place to live
   - determine your needs
   - determine your budget
   - select your favourite colour
   - seek expert advice

8. Reasons in favour of waste recycling
   - burning waste harms the environment
   - we are running out of landfill sites
   - it is wasteful
   - recycling helps our economy

9. How to pour a beer	• open the bottle gently
	• tip the glass to a 30-degree angle
	• empty the bottle fast enough to produce the desired head
	• drink with strong, steady pulls until the glass is empty
10. Comparison between the 1960s and the 1990s	• drug use
	• musical tastes
	• aspirations and ambitions of the young
	• space travel
	• personal style and fashion

Organizing Your Main Points

After you select the main points for your essay and check to make sure they are satisfactory, your final step in the planning process is to decide on the order of your main points for the best development of your topic. Some thought here can make a big difference in your readers' understanding of your instruction or explanation or argument. How you arrange your main points will determine, to a large extent, your readers' understanding of the relationship among the ideas you are presenting.

> There are four ways to order your main points: *chronological, climactic, logical,* and *random.*

Chronological Order

When you present your points in order of time from first to last, you are using **chronological order.** You will find it most appropriate in process essays, but it can be used in other essays as well. Here are two examples.

SUBJECT	MAIN POINTS
The process of getting dressed	• put on your underpants
	• pull on your socks (left first)
	• get into your shirt (button it if necessary)
	• pull on your pants
	• tuck your shirt into your pants
	• do up your pants and belt (if any)
	• put on your shoes and tie the laces (if necessary)

SUBJECT	MAIN POINTS
The evolution of a relationship	• attraction
	• meeting
	• discovery
	• intimacy
	• disillusionment

Climactic Order

Persuasion most often uses a climactic arrangement, but climactic order is also common in papers based on examples, comparison or contrast, and classification or division. In **climactic order**, you save your strongest or most convincing point for last (the climax of your argument). You lead off your essay with your second-strongest point, and arrange your other points in between, as in this example.

SUBJECT	MAIN POINTS
Advantages of a college education	• development of skills
	• friendships and contacts with compatible people
	• higher income potential for life
	• discovery of one's own potential

Logical Order

Cause-and-effect essays, or any writing in which one point must be explained before the next point can be understood, use **logical order**. The points you are making have a logical progression and you cannot take them out of order without confusing your readers. Consider the following sequence.

SUBJECT	MAIN POINTS
Main causes of juvenile delinquency	• lack of opportunity or motivation for work
	• lack of recreational facilities
	• boredom
	• quest for "kicks"

The logical links here are clear: because of unemployment, recreational facilities are needed. Because of both unemployment and inadequate recreational facilities, boredom and the quest for "kicks" become problems. Readers must grasp each point before the next can be explained and understood.

Random Order

On the rare occasions when your points can be explained in any order without affecting your readers' understanding, you can use **random order**. A random arrangement is possible only if all your main points are of equal significance and if they are not linked together logically or chronologically. In this example, all three points have equal weight.

SUBJECT

The garbage disposal crisis

MAIN POINTS

- disposal sites are hard to find
- cartage costs are high
- new technologies are not yet fully developed

EXERCISE 3.6

Choose the type of order—chronological, climactic, logical, or random—you think is most appropriate for each of the following subjects. Arrange the main points in that order by numbering them.

SUBJECT	ORDER	MAIN POINTS
1. How to brush your teeth	_____ _____ _____ _____	• use an up-and-down motion • put about 2 cm of toothpaste on the brush • brush continuously for at least 3 minutes • rinse
2. Reasons for listening to the CBC	_____ _____ _____	• it offers informative programs • your taxes are paying for it • it provides a sense of Canadian unity
3. Causes of tomato plant failure	_____ _____ _____ _____	• wet spring weather • early frost • lack of summer rain • heavy rain at harvest
4. How to get from Winnipeg to Regina	_____ _____ _____ _____	• Portage la Prairie is the first major city • go west out of Winnipeg on Portage Avenue • cross the border into Saskatchewan • Brandon, Manitoba, is the next large centre

SUBJECT	ORDER	MAIN POINTS
	_____	• about 200 km from the border you will enter Saskatchewan's capital, Regina
	_____	• Portage Avenue runs into Highway 1, which you follow all the way
5. Advantages of heating with wood	_____	• it gives a dry, comfortable heat
	_____	• it creates a pleasant atmosphere
	_____	• it costs less than other fuels
	_____	• it is a renewable resource
6. Methods of quitting smoking	_____	• laser therapy
	_____	• acupressure
	_____	• hypnosis
	_____	• cold turkey
	_____	• gradual withdrawal
7. How to train a dog	_____	• be consistent in use of commands
	_____	• be firm
	_____	• begin with easiest commands
	_____	• keep sessions short
8. Reasons for travelling abroad	_____	• meet new people
	_____	• practise and develop language skills
	_____	• see important cultural and historic sites
	_____	• practise self-reliance and "coping" skills
9. How to break into the Canadian film industry	_____	• go to acting school
	_____	• take bit parts and nonspeaking roles
	_____	• marry a producer
	_____	• get on the game shows
	_____	• work in live theatre
10. Causes of stress	_____	• change of employment
	_____	• financial problems
	_____	• death of a family member
	_____	• problems at school

In this chapter, you've learned how to identify main points, how to test them for suitability, and how to arrange them in the most appropriate order. You're ready now to go on to the next step: writing the preview statement—probably the most important sentence in your essay.

CHAPTER 4

Writing the Preview Statement

The key to clear organization of any essay is the preview statement—a sentence (or sentences) near the beginning of the paper that announces the subject and its scope. Your preview statement will be a tremendous help both to you and to your readers. It will help you plan your paper, and it will tell your readers exactly what they are going to read about.

> Specifically, a **preview statement** is one or more sentences that clearly and concisely indicate the subject of your essay, the main points you will discuss, and the order in which you will discuss them.

In fiction, telling readers in advance what they're going to find out would never do. But this "advance notice" works very well for practical, everyday kinds of writing. Essays, term papers, technical reports, research papers, office memoranda, and business letters are not suitable for suspense or surprises. Readers have expectations about these kinds of writing, and you're more likely to get and keep your readers' interest if you indicate the subject and scope of your paper at the outset. Your preview statement acts like a table of contents, giving a clear indication of what is to follow. It maps the territory covered in your paper, to keep your readers (and you) on the right track.

The number of sentences in your preview statement depends on what your subject is, how best to phrase it, how many main points you have, and how they are expressed. The preview statement is usually found in the first paragraph of an essay.

To write a preview statement, you join your subject to your main points, after you have selected them and arranged them in the most appropriate order. Here is a simple formula for constructing a preview statement:

S	**consists of**	**1, 2, 3 . . . *n*.**
(subject)		(main points)

Can you identify the subject and the main points in each of these examples of preview statements?

Success in a broadcasting career depends on a combination of personal characteristics. Winners will be talented, motivated, and hardworking.

Our trip to New York was expensive, exhausting—and exhilarating.

The United States influences Canada's foreign policy, dominates our culture, and controls our economy. In fact, Canada is little more than an American satellite.

Two cheers for democracy: one because it admits variety and two because it permits criticism. (E.M. Forster)

The most prolific producers of unnecessary jargon are politicians, sports writers, advertising copy writers, and educators.

Now try your hand at analyzing the introductory paragraphs in the exercise below.

EXERCISE 4.1

Each of the five introductions below contains a preview statement. Underline the preview statement in each paragraph.

1. Suddenly a man steps into the road in front of me. He's wearing a uniform and he's waving his hand for me to pull over to the side. My heart pounds and my pores prickle with anxiety. I feel guilty, but I don't know what I've done wrong—maybe speeding 10 km over the limit, but no more. Anyone who has been caught in a radar trap knows this momentary feeling of panic, guilt, and resentment. We fear that the police officer will be brusque and blaming, but we are often surprised. There are as many kinds of police officers as there are people. Four kinds, however, dominate the profession: the confident veteran, the

arrogant authoritarian, the cocky novice, and the friendly professional. As I roll down my window, I wonder which kind of police officer I've gotten.

2. After a hard day's work, do you relax with two or three stiff drinks? Do you enjoy a few beers while watching a game on TV? Do you believe mixed drinks make a party more fun? Do you cool off with gin fizzes on a hot afternoon? If you answered "Yes" to most of these questions, you are probably abusing alcohol. The line between excessive social drinking and a serious addictive habit is a blurry one. Most alcoholics don't know they are hooked until they try to stop drinking. What are the signs that a drinker is no longer drinking for pleasure only? If a person "needs" a drink, or drinks alone, or can fall asleep only after some drinks, and can find enjoyment only when drinking, that person is probably in trouble.

3. What does an interviewer look for in a new job applicant? Good credentials, good preparation, good grooming, and good communication skills are essential features for anyone who wants a job. No interviewer would seriously consider an applicant who comes to an interview without the required educational background and work experience, without information about the job and the company, without appropriate clothing, and without the ability to present ideas clearly in the interview.

4. Ours is a transient society. Most of us travel more kilometres in a year than our grandparents travelled in a lifetime. We move from one city to another, one province to another, and one country to another. In the course of moving, we inhabit many homes. The family home of the past might have been inhabited by several generations, consecutively or concurrently. Today's average Canadians will probably have ten or more addresses during their adult lives. Our restlessness is having numerous effects on the children in our migrating families. They have to leave familiar surroundings and friends, perhaps more than once, and they must adjust to a new environment, to new habits, and sometimes to a new language. They often have difficulty forming new relationships in a new setting. They are paying a heavy price for the mobility of modern impermanence.

5. Movie villains are a necessary evil in an adventure on the silver screen. Without them, movie heroes would have nobody to pit their strength and cunning against, nobody to save the female stars from, nobody to confront in a dramatic showdown, and nobody to defeat in the eternal battle between good and evil. This melodramatic summary of a typical cinematic contest invariably applies, in obvious or subtle form, to all Hollywood thrillers. Villains are even more important than heroes, perhaps because villains show the measure of heroes by the nature of the heroes' triumph over them.

Phrasing Your Statement of Subject

Your statement of subject should be as clear and concise as you can make it. This doesn't mean you can let it be boring, however. Beginning writers often fall into the trap of stating the obvious: "In this essay I am going to discuss . . ." or "The subject of this paper is. . . ." Your readers *know* it's your essay; you needn't hit them over the head by pointing out your authorship or the fact that the paper contains your ideas. Here are three examples of faulty subject statements and their revisions.

POOR	BETTER
In this essay, I am going to discuss violence in hockey.	Violence in hockey is misunderstood by the nonplaying public.
Canada's multiculturalism policy is the subject of this paper.	Canada's multiculturalism policy is neither practical nor desirable.
I am going to examine the three most common causes of student failure in college.	There are three important reasons for the large number of failures among first-year college students.

Phrasing the Main Points

When you combine your statement of subject with your main points to form your preview statement, be sure that all your main points are phrased in the same way, in grammatically parallel form. If point 1 is a single word, then points 2, 3, and so on must also be single words. If point 1 is a phrase, then all the points following it must be phrases. If point 1 is a clause or a sentence, then the succeeding points must also be in clause or sentence form.

The following sentence contains a main point that is not parallel with the others.

> There are many qualities that combine to make a good nurse, but the three most important are strength, intelligence, and she must be compassionate.

Rewritten to be grammatically parallel, this statement might read as follows:

> There are many qualities that combine to make a good nurse, but the three most important are strength, intelligence, and compassion.

Or, the sentence could be rewritten this way:

> There are many qualities that combine to make a good nurse, but the three most important are that she or he be strong, intelligent, and compassionate.

Try the exercise below. You may have problems now with grammatical parallelism. We will be covering it in detail in Chapter 30.

EXERCISE 4.2

In each of the lists below, one point is not parallel with the others. Rephrase the incorrect item so that all are in grammatically parallel form.

1. I enjoy
   a. reading
   b. walking
   c. to cook
   d. talking
2. We have enjoyed vacations
   a. sunbathing at the beach
   b. relaxing at our cottage
   c. European travel
3. Our doctor is
   a. full of medical knowledge
   b. competent
   c. caring
4. I've noticed that my friends are increasingly
   a. concerned about smoking
   b. interested in fitness
   c. environmental awareness
5. To upgrade our educational system we need
   a. more effective teacher training
   b. better liaison between levels of education
   c. students must be motivated to learn

EXERCISE 4.3

Correct the following preview statements so that all the main points are expressed in the same grammatical form.

1. Important steps to improve your performance in a sport are practice on non-game days, warming up before the game, and playing hard during the game.

   _____

   _____

   _____

2. Some effects of too much television viewing include increased passivity, interaction with others is reduced, and impaired imagination.

   _____

   _____

   _____

3. A newspaper has three functions in our society: to inform the public about current affairs, to entertain with features and articles, and most importantly, persuasion about our political choices.

   _____

   _____

   _____

4. All the box-office hits of last year were violent action pictures, feeble comedies about sex, or repulsive horror melodramas.

   _____

   _____

   _____

5. Common causes of failure in college are lack of responsibility, lack of discipline, and not knowing basic skills.

   _____

   _____

   _____

6. Yuppies have three characteristics. They are highly materialistic, compulsive overachievers, and affluent in a highly conspicuous manner.

   _____

   _____

   _____

7. We are victims of the fashion industry. We can buy only what the industry decides to make available; the products are shoddily made; the styles change too quickly.

   _____

   _____

   _____

8. The Goods and Services Tax has several disadvantages for low-income Canadians. Most things cost more. Manufacturers are reluctant to lower their prices. The consumer pays twice for some services.

   _____

   _____

   _____

9. Unlike American cities, Canada's large cities have low crime rates, streets that are unlittered, and graffiti-free public transit.

   _____

   _____

   _____

10. If you want to be a good nurse, you have to love the job because the hours are long, you will work hard, and the pay you get is not that high.

    _____

    _____

    _____

EXERCISE 4.4

Combine each of the following subjects with its main points to form a clear preview statement that is expressed in grammatical parallel form.

1. Factors in choosing a bicycle
   - sized to your body
   - meets your needs
   - priced to your resources

   Preview statement: _____

   _____

   _____

   _____

2. Advantages of fishing as a hobby
   - calm, relaxing activity
   - inexpensive to begin
   - can provide a delicious meal

   Preview statement: _____

   _____

   _____

   _____

3. Methods of quitting smoking
   - laser therapy
   - acupressure
   - hypnosis
   - programmed withdrawal

Preview statement: _____

_____

_____

_____

_____

4. Comparison between
   McDonald's and Burger
   King (or any other two
   fast-food restaurants)
   - food
   - atmosphere
   - service
   - price

   Preview statement: _____

   _____

   _____

   _____

   _____

5. Causes of stress
   - death of a family member
   - change of employment
   - financial problems

   Preview statement: _____

   _____

   _____

   _____

   _____

6. Steps in getting a job
   - research job advertisements
   - prepare letter of application
   - perform well in the interview

   Preview statement: _____

   _____

   _____

   _____

   _____

7. Ingredients of a
   successful party
   - friendly people
   - good music
   - tasty food
   - ample liquid refreshments

Preview statement: _____

_____

_____

_____

_____

8. Evolution of a recession
   - unemployment causes general economic slowdown
   - consumer buying decreases, resulting in inflation
   - inflation causes fear and further decrease in consumer demand

Preview statement: _____

_____

_____

_____

_____

9. Disadvantages of teenage parenthood
   - less time for fun
   - instant need for more money
   - reduced chances for a good job
   - less opportunity for higher education

Preview statement: _____

_____

_____

_____

_____

10. Effects of urban overcrowding
    - traffic jams
    - too much air pollution
    - high rate of homelessness
    - violence on the streets

Preview statement: _____

_____

_____

_____

_____

You have now covered all the steps leading up to your own construction of a good preview statement. The earlier exercises have given you practice in the skills you need to phrase subjects and main points correctly and effectively. It's now time for you to write your own "live" example.

Exercise 4.5 will walk you through the process of developing a preview statement for a subject of your own choice. As you fill in the blanks in Exercise 4.5, you will be both reviewing the contents of the first four chapters and testing your mastery of the writing tasks they presented. You may want to refer to Exercise 4.5's step-by-step outline when you are starting your next paper or research report.

EXERCISE 4.5

1. Select a subject.

   _____

   _____

2. Test whether your subject is significant, single, specific, and supportable.

3. Using either a bottom-up or a top-down approach to generate ideas, identify three, four, or five main points in support of your subject.

   _____

   _____

   _____

   _____

   _____

4. Test whether your main points are all significant, distinct, and clearly related to your subject.

5. Arrange your main points in the order that is most likely to guarantee your readers' understanding of your subject: chronological, climactic, logical, or random.

   _____

   _____

   _____

   _____

   _____

6. Now rewrite your main points so that they are grammatically parallel: all single words, all phrases, or all clauses.

_____

_____

_____

_____

_____

7. Combine your statement of subject with your main points, to produce your preview statement.

_____

_____

_____

_____

_____

CHAPTER 5

Drafting the Blueprint

Imagine for a moment that you are able to hire an architect to design your dream house. The architect produces some initial sketches, based on your wish list, but you decide you would like a wider courtyard, a southern exposure for the pool enclosure, and a larger skylight in the master bedroom. Finally, your architect creates an artist's rendering of how your house will look when it has been built to satisfy your needs and specifications. You approve the drawing and give the architect permission to proceed.

However, no builder can work from any representation of what the exterior of the building will look like when it is finished. Builders need a detailed blueprint that shows every structural component's proper place and exact measurements before they can set the first form of the foundation.

When you write, you are building words into sentences, sentences into paragraphs, and paragraphs into the written communication of your ideas. You need a blueprint when you start to structure your essay, and you should refer to it often when you write, revise, edit, and finally declare your "building" finished.

The model blueprint on the next page was drafted for building a short essay that has three main points. The blueprint can be adapted and expanded to other styles and lengths.

THE MODEL BLUEPRINT

Title _____

Introductory paragraph _____

Grabber _____
_____

Preview Statement _____
S consists of 1, 2, and 3. _____

Body paragraphs Topic sentence introducing main point 1 goes here. _____

Support of first main point _____

Topic sentence introducing main point 2 goes here. _____

Support of second main point _____

Topic sentence introducing main point 3 goes here. _____

Support of third main point _____

A statement summarizing or reinforcing your main points goes here. _____

Concluding paragraph _____

Summary _____

Clincher _____

The following essay outline was developed using the model blueprint. Preparation of an outline would precede your writing of a first draft.

After the outline, we show the final version of "Flunking with Style," matched to the blueprint.

Essay title	Flunking with Style
Grabber	Challenge traditional view of failure in school
Preview statement (statement of subject and main points)	To fail your year in grand style, antagonize your teachers, disdain your studies, and cheat on your work.
1. Topic sentence	Antagonize your teachers
Support of first main point	• show boredom • slouch in desk • wear Walkman • talk to classmates • snort at teacher's points • respond "I dunno" to questions
2. Topic sentence	Disdain your studies
Support of second main point	• don't buy textbooks until midterm and don't make notes in them • never take notes in class • don't go to class—use clever excuses
3. Topic sentence	Cheat on your work
Support of third main point	• plagiarize research assignments • copy from a classmate's paper during exams • read notes written on your forearms • consult notes hidden in washroom • send in a ringer to write the exam for you
Summary or reinforcement of main points	If you follow these guidelines, you're guaranteed to flunk your year.
Clincher	The challenge is yours. Pick up the torch and fall with it!

Flunking with Style
Nell Waldman

Introductory paragraph

Grabber

People often remark that succeeding in school takes plenty of hard work. The remark implies that failure is a product of general idleness and zero motivation. This is an opinion I'd like to challenge. My long and checkered past in numerous educational institutions has taught me that to fail grandly, to fail extravagantly, to go down in truly blazing splendour, requires effort and imagination. To fail your year in the grand style, you must antagonize your teachers, disdain your studies, and cheat on your work. Keep the following guidelines in mind.

Preview Statement

Body paragraphs
1. Topic Sentence

The first step, antagonizing your teachers, isn't difficult if you keep in mind what it is that teachers like: intelligent, interested, even enthusiastic faces in front row centre. Show that you're bored before the class begins by slouching in a desk at the back of the room. Wear your Walkman, and don't forget to turn up the volume when that teacher starts to talk. Carry on running conversations with your seatmates. Aim an occasional snort or snicker in the teacher's direction when she's putting a complex point on the board. Above all, never volunteer an answer and respond sullenly with an "I dunno" if the teacher has the nerve to ask you a question. Before long, you'll have that teacher bouncing chalk stubs off your head. Once you've earned the loathing of all your instructors, you'll be well on your way to a truly memorable failure.

Support of first main point

2. Topic Sentence

The second step, disdaining your studies, is easy to master; they're probably B-O-R-I-N-G anyway. First, don't buy your books until close to midterm and keep them in their original condition; don't open, read, or note anything in them. Better yet, don't buy your texts at all. Second, never attempt to take notes in class. Third, stop going to class completely, but have lots of creative excuses for missed assignments: "My friend's aunt died"; "My gerbil's in a coma"; "My boyfriend was in another car wreck"; "My dog ate the lab report"; "I've got mono." You can bet your teachers will be really amused by these old stand-bys. By now, you are well on your way to disaster.

Support of second main point

3. Topic Sentence

The third step, cheating, will deliver the *coup de grâce* to your academic career. Should an instructor be so sadistic as to assign a research paper, just copy something out of a book that the librarian will be happy to find for you. Your instructor will be astonished at the difference between the book's polished, professional prose and your usual halting scrawls; you're guaranteed a zero. During your exams, sit at the back and crane your neck to read your classmate's paper. Roll up your shirt-sleeves to reveal the answers you've tattooed all over your forearms. Ask to be excused three or four times during the test so you can consult the notes you've stashed in the hall or the washroom. Be bold! Dig out your old wood-burning kit and emblazon cheat notes on the desk. If you want to ensure not just failure but actual expulsion, send in a ringer—a look-alike to write the exam for you!

Support of third main point

Concluding paragraph

Reinforcement of main point

Clincher

If you follow these guidelines, you will be guaranteed to flunk your year. Actively courting failure with verve, with flair, and with a sense of drama will not only ensure your status as an academic washout but also immortalize you in the memories of teachers and classmates alike. The challenge is yours! Become a legend—pick up the torch and fall with it!

Now it's your turn to develop your blueprinting skills.

EXERCISE 5.1

Read "Of Men and Machines" (pp. 157–58) and "Lightweight Lit." (pp. 170–71). Identify in each essay the sentences that correspond to the major structural items in the model blueprint. You may not have studied some of the terms mentioned (if you're working through the units in order), but you should be able to make a good guess at identifying the grabber and the clincher.

Essay title   Of Men and Machines

Grabber _____

_____

Preview statement _____
(statement of subject
and main points) _____

_____

_____

1. Topic sentence _____

_____

*Support of first
main point* _____

_____

_____

_____

2. Topic sentence _____

_____

*Support of second
main point* _____

_____

_____

_____

3. Topic sentence _____

_____

*Support of third
main point* _____

_____

_____

***Summary or
reinforcement of
main points***

_____

_____

_____

_____

Clincher

_____

_____

_____

_____

Essay title   Lightweight Lit.

Grabber

_____

_____

Preview statement
(statement of subject
and main points)

_____

_____

_____

_____

1. Topic sentence

_____

_____

***Support of first
main point***

_____

_____

_____

_____

2. Topic sentence

_____

_____

***Support of second
main point***

_____

_____

_____

_____

3. Topic sentence _____

_____

Support of third main point _____

_____

_____

Summary or reinforcement of main points _____

_____

_____

_____

Clincher _____

_____

Writing the Paragraphs

CHAPTER 6

Understanding Form and Function

What Does a Paragraph Look Like?

Essays are divided into paragraphs. **Paragraphs** are sentence groups that are separated from each other in their physical presentation and in their thought content. They usually have an indentation at the beginning (on a typed page, the first word begins five spaces in from the left margin) and some white space at the end (the last line is left blank following the paragraph's last word). Between the indentation and the final period comes the paragraph: a group of sentences that explains a single idea or topic.

If you were to draw a blueprint for a single paragraph, it would look like this:

A sentence that introduces the **topic** (or main idea) of the paragraph goes here.

Three or more sentences that specifically support or explain the topic go in here.

A sentence that concludes your explanation of the topic goes here.

How Does a Paragraph Function?

Readers expect that a paragraph will present a unit of thought or a single, developed idea. The white space at the start of each paragraph defines your thought units and serves two other important functions. First, it provides visual cues that make your writing "reader-friendly." Imagine if the page you are now reading were one continuous block of printing: no headings, no indentations, no paragraphs. The page would look so intimidatingly difficult to read that few readers would even attempt it. Second, paragraphs divide your writing into linked but separate sections, helping both you and your readers to stay on track, always conscious of where you are in the development of the subject that is the focus of your essay. Without paragraphs, ideas would blur and blend one into another. Readers would find it difficult to identify them, let alone follow the organization and development of the writer's thoughts.

Paragraph indentations function in much the same way that commercial breaks function in TV situation-comedy shows. Review a sitcom episode in your mind. The story will have a beginning, a middle, and an end, and these will be separated from each other by commercials. Since seven or eight minutes of each half-hour show are made up of commercials, writers have developed a format that divides any script neatly into segments. The opening scene presents the characters and reveals the story problem for the episode. After a commercial break, the story problem becomes complicated and more critical. Another commercial break interrupts, just before the crisis or climax of the show. The final commercial break precedes a brief ending that solves the problem, puts everything back together, and leaves you laughing so you'll tune in to the next week's show.

The paragraphs in an essay work much the same way. The white space at the beginning and end of the paragraphs sets them apart as separate "action" sequences. In a typical essay, an introductory paragraph is followed by paragraphs that add details and complexity to the ideas set out in the introduction. A concluding paragraph brings all the ideas together again and leaves the readers with the writer's complete thinking on the subject.

Your readers will be able to tell a great deal about your thinking by just quickly glancing at your page. A number of short paragraphs on your page will indicate a series of ideas, briefly (and perhaps superficially) explained. Newspapers traditionally use very short paragraphs, many of them only one sentence long, to attract readers. Long paragraphs—half a page or longer—suggest more complex ideas that require explanation and details; they signal serious thought.

As a general rule, you explore one major idea or main point in each paragraph. When you have finished exploring one topic and wish to move on to another, you signal this shift to your readers by beginning a new paragraph.

How Long Should a Paragraph Be?

The answer to this question depends on the *topic,* your readers' *knowledge* of the topic, and your *purpose* in writing. If your topic is complex, your readers' knowledge is limited, and your purpose is to persuade readers who do not share your point of view, then you'll probably need a fairly long paragraph to accomplish your goal. On the other hand, if you're writing about a fairly common idea that your readers can be expected to be familiar with, and your purpose is simply to share your understanding of that topic with your readers, you may be able to accomplish your task in a few sentences.

E X E R C I S E 6 . 1

Read the paragraphs below. After you've finished each one, answer the following questions:

- What is the topic of the paragraph, stated in a single word or short phrase?
- How much knowledge of the topic does the writer assume the readers have?
- What is the writer's purpose in this paragraph?

1. Violence as a way of achieving racial justice is both impractical and immoral. It is impractical because it is a descending spiral ending in destruction for all. The old law of an eye for an eye leaves everybody blind. It is immoral because it seeks to humiliate the opponent rather than win his understanding; it seeks to annihilate rather than to convert. Violence is immoral because it thrives on hatred rather than love. It destroys community and makes brotherhood impossible. It leaves society in monologue rather than dialogue. Violence ends by defeating itself. It creates bitterness in the survivors and brutality in the destroyers. A voice echoes through time saying to every potential Peter, "Put up your sword." History is cluttered with the wreckage of nations that failed to follow this command.

    (Martin Luther King, Jr., excerpt from "Three Types of Resistance to Oppression," in *Stride Toward Freedom* by Martin Luther King, Jr., New York: Harper and Row, 1958, pp. 211–15. Copyright © 1958 by Martin Luther King, Jr. Reprinted by permission of Harper & Row, Publishers, Inc.)

2. Try to decide in advance from which side you want to dismount, and then *stick to your decision!* If you put off making up your mind until the last possible minute or keep changing your plans, you may find yourself unable to decide at all and end up running around in a flurry of indecision. It is surprising how quickly any panic you feel can communicate itself to the elephant, who in turn may decide to go berserk. But that's nothing compared with how quickly *his* panic can communicate itself to you.

    (Richard L. Thomas, excerpt from "How to Dismount from an Elephant." Copyright © 1967 by *Harper's* Magazine. Reprinted from the May 1967 issue by special permission.)

3. *Vinaya* means humility; it is the complete surrendering of the self on the part of the *shishya* [the disciple] to the *guru*. The ideal disciple feels love, adoration, reverence, and even fear toward his *guru*, and he accepts equally praise or scoldings. Talent, sincerity, and the willingness to practise faithfully are essential qualities of the serious student. The *guru*, as the giver in this relationship, seems to be all-powerful. Often, he may be unreasonable, harsh, or haughty, though the ideal *guru* is none of these. Ideally, he should respond to the efforts of the disciple and love him almost as his own child. In India, a Hindu child, from his earliest years, is taught to feel humble toward anyone older than he or superior in any way. From the simplest gesture of the *namaskar*, or greeting (putting the hands palm to palm in front of the forehead and bowing), or the *pranam* (a respectful greeting consisting of touching the greeted person's feet, then one's own eyes and forehead with the hands held palm to palm) to the practice of *vinaya* or humility tempered with a feeling of love and worship, the Hindu devotee's vanity and pretension are worn away.

(Ravi Shankar, excerpt from "Studying Music in India," in *My Music, My Life* by Ravi Shankar. Copyright © 1968, by Kinnara School of Indian Music, Inc. Reprinted by permission of Simon & Schuster, Inc.)

4. Take William Lyon Mackenzie King, our prime minister through the war and, so it seemed, for all time until Pierre Trudeau came along and seemed to be prime minister for all time. King held power longer than any other Western politician in this century. How did such a pudgy, mundane little man do it? The truth is, he did it deliberately. He was shrewd and self-effacing, and he told his friends that he made every speech as boring as possible because then no one would ever remember what he said and hold it against him. Twenty-two years in power, droning on and on over the airwaves, and meanwhile, he was as crazy as a loon.

(Barry Callaghan, excerpt from "Canadian Wry." Copyright © October 1985. Reprinted with permission of the author.)

5. A word about balls. The *New Columbia Encyclopedia* says, "Despite the name, the ball used is not soft," which may be the understatement of the tome's 3,052 pages. There were three kinds of softballs, and each was about as soft as anthracite. The best was simply a big baseball, with seams that were pretty well flush with the horsehide cover. Then there was a solid rubber ball with fake seams. After a while, this ball did soften up, but on grounds it no longer hurt enough for competition, it was then retired for use only in practice. Then there was the "outseam" ball. Perhaps it was not a sadist who invented it. Perhaps it was merely someone who sought durability in lean times. But the outseam was a quarter-inch ridge of leather so hard that, when you fielded a rifling, spinning grounder, the ball felt as though its real function was to rip the skin off your palms. The outseam ball was a character-builder.

(Harry Bruce, excerpt from "The Softball Was Always Hard," in *Each Moment As It Flies: Writings by Harry Bruce*. Copyright © 1984. Reprinted with permission of Bella Pomer Agency, Inc.)

CHAPTER 7

Crafting the Topic Sentence

The **topic sentence** in each paragraph is the sentence that clearly identifies your main idea in that paragraph—what the paragraph's about. The topic sentence focusses the paragraph, helps to unify it, and keeps both you and your readers on track. It ensures that both of you are starting from the same point. In some professional writing, the topic sentence is not the first sentence of the paragraph. Sometimes it is effective to wait and let the second sentence, or even the third, announce the topic of the paragraph. But professional writers, through years of practice, have earned the right to break the rules. Beginning writers should remember this: *most readers assume that the first sentence of a paragraph identifies the topic of that paragraph.* If it doesn't in your writing, you run the risk that your readers will proceed through your paragraph assuming the topic is something other than what you intended. Not only is this a waste of the readers'—and your—time, it can be frustrating for both of you. To be absolutely clear to your readers, identify your topic up front.

A good topic sentence does three things:

> 1. It introduces the topic of the paragraph.
> 2. It makes a point about the topic.
> 3. It makes a statement that is neither too broad nor too narrow.

Readers appreciate writers who get to the point quickly, make the point clearly, and support or explain it adequately. They also appreciate writers who can make their points in an interesting way. Take the time to write topic sentences that are something more than straightforward, flat announcements of your main idea. Compare the following pairs of topic sentences.

WEAK	STRONG
This paragraph is about violence.	Violence as a way of achieving racial justice is both impractical and immoral.
I'm going to tell you how to dismount from an elephant.	Try to decide in advance from which side you want to dismount, and then *stick to your decision!*
My love of "trash" is the subject of this paper.	I'm ashamed to confess my secret vice—but since we're friends, I can tell you—I *love* "trash."

A good way of introducing the topic so that it is both interesting and effective is to make a point about it. You save your readers' time and eliminate the risk of confusion if you make clear at the outset your idea about or your attitude towards your topic. Consider these examples.

WEAK	STRONG
The third step is cheating.	The third step, cheating, will deliver the *coup de grâce* to your academic career.
You should know your audience.	Knowledge of your audience will enable you to devise an effective approach to your topic.
Let us consider the idea of manhood.	I have always disliked being a man.

Finally, the topic you choose must be "the right size"—neither so broad that you cannot support it adequately in a single paragraph, nor so narrow that it doesn't require support. The 4-S test that you used to determine whether a subject was suitable for a paper can also be applied to potential paragraph topics. If your topic is single, significant, specific, and supportable, it should form the basis for a solid paragraph. Take a look at these topic sentences.

WEAK	STRONG
Good teachers share certain characteristics.	A good teacher shows respect for her students.

WEAK	STRONG
I like ink.	Despite the almost universal preference for word processors, I still prefer to write with a pen.
Canadians are different from Americans.	What Canadians should be thankful for is what genuinely makes us different.
Censorship of books and movies is a necessary evil.	Censorship of movies is a necessary evil.
Today's teenagers have a hard time.	A teen's relationship with her mother is often a difficult one.

EXERCISE 7.1

Underline the topic sentence in each of the following paragraphs.

1. Besides being time-consuming, trying to find a part-time job can be humiliating. Some employers seem to feel that it is their right, and part of the hiring process, to point out all your faults and shortcomings during the interview. Here is a person you've just met telling you how useless you are! Until you learn to cope with rejection, being turned down for a job can be pretty humiliating, too. It's very humbling to be told that you're not smart enough to sell blue jeans or strong enough to ride a courier bike.

2. Such a seemingly minor irritant as sanitation can drive a wedge between generations of new Canadians. When I approached my grand-father about his spitting, a habit he picked up in China and continued to practise on the streets of Vancouver, he waited patiently for me to finish. I explained that it is unsanitary and unhealthy to spit on the street, and that to Canadians it is a disgusting habit. He smiled and quietly asked me in Mandarin, "What do these healthy Canadians do, then? Surely they don't swallow the stuff. . . . *That* would be disgusting!"

3. No one seems able to explain the increasing death rate among loons. While some claim that acid rain has depleted the fish stock in the lakes, others maintain that mercury in the fish that loons eat is destroying their nervous systems. Evidence can be found to support both these views and several other theories as well. However, until we determine conclusively what is killing this wonderful bird, our efforts to save it will be haphazard and probably ineffective.

4. There is something magical about it. Baseball has a dimension far beyond mere athletic competition, a dimension that may encompass the mystical. *Field of Dreams*, the movie based on W.P. Kinsella's short story "Shoeless Joe Jackson Comes to Iowa," comes closest to expressing this mysterious quality of the game. A corn farmer hears a voice telling him to build a ball diamond that will attract the ghosts of long-dead players. He does, and it does. It isn't really surprising that

thousands of people every year make a pilgrimage to the baseball diamond in Iowa that was carved out of a cornfield as the setting for the movie. The voice said, "If you build it, he will come." Baseball has that kind of magic.

5.   The third consideration is perhaps the most important. Canada makes no economic sense. There may be excellent reasons for Canada's existence historically, socially, culturally, and even geographically, but the lines of trade and commerce flow north–south. If a government's chief concern is the economy, that government will naturally draw us closer and closer to the United States, cinching in those belts of commerce that bind us to our southern partner. Only governments whose prime goals are cultural or social will loosen the longitudinal ties and seek east–west bonds.

6.   The headlines in the supermarket tabloids are a revealing study of North American pop culture. For two years, "Elvis Lives!" headlines dominated the front pages. When readers got tired of seeing Elvis everywhere they turned, the headlines shifted to the always sure-selling aliens and UFOs. Some enterprising headline writers even combined the two: "Elvis Was an Alien with a Mission" and "Aliens Take Off with Elvis' Frozen Body." Roseanne, Cher, and Madonna are ever-popular subjects in the tabloids, along with deformity, depravity, and debauchery in forms previously unheard and even undreamt of. What the popularity of these checkout counter papers tells us about ourselves, or may tell future anthropologists about us, is frightening.

7.   "Why do you want it?" This should be the first question a good computer salesperson asks a prospective customer. With the huge variety of computers now on the market, the determining factor in a purchase should be the job the machine will be expected to do. While colour monitors and graphics cards, stereo sound, and joysticks are great for video games, a user who is buying a word processor needn't spend money for any of them. Home users and small businesses often get carried away with the desire for gigantic memory capacity, lightning speed, and colour graphics capability, but these are advertising gimmicks rather than useful purchases for most small users. On the other hand, it can be a costly error for a buyer to underestimate long-term computer needs and buy a machine that must be upgraded or replaced in a year.

8.   For millions of people around the world, the greatest annual sporting event is not the Stanley Cup or the Superbowl, but cycling's premier race, the Tour de France. Among the millionaire riders who compete in this gruelling contest, none is more admired and respected than Canada's Steve Bauer. From a tiny village in Ontario's Niagara Peninsula, Bauer trained on the back roads and steep hills of the Niagara Escarpment. He first came to international attention when he took the silver medal at the Olympics in 1984; he turned pro the same year, and quickly took his place among cycling's elite riders. When the greatness of many athletes is measured by their egos, and Canada's own international image is tarnished by drug use, it is refreshing to be represented in international competition by someone who so well reflects the qualities

most valued by Canadians: modesty, determination, integrity, and grit. Steve Bauer is someone in whom we can all take pride.

9. If I were unable to go to France, my next vacation choice would be Greece. A visit to Greece combines the excitement of exploring some of the world's greatest historical treasures with the joy of unequalled recreation and relaxation opportunities. From the ruins of the first Olympic stadium in Olympia to the magnificent theatre in Epidarus, from the sites of Greek mythology at Knossos and Mycenae to the wonders of Athens itself, impressive remnants of ancient Greece are everywhere. When tired of tramping through the magnificent temples and palaces of the past, one can take a break in the clear, warm waters of the Aegean Sea or lie on the white-sand beaches of Corfu. Modern Greece is one of the world's most hospitable and enjoyable recreational destinations; ancient Greece is a bonus that makes the package almost irresistible.

10. Finally, then, there is the question of appearance and whether a beard mars or improves a man's looks. In my view, a bearded man is more interesting, more mature-looking, and more attractive than his cleanshaven counterparts. It's impossible for most men to hide their feelings; emotion is written all over their bald faces. But bearded men project an air of depth, of mystery, simply because they aren't broadcasting their every feeling in the lines and frowns of their faces. Men whose chins make them appear weak, whose mouths betray indecision, whose babyish complexions make them look eternally seventeen, all can disguise their shortcomings while adding majesty and dignity with a full facial growth. There is something interesting and individual about a bearded man that his scraped and plucked friends lack.

EXERCISE 7.2

Study the topic sentences you underlined in Exercise 7.1, and determine whether each is satisfactory. Does it introduce the topic clearly? Does it make a point about the topic? Is it too broad or too narrow? Finally, rewrite the topic sentences of paragraphs 3 and 10 to make them more effective.

EXERCISE 7.3

Each of the following preview statements consists of a statement of subject and some main points. For each of these preview statements, develop the main points into effective topic sentences.

1. It is not easy for students to avoid bad eating habits, given the wide availability of junk food, the lack of time to prepare balanced meals, and the widespread ignorance about the importance of proper nutrition.

• _____

_____

_____

* _____

  _____

  _____

* _____

  _____

  _____

2. Canadians emigrate to other countries for a variety of reasons, chief among them the search for a warmer climate, the search for better job opportunities, and the search for exotic experiences.

   * _____

     _____

     _____

   * _____

     _____

     _____

   * _____

     _____

     _____

3. Though both Canadians and Americans are part of a highly affluent society, Canadians seem to be more obsessed than their southern neighbours with personal savings, life insurance, and pension plans.

   * _____

     _____

     _____

   * _____

     _____

     _____

   * _____

     _____

     _____

4. Canada's Charter of Rights prohibits discrimination on the grounds of sex, age, race, or religion.

   * _____

_____

_____

- _____

_____

_____

- _____

_____

_____

- _____

_____

_____

5. Getting the job you want requires that you prepare a flawless résumé, research the firm you are interested in, respond intelligently in the interview, and follow up the interview appropriately.

- _____

_____

_____

- _____

_____

_____

- _____

_____

_____

- _____

_____

_____

6. Because maintaining a home involves considerable amounts of both time and money, one should consider very carefully the decision to buy a house.

- _____

_____

_____

- _____
_____
_____

7. The driver who caused your accident last weekend was probably one of four types: a road hog, a tailgater, a speed demon, or a Sunday driver.

- _____
_____
_____

- _____
_____
_____

- _____
_____
_____

- _____
_____
_____

8. The thought of moving to the country is attractive to many city dwellers because of the slower pace, the cleaner air, and the more closely knit communities.

- _____
_____
_____

- _____
_____
_____

- _____
_____
_____

9. Being unemployed, being broke, and being alone all contribute to depression.

- _____

_____

_____

• _____

_____

_____

_____

• _____

_____

_____

_____

10. Though their parents may have been interested in changing the world, today's college students seem primarily interested in finding a good job and making a good salary.

• _____

_____

_____

_____

• _____

_____

_____

CHAPTER 8

Developing the Topic

After you've written your topic sentence, telling your readers what point or idea you're going to discuss in a paragraph, the next step is to develop that point or idea. An adequately developed paragraph will give enough supporting information to make the topic completely clear to your readers. Unless you are writing from a very detailed outline and have listed in front of you all the supporting material you need, a little thinking is in order at this point. Put yourself in your readers' place. What do your readers already know about your topic? Is their attitude towards your topic hostile or sympathetic? What do your readers need to know to understand your point clearly? If you ask yourself the seven questions listed below, you'll be able to decide what kind or kinds of development to use to support a particular topic sentence. The choice of development is up to you. Your topic and what your readers need to know about it will be the bases of your decision.

1. *Would telling a story be an effective way to get your idea across to your readers?* Everyone loves to read a story if it's well told and relevant to what's being discussed. Use of a personal anecdote to illustrate a point can be a very effective way of helping your readers not only understand your idea but also remember it. Below are two examples that illustrate the use of narration to develop a topic.

I first experienced culture shock when I travelled to Egypt. I was walking down the main street on the day of my arrival when it suddenly struck me that the crowds on the street were stepping aside to make way for me. It was 1980, and my height, blond hair, and blue eyes were so unusual to the Egyptians that I was an object of intense curiosity. The staring and pointing followed me everywhere. Finally, unable to cope any longer with being constantly on display, I took refuge in the Canadian Embassy and spent a couple of hours quietly leafing through back issues of *Maclean's* magazine.

I really enjoy literary discussions. I love it when people at trendy restaurants smack their lips in appreciation of the latest South American novelist, Egyptian poet, or Armenian essayist. By eavesdropping on these discussions, I can find out what's going on in the world of "great literature" so that when people ask me what I've read lately, I can pretend that I, too, am devoted to highbrow literature.

2. *Would a definition help your readers to understand?* A definition paragraph explains and clarifies the meaning of a word or an idea that is central to your topic. Use the definition paragraph to explain a term that may be unfamiliar to your readers. (Write your own definition, please. Quoting from a dictionary is an overused and boring way to start a paragraph.) Below are definitions of terms that two writers wanted to be certain their readers understood.

Culture shock is the inability to understand or cope with experiences one has never encountered before. It commonly affects travellers who journey to lands whose climate, food, language, and customs are alien to the traveller. In addition to confusion and anxiety, culture shock may even produce physical symptoms: chills, fever, trembling, and faintness.

While the flood is a single bulb, strip lighting is a series of lamps set in a rectangular trough. It can be used for general illumination, but its primary functions are to blend the acting areas, illuminate shadows, and, with the use of colour, provide tone for settings and costumes. Strips can be hung as footlights, as border lights, or as special-purpose lights to illuminate backings for windows or doors.

You should include a definition, too, if you're using a familiar term in an unusual way. Here, Martin Luther King defines what he means by "the length of life."

Now let us notice first the length of life. I have said that this is the dimension of life in which the individual is concerned with developing his inner powers. It is that dimension of life in which the individual pursues personal ends and ambitions. This is perhaps the selfish dimension of life, and there is such a thing as moral and rational self-interest. If one is not concerned about himself he cannot be totally concerned about other selves.

(Martin Luther King, Jr., excerpt from "The Dimensions of a Complete Life," in *The Measure of a Man* by Martin Luther King, Jr. Copyright © 1959. Reprinted with permission of Christian Education Press.)

3. *Would examples help to clarify the point?* Listing a number of examples is probably the most common method of developing an idea and supporting a statement. Readers can become confused or suspicious when they read unsupported statements of "fact," opinion, or ideas. One of the best ways to support your opinion or ideas is by providing clear, relevant examples. Sometimes, as in the paragraph below, a single detailed example is enough to allow your readers to see clearly what you mean.

> Culture shock can affect anyone, even a person who never leaves home. My grandfather was perfectly content to be an accountant until he retired, and was confident that his company would need his services for the foreseeable future. Computers were "silly toys" and modern business practices just "jargon" and "a new fad." When he was laid off four years before his retirement, he went into shock. It wasn't just the layoff; it was the speed of change—the idea that he was stranded in a new and unfamiliar culture for which he was unprepared, and in which he had no useful role.

A number of examples may be necessary to illustrate a point, as in this next paragraph.

> All sports may be reduced to a few basic skills, which, if learned properly at the outset and drilled until they are instinctive, lead to success. Tennis is no exception; however, few people seem willing to spend the time needed to master the basics. Having been shown the proper grip and swing for a forehand, backhand, and serve, my students seem to feel they can qualify for Wimbledon. The basics are not learned that easily. Many tennis schools are now using a system first developed in Spain that is very successful in establishing the correct stroke in new players: for the first month of lessons, they aren't allowed to use a tennis ball. For that first month, correct positioning, proper swing, footwork, and technique are drilled without any of the distractions of keeping score, winning or losing, or chasing errant balls. That's how important the basics are to winning tennis.

4. *Would a quotation or paraphrase help to convince your readers?* Occasionally you will find that someone else—an expert in a particular field, a well-known author, or a respected public figure—has said what you want to say better than you could ever hope to say it. Relevant and authoritative quotations, as long as they are kept short and are not used too frequently, are useful in developing your topic. In the paragraph below, Martin Luther King uses a famous quotation to sum up and emphasize his point.

> As long as there is poverty in the world, I can never be rich, even if I have a billion dollars. As long as diseases are rampant and millions of people in this world cannot expect to live more than twenty-eight or

thirty years, I can never be totally healthy even if I just got a good check-up at Mayo Clinic. I can never be what I ought to be until you are what you ought to be. This is the way our world is made. No individual or nation can stand out boasting of being independent. We are interdependent. So John Donne placed it in graphic terms when he affirmed, "No man is an island entire of itself. Every man is a piece of the continent, a part of the main." Then he goes on to say, "Any man's death diminishes me because I am involved in mankind, and therefore never send to know for whom the bell tolls; it tolls for thee." When we discover this, we master the second dimension of life.

A paraphrase is a summary, in your own words, of someone else's idea. Don't forget to indicate whose idea you are paraphrasing, the way King does here.

Some years ago a learned rabbi, the late Joshua Liebman, wrote a book entitled *Peace of Mind*. He has a chapter in the book entitled "Love Thyself Properly." In this chapter he says in substance that it is impossible to love other selves adequately unless you love your own self properly. Many people have been plunged into the abyss of emotional fatalism because they did not love themselves properly. So every individual has a responsibility to be concerned about himself enough to discover what he is made for. After he discovers his calling he should set out to do it with all of the strength and power in his being. . . .

5. *Would a comparison help to illustrate or clarify your point?* A comparison shows similarities between things; it shows how two different things are alike in a particular way or ways. If you have a difficult or abstract topic to explain, try comparing it to something tangible that is familiar to your readers, as this writer does.

Being left on your own in a foreign land is a bit like being forced to play a card game when you're the only one who doesn't know the rules. As the stakes get higher and the other players' excitement and enjoyment increase, you get correspondingly more frustrated and miserable. Finally, in desperation, you want to throw your cards on the table, absorb your losses, and go home.

In this next paragraph, the writer uses an **analogy**—an extended comparison—between a date and a car to make the point both clear and interesting.

The economy-model date features cramped conditions and a lack of power. The econo-date thinks that his personality can make up for the fact that you never go anywhere except for walks and never do anything that costs money. He tends to be shy, quiet, and about as much fun as an oil leak. It's not just that he doesn't have lots of money to spend; it's that he doesn't use any imagination or creativity to compensate for his lack of cash.

6. *Is a series of steps or stages involved?* Sometimes the most effective way to develop the main idea of your paragraph is by explaining how something is done—that is, by relating the process or series of steps involved. Make sure you break the process down into its component parts and detail the steps logically and precisely. Read how this writer explains the process of writing a good business letter.

> The business letter must be clear. You should have a very firm idea of what you want to say, and you should let the reader know it. Use the structure of the letter to guide the reader point by point from your introduction, through your reasoning, to your conclusion. Paragraph often, to break up the page and to lend an air of organization to the letter. Use an accepted business-letter format: there are several, and they can be found in any book of business English. Reread what you have written from the point of view of someone who is seeing it for the first time, and be sure that all explanations are adequate and all necessary information is provided (including reference numbers, dates, and other identification). A clear message, clearly delivered, is the essence of business communication.

In writing a process paragraph, you need to pay particular attention to transitions, which are discussed in the next chapter, or you'll leave your readers gasping in the dust as you gallop through your explanation. The paragraph below illustrates a simple yet effective use of transitions.

> The second step, disdaining your studies, is easy to master. They're probably B-O-R-I-N-G anyway. First, don't buy your books until close to midterm and keep them in their original condition; don't open, read, or note anything in them. Better yet, don't buy your texts at all. Second, never attempt to take notes in class. Third, stop going to class completely, but have lots of creative excuses for missed assignments: "My friend's aunt died"; "My gerbil's in a coma"; "My boyfriend was in another car wreck"; "My dog ate the lab report"; "I've got mono." You can bet your teachers will be really amused by these old stand-bys. By now, you are well on your way to disaster.

7. *Would precise, detailed information or statistics make your ideas clearer or more credible?* Providing your reader with concrete, specific, descriptive details can be an effective way to develop your main idea. In some paragraphs, numerical facts or statistics are essential to make your argument convincing or to back up your opinion. (Just make sure that your facts are 100 percent correct!)

In the paragraph below, the writer uses specific details to support a comparison of two automobiles.

> Performance of the two cars was very close, especially when you consider the tiny difference at the speeds involved. However, I was able to get the 'Vette from 0 to 100 kph in exactly six seconds, while the Porsche took more than half a second longer. In cornering, the Porsche was marginally superior, but the Corvette was the clear winner in braking. From 100 kph it came to a complete stop in 68 metres; the Porsche went almost 2 metres farther before stopping.

In this next paragraph, notice how Pierre Berton appeals to our senses in his description of the mixture he uses to season his famous baked beans:

> When it [the seasoned liquid] tastes pungent and hot (remember that the pungency will be cut by the beans), stir in a large quantity of molasses. Most people don't use enough molasses, and yet this is the essence of all good baked bean dishes. For there comes a critical moment when the sweetness of the molasses is wedded to the sharpness of the vegetables and herbs, and it is this subtle flavour, baked indelibly into the beans and mingling with the pork fat, that brings a sparkle to the eyes.
>
> _____
>
> (Pierre Berton, "Baked Beans.")

In writing your own paragraphs, you will often need to use more than one method of development to explain your point. The seven methods described in this chapter can be used in any combination you choose. Keep your readers' knowledge, attitudes, and needs in mind as you consider what kinds of development to use in support of a point.

EXERCISE 8.1

To stretch your imagination and improve your mastery of the kinds of support you can choose from to develop a topic, write a short paragraph on each of the following topics, using only the methods of development specified.

1. Chinese food	example and narration
2. Headaches	specific detail and process
3. Physical fitness	comparison and quotation or paraphrase
4. Fast food	definition and specific detail
5. Making a video	narration and process

EXERCISE 8.2

The essay below has an introduction, a conclusion, and topic sentences, but it doesn't have any support for the main points. Using a variety of the kinds of paragraph development you've learned in this chapter, write four or five sentences to support each main point. Before you begin, decide on your readers: for whom is this essay intended?

Money Matters

"Money can't buy happiness," according to the old adage. Perhaps it can't, but certainly the lack of money can bring pain. I have no aspirations to be featured on *Lifestyles of the Rich and Famous*, but I do want enough money to keep the wolf from my door. Money may not make me happy, but it will enable me to escape destitution, enjoy freedom from insecurity, and provide my family with the necessities of life.

Obviously, one needs enough money to keep off the streets and out

of the soup kitchens. _____

_____

_____

_____

_____

_____

_____

_____

_____

_____

_____

_____

Peace of mind is very difficult to come by if you don't know where

your next dollar is coming from. _____

_____

_____

_____

_____

_____

_____

_____

_____

_____

_____

_____

_____

"Enough is as good as a feast," the proverb says, and I want "enough" so that I may provide for my family. _____

_____

_____

_____

_____

_____

_____

_____

_____

_____

_____

_____

_____

Relatively few people in Canada suffer the destitution, insecurity, and deprivation that lack of money brings. But only a blind person or a fool would believe that no one in our country suffers because there isn't enough cash for basic needs. A modest bank account may not buy one ounce of happiness, but it prevents a ton of misery, and preventing misery for all should be our individual and collective goal.

CHAPTER 9

Keeping Your Readers with You

As you write your paragraphs, keep in mind that you want to make it as easy as possible for your readers to follow you through your essay. *Unity, coherence,* and *tone* can make the difference between a paper that confuses or annoys your readers and one that enlightens and pleases them.

Unity

Unity means "oneness"; the contents of a paragraph must relate to a single main idea. All supporting sentences in the paragraph must clearly and directly relate to the topic sentence of that paragraph. A paragraph is said to be unified when it contains nothing that does not contribute to its main idea.

Achieving unity takes careful planning. You want to make the points you set out to make, not revise them or introduce other points that occur to you as you are writing. The time to set down whatever happens to come to mind is in the prewriting stage, not the paragraph development stage. Any material that does not clearly support the topic sentence should be deleted or moved to another paragraph in the essay—assuming, of course, that it is directly relevant there.

Take a look at the paragraph below. It contains several sentences that spoil the unity of the paragraph, because they do not clearly relate to the topic.

I knew I wanted to return to school, but did I want to be a full-time or a part-time student? The major consideration was, not surprisingly, money. If I chose to go to college fulltime, then I would have to give up my fulltime job. The resulting loss of income would reduce my buying power to zero. Even the tuition fees would be beyond my reach. Also, my choice of program would be a difficult decision, because I still wasn't sure which career path to follow. My other option was part-time education. If I kept my fulltime job, I could at least pay for food, rent, and a modest amount of clothing. Also, I could afford the tuition fees. Going to school part-time costs less per year, because the expenditure is spread over a longer period of time than it is in the fulltime program. Therefore, I chose to educate myself part time, through continuing education courses. While working, I could learn new skills in my spare time. My career choice would still be in doubt, but I would have a longer time in which to make up my mind. Money is scarce for a fulltime, self-supporting student, but as a part-time student, I could have the best of both worlds: a steady income and a college education.

Draw a line through the sentences that do not logically and directly support the topic of the paragraph: the writer's decision whether to be a full-time or part-time student.

These are the sentences that you should have crossed out because they do not belong in this paragraph and are disruptive to its unity:

1. Also, my choice of program would be a difficult decision, because I still wasn't sure which career path to follow.
2. While working, I could learn new skills in my spare time.
3. My career choice would still be in doubt, but I would have a longer time in which to make up my mind.

EXERCISE 9.1

The paragraphs below have some irrelevant sentences. They do not support the topic sentence and thus they distract from the unity of the paragraph. Find and cross out the sentences that don't belong. (Hint: read the entire paragraph before you cross out the unrelated material.)

1. A good pizza consists of a combination of succulent ingredients. First, you prepare the foundation, the crust, which may be thick or thin, depending on your preference. I like my crusts thick and chewy. The crust is spread with a layer of basil- and oregano-flavoured tomato sauce. Next, a rich smorgasbord of toppings—pepperoni, mushrooms, green peppers, bacon, anchovies—should be scattered over the tomato sauce. *Smorgasbord* is a Swedish word meaning a buffet meal; *pizza* is Italian in origin. Last of all, a double-thick blanket of bubbling mozzarella cheese should be spread over all. Pizza is simple to make—all you need is dough, tomato sauce, vegetables, sausage, herbs, and cheese—but the combination has an unbeatable taste.

2.   Keeping a job is not easy in a tight market in which well-educated, unemployed job-seekers are plentiful. Here are a couple of hints you will find helpful in maintaining your "employed" status. First, you should not only apply your specialized knowledge on the job every day, but also continually update it by taking seminars and evening courses to enhance your skills. Doing your job effectively is difficult without falling prey to burnout. Second, good communication—with the public, your fellow workers, and your supervisor—is perhaps the most important factor in keeping you on the payroll. Upgrading your education and improving your communication skills are your best defences against the pink slip.

3.   After the divorce, I found that most of my old friends' behaviour changed. Some of them behaved as they always had, treating my former wife and me with a mixture of friendly indifference and a stoic lack of curiosity. Others avoided us because they felt, I assume, that it would have been a betrayal of one of us to socialize with the other as if nothing had happened. My wife was surprised and hurt. Those who had been closer to me withdrew from her, and those who had been closer to her disappeared from my life. I can't imagine what they are saying about me now. One thing is sure, none of our old friends is quite the same with my wife or me as they were before our divorce.

4.   Comedies are my favourite way to relax. Horror films terrify me, and adventures become tedious after the tenth chase; but comedies entertain and refresh me after a long shift at work. Woody Allen pictures, especially the early farces, help me to take my mind off the stress of the day. For example, *Bananas,* a satire about American politics in the '60s, is more relaxing for me than a double martini. It's also less fattening, and I've been trying to give up drinking. *Sleeper,* a futuristic spoof, has me laughing, on average, twice a minute. Perhaps my favourite, however, is *Annie Hall.* After viewing it, I am so weak with laughter that I can go to sleep within minutes. Now that all of Allen's comedies are available on video, I never need to feel tense and worn out for longer than it takes to insert a cassette.

5.   I admit it: word processors have me completely baffled. There is a popular myth that a word processor is merely a complicated typewriter. No way. Typing is straightforward; you hit the keys and the words appear on the paper before you. Keying on a word processor is something quite different. For one thing, the processor uses code, and you, the novice, have to learn the code before you can key in even the first word. Learning the mystifying code—and every word processor is different—requires more time and patience than it would take to carve a research essay on a piece of marble using a dull chisel. It is time-consuming and annoying to have to translate English into another "language" before beginning to grapple with this electronic monster. My problem is I was never good at languages. I studied Latin for a year and never did understand the verb endings. Hungarian or Mandarin would be easier to master than the instructions in a WordPerfect manual. No word processor for me, thank you. I'll stick to English and my old typewriter.

EXERCISE 9.2

Choose one of the topic sentences below and develop it into a paragraph. Make sure that all your supporting sentences relate directly to the topic so your paragraph will be unified.

1. Co-operative education gives you a head start in the workplace.
2. Lotteries exploit the gullibility of those who want to get rich quickly.
3. Saturday nights are fun, but you pay for them Sunday morning.
4. Exams are a nightmare for those who don't prepare well.
5. An office romance is a dangerous self-indulgence.

Coherence

Coherence means "sticking together." The sentences within each paragraph need to stick together, or cohere, as do the paragraphs within an essay. If your sentences and paragraphs are not coherent, your readers will have great difficulty trying to fit your bits of information together to make sense of the whole. Sorting out sentences as if they were pieces of a puzzle is not your readers' job. Your responsibility as a writer is to put the pieces together to form a complete and clear picture for your readers.

Coherence is achieved in two ways. First, you need to arrange the sentences in each paragraph according to an organizational principle. Remember the ways that you ordered the essay paragraphs in Chapter 3, "Managing the Main Points"? You should arrange your ideas within paragraphs in the same ways: chronological, climactic, logical, or, infrequently, random order. (You may wish to turn to pp. 41–42 to review these.)

Second, you achieve coherence by providing **transitions,** or connections between one idea and the next within a paragraph, and between one paragraph and the next within an essay. Why are transitions needed? Read the paragraph below and you'll see clearly that something is missing. The paragraph has adequate development, but no transitions.

> We were bored one day. We didn't know what to do. It was Friday. We thought about going to the library. No one really wanted to do schoolwork. We went to the mall. For a short time we window-shopped. We discussed what to do. It was agreed that we would drive to the American side of the border. We would do our shopping. It was a short drive. We went to a discount mall. The bargains were great. We spent much more money than we intended to. We went home. We discovered that with the American exchange, prices are better at home. We should have gone to the library.

Not very easy to read, is it? Readers are jerked abruptly from point to point until, battered and bruised, they finally reach the end. This kind of writing is unfair to readers. It makes them do too much of the work. The ideas may all be there, but the readers have to figure out for themselves how the ideas fit together. After a couple of paragraphs like the one above, even the most patient readers can become annoyed.

Now read the same paragraph, rewritten with transitions.

> **Last Friday we were so bored we didn't know what to do. We thought about going to the library, but no one really wanted to study, so we went to the mall and window-shopped for a while. After a long discussion about what to do next, we agreed to drive to the American side of the border for some serious shopping. A short drive later, we arrived at a discount mall, where the bargains were so great we spent much more money than we had intended. Finally, we returned home, where we discovered that, with the American exchange, prices were better at home after all. We should have gone to the library.**

Here the readers are gently guided from one point to the next. By the time they reach the conclusion, they know not only what ideas the writer had in mind but also how the ideas fit together to present a unit. The transitions make the readers' job easy and rewarding.

Transitions are necessary, and you can choose from an array of transitional devices to improve the coherence of your writing. There are five techniques to master:

1. *Repeat a key word.* This technique focusses the readers' attention on an idea and creates a thread of meaning that runs through a paragraph (or a paper), tying the whole thing together.
2. *Use synonyms.* Frequent repetition of a key word can become monotonous after a while. You can keep the reader focussed on the idea by using **synonyms,** various words that convey the same thought.
3. *Use pronoun references.* Another way of maintaining the focus but varying the wording is to use appropriate pronouns to refer back to a key noun. (This technique involves pronoun–antecedent agreement, a topic covered in Chapter 34.)
4. *Use parallel structure.* Phrasing your sentences in parallel form helps to maintain focus, reinforces the unity of your thoughts, and adds emphasis. Parallelism adds "punch" to your writing. (More punch is served in Chapter 30.)
5. *Use transitional phrases* to show the relationships between points in a paragraph as well as between paragraphs in an essay. Transitional phrases form a bond among the elements of a paragraph or a paper and allow smoother reading. They are like turn signals on a car: they tell the person following you where you're going.

Here are some of the most common transitional phrases; you can use them to keep your readers on track.

TRANSITION FUNCTION	WORDS/PHRASES USED
1. *To show a time relationship between points*	• first, second, third • now, simultaneously, concurrently, at this point, while • before, to begin, previously • after, following this, then, later, next • finally, last, subsequently • during, meanwhile, presently, from time to time, sometimes
2. *To add an idea or example to the previous point*	• in addition, also, furthermore, besides, moreover, for the same reason • another, similarly, equally important, likewise • for example, for instance, in fact
3. *To show contrast between points*	• although, nevertheless, on the other hand, whereas • but, however, instead, nonetheless • in contrast, on the contrary, in spite of, despite
4. *To show a cause-and-effect relationship between points*	• since, because, thus, therefore, hence • as a result, consequently, accordingly
5. *To emphasize or repeat a significant point*	• in fact, indeed, certainly, undoubtedly • in other words, as I have said, that is to say
6. *To summarize or conclude*	• in brief, on the whole, in summary, in short • to conclude, in conclusion, last • therefore, as a result, finally

The paragraph below is an excellent example of the use of transitional devices to achieve coherence. As you read, pay particular attention to the writer's use of repetition and parallelism.

> I want a wife who will take care of my physical needs. I want a wife who will keep my house clean. A wife who will pick up after my children, a wife who will pick up after me. I want a wife who will keep my clothes clean, ironed, mended, replaced when need be, and who will see to it that my personal things are kept in their proper place so that I can find what I need the minute I need it. I want a wife who cooks the meals, a wife who is a *good* cook. I want a wife who will plan the menus, do the necessary grocery shopping, prepare the meals, serve them pleasantly, and then do the cleaning up while I do my studying. I want a wife who will care for me when I am sick and sympathize with my pain and loss of time from school. I want a wife to go along when our family takes a vacation so that someone can continue to care for me and my children when I need a rest and change of scene.

(Judy Brady, excerpt from "I Want a Wife." Copyright © December 31, 1979. Reprinted with the permission of *Ms.* magazine.)

EXERCISE 9.3

Now it's your turn. Identify the transitional devices that create coherence in each of the sentence groups below.

1. The two women spent the whole day tramping from car dealer to car dealer. Finally, they found a used Toyota they could live with, but the price was higher than they had hoped to pay.
2. Concern was etched in the face of the priest and mirrored in the eyes of the doctor. Janis felt her shoulders tighten, and she fought to control her temper; their concern wouldn't help her now.
3. He knew that one good serve would end the match in his favour. As he walked slowly to the service line, he wondered if he had one good serve left in him.
4. Hamlet is an essentially noble man whose inaction brings about the tragedy that unfolds around him. The audience is then left with the problem of sorting out its own feelings about him.
5. The gypsy moth is invading our woodlands, killing trees that have resisted all other predators. Therefore, governments at both the local and provincial levels have begun a spraying program.
6. As he scanned the menu, Philip knew his gourmet meal would have to wait. First, the merger had to be discussed.
7. There are many jokes about cats. Unfortunately, however, in most of them the cat is either very unhappy or dead.
8. There are those who think Quebec would thrive as a separate state. On the other hand, some feel that its economic viability depends on a close relationship with the rest of Canada.

9. The Volkswagen Beetle is probably the world's most loved car. It must be, since more people have owned Beetles than any other vehicle.
10. To feel secure, you must have a company pension. A company pension can be obtained only if you're willing to take on long-term employment.

EXERCISE 9.4

In each of the following sentences, supply transition words or phrases that will help the meaning become clearer and the sentence more coherent.

1. Small pets are important members of a family. _____ they provide companionship to those who live alone.
2. My first impression of him was that he was aloof and arrogant; _____, I discovered I was wrong. He was painfully shy.
3. We had to reach the next town before dinnertime or the last motel rooms would be occupied. _____, we decided to break the speed limit.
4. At first I thought she didn't like me. _____ she confessed that she was playing "hard to get."
5. It's not hard to be a great basketball player. It helps, _____, if your parents are both seven feet tall.
6. Many best-sellers have become pathetic movies, now long forgotten. _____ many poor novels have been turned into movie classics, like *Gone With the Wind*, which last forever.
7. Many sports were discovered by accident. _____, one day at Rugby school in the 1830s, an English schoolboy, during a game of rugby, threw the ball overhand down the field. Football (as we call it in North America) was born.
8. Architecture in the twentieth century has become more streamlined, geometrical, and uniform. _____, it has become monotonous.
9. Batman and Robin were speeding off on a false lead. _____, the Joker was looting the coffers of the Gotham City bank.
10. The Fountain of Youth was rumoured to be in the swamps of Florida. _____ Ponce de Leon spent most of his remaining years looking for it there.

EXERCISE 9.5

Read the paragraphs below and underline in each the transitional devices that contribute to coherence.

1. Finally, developing the proper attitude is the true key to winning tennis. I define winning tennis as playing the game to the best of your ability, hitting the ball as well as you know you can, and enjoying the feeling of practised expertise. Winning tennis has nothing to do with

beating an opponent. Naturally, if you play winning tennis by learning the basics, practising sufficiently, and concentrating, you'll win many matches, but that is the reward of playing well, not the reason for playing well. People who swear and throw their racquets when they lose are very useful; they are the most satisfying players to trounce. But I don't understand why they play a game that gives them such pain. Tennis players who enjoy the feel of a well-hit ball and the satisfaction of a long, skilfully played rally are winners, regardless of the score.

2. While education and relaxation are important, most of us read light novels to be entertained. "Entertainment" means different things to different people. Some enjoy being frightened half to death by the books of Stephen King or his colleagues; others get satisfaction from the sugary romance of Harlequin novels; many people find science fiction absorbing and devour the works of Isaac Asimov or Jerry Pournelle. Whatever subject or style grabs you, there are literally thousands of novels to suit your taste. I'm lucky because—with the exception of popular romance—I can find enjoyment in almost any type of reasonably well-written light novel.

3. Is there any reason for optimism? There is some evidence that Canadians are becoming more conscious of the environment, and consciousness can only lead to changes for the better. In 1989, one-third of Canadians felt that the environment was the most important national issue. Only a year before that it was one in ten, and the year before that it was one in twenty. A majority of Canadians now favour tougher action against polluters, even if it means higher taxes, higher prices, and fewer jobs. However, this bit-by-bit heightening of concern is far from the concerted, all-out effort to save the planet that would result if we were threatened by an external force. How very much more difficult it is to mobilize resources and will when the enemy lies within!

Tone

As you write the paragraphs of your paper, try to be conscious of your tone. **Tone** is a word used to describe a writer's attitude towards the subject and the readers. The words you use, the examples, the quotations, and any other supporting materials you choose to help explain your main points—all these contribute to your tone. When you are trying to explain something, particularly something you feel strongly about, you may be tempted to be highly emotional in your discussion. If you allow yourself to "get emotional," chances are you won't be convincing. What will be communicated is the strength of your feelings, not the depth of your understanding or the validity of your opinion. To be clear and credible, you need to channel your enthusiasm (or your anger) into presenting your points in a calm, reasonable way.

Two suggestions may help you to find and maintain the right tone. First, never insult your readers, even unintentionally. Avoid phrases like "any idiot can see," "no sane person could believe," and "it is obvious that. . . ." Remember that what is "obvious" to you isn't necessarily obvious to someone who has a limited understanding of your subject or who disagrees with your opinion. Don't "talk down" to your readers, as though they were children or simpletons. Don't use sarcasm, and avoid profanity.

Second, don't apologize for your interpretation of your subject. Have confidence in yourself: you've thought long and hard about your subject, you've found good supporting material to help explain it, and you believe in its significance. Present your subject in a *positive* manner. If you hang back, using phrases like "I may be wrong, but . . ." or "I tend to feel that . . . ," your readers won't be inclined to give your points the consideration they deserve. Keep your readers in mind as you write, and your writing will be both clear and convincing.

EXERCISE 9.6

Rewrite the following paragraph, adding transitions where necessary and correcting any lapses in tone.

> If you like gardening, you're a wimp. It's such a dumb hobby, I don't even know where to begin listing the reasons I hate it. Flowers grow perfectly OK in the wild. Why force them into rows and beds? They claim it's relaxing. I know a guy who got a hernia from lifting manure and another who developed ulcers because his dahlias died. Inside the house, plants are a hazard. They attract insects, aggravate allergies, poison pets, and spread dirt. Gardening is a dangerous activity. Everyone I've met who likes it is a complete twit.

EXERCISE 9.7

Write a reply to this attack on gardening. Remember to keep your tone consistent, and don't forget transitions.

EXERCISE 9.8

Rewrite the following paragraph, adding transitions where necessary and correcting any lapses in tone.

> I'm no expert—in fact, I really don't know anything about it—but it seems to me that anyone who enjoys watching baseball is a masochist. I may be wrong (I usually am) but it's a very dull game, don't you think? About every third pitch the batter swings. The fielders do nothing. There are about fifteen hits in a three-hour game. The players actually do something for approximately seven and a half minutes of an entire afternoon. Home runs are dull. One man trots around the bases. The others stand and watch. An awful lot of people seem to like baseball, so

I guess there's something wrong with me. People who like baseball are probably boring people.

EXERCISE 9.9

Write a reply to this attack on baseball. Remember to keep your tone consistent, and use at least three different transitional devices in your paragraph.

CHAPTER 10

Writing Introductions and Conclusions

All of the concepts you've studied so far can be applied to any paragraph. However, two paragraphs, the first and the last in every essay, have special purposes and need extra care. All too often, the introduction and the conclusion of an essay are dull or clumsy and detract from its effectiveness. But they needn't be dull or clumsy: here's how to write good ones.

The Introductory Paragraph

The introduction is worth special attention because that's where your readers either sit up and take notice of your paper or sigh and pitch it into the wastebasket.

When we first discussed the concept of dividing a paper into paragraphs, we used the analogy of the TV sitcom, which is separated by commercials into distinct parts. The first section of the sitcom functions in ways the other parts don't. First, it attracts the viewers with a particularly funny moment, a fascinating situation, or an intriguing problem. Second, it sets the plot in motion or gets the action started. Your introductory paragraph has a similar role in your essay.

> There are two parts to an introductory paragraph:
> 1. a grabber
> 2. a preview statement

Grabbing and Holding Your Readers' Attention

Your readers must be attracted to your writing, or there's no point in putting pen to paper or fingers to keyboard. This doesn't permit you to use cheap tricks, however, like the classified ad that read:

SEX. There, now that I've got your attention, how would you like to own a 1981 Ford Comet?

The grabber must be appropriate both to the content of your essay and to your intended readers. If your audience is known for a solemn and serious approach to life and your topic is something of a serious nature (environmental ethics, for instance, or abortion), there is no point in leading off with a pun or joke, no matter how witty. Such an opening would be inappropriate and probably offensive to your readers.

Your grabber does not have to be a single sentence; in fact, good grabbers are often several sentences long. Your readers will be committing varying amounts of personal time and effort to reading your writing. You owe it to them to make your opening sentences clear, interesting, and creative.

An effective grabber should be followed by an equally effective preview statement, one that slides smoothly and easily into place. Your readers should be aware only of a unified presentation, not of the two parts you have blueprinted for your introductory paragraph.

Below are eight different kinds of grabbers you can choose from to get your readers' attention and lead up to your preview statement. In each of the illustrative paragraphs, note how the grabber and the preview statement are solidly linked to form a unified whole. To demonstrate that you can take many different approaches to a subject, depending on your purpose and your audience, we have used the same subject in all of the introductions: physical fitness, a subject that is much on the minds—and on the hips—of many Canadians.

1. *Begin with a well-phrased quotation.* You might choose a famous statement, a popular slogan, a widely known publicity gimmick, or a common saying by someone you know. Use a quotation when it sums up your point of view more succinctly and effectively than your own words could. As a rule, you should identify the source of the quotation.

"Who can be bothered?" "I'm much too busy." "I get all the exercise I need at the office." We've all heard excuses like these, excuses for avoiding regular exercise. Modern life with its distractions and conveniences tends to make us sedentary and lazy, but the human organism cannot tolerate inactivity and stress indefinitely. Eventually, it begins to break down. If you want to keep yourself in shape for the challenges of modern life, consider the benefits of working out a few times a week. Regular exercise can rejuvenate your body, refresh your mind, and improve your self-confidence.

2. *Use a provocative statement.* Sometimes a startling or surprising remark (not an insult or a false exaggeration, please) is effective in getting readers' attention. A little-known or striking fact will have the same effect.

After the age of 30, the average North American puts on 25 to 40 pounds of fat. Presumably, the cause for this startling increase in avoirdupois is a combination of metabolic changes, decreased physical activity, and hundreds of pounds of junk food ingested since childhood. It's difficult to stop the spread of middle-aged corpulence, but experts tell us we *can* resist the rise in flab by reducing our caloric intake and increasing our physical activity. Regular exercise can rejuvenate the body, refresh the mind, and improve self-confidence.

3. *Ask a question or two.* Questions are often an effective way to encourage interest because your readers will find themselves thinking of answers. Some questions are rhetorical; that is, they will not have specific answers. Others might be answered in your essay.

Have you been feeling sluggish and exhausted lately? Has your blood pressure increased along with your waistline in the past few years? Are you stalled in front of the television set every night with potato chips and a beer? If so, you are probably suffering from a common middle-aged ailment called *flabitis*. This malady strikes most people over 30: they put on unneeded pounds, have trouble concentrating, tire easily, and prefer watching sports to participating in them. Fortunately, there is a cure for flabitis: a three-times-weekly dose of exercise. With regular exercise, you can rejuvenate your body, refresh your mind, and improve your self-confidence.

4. *Point to the significance of your subject.* If its significance can catch your readers' interest, they will want to know more about it, especially if it is a subject that affects them directly.

More and more young people are dying of heart disease. Despite the statistics that say most people in our society are living longer, thanks to advances in medicine and surgery, the figures can be misleading. It is a fact that people in their thirties and forties are dying from coronary problems that once threatened people in their fifties and sixties. What has caused this change? Certainly, the increase in stress, the fatigue of overwork, the rise in obesity, and the decline in physical activity are all contributing factors. To combat the risk of cardiovascular disease, we need physical activity. Regular exercise can forestall the ravages of heart disease and promote longevity.

5. *Start with a generalization related to your subject.* Generalizations can be useful for suggesting the context and scope of your subject. They must, however, be narrowed down carefully to a focussed preview statement.

Until the twentieth century, exercise was part of the normal workday. Our ancestors were farmers, pioneers, sailors, and so on. Few of our parents, however, made their living by ploughing the land or chopping down trees. In this century, the trend in work has been away from physical exertion and towards automation. Today's generation uses technology to reduce physical activity even further: they pick up the phone, ride the elevator, and take the car to the corner store. Modern inactivity has negative consequences that only physical exercise can counter. To sustain good health, sharpen your mental edge, and have fun, you should take up aerobics or sports and use your body in the way it was intended—actively.

6. *State your intention to challenge a widely held opinion.* Perhaps your readers have also doubted the commonly held belief. Your preview statement can assert how false the opinion is, and the body of your essay can contain evidence to counter the validity of the view you are challenging.

Physical activity is for kids. Adults don't have time to hit a baseball or run around a field chasing after one, or to do aerobics and lift weights in a gym. They have to earn a living, raise families, and save money for retirement. They can leave exercise to their children. I firmly believed this until one morning when, late for work, I ran after a bus. My heart pounded; my lungs gasped; my head swam. It had been some years since my last stint of exercise, and I realized I wouldn't be around to do my job, support my family, or enjoy retirement unless I got into the habit of doing something physical to maintain my health. Regular exercise can rejuvenate your body, refresh your mind, and broaden your interests.

7. *Begin with a definition.* A definition is a good way to begin if you are introducing a key term that you suspect may be unfamiliar to your readers. If the subject of your essay depends on a personal meaning of a term that most people understand in a different way, a definition is essential.

Myocardial infarction: the very term is frightening. It occurs when a person's muscles slacken from disuse, the veins clog up with sticky fats, and the heart has to work too hard to sustain even minor exertion like raking leaves or shovelling snow. The muscles of the heart become strained to exhaustion or balloon outward because the veins cannot pass blood quickly enough. In plain English, a myocardial infarction is a heart attack. If the victim is lucky enough to survive, physicians prescribe a regimen of less stress, low fat intake, and habitual exercise.

8. *Describe an interesting incident or tell an anecdote related to your subject.* Readers like stories; keep yours short and to the point by narrating only highlights. The incident or anecdote you select might be a story from the media, an event involving family or friends, or a personal experience.

Last year, I got a free invitation to a fitness club in the mail. I responded, out of curiosity, but I needed to be convinced. After all, I was 35, had grown a little paunch, and was a bit short of breath on the stairs; ten years had passed since I had last played sports. My first workout was a nightmare. My joints ached, my muscles throbbed, and my head spun. I was in worse shape than I thought. After a few weeks, those symptoms disappeared, and I began to enjoy myself. My paunch vanished and my muscles toned up. My capacity for concentration increased. Also, I met some new people who have become friends. Obviously, ten years is too long between workouts, because exercise rejuvenates your body, refreshes your mind, and improves your social life.

EXERCISE 10.1

Each of the following paragraphs is the introductory paragraph of an essay. Using the strategy indicated in parentheses, write an appropriate grabber for each paragraph.

1. (quotation) _____

   _____

   The words of my seventh-grade teacher are still very important to me. Mrs. Patronni has been one of the most important influences on my life so far. She not only taught me, but inspired me and set an example that I will always try to live up to.

2. (quotation) _____

   _____

   Every sport has its strange expressions, just as every sport has its devoted fans, its famous teams, and its legendary heroes. A sport that gets very little attention in Canada but is very popular in many parts of the world, especially Commonwealth countries, is cricket. Like the sports that millions of Canadians follow enthusiastically, cricket is an exciting and fascinating game once you become familiar with its rules and style. In fact, it compares very favourably with baseball in skill, pace, and strategy.

3. (provocative statement) _____

_____

Canadian roads are overrun by drivers who are a danger to themselves, their passengers, and others on the road. Inept drivers demonstrate their inadequacies in so many ways that it would be impossible to list them all in one short paper. Nevertheless, bad drivers can be broadly categorized as traumatized turtles, careening cowboys, and day-dreaming dodos.

4. (provocative statement) _____

_____

For many reasons, country-and-western music is Canada's national sound. It has universal appeal from coast to coast, it is more popular than any other single kind of music, and it expresses truly Canadian themes and values.

5. (question) _____

_____

Arranged marriages are a very important part of my culture. When my family moved to Canada, we left behind many of the traditions and customs that were as natural to us as breathing. However, my parents retained their right to choose a wife for me, even though they are aware that this custom is at odds with the Canadian way of life. While their decision was at first difficult to accept, I believe there are good reasons that an arranged marriage may be best for me. The decision will be made by mature people in a thoughtful manner, uninfluenced by the enthusiasms of youth; the decision will be made by people who have at heart the best interests of our family, the bride's family, and me; and the decision will be made in accordance with a centuries-old tradition that has proven its success generation after generation.

6. (significance of subject) _____

_____

TV commercials that portray unrealistic and unattainable lifestyles should be banned. While I do not support censorship, I feel there is sufficient evidence of the damage done by these advertisements to justify eliminating them, in the public interest. The objectionable commercials promote sexual stereotyping, set up unrealistic and dangerous expectations, and encourage irresponsible consumerism.

7. (generalization) _____

_____

My first roommate was the sort of person that nightmares are made of. It's been three years since she finally moved out of our apartment, but

I still shudder when I recall our six months together. Denise was noisy, sloppy, and, worst of all, thoughtless.

8. (opinion you challenge) _____

_____

The evidence strongly suggests that overexposure to the sun can cause several forms of cancer at worst, and premature ageing at best. We can't completely avoid the sun's rays, but there are several measures we can take to prevent the damage that normal outdoor activity might cause. To enjoy the summer without fear, use an effective sun block, cover sensitive skin completely, and limit your time in the sun.

9. (definition) _____

_____

The choice of corrective lenses is an individual matter, but many people go through a tough decision process when confronting the issue. In deciding whether contact lenses or eyeglasses are more suitable, one should examine such factors as comfort, convenience, and appearance.

10. (anecdote or incident) _____

_____

Black-flies are just one of the pests that make life less than comfortable in Canada during the spring, but they tend to be the most irritating. No method of combatting the pests is foolproof, but there are several methods that can be employed, either singly or together, to repel most of them. The campaign against the black-fly begins with protective clothing, follows up with an effective repellant, and goes over the top with the secret weapon: garlic.

EXERCISE 10.2

Write an introductory paragraph for an essay on each of the following five topics. Put square brackets around your grabbers, and underline your preview statements.

1. Why I want to be a _____ (fill in your career choice)
2. Why I chose _____ (fill in your school)
3. How not to treat a friend
4. My favourite restaurant
5. The trouble with younger brothers (or sisters)

The Concluding Paragraph

Like the introduction, the conclusion of your essay has a special form. Think back to your favourite television sitcom. The last section of the show wraps up the plot, explains any details that might still be unresolved, and leaves you with a satisfying sense that all is well, at least until next week. The last paragraph of your essay has two similar special functions:

---

1. It *summarizes* or *reinforces* the main points of your paper.
2. It ends with an appropriate *clincher.*

Your **summary statement** should be as concise as you can make it, and must be phrased in such a way that it does not repeat word-for-word the portion of your preview statement that identifies the main points.

Your **clincher** is a memorable statement designed to leave your readers feeling satisfied with your essay and perhaps taking away with them something for further thought. Never end without a clincher. Don't just quit writing when your main points are covered or you'll leave your readers hanging, wondering what to make of it all.

Six strategies you can choose from in writing an appropriate clincher are described below. Each of the strategies is illustrated by a sample concluding paragraph. Try to identify the summary statement and the clincher in each conclusion.

1. *End with a relevant or thought-provoking quotation.* You can use this type of ending in two ways: repeat an earlier quotation but give it a new meaning, or give a new quote by an authority in the field, to place your subject in a larger context.

> Since I began lifting weights every second day, I have lowered my blood pressure, improved my productivity at work, and made some new friends at the fitness club. I may never be Arnold Schwarzenegger, but that isn't my goal. My muscles are pleasantly sore after a good workout, but as Arnold says, "No pain, no gain." As long as the pain is so little and the gain is so great, I will continue to enjoy my regular workouts.

2. *Offer a solution to a problem discussed in your essay.* You can plan an organization for your essay that will allow you to resolve problems or neutralize negative consequences in your conclusion.

> I've got the best intentions in the world. I know that exercise benefits me physically, mentally, and emotionally—but I still don't have the time. I didn't, that is, until last month, when I was home from work for a week because I sprained my ankle while walking the dog. That never would have happened if I had been in shape. Since then, I have forced myself to manage my time to allow for a fitness program. Four hours of exercise a week is not a very big investment of time compared with four days in bed with a bandaged foot.

3. *End with one or more relevant or thought-provoking questions.* The advantage of clinching with a question is that readers tend to mull over a question automatically; a question stimulates thought. Before they know it, readers will begin to formulate answers to your question—and that activity will automatically make them remember your points. This technique requires one caution, however: be sure your question relates *directly* to your subject.

> My life has improved considerably since I took up jogging three times a week: I'm enjoying better health, less brain-fog, and more confidence. And I'm inspired to continue jogging by the fact that coronary disease runs in my family. My father and grandfather both suffered heart attacks in their fifties. If they had done regular exercise, could they have reduced their chances of coronaries? Would they still be alive today?

4. *Point out the value or significance of your subject to your readers.* If you emphasize your subject matter at the end of your essay, you can stamp its importance on your readers' memory.

> There aren't too many ways to stay in shape, be sharp, and feel strong; regular exercise is probably the best. Furthermore, there aren't too many ways to reduce the risk of arthritis, arterial decay, and heart dysfunction. Again, exercise provides an answer. In a country where the most common cause of mortality is coronary collapse, everyone needs to consider the value of consistent exercise. It's a small daily inconvenience with large and long-term rewards.

5. *Make a connection to a statement made in your introduction.* This strategy provides your readers with a sense of closure. They will recall your earlier remarks and feel satisfied that the loose ends have been tied.

> Having exercised now for six months, I can run for the bus without losing my breath, sweating profusely, or feeling dizzy. My body is in better trim; my endurance and confidence on the job have grown. After a lapse of twenty years, I have even taken up the bicycle again: I go riding along local bike trails with friends. And now, when my children are playing baseball in the yard, I don't think, "Baseball is for kids." I'm first at the plate. Batter up!

6. *End with a suggestion for change or a prediction about the future.* Your suggestion for change will have a lasting influence if your readers have been persuaded by your arguments. Your predictions of events that *might* occur should not be misleading and exaggerated, or your readers will be sceptical of their validity. Make predictions that are possible and plausible.

> If those of us who still prefer junk food, overwork, and television don't shape up, the incidence of coronary disease will continue to rise.

Moderate exercise will benefit body, mind, and spirit. If we follow common sense and change our habits of self-pollution and self-destruction, all of us can lead long, active, and healthy lives.

EXERCISE 10.3

Each of the following is the concluding paragraph from an essay. For each paragraph, underline the summary statement and write an appropriate clincher.

1. Both games are enjoyable for spectators and create real enthusiasm among fans. High schools that chose soccer have seen no reduction in school spirit or fan support. For educational institutions to make the switch from football is really a "no-lose" proposition, because soccer provides dramatic advantages in reducing player injury, increasing player fitness, and shaving thousands of dollars from school expenses.

_____

_____

_____

_____

2. Far from fearing celibacy, young people should be enthusiastically supporting the idea. My energy is devoted to my schoolwork and two part-time jobs; my stress level is around zero; and I've got lots of money to spend on myself. These benefits and many more are easily attained by anyone strong enough to be an individual, to step off the dating–mating merry-go-round and choose, as I have done, the joys of a celibate lifestyle.

_____

_____

_____

_____

3. There's no mystery about achieving a baby-smooth face. By selecting the proper equipment, preparing your beard adequately, and following the procedures I've revealed, you, too, can have cheeks that beg to be touched. These carefully protected secrets have been used by generations of Hollywood make-up artists on the faces of the stars; now they are yours.

_____

_____

_____

4. Good friends are not easy to find. Anyone who says she has "dozens" doesn't know what a good friend is. I've been fortunate to have known four people who combine the qualities of patience, generosity, and intuition, people I'm proud and grateful to call my good friends.

_____

_____

_____

_____

5. Opinion about the two shows is pretty evenly divided, but is certainly passionate. Late-night television viewers either love them or hate them. In truth, there are more similarities than differences between the two shows, since both rely on humour and celebrity guests to attract viewers. Those who favour Letterman love his zany humour, irreverent style, and the constant surprises he springs. Leno appeals to those who enjoy more topical humour and like hearing from his impressive guest list. My own preference is for Letterman, but there are millions of North Americans who disagree.

_____

_____

_____

_____

6. While the causes of dropout among first-year students are as individual as the students themselves, the effects are easier to categorize. Conflict with parents and others whose expectations have not been met comes first, followed by a loss of self-esteem. The determination to succeed despite this unfair setback is common, but statistics show that low-paying, dead-end jobs are the norm for the college dropout. The situation is much worse, of course, for those who don't complete high school.

_____

_____

_____

_____

7. I guess that you could say my evening out in Antigonish was less expensive and more fun, but less memorable, than my evening out in Montreal. As time goes by, it's quite likely that memory will blur the events that occurred on those two evenings, and I'll probably end up telling my grandchildren wonderful tales about my Montreal adventure, while my quiet

but delightful evening in Antigonish will fade. I hope this doesn't happen, because I learned a great deal from both experiences.

_____

_____

_____

_____

8. Remember that some of the French wines we see in Canadian stores are "plonk" that the French won't drink. Dressed up in fancy labels and slapped with an impressively high price tag, they are designed to appeal to the snobbish but unsophisticated overseas buyer. At the same time, it is no longer a social blunder to present a good Canadian wine at your table. Choosing a good wine needn't be a mysterious ritual or a blind lottery. Just get good advice; don't be intimidated by packaging, price, or place of origin; and, when in doubt, let your taste guide you. Equipped with these three general rules, you should have no problem finding a wine to suit both your taste and your budget.

_____

_____

_____

_____

9. Great parties seldom just happen; they are the products of careful thought and planning. If a truly great party should occur spontaneously, then chance has brought the right ingredients together, just as chance can sometimes result in high marks on multiple-choice tests. The right people, brought together in the right place, for the right reason, will produce a memorable event every time.

_____

_____

_____

_____

10. Drinking and driving must be stopped. To stop it will require substantial commitment from all levels of government, both in terms of money and in terms of political will. The penalties for driving while under the influence of alcohol must be increased, and more money must be spent for education and publicity. But, more than these measures, it will take the individual will of every Canadian to make the promise not to drive after

drinking. Nothing will bring my sister back, but there are lots of other sisters out there—and brothers, and mothers and fathers—who can be saved.

_____

_____

_____

_____

EXERCISE 10.4

Write a short concluding paragraph for an essay on each of the following topics. Use the main points you developed for introductory paragraphs on these topics in Exercise 10.2.

1. Why I want to be a _____ (fill in your career choice)
2. Why I chose _____ (fill in your school)
3. How not to treat a friend
4. My favourite restaurant
5. The trouble with younger brothers (or sisters)

Revising the Essay

CHAPTER 11

Reworking the First Draft

No one can write in a single draft an essay that perfectly satisfies all the instructions and guidelines we've presented in Units One and Two. Nor should anyone expect to do so. The purpose of the first draft is simply to get down on paper something you can work with. Planning and drafting should take up *no more than half* the time you devote to a writing project. The rest should be devoted to revision.

Revision is the process of refining your essay until it says what you want to say in a way that enables your readers to understand your message and to receive it favourably. These two goals, *clear understanding* and *favourable reception,* are at the heart of good communication. You can accomplish these goals only if you revise from your readers' perspective. The first draft often seems all right to the writer because it reflects the contents of the writer's mind. But in order to transfer an idea *as exactly as possible* from the mind of the writer to the mind of a reader, revision is necessary. The idea needs to be reshaped and refined until it is as clear to the reader as it is to the writer. By playing the role of the intended reader of your essay, you can avoid misunderstandings before they happen.

What Is Revision?

Revision means "re-seeing"; it does *not* mean recopying. The aim of revision is to improve your writing's organization, accuracy, and style. Once you've completed your first draft, ask yourself, "How can this draft be changed to suit my audience and purpose?" Revising is a three-stage process:

1. Rework the first draft by revising content and making overall structural changes.
2. Polish later drafts by improving paragraph and sentence structure, coherence, and tone.
3. Edit and proofread to catch errors in grammar, word choice, spelling, and punctuation.

Experienced writers know that revision is essential to make their message say what they want it to say, and they usually spend more time on the first stage than they do on the second and third stages. Inexperienced writers are often reluctant to revise, perhaps because they are not sure how to go about it. Also, inexperienced writers tend to think revision means editing and proofreading. They tend to skip the first two stages and concentrate on the third, thinking to save time. Ironically, they waste time—both theirs and their readers'—because the result is writing that doesn't communicate clearly and is not favourably received.

How Do I Begin?

The first thing you need to do is to get some "distance" from your draft. It's important to be able to step back and look at what you've written as though you were seeing it for the first time. If you try to revise while the wording of the first draft is still fresh in your mind, it's easy to miss weaknesses in your reasoning and to miss inadequate or inappropriate support material. It's easy, in other words, to fool yourself into thinking you've enlightened your readers when in fact you've only confused them.

There are several ways to distance yourself from your writing. The best way is to put the paper aside for several days and then reread it. Another suggestion, if you're pressed for time, is to type out your handwritten draft. Reading your draft in a different form helps you to see it more objectively. A third way to take a fresh look at your work is to read it aloud and listen to it from the perspective of your reader. Listen to how your explanation unfolds and mark every place you find something unclear, or irrelevant, or underdeveloped, or out of order. Reading your draft aloud forces you to hear and see what you have actually written, not what you *think* you've written. Once you realize what doesn't work, you can set about developing something that does.

The First Step

Begin revising by ensuring that the content of your essay is accurate and well-organized. Now is the time to make major changes to what goes into your essay and how it is arranged. Let your writing purpose and your readers' needs and expectations guide you in deciding what to change.

As you read your paper aloud, keep in mind the three kinds of changes you can make at this stage:

---

1. You can *rearrange* your information.

Rearranging content is the kind of revision that is most often needed and least often done. Consider the order in which you've arranged your paragraphs. *From your reader's point of view,* is this the most effective order in which to present your information? Consider your introduction and conclusion: are they effective as they stand, or would they be more effective if they were altered or even reversed?

---

2. You can *add* information.

Adding new main ideas or support material is often necessary to communicate your message clearly, interestingly, and convincingly. If you're not sure where additional information may be needed, ask a friend to read your draft and identify what needs to be expanded or clarified. (Be sure to return the favour; you can learn a great deal by critiquing other people's writing.)

---

3. You can *delete* information.

Now is the time to cut out material that is redundant, insignificant, or irrelevant to your subject and audience. Be ruthless: delete *all* ideas that are only vaguely or weakly related to your overall purpose.

Your blueprint is the best place to begin checking the organization of your information. Keep it close at hand and change it as you revise your essay. Nothing you've written should be considered sacred or carved in stone. If your essay can be improved by adding, subtracting, or shifting parts of it around, go for it!

Your preview statement is your contract with your readers, so it should be the guiding principle of your essay. It should contain nothing that is not developed in the body of the essay, and there should be nothing in the essay that is not directly related to the preview statement. Be sure that you have fulfilled all the terms of your contract.

Next, check to make sure your draft includes all the major elements of an essay. Turn to Chapter 5, "Drafting the Blueprint," and match your draft against the model blueprint on p. 57. Does your essay contain everything that's noted there?

To complete this stage of the revision process, review your draft in terms of the questions below. If you have omitted any of these considerations, be sure to include them when you write your second draft.

CONTENT AND ORGANIZATION CHECKLIST

Audience

Have you a clear idea of who your readers are? Have you taken into consideration

- their level of knowledge?
- their attitude towards your subject?
- their needs in relation to the subject?

Your role

What is your purpose in this essay?

What is your attitude towards the subject?

What are your readers' expectations of you in this communication?

Accuracy

Is everything you have said accurate?

- Is the information you present consistent with your own observations and experience?
- Is your information consistent with what you have discovered through research?
- Are all your facts and evidence up-to-date?

Completeness

Have you included enough main ideas and supporting details to explain your subject and to convince your reader? Remember that "enough" means from the reader's point of view, not the writer's.

Subject

Have you defined your subject?

- Is it significant? Does it avoid the trivial or the tedious?
- Is it single? Does it avoid double or combined subjects?
- Is it specific? Is it focussed and precise?
- Is it supportable? Have you provided enough varied evidence to make your meaning clear and convincing?

Main points

Have you refined your main points?

- Are they significant? Have you deleted any trivial points?
- Are they distinct? Do any points overlap in content?
- Are they relevant? Do all points relate directly to the subject?

Have you chosen the best order for your main points? Again, "best" means from the reader's perspective: the order you choose should be the one most likely to help the reader make sense of your information.

- If they are arranged chronologically, are your main points presented in order of time sequence?
- If they are arranged climactically, have you presented the most important point last?
- If your points are logically linked, is there a clear logical progression or cause–effect connection between them?
- If your points are in random order, are they equally significant and is each logically independent of the others?

When you have considered these questions, you have completed the first step in the revision process: you have covered the "large issues" of content and organization.

EXERCISE 11.1

Read the following first draft carefully. How can it be improved? Rewrite the paragraph to communicate its point more effectively.

An elderly Ojibwa man predicted the severity of the coming winter by checking the size of his neighbour's woodpile. For decades, no one could figure out his secret. They thought he based his weather predictions on his study of animal and bird behaviour. Only when he was dying did he finally reveal his secret to one of his daughters. When people saw him out walking in the autumn, they assumed he was looking at the sky for signs or examining the leaves of the maple trees for clues. The old man became quite famous in the district for his ability to predict how severe the winter would be. He was even interviewed once by the local radio station, but he never told anyone the key to his uncanny forecasting ability.

EXERCISE 11.2

The following passage is the first draft of a paragraph. When the student had finished it, he was quite pleased with his work. He thought he had explained his points effectively and that a reader would have no difficulty in understanding his argument. Read it through, see what you think, and answer the questions that follow.

Why did I do it? This was one of those times you think something is really going to be exciting and fun, but you don't think it through to the consequences. Once I got the idea, I just got carried away and couldn't stop. I wish I had had better sense and it probably would have helped if I hadn't been drunk. If I had thought about the possible consequences, my friends would still be speaking to me and I wouldn't have to pay for the damage. I guess it could of been worse, I mean the police could have been called and instead of just paying for the repairs I could of been charged and maybe even a criminal record. My advice is to always think carefully before doing something that could get out of hand, even if it seems like alot of fun at the time.

1. Does this writer have a clear idea of who his readers are? How can you tell?
2. What is the writer's purpose in the paragraph?
3. What is the topic of the paragraph? Is it clearly stated?
4. What event or incident underlies the lesson the writer learned? Do you know? Do you need to know?
5. Rewrite the paragraph, using an incident from your own experience to support the point. Don't worry about the errors in grammar and sentence structure; just be sure the content of your paragraph is unmistakably clear and well organized from a reader's perspective.

CHAPTER 12

Polishing the Later Draft

The Second Step

In the second stage of the revision process, you examine paragraph structure, sentence structure, language level, and tone. You look closely at the construction of each paragraph and review its content for unity and coherence. You check each sentence to make sure that it is correctly constructed and that your sentences are varied in length and complexity. Readers appreciate variety as much as they appreciate clarity. If all your sentences are the same length, you'll put your readers to sleep. This is also the time to make sure your level of language is appropriate: not too casual or too formal, not too simple or too technical for your intended readers. Don't be overly concerned at this stage about spelling, punctuation, or grammatical errors. These will be considered at the editing and proofreading stage, described in the next chapter.

You should allow at least a couple of days—a week would be better—between your first revision and your second. Enough time must elapse to allow you to approach your essay as if you were seeing it for the first time. Once again, read your draft aloud, and use this list of questions to help you revise and improve it.

PARAGRAPH AND SENTENCE CHECKLIST

Introduction

Grabber

Does your essay begin with a statement designed to get the reader's attention in an appropriate way?

Is your grabber suitable both to your subject and to your audience? (Or will it turn them off or confuse them?)

Preview statement

Have you constructed a clear and comprehensive preview statement?

Is your preview statement in the most appropriate position (usually, at the end of the introduction)? If not, should it be moved?

Are the main ideas of your preview statement expressed in grammatically parallel form?

Body Paragraphs

Topic sentence

Does each paragraph have an identifiable topic sentence?

Is each topic sentence the first or second sentence of the paragraph? If not, should it be moved?

Supporting sentences

Unity

- Do all sentences in each paragraph relate clearly and directly to the topic sentence?
- Have you avoided needless repetition or redundancy?
- Is each sentence in the best position in relation to other sentences to ensure clear meaning?

Variety

- Do the supporting sentences present a variety of evidence: e.g., examples, definition, quotation or paraphrase, descriptive details?

Coherence

- Does each sentence flow smoothly into the next?
- Have you used clear transitions to signal the relationship between sentences? Between paragraphs?

Conclusion

Summary statement

Have you included a summary statement to reinforce your main points?

Have you used fresh language to avoid word-for-word repetition?

Is your summary statement in the best position (usually, at the beginning of the concluding paragraph)? If not, should it be moved?

Clincher

Does your conclusion contain a clincher that is appropriate both to what has preceded it and to your intended audience?

Sentence Structure

Are there any fragments or run-ons?

Are there misplaced or dangling modifiers?

Are all lists (whether words, phrases, or clauses) expressed in parallel form?

Are your sentences varied in length? Could some be combined to improve the clarity and impact of your message?

Language and Tone

Is your level of language consistent and appropriate to both your subject and your readers? Are there any lapses into inappropriately colloquial or technical language?

Is your tone consistent, reasonable, and courteous throughout your essay?

EXERCISE 12.1

Read the following paragraph and consider it in terms of the questions you should ask in the second stage of revising a paper. Identify all the errors you find, and then compare your paper with that of another student.

> To begin with, let's get rid of the tea bag with a string on it. This stupid American invention is the worst thing to happen to tea since the Boston Tea Party. Real tea is brewed from the leaves themselves. Which can be purchased in any good supermarket or in specialty shops. You need a kettle and a china or clay teapot. Fill the kettle with cold water. Put it on to boil. When boiling, pour some into the teapot and swirl it around. This warms the pot. An essential step in making good tea. I don't know why, but I do know that tea made in an unwarmed pot is not as good as tea made in a warmed one. Coffee doesn't need a warmed pot, but I don't really care for coffee, so I probably couldn't taste the difference anyway. Empty the water from the teapot. Put in one teaspoon of tea leaves for each cup you are serving. Add one more teaspoon of tea leaves. Take the teapot to the boiling kettle, this ensures that the water is still boiling rapidly when you put it into the pot. Pour over the tea leaves as much boiling water as is needed for the number of cups you are making. Wait five minutes. This is called steeping. Pour the tea into cups. Some people drink it with milk. Fussy tea drinkers insist that the milk must go into the cup before the tea is poured. Some like sugar. Some take both. A few people enjoy it with a slice or a squeeze of lemon. However you take your tea, it will taste better if you follow these simple steps.

EXERCISE 12.2

As a general reader, what problems do you have understanding this paragraph? Underline errors in sentence structure, language, and tone.

Car salesmen never seem to learn, you'd think that after all this time they would finally have seen the light, but they haven't. I am talking about their complete and total disregard for their women customers. When I go to look at a car and take a man along, either my dad or my boyfriend or a friend who is knowledgeable and aware of automotive detail, the salesperson ignores me and speaks over my head to the man. Even when I am the one asking the questions, the salesman (it's almost always a man) directs the answer to the man who is with me. I feel like saying, "Hey, jerk! Speak to me! It's my question you're answering and my money you're supposed to be trying to get!" Even when they do actually talk to me, which isn't very often, they talk in little simple sentences, carefully avoiding any technical terms like "engine," or "fuel injection," or "horsepower." They talk about the nice colours, the comfy upholstery, and they never fail to mention the cute dashboard. They talk to me like I'm an airhead or a small child who doesn't know anything. Men don't have these problems when they go looking for a car. I once tried to shop for a car by myself. What a disaster. When I asked to go for a test drive, the salesman said that of course I could take the car out, but why didn't I go home and get my husband first? His face is probably still red from the language I used to tell him what he could do with his car.

CHAPTER 13

Editing and Proofreading

The Third Step

At long last you've reached the final stages in the writing process: **editing**—correcting any errors in grammar, word choice, spelling, and punctuation; and **proofreading**—correcting any errors in typing or writing that appear in the final draft. By now you're probably so tired of refining the same paper that you may be tempted to skip these last steps and hand it in as is. Don't! Careful editing and proofreading are essential if you want your paper to be favourably received.

Your grammar, diction, spelling, punctuation, and neatness have an impact not only on your readers' understanding of your message but also on their impression of you. Mistakes and messiness can lead to unclear meaning, and they will certainly lead to a lower opinion of you and your work. In some kinds of writing—a letter of application, an appeal for funds, or a business proposal, to name just a few examples—irritants such as spelling errors or even misused apostrophes can be disastrous. You need to edit and proofread to ensure that the impression you convey is a positive one.

Most word-processing packages now include a grammar checker as well as a spelling checker, and it is worthwhile running your writing through these programs at the editing stage. The new ones have some very useful features. For example, they will check for passive-voice verbs; they will question—but not correct—your use of apostrophes; they will sometimes catch errors in subject–verb agreement; and they will even assess the readability of your writing. Such programs can be helpful to you as you begin to edit your work. But don't make the mistake of assuming the grammar and spelling checkers will do all your editing for you. Useful as these programs are, they cannot replace a human editor. Many errors go undetected by the computer; only you (or a knowledgeable and patient friend) can catch them. Here's an example of what we mean. The following sentences passed without comment through one of the most sophisticated grammar checkers on the market:

> The audience rose to their feet and it applauded, madly until the cast whom they so well deserved returned to the stage to take an other curtain call. They would if I had of been their in addition threw money onto the stage.

Every communication you write is judged by readers on three counts: what you say, how you say it, and how you present it. Each factor is important in getting the response you want from your readers. Whether you're writing a résumé, a love letter, or an interoffice memo, you can count on the fact that your message will be rated on appearance and style as well as on content.

EDITING CHECKLIST

Here are the questions you should ask yourself when you are editing a draft:

Grammar

Are all verbs and pronouns in the correct form?
Do all verbs agree with their subjects?
Are all verbs in the active voice unless there is a specific reason for using the passive?
Do all pronouns agree with their antecedents?
Have any vague pronoun references been clarified?
Are there any confusing shifts in the verb tense within a paragraph?
Are there any confusing shifts in number or person within a paragraph?

Words

Usage
Have you used words accurately, to communicate meaning rather than to impress?
Have you eliminated clichés, jargon, and slang?
Have you eliminated redundant (or unnecessary) words?
Have you corrected any "abusages"?

Spelling
Are all words spelled correctly?
Have you used capital letters where they are needed?

Have you used apostrophes correctly for possessives (and omitted them from plurals)?

If any words had to be hyphenated, are the hyphens in the right place?

Punctuation

Within sentences

Have you used commas where needed for clarity and deleted those that have no purpose?

Have you used colons and semicolons where appropriate?

Have you used parentheses and dashes only where appropriate?

Beginnings and endings

Does each sentence begin with a capital letter?

Are introductory words and phrases ("Similarly"; "Besides"; "In addition to") followed by commas?

Do all questions—and only questions—have question marks?

Are quotation marks correctly placed?

Tips for Effective Proofreading

By the time you have finished editing, you will have gone over your paper so many times you may have practically memorized it. When you are very familiar with a piece of writing, it is hard to spot the small mistakes that may have crept in as you produced your final copy. It is especially important, therefore, to allow some time to elapse between editing and proofreading—ideally, two or three days. If you proofread too soon after your final edit, you will read what you *think* you've written, the words that are still fresh in your mind, not what you've *actually* written, the words that appear on the page.

1. Read each sentence of your essay carefully. You can choose to do this either line by line, using a ruler to cover the next sentence, or sentence by sentence, starting at the last sentence of your essay and working forward to the first. This technique will help you focus on each sentence as a discrete unit and will help you identify any sentence errors you may have missed earlier, as well as any problems with punctuation, spelling, or typing.

2. If you've been keeping a list of your most frequent errors in this course, you can do a scan of your essay, looking specifically for the errors you know you are most likely to commit.

3. Using the Quick Revision Checklist on the inside front cover of this book, make a final check of all aspects of your paper.

Your "last" draft may need further revision after your proofreading review. If this is the case, take the time to rewrite the paper so that the version you hand in is clean and easy to read. If a word processor is available to you, use it. Computers make editing and proofreading almost painless. Since errors are so easy to correct, you can produce a clean copy with minimal effort. Regardless of how you produce your final draft, whether by hand or by machine,

> DON'T FORGET TO KEEP A COPY FOR YOUR FILES!

EXERCISE 13.1

The following paragraph has passed through the first two revision stages; it now needs editing. Using the editing checklist on pp. 121–22 as your guide, find and correct all errors in grammar, spelling, word choice, and punctuation.

In comparing and contrasting cross-country and downhill skiing, I considered four factors, and on every one of the four, cross country comes out ahead. First, cross-country skiing is much less expensive, both for the equiptment and for a day's enjoyment of the activity. Second, it is alot more convient. Unless one happens to live on a ski hill, you have to drive miles to a slope for downhill, whereas cross-country can be done anywheres. Third cross-country skiing is much better exercise since you are working steadily instead of stanidng around three quaters of the time waiting for a lift to the top of a hill. Finaly more fun is had by exploring new country, away from the crowds. The scenery can be enjoyed and there is no danger of running into other people or being run into by hotdogs or snowboarders. Yes, I'll take cross-country over downhill skiing every time.

EXERCISE 13.2

Is the following paragraph ready for submission? Go over it carefully, correcting any errors. Then get together with another student and compare your proofreading skills.

According to a recent survey in Maclean's magazine, only 43% of Canadians are satisfied with their jobs. What can you do to ensure that you will not be one of the 57% who are unhappy with the work they do. There are three questions you should consider when seeking employment that will provide satisfaction as well as a paycheque. First, are you suited to the kind of work you are applying for. If you enjoy the outdoors, for example, and like to be active, your going to be happy with a nine to five office job, no matter how much it pays. Second, is the job based in a location compatible with your prefered lifestyle. No matter how much you like your work, if you go home every night to an enviorment you are miserable in, it won't be long before you start transfering your disatisfaction to your job. If you like the amenities and coveniences of the city, you probably will not enjoy working in a small town. If, on the other hand you prefer the quiet and security of small town life, you may find the city a stressful place to live. Finally is this the kind of company you want to work for. Do you need the security of generous benifits, a good pension plan, and incentives to stay and grow with one company? Or are you an ambitous person who is looking for variety, quick advancement, and a high salary. If so you may have to forgo security in favour of commissions or cash incentives, and be willing

to move as quickly and as often as opportunities occur. Some carful self

analysis now, before you start out on your career path, will help you

chose a direction that will put you in the 43% minority of satisfied

Canadian workers.

EXERCISE 13.3

Here's another document on which you can test your editing and proofreading skills. The following item is a promotional piece that was circu-
lated to local businesses in a mid-size Canadian town. The document was
computer-produced and -printed. (We've changed the names.) Spot the
errors, correct them, and then exchange papers with another student and
compare your revisions.

Dear Sir or Madom

Please let me introduce my self to you my name is Gary kiefer, president

of the Canadian Cleaning Service Association. At C. C. S. A we take great

pride in providing our client With Superior Cleaning Service at on

affordable price. We provide service in Industrial cleaning Commercial

cleaning Residencial cleaning   We belive in giving our client prompt

personalized and proffesional service at all times, day or night. Wether

you are looking for one person, severol, or a Platoon, we can provide you

with quality profesional cleaning service you require.

The CCSA has bin operating with over 150 Independent Cleaning

Buisiness as members of the CCSA As Canada only premier cleaning

organiztion our gaol is maintain high standards of cleaning service at on affordable price to our costumes   in addition to basic cleaning other service include Carpet Cleaning Floor striping and waxing Building Maintenance services. We are interested in provide, compleat, Janitorial service to your orginazation, because we think your firm offer us on apportunity to meet a new administration challenge, and our expirence in this area of providing could be of significant intrest to you. if you are looking for a top quality cleaning company to provide top quality cleaning service to you and your organization please call us for Free estimate I am confident that your administration will find us to be an hardworking and dedecated teem of proffesional who is ready to serve and support your organization

Thank you for your consideration we are looking forward to work with you and your organazation.

EXERCISE 13.4

This exercise will serve as a review of all three stages of the revision process. Below is a first draft of an essay. Applying the principles you have learned in Chapters 11, 12, and 13, revise this essay to make it a model of good communication: complete, correct, concise, and courteous.

   We are having a garbage crisis. There is so much waste being produced in North America, we no longer have any idea of were to put it. Toronto's garbage problem is so great that they are now talking of trucking it hundreds of kilometers North of the City and putting it into abandonned mine shafts near Kirkland lake. But how long will that last?

We must act now, and we must act as individuals. We cannot wait for the Government to save us from this crisis. It is us who make the garbage, it must be us who solves the problem. In very practical, down to earth, concrete terms, here are some things we can do to reduce, recycle, and re-use.

First we must reduce the amount of garbage we produce. We can do this be refusing to buy products that are over packaged, like fast food that comes in styrafoam containers and chocolates that have a paper wrapping, a box, lining paper, a plastic tray for the candies, and foil wrap around each chocolate. By not purchasing such wasteful items, we say to the manufacturer, Either reduce the packing in your product or lose buisness to your competition. We can also be less wastful in our own habits by carpooling, for example, or by using cloth diapers instead of disposables.

We must recycle everything we can instead of sending it to the dump. Old cloths can be sent to the Salvation Army, the Scott mission, or other charitable organizations. As can furniture, appliances, books, and most other household items. There are dozens of ways to make useful items from packaging that would otherwise be thrown away, such as bird feeders from plastic jugs, braided rugs from old rags, and fire logs from newspapers. We don't need to consume as much as we do, and it won't hurt us to use things longer instead of buying new items before the old ones are completely worn out. Many companies now manufacture products from recycled goods, and we should be on the lookout for their products to support their efforts and to reduce the waste that is dumped into landfills.

Third, we can re-use most things. Composting vegetable garbage is a good way to put waste to valuable use. Or we can offer the things we no longer wnt to others through lawn sales and flea markets.

This is an absolute necessity. If we do not stop producing so much waste, we will inevitibly destroy our own enviornment. Unlike most efforts to improve things, the move to recycle, re-use, and reduce has one other advantage: it doesn't cost any money. In fact, it can save each household that practices it hundreds of dollars every year.

Developing the Essay

CHAPTER 14

Description

College essays and most reports fall into three broad categories:

1. Descriptive and narrative writing
2. Expository writing
3. Persuasive writing

These categories are not separate and distinct. In general-interest, business, and technical prose, they often overlap. (In fact, one could argue that *all* writing is persuasive, since all writing attempts to convince readers that the information the writer is presenting is reasonable and true.) It is useful, however, to consider the three categories one at a time and to learn the techniques involved in each separately, before you attempt to combine them in an essay or report.

All effective writing depends to some extent on *description* and *narration*, the techniques that are the subjects of this and the next chapter. Expository writing includes *process analysis, classification and division, cause and effect,* and *comparison and contrast.* These patterns of development are covered in Chapters 16 to 19. Persuasive writing is introduced in Chapter 20. The final chapter of this unit shows you how to develop your main points using quotations, paraphrases, and summaries, all of which can help support main points in each of the three broad writing categories.

After you have identified your subject and main points, it is time to consider how best to explain those points to your reader. The various patterns of organization we present and illustrate in this unit represent different ways of looking at your subject. Which organizational pattern you choose for a particular writing task will depend on what you want your readers to know or believe about your subject. In getting your message across to your readers, how you organize your ideas and how you develop them are as important as the words you choose.

What Is Good Description?

Description covers many writing applications, from the creative prose you might use to describe scenery, to the precise and concrete descriptions needed by law enforcement officers, medical staff, and emergency personnel to provide detailed reports. A description is a verbal picture of an object, a scene, a person, or an event. In all descriptive writing, the objective is to provide readers with a picture of what it was like to be there.

By learning to write good description, you will become better at all kinds of writing. Making your readers see what you have seen, even in your imagination, is the essence of communication.

Tips on Writing a Description Essay

1. Engage all the senses, if possible: sight, sound, smell, touch, and taste.
2. Describe precisely, using words that create specific images. Don't say that something is "beautiful" or "impressive" or "wonderful," without telling your readers specifically how the object or event exhibited those qualities.
3. Select words with care. Never use a general word where a more specific, descriptive one could be used.

   Example: He walked towards the large figure sitting in the shadows.

   Examples, with descriptive words replacing nonspecific ones:
   He strutted towards the large figure cowering in the shadows.
   He crept towards the large figure hulking in the shadows.
   He bounded towards the large figure poised in the shadows.
4. Choose a viewing point for your description. As the describer, you must take a position and describe what you see from that spot. Tell what is visible from left to right or from far to near, or "walk" your readers around an object or along a defined pathway; but don't confuse them by changing your viewing point unnecessarily.

EXERCISE 14.1

Read the following description essays and answer the questions that follow each essay.

Diamonds Are Forever

Montreal's "Big O" and Toronto's SkyDome are wonderful places for loyal subjects to pay homage to baseball's royalty. We can watch the game in air-conditioned comfort, fearing neither rain nor cold, just as though we were at home viewing the proceedings on TV. While modern stadiums are fittingly lavish for highly paid major-leaguers to perform their feats, baseball for most Canadians has a much different atmosphere. Many of us have in common the sights, sounds, smells, and "feel" of the dirt diamonds, grass outfields, wooden bleachers, and home-town crowds of small-time baseball.

Where I grew up, baseball meant the home-town "Star Cleaners" in their white uniforms with red trim. The infield of our diamond was hard red clay, raked over and loosened prior to game time so that by the middle innings the players were covered in fine rust; latecomers could tell what inning it was by the degree of colour in the uniforms. A fastball would explode into the catcher's mitt in a satisfying cloud of dust, while a slide at second would sometimes be obscured from the bleacher crowd. In the early part of the season, the outfield grass was always bright green and as lush as a cemetery lawn. As the dry weather of August approached, however, brown patches would appear, until, by playoff time, the outfield was straw brown relieved by the odd green patch.

The newly mown outfield grass and, especially, the perfume of fried onions from the Lions Club snack bar behind the stands remain the most vivid scents of summer, and the *thwack!* of ball hitting leather the most exciting sound. The yelling of the home-town fans stirred excitement, and the hilarious jibes of the local wit in the back row of the bleachers brought comic relief, but the sounds on the field were what we were all there for. The smack of the bat on a well-hit ball, the umpire's guttural exclamations, the grunt of a player's effort, cries of encouragement from the players' benches: all these blended together in a happy symphony. But the slap of the ball into the leather of the first-baseman's glove, that breathless moment when so much is at stake—that's the sound that I crouched in the front row of the bleachers to hear.

Individual great plays still raise the hair on the back of my head when I recall them: "Moose" Christie catching a line drive in his bare, pitching hand; the reserve player/coach (his name now forgotten) who came off the bench in the sixteenth inning to hit a game-winning triple; my fifth-grade teacher, "Squirt" Dunsmore, striking out the side in the ninth inning; the entire, delirious game on a sunny Sunday when the "Star Cleaners" won the provincial championship. I love the Expos and adore the Blue Jays, and I live and die with them all season long. But somehow, their game is plastic, artificial, and remote beside the baseball being played on dirt diamonds by men and women who play for the love of it.

1. Sight, sound, and smell are the senses engaged in this essay. Identify specific words the author used to appeal to each of these senses.

    Sight: _____

    _____

Sound: _____

_____

Smell: _____

_____

2. What is the author's viewing point in this description?
3. This essay has elements of comparison/contrast. How do they add to the description?
4. In the introduction, the author begins with a brief description of other places before shifting to the real theme of the essay. Is this an effective way to start? Why?
5. Blueprint the essay, highlighting major and minor points.

The White Darkness
Wade Davis

The challenge of travel is to find a way to isolate and understand the germ of a people, to measure and absorb the spirit of place. In Haiti one begins in Port-au-Prince. The capital lies prostrate across a low, hot, tropical plain at the head of a bay flanked on both sides by soaring mountains. Behind these mountains rise others, creating an illusion of space that absorbs Haiti's multitudes and softens the country's harshest statistic: a land mass of only ten thousand square miles inhabited by six million people. Port-au-Prince is a sprawling muddle of a city, on first encounter a carnival of civic chaos. A waterfront shantytown damp with laundry. Half-finished public monuments. Streets lined with *flamboyant* and the stench of fish and sweat, excrement and ash. Dazzling government buildings and a Presidential palace so white that it doesn't seem real. There are the cries and moans of the marketplace, the din of untuned engines, the reek of diesel fumes. It presents all the squalor and all the grace of any Caribbean capital.

Yet as you drive through the city for the first time, down by the docks perhaps, where the shanties face the gleaming cruise ships and men with legs like anvils haul carts loaded with bloody hides, notice something else. The people on the street don't walk, they flow, exuding pride. Physically, they are beautiful. They seem gay, jaunty, carefree. Washed clean by the afternoon rain, the entire city has a rakish charm. But there is more. In a land of material scarcity, the people adorn their lives with their imagination—discarded Coke cans become suitcases or trumpets, rubber tires are turned into shoes, buses transformed into kaleidoscopic *tap-taps*, moving exhibits of vibrant, naive art. And it isn't just how things appear, it is something in the air, something electric—a raw elemental energy not to be found elsewhere in the Americas. What you have found is the lens of Africa focused upon the New World.

_____

(Wade Davis, "The White Darkness," from *Shadows in the Sun: Essays on the Spirit of Place*. Edmonton: Lone Pine, 1992, pp. 50–51. Reprinted by permission of the author.)

1. Consider how the author has arranged the details of his description. How does he ensure that readers will find it coherent and well organized?
2. What overall impression of Haiti does Davis convey? List at least five negative details and five positive details that contribute to this impression. What single sentence best sums up the paradoxical nature of this island?
3. Underline the specific descriptive phrases you find most effective in contributing to the vivid verbal picture Davis paints in these paragraphs. Which of the physical senses does he appeal to?
4. The first paragraph contains a number of sentence fragments. How do these fragments help contribute to the dominant impression the writer wishes to communicate?
5. What does the last sentence mean? Why is it an effective conclusion?

Ode to a Café
Danielle Crittenden

There is a café in Toronto that I do not visit as much as I should since I moved from the neighbourhood. It is in an area known as The Beaches, where it has recently become impossible to buy a drink without a parasol in it. This was once a quiet district of clapboard cottages and empty stretches of sand, until the men with the pink neon and the white sportscars moved in. Now it looks something like a seaside village in drag. There are many cafés, and unless you are of a certain romantic temperament, it is unlikely you would wander into this particular one on your own. It is very small, about the size of a dry-cleaning outlet. On some days, depending upon the mood of the proprietress, only a few dishes are available.

Most prefer the café across the street, larger and more fashionable, decorated, like the rest, with black bentwood chairs and marble tables, and modern graphics on the walls. I have watched many people who go there, and it seems to be the choice of the Bohemian set. They sit by the windows wearing their berets and smoking French cigarettes, speaking of whatever is new.

Once, when my favourite café was closed, I had no choice but to eat lunch there. I listened to a couple near me discuss a significant development in art: a sculptor who coated small plywood houses with chewed bubblegum. The man was rapturous as he described the metaphysical repercussions this technique could have on the art world. The woman listened intensely, stirring her *espresso* absently many times before she finally sipped it. The waitress appeared to be an unemployed actress, because she put much theatre into taking the orders, rattling off the specials of the day like a succession of memorized lines, sighing dramatically if one took too long to decide, bringing and removing plates with great swoops and arabesques. The bill for a stale, paltry amount of food was large (including, I assume, the price of the show), and she was insistent that I pay it immediately and vacate, as she was going "off shift."

It made me realize that there are few really good cafés in this city, or any Canadian city. We are not a café society in the tradition of Europe; our eateries are efficient, productive places that use loud music to discourage lingering or prolonged discussion; staff are trained like chained bull terriers. In Paris one can rent a table for several hours for the price of a single cup of coffee, and sit there, watching the other customers in the greasy mirrors along the walls or the passers-by outside as they bustle home in the dying autumn light.

There is a photograph that I love, taken in Paris in 1950, of a couple embracing in front of an outdoor café. The two lovers and a nearby table are the only objects in focus—the rest of the world around them is blurred, a mad, monochromatic rush. To me it illustrates what a good café should be, an oasis amidst the swirling, arid winds of society. In North America, we want everything at a fast pace, and our cafés are indicative of this. They are sleek, impressive, and modern, but unwhimsical. The culture they serve is like a bland patty shaped by a production line and fried until flavourless. It sells, people eat it, but ultimately, it is fattening and unhealthy.

I had long given up on finding a European-style café in Toronto, until the day i went into the smaller place. It had a large window with "Café Natasha" painted on it in gaudy yellow, next door to a beauty salon and a gourmet candy shop. Inside were eight small tables covered in blue cloths, all taken, except for one seat at a table for four. The woman who appeared to be Natasha looked at me sympathetically, and waved her hand to the empty chair.

"Perhaps you would like that one?" she said in a dense accent, and as I opened my mouth to say "No," she was already announcing my arrival to the three diners. They looked up cheerily and waved me over, and I spent the evening with them in a conversation of some sort which was eventually lost in drink, as most good conversations are.

It took me many more trips to the café to learn about the woman who ran it. Occasionally, when she was not busy, she would sit with me by the window and smoke one of her skinny brown cigarettes and muse on the colour of the sky. On evenings when I stopped by for a glass of wine before closing, the lights would be dimmed, and the woman shimmied softly by herself to an old jazz tune.

Her age was somewhere between precocious and refined, forty, I think, but it doesn't matter. She belonged in another era: a Berlin coffee house in the 'thirties, perhaps, or a Paris dance hall during the 'twenties. She had deep red hair cut along the line of her chin, and black eyes which reflected the light, or absorbed it, depending on her mood. On a fine day she would be wearing an outrageous, colourful costume with a wide leather belt and lace-up shoes. On bad days she would dress bleakly, her hair would be rumpled, and she would smoke her dreadful cigarettes with particular ferocity. Most of the time I saw her she was between these two extremes, a lyrical creature arranging fresh flowers in a chipped, ceramic jug, or exclaiming about the seasons.

It was not her dress or the way she wore her hair that defined Natasha. Something about her reminded me of an exotic, uncatalogued species of bird, next to whom one felt flightless. When she moved, she danced, even to fetch a spoon. The music she played constantly in her café was the kind that evoked memories of other places, and other times. In the spring, it was always Vivaldi; in the hot summer, it would be the sultry pining of Billie Holiday; by autumn, red wine and Piaf; throughout winter, the blues of Bessie Smith.

Eventually, I learned that Natasha had left Yugoslavia with her husband many years ago to come to Canada. On the walls she had hung small mirrors and black and white photographs, and a few girlish sketches of people she had drawn at college in Dubrovnik. Natasha worked from eleven in the morning to eleven at night, cooking in the back and serving people out front. She offered simple food which she knew how to cook well: schnitzels and goulash, perogies and chicken soup, with thick, fresh bread. Half of the menu was available at any moment, as long as the dishwasher had not quit earlier that day, or the stove had not broken down, which happened rather frequently. At these times Natasha would be flying around the café like a startled, frantic sparrow, flapping her arms and calling out in her accented English.

Yet those who came did not do so for the food but to visit Natasha, and she developed a regular, eclectic clientele who dropped by to drink and to talk. One pleasant gentleman would take a side table, order a carafe of wine, and sit for hours reading paperback novels. An older woman who lived alone dined every night at the café and often stayed until closing, watching the other customers benignly like an aged cat. One Eastern European fellow was there frequently, a bulky man who wore a dark jacket, steel-toed boots, and had a face like moulded concrete.

"Who is that?" I asked Natasha one day.

"Shhh," she said furtively. "KGB."

Sometimes she would stop in the middle of carrying out plates to the kitchen and gaze at her café with fond amusement. There might be an argument going on at one table, drunken outbursts of laughter from another, and two lovers in the corner watching each other as they ate. You could easily spot the new customers. They would sit watching with uncertain grins on their faces. "You know," she would say with great pride, "this has become my private smoking and drinking club."

Mostly, though, there were conversations, hundreds of them, now scattered. We would sit with wine, and smoke and speak frivolously, which one does when one is drunk. Sometimes she would shut the café so we could dance late at night, or she would put up the closed sign so we could have privacy to drink in the afternoon. One forgot other things when around her, the world shrank until it could fit in her front window.

I left the city for several months, and when I returned, I found a flat in a different neighbourhood. When I saw her again recently, she scolded me for not coming by as often as I did when I lived near the café. I apologized, and we drank quietly, with the resigned understanding of friends who know that nothing can be done to change the circumstances. She is open less frequently now, and on some days, I have gone by and found the café dark, with a handwritten note taped to the door: "Sorry, dear friends, you are here but I am not."

I noticed that she has been sadder lately, the light catching only the shadows of her eyes. She speaks often about selling the café, opening one in Casablanca, or Havana, or Montparnasse. She knows they are all lost places, but then so are many dreams, and Natasha's café has become more of a state of mind than a place to eat. If she closes, there will be nowhere else. As we talked, I looked out the window at the café across the street. It was full.

Suddenly Natasha grasped my hand. "But my goodness, look how serious you and I have become!" she exclaimed, standing to fetch more wine. "Come, let's dance. . . ."

(Danielle Crittenden, "Ode to a Café," *The Idler*, May/June 1987. Reprinted by permission of the author.)

1. Crittenden uses contrast frequently to help her description. What points of difference does she give in comparing cafés in Europe with cafés in North America?
2. The description of Natasha is vivid on many levels; Crittenden describes her appearance, her manner, and her attitudes. How is Natasha's personality reflected in the atmosphere of her café?
3. What is the atmosphere of the café? Is the author's description effective? Does the description of the café's customers contribute to the overall picture?
4. Contrast Natasha's café with the café across the street. Why does Crittenden prefer Natasha's café?
5. What is Crittenden's purpose in this essay? Who are her intended readers?

EXERCISE 14.2

A list of general or nonspecific words is given below. Write at least three verbs that could replace each word listed, to provide readers with a clearer image of the activity.

look   (*Example:* stare)   _____   _____

talk   _____   _____   _____

cut   _____   _____   _____

fall   _____   _____   _____

laugh   _____   _____   _____

EXERCISE 14.3

For each of the verbs you provided in Exercise 14.2, write an effective sentence. Vary the subject matter as much as possible.

EXERCISE 14.4

For one of the persons listed below, brainstorm until you have at least ten characteristics. Put the characteristics in order and then develop them into a good paragraph. Have a specific person in mind, not simply an abstract "character."

a class clown   a grandparent
a fitness instructor   your favourite comedian
your girlfriend/boyfriend, past or present your present boss
a small child   a street runaway
a teacher   a transit employee

EXERCISE 14.5

Choose a scenic photograph or painting that appeals to you, and write a paragraph describing in detail exactly what you see. As you write, imagine that a friend will be listening to your description over a telephone, in another city.

EXERCISE 14.6

To the paragraph you wrote in Exercise 14.5, add a paragraph that describes the sounds and smells that you might experience if you were in the scene depicted in the photograph or painting.

EXERCISE 14.7

Write an essay describing an interesting person you know. Remember that your objective in description is to make your subject come alive for your readers. Specific details (including mannerisms, possessions, and activities) will bring the character to life more than abstract descriptions of his or her personality, and a very detailed physical description will help to convey a clear impression.

EXERCISE 14.8

Write a description essay about a place that is particularly memorable to you, not because a significant event occurred there, but because the place itself was interesting and unique. Try to isolate the place into a sharply defined "snapshot," rather than a "panorama." The locations listed below may remind you of a particular memory spot.

a stadium after a rock concert	a train (or bus) station
a cemetery	a junkyard
an all-night diner	a garage sale
a hospital waiting room	a highway at night
a classroom during an exam	a church, temple, or synagogue

EXERCISE 14.9

We can learn a lot about people if we know what possessions they have and what activities they engage in. What might you infer about the character of a woman who writes with an engraved, gold-plated fountain pen? One who writes with a stubby pencil? Describe *one* person and convey that person's character in a paragraph that includes description of each of the following.

means of transportation	ring(s)
writing implement	lunch
favourite drink	wristwatch
favourite TV show	wallet or purse
shoes	leisure activities

CHAPTER 15

Narration

Narration is the kind of writing you do when you want to tell your readers how something happened. Your purpose in telling a story may be to illustrate a point, persuade, or entertain, but all good narrative essays follow a basic pattern. The introduction presents a thesis, an overall theme for the story. The story then unfolds, usually in chronological order, with sufficient detail and description that your readers can experience the events along with you. The conclusion brings the story to a satisfying end and reinforces its point.

Like description, narration is seldom found in its "pure" form in academic or professional writing. It is usually used in combination with other kinds of development. For example, explaining a process (how something works) is a special kind of narration; explaining a cause–effect relationship frequently involves narration, and so does arguing a position or persuading. Almost everything you write will include at least some description and narration; that is why we are dealing with these two forms first. Because they are specific rather than general, narration and description add interest to whatever kind of writing you do. They enable readers to *see* and *feel* what you are saying, so your ideas are easier to understand and remember.

Tips on Writing a Narration Essay

1. The story you tell must have a clear purpose; it must have a point. Good narration tells who did what to whom, where, when, and how. It also states or clearly implies why the event or incident is significant. Remember: the subject of your essay is the point you are making, not the story you are telling.

2. Blueprint your ideas, and then fill in descriptive details. Blueprinting will help you to arrange your events in chronological order and to group the events appropriately. Begin each paragraph after a natural break in the narrative. Use transition terms to help the coherence of your narrative.

3. Make sure that your opening paragraph introduces the scene and major characters fully enough that your readers are not confused. In your closing paragraph, draw the strings together to leave your readers with a feeling of satisfactory closure.

4. Dialogue is a common device in narration, but use it sparingly. Traditionally, each exchange of dialogue is given a separate paragraph.

5. Don't use so much description that events are drawn out beyond their natural length; you may make your readers impatient.

6. Don't try to include too many events in a short narrative.

EXERCISE 15.1

Read the three narration essays that follow, and answer the questions after each essay.

The Incomplete Angler

While visiting a kind and well-meaning friend in Sarnia, I revealed myself to be an avid, if not very expert, sports fisherman. My friend confessed that he found fishing slightly less enthralling than watching algae grow in his swimming pool, but he had a pal who was a fishing fanatic. A phone call later, I was to be the special guest of "Ol' Jack" on an all-day fishing expedition to the Thames River the very next day. It has taken me four years to recover sufficiently from this adventure to tell you about it.

On the fateful day, Ol' Jack picked me up at 5:30 AM in his monstrous blue four-wheel-drive truck. Attached to the trailer hitch on the bed was a fourteen-foot aluminum tub with an outboard motor of adequate horsepower to push the *Queen Mary*. In the back of the truck about twenty fishing rods lay tangled together in a heap, together with assorted tackle boxes, coolers, paddles, and hip waders. Surmounting this mess of miscellaneous gear was a green fishing net that could comfortably have held Moby Dick. I was beginning to get a picture of the kind of fisherman Ol' Jack was.

I credit a tough constitution and my battered fishing hat for my survival during our trip to the river. Even with the protection of the hat, by the time we pulled up at the dock I was nursing a scalp wound and two goose-eggs on my skull from being tossed around the cab. Jack hurled the mound of fishing paraphernalia into the back, launched the boat, and we were off; no one was going to beat us to the "good spots." As we tore up the river, leaving a four-foot wake on either side, Jack pulled out a vodka bottle filled with an evil-looking red liquid. After taking a long swig, he handed me the bottle. "Bloody Mary," he said. "Just the thing to start the day." Gingerly, I sniffed the contents and took a tiny taste. Jack laughed as I recoiled and spat the stuff over the side. "Didn't have any tomato juice," he howled, "so I just dropped a little ketchup in the vodka!"

For the rest of the day, we thrashed up and down the river, dragging various strange devices behind us in a futile attempt to attract a fish. While Jack stood tall in the cockpit, handling throttle, wheel, fishing rod, and bottle, I huddled miserably in the stern, hoping I would not be recognized by any of the canoeists or fishermen we were swamping in our wake and sending scurrying for shore with our erratic trolling. Jack waved jauntily at the shaken fists and obscene gestures directed our way and tipped his baseball hat to those who favoured us with shouted curses.

Noon found me trying to decide whether sunburn, hunger, and exhaust fumes from the leaky outboard motor would end my misery before the inevitable collision and death by drowning or lynch-mob. I favoured whichever end would be quicker. By mid-afternoon Jack had decided we weren't using the right lures, so we swept up to several anchored boats to find out what was working. These manoeuvres added seasickness to my list of woes. When anyone admitted to having caught a fish, Jack offered to buy the successful lure on the spot. However, even with these measures, he failed to entice any fish into attaching themselves to our lines. By supper time, even Jack was ready to admit defeat and head for the dock. I was beyond caring.

Back in Sarnia, Jack dropped me at my friend's house and roared off with the promise to pick me up the next morning at 4:30. I staggered into the house and, when the trembling stopped, told the story of the day's fun on the river. Later, as I was helped up the stairs for a hot bath and long night's sleep, I begged my friend to call Jack with the news that I had come down with a potentially fatal attack of presbyopia and would be unable to join him in the morning. I haven't killed, caught, or eaten a fish since.

1. The narration in this essay begins with the first sentence. There is no general introduction, but the thesis is clearly implied in the first paragraph. State the thesis of the essay in a short sentence.

_____

_____

2. You learned in studying descriptive writing that a person's possessions and actions can tell us a great deal about his or her character. List some of Ol' Jack's more significant possessions and actions and the characteristics they reveal about Ol' Jack.

POSSESSION/ACTION   CHARACTERISTIC

_____   _____

_____   _____

POSSESSION/ACTION   CHARACTERISTIC

_____   _____

_____   _____

_____   _____

3. This story is entertaining, but is there any moral that can be learned from the narrative? What did the author learn from his experience?
4. Who are the author's intended readers?
5. The author shows himself as the victim of this humorous escapade. What is his role? What is his purpose?

How I Lost My Faith
Mark Twain

My school days began when I was four years and a half old. . . . Mrs. Horr was a New England lady of middle age with New England ways and principles and she always opened school with prayer and a chapter from the New Testament; also she explained the chapter with a brief talk. In one of these talks she dwelt upon the text "Ask and ye shall receive," and said that [whoever] prayed for a thing with earnestness and strong desire need not doubt that his prayer would be answered.

I was so forcibly struck by this information and so gratified by the opportunities which it offered that this was probably the first time I had heard of it. I thought I would give it a trial. I believed in Mrs. Horr thoroughly and I had no doubts as to the result. I prayed for gingerbread. Margaret Kooneman, who was the baker's daughter, brought a slab of gingerbread to school every morning; she had always kept it out of sight before, but when I finished my prayer and glanced up, there it was in easy reach and she was looking the other way. In all my life I believe I never enjoyed an answer to prayer more than I enjoyed that one; and I was a convert, too. I had no end of wants and they had always remained unsatisfied up to that time, but I meant to supply them and extend them now that I had found out how to do it.

But this dream was like almost all the other dreams we indulge in in life; there was nothing in it. I did as much praying during the next two or three days as anyone in that town, I suppose, and I was very sincere and earnest about it too, but nothing came of it. I found that not even the most powerful prayer was competent to lift that gingerbread again, and I came to the conclusion that if a person remains faithful to his gingerbread and keeps his eye on it he need not trouble himself about your prayers.

_____

(Mark Twain, "How I Lost My Faith," from *The Autobiography of Mark Twain*, first published 1924, edited by A.B. Paine; 1960 London edition, Charles Neider, editor, reprinted in Penelope Hughes–Hallett, editor, *Childhood: A Collins Anthology*. London: Collins, 1988, p. 353. Reprinted by permission of Penelope Hughes–Hallett.)

1. What is the point of Twain's story? Explain it in your own words.
2. How does the first paragraph serve to introduce this story effectively?
3. Is the conclusion satisfying? Why?
4. Identify, in order, the main events in this narrative.
5. What is the tone of this piece? How does it help establish a positive relationship between the writer and his readers?

The next selection is an excerpt from a longer work. On a student exchange to Thailand, Karen Connelly makes a phone call home to Canada and discovers that her boyfriend is in love with someone else. Her Thai friends try to comfort her:

Beed saves me from feeling sorry for myself. . . . I walk slowly up Yantrak (I've been walking slowly for several days now), wanting only to speak to someone who will understand me, who will listen. I reach the gas station, but Beed is not alone. The entire family is out in front, having an argument about geraniums. . . .

Everyone hushes to a whisper when I appear: it's all over Denchai that the *falang* [foreigner] has been somewhat hysterical these last few days, has even been seen crying in public. Paw Prasit comes to see me every day to make sure I'm not dying.

Beed's father smiles and asks if I've been swimming; my eyes are so red. I'm not sure if this is a joke or not. I begin an attempt at calm explanation but it quickly turns into English and Thai gibberish verging on tears. For a moment, Beed, her husband and her parents are silent. Little Poun, who did not notice me until I began to sputter, also begins to cry, which fortunately takes everyone's attention away from me. I blow my nose. (Finally I am remembering handkerchiefs.)

A truck has pulled up at the pumps and before going to fill it, Samat makes a strange clicking noise with his teeth and says, "Kalen, kohn soo-wai, mai pen lai." Beautiful one, never mind. I laugh in spite of myself; the last thing I am now is beautiful. Beed takes me by the hand and leads me to the office, with still-snivelling Poun perched on her hip. Her parents follow close behind. Once inside the sunny office, Koon Meh takes down a Chinese checkerboard. The little grease-monkey named Chet comes in to play with me.

"There are a thousand good men in Canada," Beed tells me.

"And many millions of great Thai men right here," says her father.

"You should find a new Thai boyfriend who is not rai-jai," Beed's mother says. *Rai-jai* means many-hearted, without one true heart. "We all love the people who are closest to us. You are very far away. But don't worry. You are young and will be close to many."

"You should marry my brother," chirps Chet, who is quite small, even for a Thai. "He's a policeman who will take good care of you."

Out of eight matches of Chinese checkers, I win only twice, when Beed's mother plays. She lets me win. I don't care. I'm not even angry that they don't take this very seriously. Samat says "Mai pen lai" every time my face begins to crumble. "Don't think," advises Beed's father. "First it will give you a headache, then it will make you old." I play checkers until I am half blind, then, without thinking, I walk home through the green-gold light of dusk. After my chicken and rice and a discussion with Pee-Moi about duck eggs, I go to bed, sleeping deeply for the first time in weeks, without a memory of dreams.

_____

(Karen Connelly, excerpt from *Touch the Dragon.* Winnipeg: Turnstone Press, 1987, pp. 47–48. Copyright © 1987 Karen Connelly. Reprinted by permission.)

1. What is the point of this story? Where in the narrative do you learn the point?
2. How do the last two sentences reinforce the point?
3. Study Connelly's use of dialogue. What is the guiding principle that determines whether or not a piece of dialogue is set off in a separate paragraph?
4. Because this is an excerpt from a longer work, there is no introductory paragraph. Write an introduction to set the scene and point to the purpose of this story.

EXERCISE 15.2

You hear narration every day, when your friends, family, classmates, and teachers tell you about incidents that happened to them. Most of these are insignificant incidents that seemed important at the time but are soon forgotten. What makes a narrative memorable? What kinds of stories stick in your mind long after you have heard them? Why?

EXERCISE 15.3

Narration relies on the same principle as description: a detailed account that appeals to the senses. However, good narration adds the answer to the question "What did it feel like to be a participant?" Imagine yourself as the central figure in a major event. Write a paragraph that will convey to your readers some of the emotion of the event. You might start with "As I walked from the on-deck circle towards the plate . . ." or "The director motioned for action, and I moved forward into the arms of Richard Gere. . . ."

EXERCISE 15.4

Using the same incident that you created in Exercise 15.3, write the narration as it might have been seen and felt by a minor participant, perhaps the mascot in the first example, or a lighting technician in the second.

EXERCISE 15.5

In good narration, the story told is often used as an example to illustrate a theme or point of view. Briefly blueprint a story you might tell from personal experience to demonstrate one of the following themes.

loneliness	overcoming great odds
friendship	loss
panic	jealousy
peer pressure	a close call
victory	obsession

EXERCISE 15.6

Using the blueprint from Exercise 15.5, write a narration essay. Remember that good stories are carefully planned and structured; poor ones are often the products of writers who begin at the top of the page and stumble downward until the story comes to an end.

EXERCISE 15.7

Embarrassing incidents often make good narratives, both because most are entertaining and because listeners and readers can often learn a lesson from the embarrassing mistakes of others. Briefly rough out, in point form, a narrative of the most embarrassing thing that has ever happened to you. This may make a good essay when you are assigned a narrative to write. It might also be good therapy!

EXERCISE 15.8

Narrate the plot of a movie that you enjoyed and remember clearly. Give important details, beyond the simple facts of the story. Try to make the experience of reading your essay as vivid and interesting as viewing the movie itself.

EXERCISE 15.9

Your life is full of experiences that you share with many others: your first day at school, your first day at work, your wedding day, a memorable vacation, and so on. However, no two of these experiences are the same; each person has a unique version. Below is a list of "first" or "last" or "only" experiences. Only *you* can narrate how yours happened. Plan and develop *one* of these events into a full essay. Remember to focus on a limited length of time and give most attention to highlights.

a speeding ticket	a surprise birthday party
my first car purchase	my first time skiing (*or* another sport)
my first love affair	moving day
the last day on a job	betrayal by a friend
the birth of a child	my first speech

CHAPTER 16

Process

A **process essay** explains to your readers how to make or do something or how something works. It presents, in the order in which they must happen, the steps or stages necessary to perform a task or achieve a goal. A process-essay subject may be very concrete, such as "How to fix a flat tire" or "Getting to the Resource Centre from the Registrar's Office"; or it may deal with something more abstract, such as "Surviving the first week of college" or "How to get along with a difficult boss."

When you write a process essay, keep your language simple and clear. Your readers must be able to understand your instructions in order to follow them. The following instructions accompanied a simple box designed for preparing newspapers for recycling.

> This paper recycler has been thoughtfully designed for ease of use and practical serviceability. Slide recycling binder material into recycling binder material placement slot in the upper frame opposite recycling binder material spool. Reel off sufficient recycling binder material to line the inside of the vertical housing unit and rest on the support struts. Place newspapers to be recycled lengthwise across support struts between vertical housing units, on top of recycling binder material. When newspaper stack reaches a height of 40 cm reel off approximately 20 cm of recycling binder material, remove end from recycling binder material placement slot, and tie securely. Cut off recycling binder material, remove newspaper bundle, and repeat.

The instructions break the process down into simple steps organized in chronological order, but the writer has forgotten the most basic rule of good writing: *remember your readers.* Even the most determined environmentalist would be dismayed and discouraged by these directions. A successful process essay takes into account the readers' familiarity (or lack of it) with the process, their experience, and their level of vocabulary, and communicates the steps of the process in a way that holds their interest.

You should be knowledgeable about the process you are describing, but remember that your readers don't share your knowledge. One of the most difficult aspects of writing a process paper is making sure you have included all the necessary steps. Try to imagine yourself in your readers' place: a novice, reading the instructions for the first time.

Tips on Writing a Process Essay

1. List all the steps in the process in logical or chronological order. Include *everything* that your readers need to know. (See p. 41 and p. 42 for definitions of chronological order and logical order, respectively.)
2. Write a preview statement that makes it clear what your readers are about to learn and what major steps are involved in the process.

   Example: To become a truly healthy person, you must follow a fitness program, develop good eating habits, and control stress.

3. In developing your points into paragraphs, be careful to use transitions within and between the paragraphs.
4. When editing and revising, put yourself in the position of a novice and test whether you can follow the instructions as they have been written; or have someone who really is a novice try to follow your directions.

EXERCISE 16.1

The following three essays show clearly how to direct readers through a step-by-step process. Read each one and answer the questions that follow.

How to Play Winning Tennis

As a tennis instructor for the past three summers, I've watched many people waste their money on hi-tech racquets, designer outfits, and professional lessons, and then loudly complain that in spite of all the expense, they still can't play the game. Unfortunately for them, a decent backhand is one thing that money can't buy. No matter what level of player you are, though, or what level you wish to be, there are four steps to accomplishing the goal of winning tennis. They can be summed up in four words: basics, practice, concentration, and attitude.

All sports may be reduced to a few basic skills, which, if learned properly at the outset and drilled until they are instinctive, lead to success. Tennis is no exception; however, few people seem willing to spend the time needed to master the basics. Having been shown the proper grip and swing for a forehand, backhand, and serve, my students seem to feel they can qualify for Wimbledon. The basics are not learned that easily. Many tennis schools are now using a system first developed in Spain that is very successful in establishing the correct stroke in new players: for the first month of lessons, they aren't allowed to use a tennis ball. For that first month, correct positioning, proper swing, footwork, and technique are drilled without any of the distractions of keeping score, winning or losing, or chasing errant balls. That's how important the basics are to winning tennis.

Having acquired the basics, a beginning player must now practise and practise and practise to remember and refine those important skills. It isn't very much fun sometimes to play against a ball machine that never swears or sweats, and doesn't care whether you hit a winning return. Drills and exercises won't do much for your social life while your friends are on the next court playing "pat-a-ball" with a couple of good-looking novices. Those basic strokes that you must keep hitting correctly hundreds of times a day aren't as impressive as the sexy spins and tricky between-the-legs shots the club players are perfecting . . . but if you're going to play winning tennis, practice is vital. Your feet must move instinctively to get you to the ball properly positioned for an effective stroke; a smooth backhand must become automatic from everywhere on the court; a crisp forehand, hit with accuracy, must be as natural as breathing.

When you're finally ready for competition, everything seems calculated to make you forget all you've learned. It requires enormous concentration to shut out the distractions and continue to practise the basics that are essential to your game: watch the ball, keep your head down, turn 90 degrees from the path of the ball, keep your feet moving, and so on and so on. With an opponent opposite you, people watching, and your own self-esteem on the line, it's very difficult to keep your mind from wandering. Tennis is about 50 percent mental. Successful players are able to block out distractions and concentrate on making the racquet meet the ball with precision.

Finally, developing the proper attitude is the true key to winning tennis. I define winning tennis as playing the game to the best of your ability, hitting the ball as well as you know you can, and enjoying the feeling of practised expertise. Winning tennis has nothing to do with beating an opponent. Naturally, if you play winning tennis by learning the basics, practising sufficiently, and concentrating, you'll win many matches, but that is the reward of playing well, not the reason for playing well. People who swear and throw their racquets when they lose are very useful; they are the most satisfying players to trounce. But I don't understand why they play a game that gives them such pain. Tennis players who enjoy the feel of a well-hit ball and the satisfaction of a long, skilfully played rally are winners, regardless of the score.

1. Describe typical readers the author may have been thinking of. Consider their interests and goals.
2. What is the role of the author?

3. What are the main points the author covers in explaining the steps of improving performance in the game? Blueprint the main and supporting points that were employed while constructing this essay.
4. What functions does the introductory paragraph serve in this essay?
5. Discuss the final paragraph as an effective conclusion to the essay.

How They Get Pancake Sauce from Trees
Geoffrey Rowan

Soon the sap will be running—which is not a comment on the base-stealing abilities of any specific Toronto Blue Jay. It's maple sap we're talking about, for maple-syrup season is upon us. For centuries, people have been tapping maple trees, drawing off sap, and boiling it down into sweet, sticky, amber syrup that's a perfect sauce for pancakes, French toast, and waffles. Making maple syrup can be extremely low-tech, requiring little more than a bucket, a pan, a wood fire, and, of course, a maple tree or two. Making lots of maple syrup takes a bit more technical sophistication.

First, something about the trees. Most maple syrup comes from the sugar or rock maple (*acer saccharum*), found only in North America, and the black maple (*acer nigrum*). It takes a maple 20 to 80 years to grow to a tappable diameter of 25 centimetres. The sap, which is mostly water and about 2 to 4 per cent maple sugar, is formed through the process of photosynthesis: the tree draws water from the ground and carbon dioxide from the air, and uses the energy of sunlight, absorbed through its leaves, to manufacture organic compounds, including sugar, from the water and carbon dioxide. In winter, the sap retreats to the tree's roots. When the temperature gets above freezing, the sap start to rise. Maple-syrup producers say the optimum conditions for drawing sap are below-freezing nights and above-freezing days, which create a sort of pump action over the 4- to 6-week-long sap season. Worst is a warm spell, which produces a gush of sap for a few days and then nothing for the rest of the season. It can also give the sap a bad taste. Sap production varies greatly from tree to tree, but producers say they like to get 1 to 2.5 litres of syrup per tap. It takes about 40 litres of sap to make 1 litre of syrup.

Once a tappable tree has been identified, a tap—called a spile—is driven 3.5 centimetres into the tree. A spile is simply a small tube, tapered at one end. Some have a little hook hanging below the lip of the exposed end for hanging a bucket. But big syrup producers don't use buckets anymore. They run plastic tubing from trees to feeder lines to main lines and back to a collection centre, creating a bizarre cat's cradle in the woods. The problems with tube collection are deer, elk, and moose, which can pull tubing down as they wander among the trees, and squirrels, which chew holes in it. (Who knows why squirrels do anything?) Some producers arrange the lines so gravity will pull the sap through the tubes to storage tanks. Others use pumps to create a vacuum that draws the sap along the lines. Vacuum power can suck about 50 per cent more sap out of a tree than gravity.

From a holding tank in the sugar house, the sap flows into an evaporator, which is basically a pan with a corrugated bottom. The ridges on the bottom create more surface area, making it more efficient to apply heat to boil away the water. The most sophisticated evaporators have automatic draw-off systems. Sensors monitor the density and temperature of the syrup and start the draw-off at the proper time. Less sophisticated systems rely on producers paying careful attention to their thermometers and density metres. Some large producers have introduced a step between the storage tank and the evaporator. They pump the sap through a reverse-osmosis unit, which contains a semi-permeable membrane that can remove up to 75 per cent of the sap's water. Once in the evaporator, the sap is kept over the fire until enough water has boiled off to make it 66 per cent sugar. At this point it has become maple syrup and is drained off, filtered through felt, and poured into hot bottles.

Then there are the really unsophisticated systems for small-scale hobbyists, systems that are closer to the time-honoured process involving buckets and pans and hardwood fires than to the high-tech procedures today's producers employ. Maple-syrup kits are available that include spiles and an evaporator that will fit on a gas barbecue. All you need is a couple of productive, healthy maple trees. A word of caution: don't try to boil down your sap on the stove or in the oven unless you want a sticky, sugary coating over everything in the house.

_____

(Geoffrey Rowan, "How They Get Pancake Sauce from Trees," *The Globe and Mail*, March 15, 1994, A11. Adapted with permission.)

1. What is the author's purpose in this article: to tell readers how to make maple syrup, or to tell readers how syrup is made?
2. Where in the article does Rowan clearly identify his subject? Why does he not also outline the major steps in the process?
3. What do you think of the author's grabber? Is it effective?
4. Outline the main points of the process Rowan describes. Are they arranged in logical order or in chronological order? Why did the author choose this arrangement?
5. What purpose does the second paragraph serve? Would the article be equally effective if this paragraph were omitted?
6. Consider the concluding paragraph: how does it bring the article to a satisfying close?

Lasting Impressions

Dating is a very important part of college life. In our quest to be educated people, most of us must undergo some humiliation and embarrassment as part of the maturing process. As a male who has gone through this horrible ritual more times than he cares to remember, I have some observations to offer to those women who are planning to gamble their self-esteem for the chance of winning a partner. I'm twenty-four (next month, the big "two-five"), so my advice can be seen as coming from one who is experienced. To make a lasting impression on that all-important first date, it's important for a woman to be late, self-centred, and unappreciative.

The best way to get the date off to a good start is to keep your new prospect waiting for at least half an hour . . . longer if you can manage it. This cooling-off period will make him appreciate you all the more when you finally do put in an appearance. He will have had time to reflect on how lucky he is to be going out with someone who is so careful about her make-up that it takes 45 minutes to apply. His anticipation will build and build to a fever pitch, so that by the time you present yourself, he will be speechless with eagerness to impress you.

Once your prey has been properly softened up by his long wait, he is ready to hear about your qualities and accomplishments. Now is not the time to keep him in suspense, so get started right away and give lots of detail. Tell him all about the many men who have sought your favour over the past two or three years, the teachers who have given testimony to your brilliance, the firms that have begged you to return to their employ, the girlfriends who have turned their backs on you because they were unable to compete. Your date will be enthralled with your résumé of triumphs. After all, if you don't tell him how lucky he is, how will he know?

By now your new man should be thoroughly infatuated with you, so don't spoil the good impression you've created by showing any appreciation for his efforts on the date. In fact, it is an excellent tactic to complain about as much as possible so that in future he will try to do better. Be sure to mention that his car is old-fashioned (or underpowered, or overpriced, or uncomfortable) and that other men you've dated drove much better vehicles. Criticize the meal if he has taken you to an expensive restaurant, and complain miserably about the band or the movie or the play or his friends, depending on what he has chosen for your entertainment. Your high standards will tell him all he needs to know about your style and expectations.

By following these simple steps you'll have no problem making that all-important first impression. You'll know, when he drops you at your door and takes off in a screech of tires, that he's trying in his own way to impress you, too. Being late, self-centred, and unappreciative are three important building blocks to creating a firm foundation for a relationship that will last minutes. Take it from one who knows.

1. This writer says that his purpose is to reveal how to make a lasting impression on a first date. What do you think his real purpose is in writing this essay?
2. What other main points might the author have used to add to his list of instructions?

3. List as many main points as you can for an essay on the same subject written from the female perspective. In other words, use the same technique to instruct a male on how to make a lasting impression on a first date.
4. Select three good main points from your list in question 3 and blueprint an essay on the subject.
5. Process essays often use irony (saying one thing but meaning something else). Think of as many subjects as you can that would make good ironic process essays. (Example: "How to lose friends")

For each of the exercises below, brainstorm your idea and use a question as your grabber. Devise a strong preview statement, and then draft a clear blueprint for the rest of the essay.

EXERCISE 16.2

A friend from a distant town is staying with you and needs instructions on how to travel from your home to the building where this course is given, to meet you after class. In point form, describe how to get from your home to your classroom. On your next trip into class, test whether your instructions were complete.

EXERCISE 16.3

You have some expertise that is not shared by others; though others may be able to do it, no one does it as well as you. Your skill may be in serving customers, fly-fishing, sleeping, eating spaghetti, or baby-sitting. Choose an activity at which you excel, and write a set of instructions for someone who wishes to become as expert as you are. For now, write your instructions in point form.

EXERCISE 16.4

Use the points you wrote for Exercise 16.3 to develop an essay. Remember to consider your readers, to select and arrange your main points, and to develop the essay in paragraph units. Include an introduction and a conclusion.

EXERCISE 16.5

Write a process essay on one of the following subjects, observing all the guidelines for proper essay development.

How to cure a hangover
How to get fired
How a liar prospers

How to be popular

How to get a bargain

How to win an argument

How to unwind after a long day's work

How to make stir-fry/curry/baklava/Nanaimo bars/any dish you like

How a biological process works (e.g., how skin heals, how the lungs function)

How a TV converter (*or* any other electronic or mechanical device) works

CHAPTER 17

Classification and Division

Classification and **division** are based on the natural human instincts for arranging and analyzing things. We group things that are alike into categories or classes, and we identify the component parts of something in order to understand them better. For example, college students might be classified into undergraduates and graduates. The undergraduate class might be divided into programs or majors such as engineering, nursing, arts and science, and so on. When you look at a menu in a restaurant, you note that the dishes offered are classified into categories such as appetizers, entrées, desserts, and beverages. And when you order your meal, it might be divided into courses: soup, salad, entrée, dessert.

The process of **definition** involves both classification and division: we define a concept (e.g., a good student) by identifying the features or characteristics that are shared by all members of the class to which it belongs: a good student is one who is hard-working, interested, and creative. Writing a classification essay requires grouping similar things together to identify them as belonging to one of several categories; writing a division essay requires examining one entity and breaking it down into constituent parts, or features, or characteristics. Here are some examples of classification and division topics:

CLASSIFICATION		DIVISION	
Saturday AM TV programs	• cartoons • sports shows • interview programs	Saturday AM TV	• informative • infuriating • infantile

156

CLASSIFICATION		DIVISION	
Patients doctors hate to treat	• clingers • deniers • demanders • help-rejecters	The ideal patient	• co-operative • knowledgeable • emotionally supported by family
Types of bad parents	• overprotective • uninterested • disengaged	A good parent	• kind • firm • consistent

Tips on Writing a Classification or Division Essay

1. The key to a good essay is choosing your main points carefully. Make sure that all points are of approximately equal weight and importance, that you have included *everything,* and that the points do not overlap.
2. Set out clearly in the introduction your reasons for choosing your main points. Are any aspects of the subject deliberately left out? If so, you must explain to your readers why you have limited your coverage.
3. Your preview statement should set out your subject and its main points, as in the following examples.

> Inanimate objects can be classified into three major categories—those that don't work, those that break down, and those that get lost.

> The perfect outfit for school is comfortable, easy to get (and keep) clean, and, within limits, distinctive.

> Our softball team is made up of has-beens, might-have-beens, and never-weres.

EXERCISE 17.1

The following three essays illustrate classification and division. In the first essay, the subject is defined by a description of its characteristics. The second and third essays show how subjects (here movie-goers and dates) can be classified into categories. Read the essays and then answer the questions that follow each.

Rock of Ages

There are not many rock bands that can be defined as truly great. The history of rock is full of "one-hit wonders" and cult favourites, but very few groups have achieved both popular success and staying power. To be considered great, a rock band must have broad popular appeal, an exciting stage performance, and the ability to evolve with tastes and times.

Popularity is an important consideration in determining the greatness of a band, but because popular taste is so changeable, it can't be the only criterion. It takes great talent to produce lyrics and music, a style, and a personality that will keep a band in the public's favour for any length of time. Some bands manage to stay in business for years with a small, specialized following; others produce one platinum hit and are wildly popular for a few months before disappearing forever. But neither type of band qualifies for greatness.

Although popularity can be achieved with studio releases, a necessary ingredient in greatness is live performance. Studio bands can produce wonderful effects and a polished sound, but unless they can go on the road and demonstrate their abilities on stage, they will not be able to hold their audience beyond one or two albums. A stage performance need not be hi-tech or fantastically expensive to be successful; in fact, many groups who indulge in an excess of light shows and explosives to impress their fans are covering up for a lack of substance in the music. Great music well played, visually interesting performances, and appealing personalities are the characteristics of a great live performance.

Staying power is, in part, a product of popularity and performance, but versatility and adaptability are also needed if a band is going to have a long enough life span to qualify for greatness. Some bands that qualified under the other two categories fell apart over personality differences, money, drugs, or music style before they could become truly great. Others didn't have the talent to change their style or adapt their themes as musical tastes evolved. Truly great bands possess the musical ability and the collective strength to shape and set style, rather than labour to catch up with what's popular.

Naturally, personal tastes will differ, but no one can deny that popular appeal, spectacular live performance, and versatility and adaptability are the factors that made the Beatles, the Stones, Dire Straits, and others like them the great bands of rock.

1. Describe the audience this writer had in mind when writing the essay. Include age, education, interests, musical knowledge, and any other details you can.

2. What are the essential characteristics of "greatness," according to this writer?

   - _____
   - _____
   - _____

3. What other characteristics could have been used in writing an essay on this subject?

   - _____
   - _____
   - _____

4. Write a one-sentence explanation of the *function* or *purpose* of each of the five paragraphs in "Rock of Ages."

   • _____

   _____

   • _____

   _____

   • _____

   _____

   • _____

   _____

   • _____

   _____

5. "Rock of Ages" is about the factors that make a rock band "great." Think of three other topics that include the word "great," such as "Great Canadian vacation spots" or "Great movies of the 1990s." Provide at least three kinds or parts or characteristics for each topic.

   Topic 1 _____

   a. _____

   b. _____

   c. _____

   Others _____

   _____

   Topic 2 _____

   a. _____

   b. _____

   c. _____

   Others _____

   _____

   Topic 3 _____

   a. _____

   b. _____

   c. _____

Sit Down and Shut Up or Don't Sit by Me
Dennis Dermody

All right, I admit it: I'm a tad neurotic when it comes to making it to the movies on time. I have to be there at least a half hour before the feature begins. Not that I'm worried about long lines at the box office, either. The movies I rush off to see are generally so sparsely attended you can hear crickets in the audience. It's just a thing I do.

Of course, sitting for 30 minutes watching a theater fill up is pretty boring, but through the years I've amused myself with a Margaret Mead–like study of the way people come in and take their seats and their antics during a movie. I felt I should share my impressions lest you find yourself succumbing to these annoying traits.

. . . For some people, choosing a seat takes on moral and philosophi-cal implications. Sometimes they stand in the middle of the aisle jug-gling coats, popcorn, and Cokes, seemingly overwhelmed by the prospect of choice. Should I sit down front, or will that be too close? Is this too far back? That man seems awfully tall, I bet I couldn't see the movie if I sat behind him. I'd love to sit somewhere in the middle but would I be too close to that group of teenagers shooting heroin into their necks? If I sit on this side, will the angle be too weird to watch the movie? Is that seat unoccupied because it's broken? Good Lord, the lights are dimming and I haven't made up my mind and now I won't be able to see where I'm going.

Many, upon choosing their seats, find they are unsatisfied and have to move. I've watched many couples go from one spot to another more than a dozen times before settling down—it's like watching a bird test different spots to build a nest.

As the lights begin to dim and the annoying theater-chain logo streaks across the screen, lo and behold, here come the *latecomers!* Their eyes unaccustomed to the dark, in a panic they search for friends, for assis-tance, for a lonely seat. Just the other day, I watched an elderly woman come into the darkened theater 10 minutes after the movie had begun and say out loud, "I can't see anything!" She then proceeded to inch her way down the aisle, grabbing onto what she thought were seats but were actually people's heads. I saw her sit down right in the lap of some-one who shrieked in shock. After the woman stumbled back into the aisle, chattering wildly, someone mercifully directed her to an empty seat. Then, after a great flourish of getting out of her bulky coat, she asked spiritedly of the grumbling souls around her, "What did I miss?"

I also must address the behavior of people *during* the movie. The *chatterers* comment blithely on everything that is happening on the screen. Like Tourette's Syndrome sufferers unable to control what they blurt out, these people say anything that comes into their heads. "What a cute puppy," they say when they spy an animal ambling off to the side of the frame. "I have that lamp at home," they exclaim. And add, five minutes later, "But mine is red."

The *krinklers* wander down the aisle with a million shopping bags and wait for a key sequence, then begin to forage in their bags for the perfect and most annoying plastic wrap, which they use to make noise with sadistic relish. You try to focus on the screen but the racket starts up again with a wild flourish. I've seen grown men leap to their feet with tears streaming down their face and scream, "Will you stop shaking that motherfucking bag!"

The *unending box of popcorn people* sit directly behind you and start masticating during the opening credits. It's bad enough having the smell of cooked corn wafting around you, but the sound is enough to drive you mad. You tell yourself that eventually they'll finish, but they never do. They keep chewing and chewing and chewing and you're deathly afraid that next they'll start on a four-pound box of malted milk balls.

So in summary: Get to the movie theater early and scout out the territory. It's a jungle in there, filled with a lot of really stupid animals. Know the telltale signs and act accordingly. And then sit down and shut up.

(Dennis Dermody, "Sit Down and Shut Up or Don't Sit by Me," from *Paper*, April 1993, reprinted in *Utne Reader*, July/August 1993, pp. 135–37. Reprinted by permission of the author.)

1. In paragraph 2, the author identifies his subject, but does not name the categories into which he intends to classify it. Into how many categories does he classify the movie-going audience? (Be careful: he specifically labels only four of them.)
2. Movie-goers can be classified any number of ways. Draft at least two preview statements that identify classifications different from the one Dermody has identified.
3. Dermody's language in this piece is colloquial, slangy, even profane. What kind of audience is he addressing? What is his purpose in writing this article?
4. Most readers either love this piece or hate it. How do you react to it? Underline the phrases that most delight/offend you.

Of Men and Machines

There has got to be a better way! The North American system of mate selection by dating is so inefficient that I wonder why it works even as often as it does. If we selected cars using the same methods we employ to choose a mate, few of us would bother driving. Dates, like cars, have a few basic things in common: a body, an image, and (if you're lucky) insurance. Beyond the basics, however, each model is so individual that making a selection becomes a matter of guesswork. Nevertheless, for research purposes, we can classify cars and dates into these general types: the economy model, the standard North American model, and the exotic sports model.

The economy-model date features cramped conditions and a lack of power. The econo-date thinks that his personality can make up for the fact that you never go anywhere except for walks and never do anything that costs money. He tends to be shy, quiet, and about as much fun as an oil leak. It's not just that he doesn't have lots of money to spend, it's that he doesn't use any imagination or creativity to compensate for his lack of cash. The economy model's greatest ambition is someday to move up and compete with the standard North American model.

The standard North American date is big on comfort and appearance, but short on quality. He'll pay big money for an ordinary meal, then tip lavishly for poor service, thinking he's impressing you. He is loud, confident, showy, and sure he is the best thing that could happen to you. Unfortunately, he can't carry on a conversation about anything but himself and, occasionally, sports. While he would never admit it, he secretly wants desperately to grow up to be an exotic sports type.

The exotic, high-powered sports date is rich, sophisticated, gorgeous, and nasty. If you should get a date with one of these creatures, you will be the envy of all your friends. Unfortunately, he has cultivated his vanity like a fine art, and your value to him is purely ornamental. Equality of the sexes is something he either doesn't understand or reserves for his equally wealthy and attractive friends. My mother always reminded me that "beauty is only skin deep;" the exotic sports date is proof that she was right.

If this sounds terribly pessimistic, I guess it is. If only we could select mates as intelligently and carefully as we choose cars! Of course, with my luck, I'd probably end up with something that has the power of an econo-model, the quality of the North American standard, and the repair bills of an exotic.

1. While planning "Of Men and Machines," the author had an audience in mind. Who were they?
2. Into what categories are dates classified in "Of Men and Machines"?

   * _____

   * _____

   * _____

3. "Of Men and Machines" uses the technique of analogy. It makes a statement about types of men by comparing them to types of cars. Is this analogy accurate? Is it effective?
4. The conclusion makes a serious point. What is it? Does it work?

EXERCISE 17.2

This exercise is designed to improve your skill in identifying *unity* within a classification or division. In each of the following preview statements, cross out the one point that doesn't belong.

1. A good teacher doesn't bark at his students, give last-minute assignments, study for a test the night before, or grade unfairly.

2. The last movie I saw in the theatre was a boring mixture of unnecessary violence, annoying commercial interruptions, shallow characterizations, and nauseating sentimentality.
3. Newspapers are her main source of information. Every morning she reads *The Halifax Gazette, Le Devoir, The Calgary Sun,* and *People Weekly.*
4. Toronto is noted for several landmarks: the CN Tower, good civic government, the Royal York Hotel, and the SkyDome.
5. It's not easy to work for a perfectionist. She wants perfect results, double the work in half the time, unpaid overtime, and memos for almost everything.
6. Food is significant for several reasons. It is a biological necessity, a pleasant focus for social activities, a sensual experience for gourmets, and a cause of environmental damage.
7. Baseball pitchers can be divided into four kinds: neurotic celebrities, stoic workhorses, speedy infielders, and anxious newcomers.
8. A media person has four important tasks to perform: to report news accurately, to collect a big salary, to prevent government control of information, and to entertain with social information.
9. There are several civic holidays during the spring and summer: Victoria Day, Canada Day, Labour Day, and Thanksgiving.
10. Tonight's entertainment consists of dinner at Maison Duchamp, a movie at the Bollinger cinemas, a midnight ferry-ride through the islands, and a miserable hangover in the morning.

EXERCISE 17.3

Humans have a strong instinct to classify everything. List at least ten classifications to which you belong.

EXERCISE 17.4

To help explain exactly what things are, we usually divide them up into their constituent parts. For each of the following terms, list several characteristics that would help to define it.

- a good teacher
- a successful résumé
- an ideal girlfriend/boyfriend
- a worthwhile course of study
- a good TV program

EXERCISE 17.5

Select one of the terms you used in Exercise 17.4 and expand your list of characteristics into an essay.

EXERCISE 17.6

Think of an example of a test question on a recent exam that required you to classify or divide in order to explain, or make up a possible test question that would require a classification or division essay in response.

EXERCISE 17.7

Sports analogies are very common ("He can't get to first base," or "Just when she was making the right moves, she dropped the ball"). For each of the following subjects, give an analogy and an example that would help your readers' understanding in a classification or division essay.

SUBJECT	ANALOGY	EXAMPLE
Overwork	electronics	When the brain's circuits are overloaded, a fuse can blow, resulting in nervous breakdown.
Personal health	auto mechanics	_____ _____ _____
Marriage	travel	_____ _____ _____
Fashion	_____	_____ _____ _____

EXERCISE 17.8

Focus each of the following general subjects into a topic suited to a classification or division essay. For each, identify three types or categories; or three parts, characteristics, functions, or features.

Restaurants   Topic _____

- _____
- _____
- _____
- _____

Work   Topic _____

              • _____

              • _____

              • _____

Commercials   Topic _____

              • _____

              • _____

              • _____

Hobbies   Topic _____

              • _____

              • _____

              • _____

Soft drinks   Topic _____

              • _____

              • _____

              • _____

EXERCISE 17.9

Here is a blueprint for an essay on the characteristics necessary for career success. The preview statement and topic points are provided. Fill in appropriate topic sentences and support. When you are satisfied, turn your blueprint into a full essay.

                          Career Success

Grabber   _____

                          _____

                          _____

Preview statement   To be successful in your career, you must pre-
                          pare adequately in college, work hard on the
                          job, and communicate well with employers, col-
                          leagues, and the public.

1. Topic sentence: _____
   (Preparation)   _____

Support: _____

_____

_____

_____

2. Topic sentence:
(Hard work)   _____

_____

Support: _____

_____

_____

_____

3. Topic sentence:
(Communication)   _____

_____

Support: _____

_____

_____

_____

Summary   _____

_____

_____

_____

Clincher   _____

_____

EXERCISE 17.10

Write an essay on *one* of the following subjects.

The main kinds, types, or categories of
- employees
- restaurants
- prime-time TV shows
- bicycles
- sports fans
- pets
- your peers
- Americans

The characteristics of

- an ideal job
- an ideal marriage
- a bad film
- a bad actor
- a good athlete
- a good TV commercial
- a good book
- a good evening's entertainment
- an average Canadian

The component parts of

- a newspaper
- a five-course meal
- a sci-fi movie
- a citizenship review
- a love affair
- a winning hockey team
- a golf swing
- a successful party

CHAPTER 18

Cause and Effect

- What are the causes of unemployment?
- What are the causes of acid rain?
- What are the effects of drug addiction?
- What are the consequences of bad posture?
- What are the results of a well-conceived business plan?

These are the kinds of subjects often discussed in **cause essays** and **effect essays.** On some occasions, cause and effect may be combined in one essay or report, but its length and complexity would put it out of the range of our introductory discussions here. Examples of such subjects might be "A discussion of hypertension" or "Share-splitting: a corporate strategy." For these topics, writers would likely include both the causes of the condition or activity and its probable effects. It is more usual, however, for essays to concentrate either on causes or on effects.

The most common problem found in student cause or effect essays is oversimplification. In the absence of solid facts, figures, or evidence, student writers have a tendency to generalize and to substitute unsupported opinions for reasons. This problem often originates from choosing a topic that is too big for the length of the paper. For example, one student decided to do an effect paper on Canada's immigration policy, a subject so big and so complicated that he could do nothing more than give vague and unsupported opinions. The result made him seem not only bigoted, but also ignorant and foolish. You can avoid this pitfall by choosing your subject carefully, focussing it into a limited topic, and supporting each main point with lots of evidence.

Tips on Writing a Cause or Effect Essay

1. Your preview statement should clearly indicate whether you are tackling cause or effect, and should present your main points in order. Consider these examples.

   > The chief causes of dissatisfaction among the workers in the office where I spent my placement are low wages, sexual harassment, and boredom.

   > The beneficial effects of my annual canoe trip include reduced stress and increased fitness.

2. Fully support your statements. You must provide proof of what you say, in the form of examples, facts, statistics, quotations, anecdotes, etc. (See pp. 77–82.)

EXERCISE 18.1

The following three essays demonstrate writing that discusses causes and/or effects. In the first essay, the writer employs facts to support statements of cause; in the second, effects are illustrated with examples; in the third, the writer uses facts, examples, statistics, and summaries as support in an effect essay. Read each essay and answer the questions that follow it.

"We Have Met the Enemy, and They Is . . . Us"

Our planet is being destroyed. If the cause of its destruction were some external force, such as aliens or a rogue comet, then we humans would band together and fight the threat with every resource at our disposal. We wouldn't count the cost in lives, effort, or money; we would throw every ounce of our strength and will into the effort. However, while the threat is just as real as if it came from space ships bombarding us with poison rays, we aren't doing much to save ourselves from destruction, because the evildoers are much closer to home. We see them daily in our mirrors. Motivated by greed and ignorance, we are wrecking our own environment with ruthless efficiency.

Greed—industrial, commercial, and personal—has motivated us to rape the earth's resources without giving thought to the consequences. A supplement appeared recently in a Canada-wide chain of newspapers. Printed on recycled paper, it outlined some of the environmental changes brought about by human greed. Since the industrial revolution, two-thirds of the world's rain forest has been cut or burned. The rain forest is (was?) the largest single source of the earth's oxygen supply. Around the world, we pave over, build on, or otherwise destroy one hectare of agricultural land every 14 seconds. In Canada, we fill our

rivers with chemicals and sewage, kill our lakes and forests with industrial pollutants, poison the soil and the water table with toxic waste, all
in the name of industrial growth and the jobs it creates. And we're one
of the luckier nations. We are relatively rich in natural resources and, in
the short term, can survive our attacks on the environment.

Often linked with greed, ignorance is the other prime motivator in
our self-destruction. Ignorant and uncaring, we cling to our "freedom
machines." Automobiles are the primary source of air pollution, and
there are more than twice as many cars on Canadian roads today as
there were twenty years ago. Canadians throw away some 275 000
tonnes of disposable (and nonbiodegradable) diapers every year. We
munch our fast food in its environmentally harmful containers; demand
that our paper products be bleached pure white despite the horrific
pollution of our rivers that is caused by the bleaching process; recycle
glass and plastics and papers reluctantly, if at all; and cheerfully
accept—even demand—the plastic packaging, plastic bags, and plastic
products our supermarkets peddle.

Is there any reason for optimism? There is some evidence that Canadians are becoming more conscious of the environment, and consciousness can only lead to changes for the better. In 1989, one-third of
Canadians felt that the environment was the most important national
issue. Only a year before that it was one in ten, and the year before that
it was one in twenty. A majority of Canadians now favour tougher action
against polluters, even if it means higher taxes, higher prices, and fewer
jobs. However, this bit-by-bit heightening of concern is far from the
concerted, all-out effort to save the planet that would result if we were
threatened by an external force. How very much more difficult it is to
mobilize resources and will when the enemy lies within!

1. What is the main problem identified in "'We Have Met the Enemy . . . ,'"
   and what are its two causes?

   The causes of _____ are

   _____ and

   _____ .

2. Look at the concluding paragraph of the essay. How does it affect you as
   a reader? What is its purpose?
3. Describe the role that the author has assumed in developing this essay.
   Be as precise as you can.

Lightweight Lit.

I really enjoy literary discussions. I love it when people at trendy restaurants smack their lips in appreciation of the latest South American
novelist, Egyptian poet, or Armenian essayist. By eavesdropping on
these discussions, I can find out what's going on in the world of "great

literature" so that when people ask me what I've read lately I can pretend that I, too, am devoted to highbrow literature. I'm ashamed to admit my secret vice . . . but, since we're friends, I can tell you . . . I *love* "trash." I'm embarrassed about it, and I know that my intellectual friends would ridicule me if they found out. Still, I have very good reasons for enjoying "light" literature so much. I find it educates, relaxes, and entertains in a way that more cerebral reading doesn't—at least, not for me.

The educational nature of popular or "junk" literature is often overlooked. From reading countless police novels, I know the workings of the Los Angeles and New York police departments inside out. I have a thorough grounding in the operations of the CIA, the KGB, MI6, and any number of less illustrious spy agencies. I'm eagerly awaiting the first novel about a hero from Canada's CSIS. Science-fiction books have detailed for me the ways of life, war, travel, and even agriculture in outer space. My education even includes the laws of nature in alternative universes: I know about the society of Gor, the politics of Fionavar, and the nature of good and evil in a hundred other worlds.

Acquiring all this knowledge may sound tiring, but light novels are actually extremely relaxing. The way I read this kind of literature is slouched in my favourite chair with my feet up and a comforting drink close at hand, and, since I can't do anything else while I read, the overall effect is complete physical relaxation. Also, an absorbing novel will take me away from the concerns and stresses of everyday life, allowing me to escape to a world created by the writer. Since I can have no effect on this world, I can, with a completely clear conscience, let things unfold as they may and assume the relaxing role of observer.

While education and relaxation are important, most of us read light novels to be entertained. "Entertainment" means different things to different people. Some enjoy being frightened half to death by the books of Stephen King or his colleagues; others get satisfaction from the sugary romance of Harlequin novels; many people find science fiction absorbing and devour the works of Isaac Asimov or Jerry Pournelle. Whatever subject or style grabs you, there are literally thousands of novels to suit your taste. I'm lucky because—with the exception of popular romance—I can find enjoyment in almost any type of reasonably well-written light novel.

None of the novelists I read will ever win the Nobel prize for literature, and few of them will be studied in university literature courses. However, many writers have become wealthy from selling their fantasies to those millions of readers like me who seek entertainment, relaxation, and education from the novels they enjoy—even if they have to enjoy them in secret.

1. What is the main topic identified in "Lightweight Lit.," and what are its three effects?

The effects of _____ are

_____ , _____ ,

and _____ .

2. What view is the author promoting to the audience? What role does the author perform in this essay?
3. Who are the readers? What do they expect from the essay? Will they be convinced of the causes for the author's literary preferences?
4. What purpose is served by the author's supposed embarrassment? How does this device affect you as a reader?
5. The author uses specific examples to demonstrate each point under the headings "Education," "Relaxation," and "Entertainment." List the examples used to illustrate each point.

Overstuffing Africa

All too often in Africa, outsiders give charity with one hand and deliver a slap with the other. Farmers are usually the victims. Many African farmers who are helped by Western aid agencies to improve their crops find that they cannot sell what they grow because local markets are swamped by cheap Western imports—or by food aid. Two reports . . . describe the destructive impact of such policies, one on farmers in Somalia, the other in West Africa.

Most aid specialists agree that, once the worst of a famine is over, the distribution of free food should be kept to a minimum to avoid flooding local markets. In Somalia . . . this wisdom seems to have been forgotten. The price of cereals in Somali markets [according to African Rights, a British human-rights group] had fallen back to their seasonal levels even before American soldiers arrived [in December 1993]. Somali aid workers gave warning that, if imported food aid continued to flow in, local farmers would have difficulty selling their own produce.

The warnings were ignored. By March [1994] the price of sorghum, wheat and maize in local markets had been depressed so far that farmers were complaining. One farmer told the authors that it cost him 194,000 Somali shillings ($74) to grow 100 kilos (220 lbs) of maize, which he could sell for a mere 55,000 shillings at the local market. He said he would not start planting again unless prices rose. Pushing down the high price of food during a famine is desirable. But if prices continue to drop because food aid continues to be pumped in, the fragile livelihoods of farmers can be harmed.

One logical solution . . . would be to stop shipping in Western grain and to start buying Somali farmers' crops instead. Yet this would bump up against the Western world's self-serving policy of subsidised farming, which explains a lot of its enthusiasm for shipping grain to Africa.

[A report] from Christian Aid, another British charity, shows how the West's policies of subsidised farming can inflict damage on African farmers in good times as well as lean. Cattle farmers in the poor countries of the Sahel walk for days to bring their animals to market. Until the mid-1980s, merchants bought their cattle and drove them south, where the climate is less favourable to cattle rearing. Nowadays, however, the merchants are gone. This is because the European Community dumps low-quality beef, at great cost to the European taxpayer, on West African markets, where it sells at half the price of locally produced beef.

Naturally, Africans cannot compete. In 1975 . . . cattle from the Sahel accounted for two-thirds of the beef eaten in Cote d'Ivoire. Now it accounts for less than a quarter. In 1991 alone, the EC dumped 54m tonnes of frozen and chilled beef in West Africa, much of it from France and Holland. This impoverishes the 4m Sahelians, most of whom have no alternative to cattle farming. It can also damage the health of towns-people in the south, few of whom understand the risks associated with defrosting frozen food. The stuff dumped in Africa is of particularly poor quality: the EC offers extra subsidies for exports of the sort of fatty beef European shoppers increasingly turn their noses up at.

Some African countries have tried to fight back. In 1991 Cote d'Ivoire slapped an import tax on frozen beef. But European exporters simply thawed their beef before unloading. Others shipped it to Ghana and smuggled it over the border. West Africa, which includes the poor Sahe-lian countries, is a vulnerable target: the EC offers no special subsidies for beef exports to America, Japan, Latin America, or other bits of Africa.

The absurdity of beef dumping is all the greater because the EC claims to be trying to support African cattle farmers. At the same time as ship-ping packs of frozen fatty beef carcasses to West Africa, it spends aid money on improving cattle breeds in Mali and Senegal, on refrigerating abbatoirs in Burkina Faso and on fattening cattle in Cote d'Ivoire.

1. The writer of this essay has a firm point of view. What role does he use to support it?
2. Who is the audience for this piece? Will the readers see the *causes* that have encouraged the writer to take this stand? Will they be convinced by the information that backs it up?
3. While organized along cause–effect lines, this essay is intended to be primarily persuasive. List the effects that are intended to persuade read-ers that the West's food-aid policies in Africa are misguided.
4. The last paragraph reinforces the subject of this essay, but it does not pack much of an emotional punch. Can you write a concluding sen-tence that would have an emotional impact on readers?

EXERCISE 18.2

Develop each of the following preview statements by adding three good main points.

1. The main causes of divorce in adolescent marriages are _____

_____ ,

_____ , and

_____ .

2. The effects of secondary smoke inhalation by nonsmokers are serious; they include _____

_____,

_____, and

_____.

3. Obesity, a common problem in North America, is the result of three major causes: _____

_____,

_____, and

_____.

4. The positive effects of professional day care upon preschool children are _____

_____,

_____, and

_____.

5. There are several causes for unemployment in Canada: _____

_____,

_____, and

_____.

6. The major causes of air pollution are _____

_____,

_____, and

_____.

7. The fitness craze was prompted by these causes: _____

_____,

_____, and

_____.

8. Violence in professional hockey has several negative effects upon young hockey players: _____

_____,

_____, and

_____.

9. There are several causes for the increase in numbers of full-time workers returning to college for part-time study: _____

_____ ,

_____ , and

_____ .

10. Three effects of superior Japanese technology in the North American marketplace are

_____ ,

_____ , and

_____ .

EXERCISE 18.3

Begin with the question "What are the causes of _____ ?" and fill in five topics that you know enough about to list at least three causes.

EXERCISE 18.4

Repeat Exercise 18.3, using the question "What are the effects of _____ ?"

EXERCISE 18.5

Choose one of the topics that you have developed in either Exercise 18.3 or Exercise 18.4 and work that topic into a full essay, taking care to select a subject about which you know enough to support your ideas.

EXERCISE 18.6

Write a cause essay or an effect essay on one of the following subjects. If you don't know enough to fully support your ideas, be prepared to do some research.

Causes
Adjusting to college was not as easy as I'd thought it would be.
Many people look forward to early retirement.
Adolescence can be painful.
My first job was a good (or bad) experience.
Generation X (people between 18 and 24) is a "lost generation."
Vandalism is a symptom of adolescent frustration.
Many criminal offenders are given probation rather than a jail sentence.

Eating disorders are a growing problem among young women.
Homelessness is widespread in large cities.
Runaways prefer the street to a dysfunctional home life.

Effects
Unemployment can be devastating.
Technology is making us lazy.
A bad boss has a big influence on his or her employees.
Credit cards can be dangerous.
Music can reduce tension.
Being an only child is a difficult way to grow up.
Poor driving skills are a hazard to everyone.
Caffeine is a harmful substance.
Injuries resulting from overtraining are common among athletes.
Worrying can age you prematurely.
Losing your job can be a positive, liberating experience.

CHAPTER 19

Comparison and Contrast

The difference between comparison and contrast is quite simple: if the similarities between two things (or ideas or concepts or points of view) are being emphasized, it's a **comparison essay;** if the differences are being emphasized, it's a **contrast essay.** Many people use the term "comparison" to cover both, and similarities *and* differences are often discussed together in an essay.

You can choose from two approaches when you are organizing a comparison essay. In the first option, you discuss one item fully, and then turn to the other item. This approach is sometimes called the **chunk** or **block method** of organizing. The alternative option is to compare your two items point by point. This approach is sometimes called the **slice** or **point-by-point method.** For example, suppose you decided to compare Jean-Claude Van Damme and Arnold Schwarzenegger. You might identify the following three points:

- physical appearance
- acting technique
- on-camera heroics

Using the chunk method, you would first consider Van Damme in terms of these three points; then you would do the same for Schwarzenegger. You would need to blueprint only four paragraphs for your essay:

1. Introduction
2. Van Damme's physical appearance, acting technique, and on-camera heroics

3. Schwarzenegger's physical appearance, acting technique, and on-camera heroics
4. Conclusion

The chunk method works best in short papers, where the points of comparison are easy to understand and remember. As comparisons get more complex, your readers will be able to see your points better if you present them side by side, using the slice method. You would then need to blueprint five paragraphs for your essay:

1. Introduction
2. Physical appearance of Van Damme and Schwarzenegger
3. Acting technique of Van Damme and Schwarzenegger
4. On-camera heroics of Van Damme and Schwarzenegger
5. Conclusion

The introductory paragraph in the comparison or contrast essay usually tells readers what two things are to be assessed and what criteria will be used to assess them. The concluding paragraph may (or may not) reveal a preference for one over the other.

Tips on Writing a Comparison or Contrast Essay

1. Make sure that the two items you have chosen are appropriately paired; to make a satisfactory comparison or contrast, they must have something in common. Both might be baseball teams or both world leaders; but to compare the Montreal Expos and the Calgary Stampeders or to contrast Queen Elizabeth and your Aunt Agatha would be futile and meaningless.
2. Your main points must apply equally to both items in your comparison. Reject main points that apply to one and have only limited application to the other. For example, in a comparison of typewriters and word processors, a category for screen colour would be pointless.
3. Your preview statement should clearly present the two items to be compared or contrasted and the basis for their comparison. This is a tricky job and deserves some time. Consider these examples.

The major points of comparison in automobiles are performance, comfort, and economy, so I applied these factors to the two cars in the running for my dollars: the Corvette and the Porsche.

In comparing the top-of-the-line running shoes from Nike and Brooks, I looked at fit, cushioning, stability, and price.

EXERCISE 19.1

The following three essays demonstrate different approaches to writing comparisons or contrasts. After reading each essay, answer the questions that follow it.

The Canadian Climate

The student who comes to Canada from a tropical country is usually prepared for the cold of the Canadian winter, a sharp contrast to the hot northern summer. What the student may not be prepared for is the fact that Canadian personalities reflect the country's temperature range but are not quite so extreme. Canadian personalities fall into two categories: warm and cool. The two groups share the Canadian traits of restraint and willingness to compromise, but they are dissimilar in their attitudes both to their own country and to the foreign student's country of origin.

Warm Canadians are first of all warm about Canada, and will, at the first sound of a foreign accent, describe with rapture the magnificence of the country from the Maritimes to the West Coast, with loving descriptions of the Prairies, the Rockies, and even the "unique climate of the far North." Canadian leisure activities are enthusiastically explained, with a special place reserved for hockey. "You must come out with us. So you've never skated? You'll learn. You'll have a great time." The Warm Canadian wants the newcomer to participate fully in the pleasures of life in Canada. When he turns his attention to the foreign student's homeland, he seeks enlightenment, asking questions about its geography, social and economic conditions, and other concerns not usually addressed in travel and tourism brochures. The Warm Canadian understands that the residents of these countries are not some tribe of wonderfully exotic flower children who sing and dance and have natural rhythm, but are individuals who, like people in Canada, face the problems of earning a living and raising a family.

Compared to the Warm Canadian, who exudes a springlike optimism, the Cool Canadian is like November. Conditions may not be unbearable for the moment, but they are bound to get much colder before there is any sign of a thaw. The Cool Canadian's first words on hearing that the foreign student is from a warm country are, "How could you leave such a lovely climate to come to a place like this?" Not from him will one hear of Banff, or Niagara Falls, or anything except how cold and dark and dreary it gets in the winter. It sometimes seems that the Cool Canadian's description of his own country is designed to encourage foreign students to pack their bags and return home at once. As for the foreign student's country of origin, the Cool Canadian is not really interested, although he may declare, "I hear it's beautiful. I'd love to go there." Beyond that, however, he has no desire to receive information that may shake the foundations of his collection of myths, half-truths, and geographic inaccuracies. This type of Canadian, if he does travel to a tropical country, will ensure that he remains at all times within the safe confines of his hotel and that he returns to Canada with all his preconceived ideas intact.

The foreign student should not be upset by Cool Canadians; he should ignore their chilliness. Besides, like a heat wave in March, an unexpected thaw can occur and create extraordinary warmth. Likewise, a Warm Canadian may become a little frosty sometimes, but, like a cold spell in June, this condition won't last. When the weather changes, the foreign student is given a wonderful opportunity to display his own qualities of understanding, tolerance, and a fine "Canadian" acceptance of others as they are.

1. What are the main points of contrast in "The Canadian Climate"?

    _____

    _____

    _____

2. Which method of contrast has the author of "The Canadian Climate" chosen for his subject, chunk or slice? Is it the better method?
3. Why did the author choose this approach? Would the essay work as well if it were organized the other way? Blueprint the main points of contrast as they would look in the other style.
4. What other points of contrast between the two kinds of Canadians can you think of?

    _____

    _____

    _____

5. What audience does this foreign student have in mind? What effect do you think the essay is likely to have on the readers?

Car Wars

Recently I was assigned an unusual project in my economics class: assuming money was no problem, decide which car to buy. Professor Wright has taught us to be careful consumers, so I spent many hours of research before I made my decision. The major points of comparison in automobiles, I discovered, are performance, comfort, and economy, so I applied these factors to the two cars in the running for my imaginary dollars: the Chevrolet Corvette and the Porsche 944 Turbo.

Performance of the two cars was very close, especially when you consider the tiny differences at the speeds involved. However, I was able to get the 'Vette from 0 to 100 kph in exactly six seconds, while the

Porsche took more than half a second longer. In cornering, the Porsche was marginally superior, but the Corvette was the clear winner in braking. From 100 kph it came to a complete stop in 68 metres; the Porsche went almost 2 metres farther before stopping.

Comfort was my next concern, and here I gave a slight edge to the 944. Both have luxurious seats that provide support and comfort no matter what kind of twists and turns the car performs. The dash and instrumentation are a matter of personal preference, and I like the no-nonsense clarity of the European gauges better than the somewhat cluttered and flashy appearance of the Corvette interior. Fit and finish are superior in the Porsche, and the sound systems are pretty close, though I gave the nod to the 'Vette in this category after playing k.d. lang's "Absolute Torch and Twang" album at full volume on the built-in CD player in both cars.

Finally, keeping my economics class in mind, I examined the financial implications of each purchase. The list price is in the Corvette's favour by about $3000, and it gets almost one kilometre more for every litre than the German car. A quick check of typical repair bills and the cost of replacement parts sealed this category firmly in the Corvette's corner.

If I were to put all the factors on a balance sheet and make my decision based on the totals at the bottom of the page, I would purchase a Corvette without hesitation. However, there are many intangible factors that weigh heavily in a decision about cars. Prof. Wright would never understand (he drives a seven-year-old Hyundai), but if my bank balance permitted, I'd order the Porsche. The sales rep would understand.

1. Which method of organization has this writer used for his comparison? Is it the most appropriate one in this case?
2. Blueprint the essay as it would appear in the other method.
3. What other points might the writer have chosen in comparing two sports cars?
4. What audience does this writer have in mind for his essay? What is his purpose in writing?
5. What purposes does the last paragraph serve? What was your reaction to the writer's conclusion?

Memories of Guilt-Free Eating
Joan Frank

The end of my youth has served formal notice. It's the mother of all turning points. Big-time loss. Big-time transition. I mourn. Forget high culture. Forget nouvelle, forget five-star. I mean simple, regular eating. What is purer, more primal, more sensuous, more unilaterally endorsed? We eat, therefore we live.

So it is tragic to arrive at the moment of adulthood when I need only look in the direction of delicious food for it to leap into my mouth and lodge in great lumps at strategic places under my skin. There it bulges buoyantly, while I claw through the closet, breathing hard, for the Liz Claiborne tent dress that looks like a choirboy's cassock. I work out like an Olympian, and what faces me in the mirror is a very tired Amazon. It's no secret, but when it happens to you, it's news. After a certain point, you wear what you eat.

Once this wasn't so. Once, the chemistry of eating was hot and clean. Bodies metabolized whatever we put in, fast. We could pack it away—and it was wholesome, charming, a signal of health and vigor; the world smiled warmly on us while we ate with abandon. I looked and felt terrific. . . .

Return with me now to the early years . . . . [B]urgers, malts, and candy were definitive food groups. Our eyes shone; our skin was smooth and clear. College meant bowls of granola, huge fudge sundaes; gigantic greaseburgers, ghastly quantities of liquor and drugs. We put it in our mouths first, and asked what it was later. Next morning we sprang forth shiny as new pennies. Burrito for breakfast? Hey, thanks, man. On to cocktail-waitressing days, when I swam all afternoon, rode my 10-speed bike across town to the bar, slung the suds till 3 AM, toasted my colleagues good night with a Black Russian, and pedaled home under the early morning stars, stopping for a bag of doughnuts and a quart of milk at the 7-Eleven. I was *en forme*.

Today, to fit that *forme* into its clothes and sprint it upstairs without sobbing for breath, I may enjoy one modest meal per day. The rest of the time I must sublimate, sloshing down herb teas and chomping sugarless gum. When I slip, and start building mountains on my salad bar tray that make checkout clerks' eyebrows waggle, I know it is time to chant my mantra: resist, sublimate, and, failing all else, build in antidotes. These code words address each phase of the compulsion. If one is plucky, one makes it through with maybe a few extra pieces of fruit in one's belly instead of a quart of Häagen-Dazs.

I assure you of this: when you see one of those exquisitely thin sylphs onscreen or in magazines, draped artfully against the ship's railing or the silk sheets, a delicate glass of something pale in her slender little hand, don't kid yourself. That babe longs to grind an entire pizza, and wash it back with a few malt liquors or a tall chocolate shake. How she sublimates may not be pretty. Let us also grant right now that this is the nonproblem of a decadent and corrupt patriarchal, imperialist culture. Shame on us.

That said, one turns heavily back to the task, a sad Sisyphus slogging uphill, never done with it. Pushing the boulder of Moderation, steeling herself against beckoning sights and smells—and oxymoron television images like the nymphette in denim short shorts taking a faked hearty bite of the big fat burrito.

There: I said the F-word. For the last time, too—I swear it.

(Joan Frank, "Memories of Guilt-Free Eating," first published in *The San Francisco Chronicle* magazine *This World*, September 6, 1992. Adapted by permission of the author.)

1. Identify the two main points of contrast in this piece. How are they organized?
2. What do you think the writer's purpose is in presenting this contrast?
3. Much of the impact of this piece depends on the writer's use of language. Underline ten phrases you find particularly effective.
4. What is the tone of this piece? How does it affect the writer's relationship with her readers?
5. If you were to write an essay on the differences between youth and middle age, what points would you choose as the basis for your contrast?

EXERCISE 19.2

Briefly list (in point form) the characteristics of two people you know. Examine your lists and choose characteristics of each person that would make a basis for a comparison between the two. Then go back over the lists and choose characteristics that would make a basis for contrast.

EXERCISE 19.3

Contrast essays often turn persuasive, but they don't have to. When you are presenting a contrast, try not to be influenced by your own opinion. List the arguments on both sides of three of these controversial issues.

gun control
the use of animals in medical research
nuclear power
physician-assisted suicide
legalizing prostitution

EXERCISE 19.4

For one of the topics you worked on in Exercise 19.3, write an essay contrasting the views held by the two sides. Some research may be necessary, to find out exactly what the opposing arguments are and to explain those arguments to your reader.

EXERCISE 19.5

Write a comparison or contrast essay on one of the following subjects. Be sure to follow the guidelines for proper essay development, from selecting a subject, through managing your main points, to blueprinting your paper and writing your paragraphs.

Cycling and driving
Two beverages (two beers, two soft drinks, two wines, etc.)

Gardening and marriage
Two actors
Two concerts
Jogging and weight training (*or* rowing, *or* walking, etc.)
Two vacation destinations
Two bosses
Two business environments
Two careers

EXERCISE 19.6

Construct a comparison essay or a contrast essay, using one of the suggestions given below. Develop a preview statement that reflects the relationship of the two subjects. Before you begin writing, blueprint your thoughts, using either the chunk method or the slice method.

Two provinces in Canada
Your spouse with the fantasy you had of a spouse before you were married
Two objects that have sentimental value for you
Two newspapers' coverage of a news event
Your life now with your life five (or ten or twenty) years ago
Full-time and part-time education
Living in an apartment and living in a house
A nurse's duties and a doctor's duties
Views of fidelity held by women and held by men
Two ways in which one of these pairs of products is advertised on television: beer and laundry soap; deodorants and diapers; candy bars and muffler repairs.

CHAPTER 20

Persuasion

In a **persuasion essay**, you go beyond simply trying to get your readers to understand and respect your ideas. You attempt to bring your readers over to your point of view or to motivate them to take an action of some kind. For either task, thorough knowledge of your audience is necessary before you begin.

If you are trying to get your readers to agree with you, you must know (or be able to make an educated guess about) what opinions they already hold, or to what degree they disagree with your views. If, for example, you want to convince your readers that urban living is more interesting than rural life, your approach will differ greatly, depending on the background, present location, and probable views of your readers. Do they love the city, hate it, or have no opinion?

If your readers are likely to disagree with your view or are known to oppose it, it is best to build your case with examples, illustrations, definitions, and the like *before* strongly stating your own opinion. Readers who are confronted early by a statement they disagree with are often less open to persuasion; instead, they are inclined to read the rest of the essay thinking of rebuttals and trying to pick holes in the arguments.

To win your readers' agreement with your point of view, you will need both an understanding of your readers and an ability to adapt your approach to them so that your essay will have the greatest possible impact. Persuading your readers to take action—to donate to a charity, lose weight, vote for the Green Party, or drink Canadian wines, for example—enlists the same knowledge and ability but may require a subtler technique. Readers who may be resistant to your views must be approached gently and convinced with facts before receiving your "pitch."

The following subjects lend themselves to development of a persuasion essay. Imagine a specific group of readers for each subject. Then decide whether you would use the direct approach (D) in your essay, because your readers are neutral or sympathetic to the argument, or the indirect approach (I), because your readers are going to be difficult to persuade.

SUBJECT	APPROACH (D or I)
Our public school system needs drastic reform.	_____
Buy a North American– built car.	_____
AIDS education should begin in primary school.	_____
Winter in Canada is the best time of year.	_____
The government should not restrict the distribution of pornography.	_____

You can use several techniques, in varied combinations, to persuade your readers. First, you may choose to use "facts and figures" to support your argument. Many readers are suspicious of statistics (usually, amounts expressed as percentages) because it's well known that they can be used to prove almost anything. If your statistics are accurate and presented fairly, however, they can be helpful in convincing your readers. When you read this chapter's sample essays, notice that the authors do not use numbers or statistics. They persuade with expression of ideas and presentation of facts. What numbers or statistics might each have included to help persuade readers? Would their inclusion have improved or cluttered the essays?

Second, you might use logic as a method of persuading, but be careful. Logical reasoning can be convincing if it is correctly presented, but it is also subject to all kinds of abuse and errors. The most common mistake is overgeneralization. "A is true; B is true; therefore C is true." Consider these examples:

All dogs have tails; Digger is a dog; therefore Digger must have a tail.

Everyone knows that hockey players are violent; Vince is a hockey player; therefore Vince must be the one who started the fight.

Which item in each set is overgeneralized?

Third, you can try to persuade your readers by citing an authority who supports your opinion. The trouble with this approach is that it's very likely that another authority, or a host of authorities, can be found to support the other side. It's also possible that the reputation and ability of your authority can be challenged, thereby weakening your "proof."

"I know it's true because I read it in *The Globe and Mail*," you say.

"But," say your opponents, "*The Globe and Mail* is a conservative newspaper and therefore an unreliable source on this issue."

"Is not," you cleverly reply.

"Is too," say your antagonists.

Your argument has been sidetracked. Instead of focussing on the issue and the validity of your case, your readers dispute the credibility of your "authority" and dismiss your argument. Choose your authorities carefully and provide ample proof that what they say can be believed.

The keys to good persuasion are to think carefully about what you are saying and to present honestly your reasons for believing it—*after* you have carefully analyzed your readers' level of knowledge, possible biases or prejudices, and degree of commitment to one side over the other. To persuade successfully, you need to be not only well organized and informative but also *tactful*, especially if your readers are likely to hold an opposing opinion.

Tips on Writing a Persuasion Essay

1. Thinking about your intended reader helps you to decide on a direct or an indirect approach for your persuasion.
2. In structuring your essay, remember that persuasion can come in several forms. Comparison/contrast or cause/effect essays can also be persuasive. Choose the organizational structure that will be most effective in persuading your readers.
3. Remember that there is another side to the argument. You can help your own cause by presenting the opposing viewpoint and refuting it.
4. For the direct approach, your preview statement should clearly present your opinion and the main points that support it.

   Example: The United States should switch immediately to full metric measurement because it is a more logical system, and it is now the world standard.

   For the indirect approach, your preview statement should still state the main points you will be discussing. However, you should keep your opinion to yourself at the outset. In the course of your essay, you should win your reader over to your side.

   Example: In choosing which candidates to vote for, we must consider their records, their platforms, and their characters.

EXERCISE 20.1

The following three essays illustrate three different persuasive approaches. Read the essays and answer the questions that follow each.

Let's Get Physical

As institutions where "education" is supposed to take place, colleges and universities are shirking their responsibility. By concentrating almost exclusively on intellectual development, they are only half educating their students. Physical development is important, too: it helps to make students healthier, happier, and even smarter. Physical education should be a significant part of every postsecondary-school curriculum.

Let's acknowledge the obvious: training in physical fitness will produce healthier individuals. Cardiovascular development increases stamina for any task or activity and makes the recovery rate after exertion much shorter. It leads directly to a longer, more productive life and reduces time lost in sickness. In addition, a sound physical education includes attention to diet and promotes the elimination of harmful habits such as excessive caffeine, sugar, and nicotine intake, thereby significantly increasing the life span and productivity of the individual.

A healthier individual is a happier individual. With improved fitness comes an increased sense of well-being and enhanced self-esteem. Recreational and social activities multiply, and a more rounded and satisfying lifestyle commonly results from higher levels of fitness. Many people who participate in a college or university physical education program develop a lasting enthusiasm for specific games or fitness activities, such as swimming or jogging, that enhance their social, professional, and personal lives.

Healthier, happier, and—yes—smarter people are produced by good physical education. The brain, like the heart, the lungs, and the liver, is a physical organ that functions better when the entire organism is healthy. Oxygenated blood supplies the brain and removes wastes. A strong heart, healthy lungs, and unclogged veins and arteries have a direct impact on the brain's performance. Caffeine, nicotine, and other harmful substances impair the brain's ability to function, so their removal or reduction can enhance the organ's capability. A sense of confidence and well-being also helps to minimize the stresses and pressures that can have a negative effect on our ability to receive, process, and retain information.

We sometimes hear the argument (especially when budgets are tight) that educational institutions should concentrate on the development of the mind and leave development of the body up to the individual student. The division of the organism into separate compartments is not only poor zoology, it is harmful to the very process it attempts to promote: increased intellectual ability. For postsecondary institutions to ignore physical development in favour of intellectual development is to impair the health, happiness, and even the intelligence of the students whose interests they claim to serve.

1. Describe the readers whom the author of this essay has in mind. What are their attitudes, their goals, their levels of vocabulary?
2. Identify the essay's subject and main points. Draft a blueprint that the author might have used to construct the essay.
3. Did you find this essay persuasive? If not, why?
4. The author takes a very direct approach to persuasion. How might this essay have been structured if the author had wanted to be more subtle and to present the arguments before revealing a particular point of view? Draft a blueprint for such an essay.
5. The topic sentences in this essay refer to previous topic sentences each time they appear. What are the advantages of this technique?

Making the Punishment Fit the Crime
Julian V. Roberts

Sentencing statistics released by Statistics Canada [in 1993] offer an all-too-rare glimpse into sentencing practices across the country. There [is], for a start, considerable evidence of variations in sentencing. The incarceration rate for impaired driving—the percentage of those who went to jail—ranged from 6 per cent in Nova Scotia to 97 per cent in Prince Edward Island. For breaking and entering, rates of imprisonment ranged from 55 per cent in Quebec to 85 per cent in PEI. Half the offenders convicted of sexual assault in Ontario were imprisoned, compared with more than 80 per cent convicted of this crime in Yukon or PEI.

The second important finding was that crimes against property frequently result in higher incarceration rates than crimes of violence. Many property crimes, such as theft over $1,000, resulted in harsher penalties than assault causing bodily harm or assaulting a police officer. Fifty-five per cent of convictions for possession of stolen goods resulted in a prison term, the average length being more than five months. But only 21 per cent of convictions for assault resulted in a prison term, the average length being less than two months.

What do such findings mean? They underline the need to reform sentencing in this country. We have been talking about this for years, with little or no progress. In 1987, a parliamentary committee also recommended substantial changes. In 1992, the federal government introduced a draft reform bill that was awaiting parliamentary review when [the 1993 federal] election was called.

At least three steps should be taken to reform the system. First, Parliament should place a statement in the Criminal Code specifying the purpose of sentencing. At present there is no such statement. Judges are free to follow any of a number of sentencing purposes, including deterrence, punishment, rehabilitation and incapacitation. If there are many purposes, and little guidance as to which one is relevant in a particular case, is it any wonder that sentences vary according to the views of the judge?

Second, judges need more guidance about the kind of sentence to impose in specific cases. One solution is to have sentencing guidelines. . . . In some foreign jurisdictions, including many U.S. states, there is a recommended range of sentences for each crime. For breaking and entering, say, the range may be between three months and three years. If a judge feels the recommendation is not appropriate in a particular case, that judge can impose a harsher or a more lenient sentence, as long as he or she gives reasons why the recommended range is not appropriate. The guidelines are not carved in stone; they can be revised periodically to reflect changing needs. Such a system has been advocated for Canada by many people, including those on the Canadian Sentencing Commission. It would help remove the anomalies identified in the recent Statistics Canada report. And it would give back to law-makers, and through them the public, a great deal of control over the sentencing process.

Third, there needs to be a thorough revision of the maximum-penalty structure to remove the incongruities that riddle the current Criminal Code. Should forgery or certain kinds of fraud really have the same maximum penalty as sexual assault with a weapon? The maximum penalties are also much too high; most were created many decades ago, when our perceptions of the seriousness of various crimes differed from those today. The maximum penalty for breaking and entering is life imprisonment, for example, but in practice the average sentence is well under one year. This is called "bite and bark" sentencing; the system barks more loudly than it bites, and creates false expectations among the public.

Canada needs a more rational and equitable sentencing system. The new Justice Minister should make sentencing reform a priority.

(Julian V. Roberts, "Three Steps to Make the Punishment Fit the Crime," *The Globe & Mail*, December 7, 1993, p. A25. Adapted with permission of the author.)

1. Summarize this article by writing a preview statement that includes both the subject and the main points of his argument.
2. Review the three persuasive techniques explained on pp. 186–87. Which ones does the author employ in this article? Which do you find most effective in convincing you to share his point of view?
3. What other sorts of evidence could the author have drawn on to make his argument more strongly persuasive?
4. The conclusion of this article is very abrupt. Write a more effective concluding paragraph, one that would clinch the writer's argument.

Resisting the Revolution
David Suzuki

For years now, I have resisted the pressure to buy a personal computer. I am not mesmerized by technology, nor am I a technophobe (as proof, I have two VCRs and love my stereo system). I do admit to being intimidated by the hackers and the video parlour freaks. But having watched my secretary (I can't reveal her age lest she quit, but she is older than I and I'm almost 50) take to a word processor easily, the crunch has now come. I've rationalized my lack of interest in computers because I couldn't see a valid use for them but word processing is definitely something I now need. By the time this article is out, I am absolutely sure I'll find a portable word processor, with modem, indispensable.

One of history's remarkable lessons is the incredible seductiveness of technology. At first it's just convenient; but once we overcome initial reticence and conquer it, it becomes indispensable—it turns around and conquers us. I get annoyed as hell when my phone calls from Toronto to Vancouver don't go through right away—yet not long ago, I'd have to go through an operator and wait quite a while to make a transcontinental call. Indeed, we now take direct overseas dialing for granted. Yet in 1945, there was no transatlantic telephone cable at all; and until communications satellites went up in the '60s, there were fewer than 300 channels for all transatlantic calls. Does anyone out there remember when we had to book them days in advance?

I was once waiting at the airport with a friend when his mother (originally an immigrant from Europe) arrived on the plane from New York. The jet had been full and the airport crowded, so it took almost an hour before her baggage arrived—and she spent the entire wait complaining bitterly about the inefficiency of the airlines. I found it amusing to think that it once took her two weeks to get from London to Montreal by boat; here she had just reached Vancouver in a 747 in six hours, yet felt enormously put out by an hour's inconvenience.

Once a technology is available, we rapidly forget what life was like before it, and simply take it as the norm. Today, we complain that amniocentesis takes up to four weeks for a diagnosis; yet twenty years ago, it wasn't possible to do any such analysis before birth. I get furious at the CBC office because our videotape machine is so "old." I can't rewind and view a tape at the same time, and it takes "so long" (meaning 15 seconds or so) to go back and forth from shot to shot. When our copier breaks down, I rant and rave without remembering all those smudged hands from ink and gels and stencils.

These technologies have transformed society beyond recognition from the one I knew as a child. My children grow up thinking of my childhood as an ancient way of life, long extinct. (Why, their dad is so old, there was no television when he was a kid!) And in spite of ourselves, we have been changed by technology in our values, in our expectations, and in the "needs" we feel.

In the summer of 1983, I spent time with the nomadic San people of the Kalahari Desert. One night, after they had slaughtered a cow we presented to them, they began to dance while we filmed the spectacle. As the camera zoomed in on a group of singers, we were astounded to find a huge, battery-driven cassette tape recorder blasting away. Where they got the machine, and how they got batteries for it, days away from the nearest settlement, is beyond me. But even they found value in its technology, thus ensuring that a chunk of their millennia-old culture will soon disappear.

We operate on simple faith that if we find any new technologies to have serious deleterious effects, we can always prohibit them. But when in history have we ever done that? Some suggest supersonic transport was scrapped because of its potential effect on the ozone layer. Nonsense! The Americans saw the enormous deficits it would pile up, and the Concorde is certainly proving them wise. Well, how about DDT? Yes, it was ultimately banned—in the industrialized countries—not so that we'd become less dependent on chemical technology, but only because there were alternative chemical pesticides. Technologies are too useful and convenient, and compel us ever onward. This leads us to depend on technological solutions to technological problems, thus assuring there will always be a price to be paid for the benefits.

And where does it all end? I am appalled at the effort that has gone into the development of embryo transplants for women. In a time when overpopulation, malnutrition, and parasitic disease cause global problems, medical science pursues non-life-threatening "problems" to satisfy desires. And once the new technology is in place, it is impossible to resist its use. Aside from the issue of whether it's a worthwhile use of medical expertise, the technology of embryo transplants has a deep impact on the very nature of biological lineage, by separating the "egg mother" from the "uterine mother" from the "social mother." Where that leads I have no idea, but it's not a trivial problem. I have watched, in horror, as parents pled for a liver to transplant into their mortally ill child—horrified at how far humans are prepared to go to fight nature, but also at the realization that were my child to develop a lethal liver condition, I would feel the same urge as those other distraught parents, now that the technology exists.

So, cognizant of and grateful for the utility of technology, I nevertheless feel that we ought to spend far more time weighing its benefits against its possible social costs. Does anyone out there agree or disagree?

(David Suzuki, "Resisting the Revolution," *Science Dimensions*, 1985, Volume 17, Number 3. Copyright © 1985 David Suzuki. Reprinted by permission of the author.)

1. The author of this essay does not use a precise preview statement. What, exactly, is the essay about? Write a preview statement for it.
2. Several incidents are used as examples. For each of these anecdotes, state the main point that it illustrates.
3. Comment on the tone of this essay. Describe the audience for whom you think it was intended.
4. We have seen that there are two main types of persuasion essay: one tries to convince readers to agree with the author, and the other tries to get readers to take an action. Into which of these categories does this essay fall? What is the author's purpose?

EXERCISE 20.2

Many people have firm convictions, yet few are willing to take action to uphold them. Everyone agrees, for example, that cancer should be cured, but not everyone donates to the Cancer Society. The same may be said for many other charitable causes. Choose a charitable cause in which you believe and list all the reasons why people should give money to support it. Then list all the excuses people would give for not donating.

EXERCISE 20.3

Write a few main points to support each of the following statements of subject. Make sure your points are persuasive.

Canada should increase (*or* decrease) its level of immigration.

There should be a uniform tax percentage for all citizens, regardless of their income.

College courses should be graded on a pass/fail basis.

Music lyrics should be strictly monitored and censored.

The number of children in a family should be limited.

TV sitcoms can be surprisingly educational.

Public schools should impose a dress code on students.

Radio is a better news medium than television.

College teachers are overpaid (*or* underpaid).

David Letterman is the King of Talk Shows.

EXERCISE 20.4

Choose a subject from the list below. Plan your preview statement, and blueprint your essay carefully. Make sure you have a strong point of view and valid reasons to support it. The statements are worded to allow a positive *or* a negative viewpoint. *Choose one side only.*

Women are (*or* are not) advancing in the workforce at an appropriate rate.

Life in the city is better (*or* worse) than life in the country.

Trial marriage is (*or* is not) a useful preparation for a legal union.

Pornographic magazines exploit (*or* do not exploit) the women who pose in them.

The attitudes of adult players have (*or* haven't) had a negative effect on junior sports players.

The greenhouse effect is (*or* is not) a serious threat to global survival.

All students should (*or* should not) be obliged to take mathematics courses in college, regardless of their program.

The government is (*or* isn't) avoiding its responsibilities to the Native population.

Cheaters never (*or* always) prosper.

Blonds do (*or* do not) have more fun.

EXERCISE 20.5

Often, in an argument, we do not simply oppose or defend a certain point of view. Rather, we consider the degree to which a point of view can be upheld. For example, most North Americans agree that there should be a legal drinking age, but passionate debates are held to determine what that age should be. For the following subjects, a debate centres about *degree*. Choose three of the subjects, determine your own feelings, and then list the reasons and evidence that you have for supporting your position.

The age at which people may buy alcohol (*or* tobacco)

The age at which people are allowed to drive

The age at which people may marry

The amount of foreign ownership of Canadian business

Where smoking should (and should not) be allowed

EXERCISE 20.6

Expand your notes for one of the subjects in Exercise 20.3 into a persuasion essay. Remember to work through selecting a suitable subject and then identifying, editing, and ordering your main points. Decide on an approach (direct or indirect) for your arguments, based on your analysis of your readers' opinions on the subject.

EXERCISE 20.7

Write a persuasion essay on a subject of your choice—one you feel strongly about. Aim your communication at a specific group of readers, and choose accordingly the approach you will take. If you don't feel strongly about anything, write about one of these subjects:

Tobacco products should be banned.

Seatbelt use should not be mandatory.

Quebec should (*or* should not) become an independent state.

Newfoundland should (*or* should not) become an independent state.

Same-sex couples should (*or* should not) be entitled to the same benefits heterosexual couples enjoy.

Parenthood should (*or* should not) be strictly controlled and licensed, like driving.

Professional boxing should be banned.

Canadians are (*or* are not) just cold Americans.

Canada's heart lies in Saskatchewan (*or* _____).

Movies should be completely uncensored.

CHAPTER 21

Quotation, Paraphrase, and Summary

Quotations, paraphrases, and summaries are special kinds of examples you can use to develop a topic sentence or support a preview statement. If you use them skilfully, they will add credibility, variety, and interest to your writing. When you **quote,** you reproduce the exact *words* of another speaker or writer; when you **paraphrase** or **summarize,** you restate in your own words the *idea(s)* of another speaker or writer. Let's look at these techniques in turn.

Using Quotations

Occasionally you fill find that someone else—an expert in a particular field, a well-known author, or a respected public figure—has said what you want to say better than you could ever hope to say it. In such cases quotations, so long as they are kept short and not used too frequently, are useful in developing your topic. Carefully woven into your paragraph, they help convince the reader of the validity of what you have to say. They also tend to heighten your reader's interest in your writing. It never hurts to show that at least one respected authority agrees with you.

You can choose quotations from two sources:

1. people you know, or have heard, or have interviewed; and
2. printed or recorded materials (e.g., books, articles, films, tapes).

In either case, it is important to select your source with care. Readers are more likely to be convinced by a quotation from an authoritative, objective source than by a quote, no matter how brilliant or wittily phrased, from an unknown or biased one. For example, if you were writing a paper on Canada's prospects for economic growth over the next decade, your reader would probably find an observation from a well-known economic analyst such as Abraham Rotstein or Judith Maxwell more pertinent and persuasive than a quote from your brother in Scarborough who has been unemployed for the last three years. Most newspapers and magazines have an editorial bias for—or against—particular political philosophies and the parties that represent them. When you quote from an article, you should assume your reader is aware of this bias and will "consider the source" when evaluating the credibility of your quotation. If you choose to support your topic with quotations from a publication like *People Weekly*, or *Frank*, don't be surprised if your reader dismisses your argument as not worth serious consideration.

One skill you need to master is fitting quotations smoothly into your own writing. It isn't difficult, but it does require sensitivity to the sound as well as the sense of what you're saying. How you incorporate a quotation into your sentence or paragraph depends on whether your quote is a **block** or a **spot.** A block quotation is several sentences long: usually more than forty words or four typed lines. After you've introduced it, you begin the quoted passage on a new line and indent all lines of the quotation ten spaces from the left margin. The ten-space indentation is the reader's visual cue that this portion of the paragraph is someone else's words, not yours. Here's an example:

> Committees put a lot of thought into the design of fast foods. As David Bodanis points out with such good humor in *The Secret House*, potato chips are
>
>> an example of total destruction foods. The wild attack on the plastic wrap, the slashing and tearing you have to go through is exactly what the manufacturers wish. For the thing about crisp foods is that they're louder than non-crisp ones. . . . Destructo-packaging sets a favorable mood. . . . Crisp foods have to be loud in the upper register. They have to produce a high-frequency shattering; foods which generate low-frequency rumblings are crunchy, or slurpy but not crisp. . . .
>
> Companies design potato chips to be too large to fit into the mouth, because in order to hear the high-frequency crackling, you need to keep your mouth open. Chips are 80 per cent air, and each time we bite one we break open the air-packed cells of the chip, making that noise we call "crispy." Bodanis asks:
>
>> How to get sufficiently rigid cell walls to twang at these squeaking harmonics? Starch them. The starch granules in potatoes

> are identical to the starch in stiff shirt collars. . . . [Also,] all chips are soaked in fat. . . . So it's a shrapnel of flying starch and fat that produces the conical air-pressure wave when our determined chip-muncher finally gets to finish her chomp.

(Diane Ackerman, adapted from *A Natural History of the Senses.* New York: Random House, 1990, pp. 142–43. Copyright © 1990 by Diane Ackerman.)

Note that Ackerman is careful to tell her readers the source of her quotations. To introduce the first quote, she gives the author's full name and identifies the title of his book. To introduce the second quote, which is from the same work, Ackerman doesn't repeat information unnecessarily, but simply identifies the author by surname. Thus she doesn't leave her readers wondering where the quotations came from. The only information missing is the publication data—city, publisher, and date—which can be presented at the end of the paper in a Works Cited list or in a footnote. (See Unit Five for information on documenting your sources.)

In addition to illustrating how to introduce and format chunk quotations, Ackerman's paragraph also shows you how to modify a quotation to fit your space and suit your purpose. While *you must quote exactly and never misrepresent or distort your source's intention,* you may, for reasons of conciseness and smoothness, leave out a word or phrase or even a sentence or two. You indicate the omission by replacing the words you've left out with three spaced dots called **ellipses** (. . .). If the omission comes at the end of a sentence, add a fourth dot as the period. The whole passage should read smoothly; the quotation should seem to be an extension of your own writing.

Sometimes you need to add or change a word or words to make the quoted passage more readable in the context of your paragraph. For example, if you have omitted some words from the original, you may need to add a transitional phrase or change the first letter of a word to a capital letter. One common reason for changing words in a quoted passage is to keep the verbs consistent in tense throughout your paragraph. For example, if you are writing in the present tense and the passage you are quoting is written in the past tense, you can change the verbs to present tense (so long as the change doesn't distort the meaning), but you must signal to the reader that you have made these changes. Use square brackets [around whatever you add or change], as we did above when we added the transition "Also," to form a link between the starch and the fat added to potato chips.

Modifying quotations to make them fit smoothly into your own sentences without altering the author's meaning takes practice. Try this approach. In your first draft, write out the quotation exactly as you found it. When you revise, read your draft with the quotation in it aloud and mark any places that sound awkward or jarring. Now experiment with introductory phrases, ellipses, and square brackets until the whole paragraph reads like one seamless unit. Remember: alter only what you must in order to achieve coherence, and *never* add or omit anything that would change your source's original meaning. (To take the most obvious example, you may never add or leave out a "not.")

A *spot* quotation is a short quotation—a word, a phrase, or a short sentence—that can be worked into one of your own sentences. You put quotation marks around a spot quote. They signal the reader that these aren't your words: a new voice is speaking. Here's an example of a paragraph containing several spot quotations:

> "You are what you quote," in the words of the American essayist Joseph Epstein, himself a heavy user of quotations and the writer who introduced "quotatious" into my vocabulary. Winston Churchill understood the value of a well-aimed quotation: as a young man he read a few pages of *Bartlett's Familiar Quotations* every day, to spruce up his style and compensate for his lack of a university education. He transformed himself from a quotatious writer into the most quoted politician of the western world, establishing a reputation [that] will survive even the frequent use of his words by Ross Perot. As for Perot, [he is an example of someone using quotations as] a way of showing off. Fowler's *Modern English Usage* warns against quoting simply to demonstrate knowledge: "the discerning reader detects it and is contemptuous," while the undiscerning reader finds it tedious. A few years ago Garry Trudeau made fun of George Will's compulsive quoting by inventing a researcher who served as "quote boy" in Will's office: "'Quote boy! Need something on the banality of contemporary society.' 'Right away, Dr. Will!'" . . . As for me, I say don't judge, because you might get judged, too. That's how the quotation goes, right?
>
> _____
>
> (Robert Fulford, adapted from "The Use and Abuse of Quotations," *The Globe & Mail*, November 11, 1992, p. C1. Adapted with permission of the author.)

Notice that to make Fulford's paragraph slightly shorter and easier to read, we made a couple of minor alterations to the original. The signals to the reader that something has been left out or added are the same as those used in a chunk quotation: ellipses and square brackets.

Tips on Using Quotations in Your Writing

1. *Use quotations sparingly and for a specific purpose,* such as for emphasis or to reinforce an important point. There are two reasons for this. First, if your readers don't interpret your overuse of quotations as showing off, they are likely to interpret it as a sign of your having nothing of your own to say. Second, your responsibility as a writer is to communicate *your* ideas. Quotations, like other kinds of support, should be used to back up what you have to say, not to substitute for it. Unsure of their responsibility, inexperienced writers sometimes produce paragraphs that are little more than

jigsaw puzzles—bits and pieces of other people's writing stuck together to look like an original work. Such paragraphs do little to help the reader form a positive impression of the quality of your thinking.

2. *Choose your quotations from the writings of acknowledged authorities or experts.* You'd be wise to consider when the work was written, too. The date may be as important as the writer's reputation. For example, a quotation from Ed Sullivan about the influence of television on popular culture would be useful only in an essay looking at television from a historical perspective, not in one discussing its influence on people today.

3. *Make sure your quotations are **accurate** reproductions of the original passage.* If you must change or omit a word or words, indicate those changes with ellipses or square brackets, as appropriate.

4. *Make sure your quotations are **relevant**.* No matter how interesting or how well-worded, a quotation that does not directly and clearly relate to your subject does not belong in your essay. An irrelevant quotation will either confuse your readers or annoy them (they'll think it's padding), or both.

5. *Be sure to make clear the link between the quotation and your controlling idea.* Don't assume readers will automatically see the connection you see between the quote and your topic sentence. Comment on the quotation, so they will be sure to make the connection you intend. If you have used a chunk quotation, your explanatory comment can sometimes form the conclusion of a paragraph.

6. *Introduce your quotations smoothly, with appropriate punctuation.* When you use a spot quotation, you can introduce it with a phrase such as "According to X" or "Y writes (*or* states, *or* comments, *or* observes, *or* says)," followed by a comma. Consider these examples:

> According to Oscar Wilde, "All women become like their mothers—that is their tragedy; no man does—that's his."

> Oscar Wilde observes, "Children begin by loving their parents; as they grow older they judge them; sometimes they forgive them."

Use a variety of introductory phrases. The repetitive "X says," "Y says," "Z says," is a sure way to put your readers to sleep.

When your spot quotation is not a complete sentence, you normally introduce it without a comma. For example:

> Oscar Wilde defined fox-hunters as "the unspeakable in full pursuit of the uneatable."

Wilde believed that people "take no interest in a work of art until they are told that the work in question is immoral."

If your introductory statement is a complete sentence, put a colon (not a comma) between it and the quotation:

George Bernard Shaw's poor opinion of teachers is well known: "Those who can, do; those who can't, teach."

Oscar Wilde's observation on education is less famous but even more cynical than Shaw's: "Everybody who is incapable of learning has taken to teaching."

Chunk quotations are normally introduced by a complete sentence followed by a colon (for example, "X writes as follows:"). Then you reproduce the quotation, beginning on a new line and indented ten spaces. If your introductory statement is not a complete sentence, use a comma or no punctuation, whichever is appropriate. The paragraphs by Ackerman and Fulford (on pp. 197–98 and p. 199, respectively) provide examples of both ways to introduce chunk quotations. Reread them now. Can you explain why a colon or no punctuation mark was used in each case? (See Chapter 36 for more information about quotations and for practice in punctuating them.)

7. *Remember to identify the source of the quotation.* This can be done by mentioning the name of the author and, if appropriate, the title of the book or article in which you found the quotation, or it can be done in a parenthetical citation or a footnote. (Chapter 24 covers the basics of documenting sources in your writing.) Follow the format your instructor prefers.

EXERCISE 21.1

For each of the following quotations, make up three different sentences:

a. Introduce the *complete quotation* with *a phrase followed by a comma.*
b. Introduce the *complete quotation* with *an independent clause followed by a colon.*
c. Introduce a *portion of the quotation* with *a phrase or statement that requires no punctuation between it and the quotation.* Use ellipses and square brackets, if necessary, to signal any changes you make in the original wording.

Example: Education is the ability to listen to almost anything without losing your temper or your self-confidence. (Robert Frost)
a. According to Robert Frost, "Education is the ability to listen to almost anything without losing your temper or your self-confidence." (complete quote introduced by phrase + comma)
b. Robert Frost had a peculiar opinion of the value of higher learning: "Education is the ability to listen to almost anything without

losing your temper or your self-confidence." (complete quote introduced by independent clause + colon)

    c. Robert Frost defined education as "the ability to listen to . . . anything without losing [one's] temper or [one's] self-confidence." (partial quote introduced by phrase requiring no punctuation; changes indicated with ellipses and square brackets)

1. I find the three major administrative problems on a campus are sex for the students, athletics for the alumni, and parking for the faculty. (Clark Kerr)

2. Education is not a *product:* mark, diploma, job, money—in that order; it is a *process,* a never-ending one. (Bel Kaufman)

3. School days, I believe, are the unhappiest in the whole span of human existence. (H.L. Mencken)

4. In the first place, God made idiots. This was for practice. Then he made school boards. (Mark Twain)

5. Education makes a people easy to lead, but difficult to drive; easy to govern, but impossible to enslave. (Lord Brougham)

EXERCISE 21.2

Read the passages below and answer the questions following each.

1.   Whenever college teachers get together informally, sooner or later the conversation turns to students' excuses. The stories students tell to justify absences or late assignments are an endless source of amusement among faculty. These stories tend to fall into three broad thematic categories.

    Accident, illness, and death are at the top of the list. If the stories were true, such incidents would be tragic, not funny. But how could any instructor be expected to keep a straight face at being told "I can't take the test Friday because my mother is having a vasectomy"? Or "I need a week's extension because my friend's aunt died"? Or—my personal favourite—"The reason I didn't show up for the final exam was because I have inverse testosterone"?

    Problems with pets rank second in the catalogue of student excuses. Animals take precedence over tests: "I can't be at the exam because my cat is having kittens and I'm her coach"; and they are often responsible for a student's having to hand in an assignment late. The age-old excuse "My dog ate my homework" gets no more marks for humour than it does for originality, but occasionally a student puts a creative spin on this old chestnut. Would you believe "My paper is late because my parrot crapped in my computer"?

    In third place on the list of students' tales of extenuating circumstances are social commitments of various sorts. "I was being arraigned in Chicago for arms dealing"; "I had to see my fence to pick out a ring for my fiancée"; and "I can't take the exam on Monday because my Mom is getting married on Sunday and I'll be too drunk to drive back to school" are just three examples collected by one college teacher in a single semester.

An enterprising computer programmer could easily compile an "excuse bank" that would allow students to type in the code number of a standard explanation and zap it to their professors. I suspect, however, that there would be little faculty support for such a project. Electronic excuses would lack the humour potential of live ones. Part of the fun comes from watching the student confront you, face to face, shamelessly telling a tale that would make Paul Bunyan blush.

1. Are all the quotations relevant to the subject of this brief essay? Are they sufficiently limited, or could the essay be improved by leaving any out?
2. Underline the specific connections the writer makes between her quotes and her controlling idea.
3. What purpose does the concluding sentence serve? Would the essay be equally effective without it? Why?

2.   U.S. federal drug policy, especially the mandatory minimum sentences for drug offenders enacted by Congress in 1987, has so distressed federal judges that approximately 10 percent of them will not hear drug trials. Judge Jack B. Weinstein of Brooklyn, N.Y., is a case in point. In an April 1993 memo to all the judges in his district, he announced that he would no longer preside over trials of defendants charged with drug crimes:

> One day last week I had to sentence a peasant woman from West Africa [with four dependent children] to forty-six months. . . . On the same day I sentenced a man to thirty years as a second drug offender—a heavy sentence mandated by the Guidelines and statute. These two cases confirm my sense of frustration about much of the cruelty I have been party to in connection with the "war on drugs" that is being fought by the military, police, and courts rather than by our medical and social institutions.
>
> I myself am unsure how this drug problem should be handled, but I need a rest from the oppressive sense of futility that these cases leave. Accordingly, I have taken my name out of the wheel for drug cases. This resolution leaves me uncomfortable since it shifts the "dirty work" to other judges. At the moment, however, I simply cannot sentence another impoverished person whose destruction can have no discernible effect on the drug trade. I wish I were in a position to propose a solution, but I am not. I'm just a tired old judge who has temporarily filled his quota of remorselessness.

The sentencing guidelines that Congress requires judges to follow are so harsh they cause, in Weinstein's words, "overfilling [of] our jails and . . . unnecessary havoc to families, society, and prisons." As a senior judge,

Weinstein can choose the cases he hears. But 90 per cent of judges are not so fortunate. After they have imposed on a low-level smuggler or a poverty-stricken "mule" a sentence far harsher than those mandated for someone convicted of rape or manslaughter, one wonders how—or if—judges can sleep at night.

(Excerpt from "The War on Drugs: A Judge Goes AWOL." Copyright © 1993 by *Harper's Magazine*. All rights reserved. Adapted from the July issue by special permission.)

1. This writer uses both chunk and spot quotations to develop her point. Where does she make clear the connection between the chunk quotation and her topic?
2. The original passage from which the writer extracted her spot quotation reads as follows: "Most judges today take it for granted, as I do, that the applicable guideline for the defendant before them will represent an excessive sentence. The sentencing guidelines result, in the main, in the cruel imposition of excessive sentences, overfilling our jails and causing unnecessary havoc to families, society, and prisons." Why did the writer modify the quote the way she did?
3. In Tip 5 (see p. 200) we advise you not to introduce a quote and just leave it hanging, but rather to comment on it. Where does this writer comment on the quotations she has used?

Writing Paraphrases and Summaries

When you **paraphrase,** you restate someone else's idea in your own words. The usual purpose of a paraphrase is to express another's ideas more clearly and more simply—to translate what may be complex in the original into easily understandable prose. A paraphrase may be longer than the original; it may be about the same length; or it may be shorter than the original statement. If it is considerably shorter, it is a **summary.** Whatever its length, a good paraphrase satisfies three criteria:

1. It is clear, concise, and easy to understand.
2. It communicates the main idea(s) of the original passage.
3. It doesn't contain any idea(s) not found in the original passage.

Let's look at the three different kinds of paraphrase in turn. Occasionally you may need to clarify technical language or explain a short, pithy statement—an aphorism, a proverb, a maxim, or another traditional saying that states a principle, offers an insight, or teaches a point. Statements that pack a lot of meaning into few words can be explained only at greater length. For example, one of the principal tenets of modern biology is "ontogeny recapitulates phylogeny." It simply isn't possible to paraphrase this principle in three words. (It means that as an embryo grows, it follows the same pattern of development that the animal did in the evolutionary process.)

EXERCISE 21.3

As simply and concisely as possible, explain each of the following expressions in your own words.

1. Seeing is believing.
2. A stitch in time saves nine.
3. Money talks.
4. More haste, less speed.
5. Birds of a feather flock together.
6. Too many cooks spoil the broth.
7. As the twig is bent, so is the tree inclined.
8. Procrastination is the thief of time.
9. Nothing ventured, nothing gained.
10. Garbage in, garbage out.

Much of the writing you now do in college and will do on the job, especially if you are in management, requires you to express in your own words the facts, opinions, and ideas you find in your reading. If you're like most students, you find paraphrasing a real challenge. Part of the problem may be that you are uncertain of the differences between paraphrasing and **plagiarism,** which means presenting words or ideas that come from another source as your own. Plagiarism is easy to avoid; all you have to do is (1) identify the source of any words or ideas you have borrowed and (2) use visual cues—quotation marks or indented lines—to mark any words taken directly from that source. (See pp. 218–20 for more information on avoiding plagiarism.)

To paraphrase a passage, you need to dig down through your source's words to the underlying ideas and then reword those ideas as clearly and simply as you can. This skill is not an inborn talent; it takes patience and a lot of practice to perfect it. But the rewards are worth your time and effort. First, paraphrasing improves your reading skill as well as your writing skill. Second, it improves your memory. In order to paraphrase accurately, you must thoroughly understand what you've read—and once you understand something, you're not likely to forget it.

Let's look now at an example of how *not* to paraphrase. Read through the following paragraph.

> The site and how the building relates to it is a critical determinant in the calculation of energy consumption. The most profound effects, and the ones the individual has least control over, are the macro-climatic (regional) factors of degree days, design temperature, wind, hours of bright sunshine, and the total solar insolation. Other factors which can have an enormous effect on the energy consumption of a house are micro-climatic. These include the topography of a site, the sun path, specific wind regime, vegetation, soil, and the placement of other buildings.
>
> (Robert Argue, excerpt from *The Well-Tempered House,* Toronto, 1980, p. 14. Reprinted by permission of Renewable Energy in Canada.)

Now let's assume we are writing a paragraph on designing an energy-efficient home. There are two pieces of information in Argue's paragraph that we want to include in our own paragraph:

1. Some of the factors influencing energy consumption relate to the climate and weather patterns of the region (macro-climatic factors).
2. Some of the factors influencing energy consumption relate to the specific characteristics of the building site (micro-climatic factors).

If we are not careful, or if we don't have much experience with paraphrasing, our paragraph might look something like this:

> In *The Well-Tempered House,* Robert Argue explains that a designer must consider two critical determinants in building an energy-efficient home. The most important factors, and the ones the individual has least control over, are the macro-climatic (regional) factors of degree days, design temperature, wind, hours of sunshine, and the total solar insolation. The other significant factors are the micro-climatic ones, which include the topography of the site, the sun path, wind regime, vegetation, soil, and the location of other buildings on or near the site.

This is plagiarism. Although we have indicated the source of the information, we have not indicated that the wording is almost identical to that of the original. Of the total 90 words, 50 come from the source. There are no visual or verbal cues to alert the reader that these are Argue's words, not ours. Let's try again:

> In *The Well-Tempered House,* Robert Argue identifies two significant influences the cost-conscious home-builder must consider in designing an energy-efficient house. The first and strongest influence is the typical weather of the region. The designer must be familiar with such "macro-climatic factors" as "degree days" (the difference between the indoor comfort temperature and the average daily outdoor temperature), "design temperature" (the lowest temperature to be expected during the heating season), wind, and the total effect of the sun. The other influences are called "micro-climatic factors" and include the site's topography (elevation and slope of the land), sun path, prevailing wind pattern, and the presence or absence of vegetation and nearby buildings.

While this draft is technically a paraphrase rather than plagiarism, it doesn't demonstrate very much work on our part. We have replaced the source's words with synonyms and added explanations where the original is too technical to be easily understood by a general reader, but our paragraph still follows the original too closely. Paraphrase is *not* a method for passing off someone else's ideas as your own by changing a few words and sentences. A good paraphrase goes farther. It uses source information, but rearranges it, rephrases it, and combines it with the writer's own ideas to create something new. Let's try once more:

> The cost-conscious home-builder must consider a number of fac-tors that will affect the energy consumption of his or her new home. The exterior design of the house should take advantage of the natural slope of the land, the presence of sheltering vegetation, prevailing wind patterns, the path of the sun, and other characteristics of the building site (Argue 14). In addition to sufficient insulation, the inte-rior should feature appropriate heating and cooling devices to keep the family comfortable during the coldest winter days and the hottest summer days. To keep costs down, these devices should take advan-tage of the natural energy sources available: wind, sun, and seasonal fluctuations in temperature can all be used to harness and conserve energy. With careful planning, a new home can be designed to max-imize the advantages of even an apparently unlikely site, minimize the negative effects of temperature and weather, and cost surprisingly little to maintain at a comfortable temperature year-round.

Here we have used paraphrase to incorporate information from a published source into a paragraph whose topic and structure are our own. This is how paraphrase can be used both responsibly and effectively. If you want to take ideas more directly from a source, retaining the original arrange-ment and some of the wording, use spot quotations—but remember to inte-grate them smoothly into your own sentences.

Finally, let's look at the third kind of paraphrase, the **summary.** It's hard to overstate how valuable the ability to summarize is. Note-taking in col-lege is only one form of summarizing. Abstracts of articles, executive sum-maries of reports, market surveys, legal decisions, research findings, and records (called "minutes") of meetings, to name only a few kinds of formal documents, are all summaries. Topic sentences and preview statements are essentially summaries; so, often, are conclusions. In speaking, you rely on your summarizing skills in every conversation you have. In committee, group, or team work, imagination and creativity are desirable, but the abil-ity to summarize is crucial. There is no communication skill that you will need more or use more than summarizing. Again, this is a skill that doesn't "come naturally." *You need to practise it.* Remember: you summarize for yourself and for others all day long. You'll improve very quickly if you make an effort to think about what you're doing—that is, if you're con-scious rather than unconscious of the times and the circumstances in which you need to call on summarizing skills.

A summary is a clear, concise, orderly statement of the contents of a writ-ten or spoken message. It is a communication boiled down to its essence or gist. Like frozen juice concentrate, it contains the distilled essence of the original in a smaller package. Consider the following passage, which contains a highly concentrated summary of another writer's ideas:

> One of Edward de Bono's books is called *Six Thinking Hats*. [In it] he proposes that you adopt six different mind sets by mentally putting on six different coloured hats. Each hat stands for a certain way of thinking about a problem. By "putting on the hat" and adopting a certain role, we can think more clearly about the issues at hand. Because we're only "playing a role," there is little ego riding on what we say, so we are more free to say what we really want to say. De Bono likens the process of putting on the six hats one at a time to that of printing a multicoloured map. Each colour is not a complete picture in itself. The map must go through the printing press six times, each time receiving a new colour, until we have the total picture.
>
> _____
>
> (Timothy Perrin, excerpt from "Positive Invention," in *Better Writing for Lawyers*, Toronto: The Law Society of Upper Canada, 1990, p. 51.)

Notice that Perrin is careful to tell his readers the source of the ideas he is paraphrasing: both the author and the book are identified up front.

Tips on Summarizing

1. Read the passage carefully, looking up any words you don't understand. Then read it through again, often enough to grasp the main ideas and form a mental picture of their arrangement. Make notes of the main ideas in the order in which they appear. Omit any repetitions and most or all of the supporting material. If the original passage contains quoted material that is essential to its meaning, turn the quotation into indirect speech (see Chapter 36), condensing it as much as possible.
2. Put the original and your notes away for a day or two, and let your unconscious mind go to work on what you've read.
3. Working from your notes, write out the main ideas in your own words. Do not introduce any ideas that were not in the original.
4. Revise your draft until it is coherent, concise, and makes clear sense to someone who is unfamiliar with the original passage. It's a good idea to get someone to read through your summary to check it for clarity and completeness.
5. Don't forget to acknowledge your source, either in your paragraph or in a footnote.

Here's an example of summarizing in action. Turn back to pp. 197–98 and reread Diane Ackerman's paragraph on potato chips, underlining the main ideas as you read. Now read our summary, below, and see how close you came to what we think is the essence of her paragraph.

> Diane Ackerman explains in *A Natural History of the Senses* (1990) that fast foods are designed and packaged to appeal to consumers' senses. Quoting David Bodanis' research, Ackerman uses potato chips to illustrate her point. To satisfy consumers' desire for crispiness in chips, manufacturers add laundry starch and fat to their product and make the individual chips so large that one has to bite into them, producing the desired "crispy" sound, to fit them into the mouth. Even the plastic packaging is designed to crackle noisily when opened, enhancing the product's appeal to the sense of hearing as well as taste.

This paraphrase (100 words) is slightly less than half the length of the original (228 words), yet it contains all of Ackerman's main points. It could be shortened still further, if our purpose and context required a really brief summary:

> Diane Ackerman uses potato chips as an example of the sensory appeal of fast foods. Chips appeal to our hearing as well as to our taste: both the chips themselves and the packages they come in are designed to make the maximum amount of noise during consumption.

While these two sentences (47 words) capture the gist of the original paragraph, there's not much "flavour" left. Summaries are useful for conveying an outline or a brief overview of someone else's ideas, but by themselves they aren't very memorable. Details and specifics are what stick in a reader's mind, and these are what your own writing should provide.

EXERCISE 21.4

Using the five Tips on Summarizing (see p. 208) as your guide, reread the paragraphs in Exercise 21.2, pp. 202–204. Paraphrase each one to make it approximately one-third to one-half as long as the original. Each paraphrase should be about 100 to 125 words.

EXERCISE 21.5

Condense each paraphrase you prepared in Exercise 21.4 to two or three sentences (no more than 50 words).

EXERCISE 21.6

Choose three of the paragraphs from Exercise 6.1 in Chapter 6 (pp. 66–67). Paraphrase each one, making it approximately half as long as the original.

Then, in as few words as you can, condense each paraphrase into a summary.

EXERCISE 21.7

Choose an article that interests you from one of the regular sections (e.g., Business, Medicine, Education, Music, Art) of a general newsmagazine such as *Time, Maclean's, Newsweek,* or *The Economist.* Summarize the article for a friend who is not an expert in the field and who has not read it. Do not evaluate the article or give your opinion about it. In a paragraph of about 150 to 200 words, simply inform your friend of its contents.

EXERCISE 21.8

Read an article from a professional journal in your field. Reduce each paragraph to a single-sentence summary. Assume your reader is a professional in the field.

Additional Suggestions for Writing

1. Interview someone two generations removed from you (e.g., a grandparent, an elderly neighbour) about his or her life as a young person. What were the sources of entertainment? Leisure activities? Work? Family responsibilities? Major concerns? Goals? Write an essay in which you tell this person's story, using quotation and paraphrase to develop your main points.
2. Interview a friend, classmate, or relative on one of the following topics. Then write an essay using quotation and paraphrase to help tell your reader how your interviewee answered the question.
   a. If you were to live your life over knowing what you know now, what would you do differently?
   b. What being Canadian (or a parent, or childless, or unemployed, or successful, or a member of a particular religious group) means to me.
   c. Once I was _____; now I am _____.
3. Research a topic of particular interest to you and write an essay using quotation and paraphrase to develop your main points.
4. Select a news article or a group of articles dealing with a current issue in the scientific, business, arts, or medical community. In a paragraph of approximately 200 to 300 words, summarize the issue for your instructor, who has just returned from spending six months in the wilderness without access to either print or electronic media.

The Research Paper

CHAPTER 22

Writing a
Research Paper

When you write a short essay, you can often rely on what you already know about a subject to generate the main points and supporting detail your readers need to understand your message. When the subject of the essay is unfamiliar or complex, however, or when you want to make your argument more convincing, you will need to do some research.

Writing a research paper is not usually a more difficult task than writing an essay, but it *is* more time-consuming. Remember that it takes longer, and plan your time accordingly. The major difference between the two is that a research paper includes **source material**—information taken from other writers—to support a discussion. Think of the options you'd have if you were asked to give a speech on a subject. You could stand up there and talk all by yourself—the oral equivalent of an essay—or you could gather together a panel of experts and act as the panel's moderator by leading the discussion. A research paper is comparable to a panel discussion.

You can't just gather your panel of experts together and then excuse yourself and go home. The research paper isn't simply a collection of what other people have had to say on the topic. It is your responsibility to shape and control the discussion, make sure that what the experts add is both interesting and relevant, and make observations and comments on the validity or significance of their remarks. It's *your* paper, *your* subject, *your* main points; the quotations and ideas you include from your sources should give valid support for *your* topic sentences.

A research paper gives you the advantage of not having to face your readers alone, but it creates the problem of clearly separating your ideas from those you took from your sources. Readers can't hear the different "speakers" when ideas are put on paper; you have to show clearly who "said" what. To separate your sources from one another and from your own ideas, research papers require **documentation**—a system of acknowledging your sources. Your documentation will give your readers a guide to the sources of the information contained in your research paper—a play-by-play of who is "speaking."

You may prefer writing research papers instead of essays. You may find it easier to develop an argument when you can use source material, and more interesting to discover and use new information than to discuss what you already know. As a bonus, the skills you develop while doing research-paper assignments will be useful when you want to do research for your own interests or to solve an on-the-job problem.

Generally, research papers are longer than essays. Therefore, the time you are allowed to complete a research assignment is usually longer than the time you are given to complete an essay. This extra time can work to your advantage. In addition to being able to find material that makes what you say about your subject more interesting and credible, you have more time to polish your writing. A research paper allows you to demonstrate both your research skills and your writing skills.

Tips on Writing a Research Paper

1. Manage your time carefully. You need to allow yourself time to complete both the research and the writing stages of the paper.
2. Divide the work into a number of smaller tasks, and work according to a schedule. Last-minute cramming may give you an "adrenalin rush," but it does not produce a well-written paper.
3. Clearly define your subject before beginning your research, but be prepared to modify, adapt, and revise it as you research and write your paper.
4. Find out where to locate appropriate information.
5. Incorporate your information into your paper as smoothly as you can.
6. Write your research paper as clearly and correctly as you would write any other essay. Without careful attention to your writing skills, your effort will be wasted, not rewarded.

CHAPTER 23

Researching Your Subject

Your first step in writing a research paper is the same as your first step in any writing task: select a suitable subject. Whether you choose your own subject or are assigned one for your paper, don't rush off to the library right away. Take a little time to think about your subject carefully. If it has been assigned and you're not sure what the instructor expects, clarify what is required of you.

Check your subject with the 4-S test: is it significant, single, specific, and supportable? If not, refine it by using the techniques discussed in Chapter 2.

Next, consider what approach you might take in presenting your subject. Does it lend itself to a comparison? Process? Cause or effect? Deciding up front what kind of paper you're going to write will save you hours of time, both in the library and at your writing desk.

When you're sure your subject is appropriate and you've decided, at least tentatively, on the approach you're going to take, you've already begun to focus on the kind of information you're going to look for in your research. For example, if the subject is "Word processing programs make writing easier," you don't need to discuss the history of computers, computer crime, or the best accounting programs. You can focus your research in areas that will be relevant to your specific subject.

Once you have an idea of the information you will need to help develop your subject, it's time to find the best information you can. There are many places to find information, but the library is the most obvious place to begin.

Using the Library

Does your library intimidate you because you don't know how to find quickly the information you need? Your library will be less overwhelming when you realize that all of its contents are organized and classified to simplify finding specific information. All you need to do is figure out the organizational system your library uses, and you'll have the key that unlocks the information gates.

Books

The books in libraries are catalogued by subject, title, and author. This system means you can track down a specific book three ways. The library may have its catalogue on cards in file drawers, on microfiche, or on computers. No matter how the information is stored, the catalogue headings will be the same.

You could begin your search by looking under a subject heading, such as "Computers." Or, if you know the title of the book you want, you can go directly to the title headings and look up the title—*Computer Wimp*, for example—and find where the book is located in the library by using the call number given. If you know that John Bear wrote a book on computers, but you aren't sure of the title, you can look under the author headings to find "Bear, John."

Books are arranged on library shelves in a sequence of call numbers. The call numbers that catalogue the subject of each book originate from the numbers assigned under the U.S. Library of Congress classification system. (Some small libraries still use the Dewey decimal system of classification, but most college and university libraries follow the Library of Congress system.)

When you arrive in a new library, look for a map showing where the various categories of books are located. When you have noted from the catalogue files the call numbers of the books you want, use the map to find the shelves where the books are stored.

Periodicals

Your library's collections of **periodicals**—journals, magazines, and reviews—may contain useful articles on the subject you are researching. In fact, articles may be more useful than books because they are more recent and up-to-date. To find the specific articles you need, use the periodical indexes; these list articles according to subject, author, and title.

There are many different indexes to journal and magazine articles. The most comprehensive index is the *Readers' Guide to Periodical Literature*, which lists most of the popular magazines. Other general indexes include the *Canadian Periodical Index* and the *New York Times Index*. Specialized areas have their own indexes, such as the *Social Sciences Index, Applied Science and Technology Index, Art Index, Business Periodicals Index, Canadian News Index, Education Index,*

Humanities Index, and *Music Index.* Once you've found the listings for the articles you want, check to see whether the library subscribes to the magazines or journals that published the articles. A list of the periodicals held in the library is often posted in the section where the indexes are shelved.

Encyclopedias

Another useful source of *general* information on a topic is an encyclopedia. There are many different types of encyclopedias. Some of the general ones include *The Canadian Encyclopedia, Collier's Encyclopedia, Encyclopedia Americana,* and *Encyclopaedia Britannica.* Specialized encyclopedias include the *Encyclopedia of Music in Canada, Encyclopedia of World Art, International Encyclopedia of Social Sciences,* and *Encyclopedia of Computers and Data Processing.* An encyclopedia article on your topic may give you a good overview and a bibliography to guide you to further reading. Encyclopedias do *not* contain current, up-to-the-minute information, however.

Other Sources

Your library may have a vertical file that contains newspaper clippings, short articles, and brochures related to your topic. This material *is* current. The vertical file cabinet will have information listed according to general subject categories. A list of the categories is usually kept near the file.

Finally, don't overlook the possibility of finding information from the audio-visual materials held in the library—video tapes, films, recordings, or slide presentations. Check the catalogue for these items.

The library is not the only source of information you can use. Interviews with people who are familiar with your subject are good sources because they provide a personal view and they ensure that your paper will contain information not found in any other paper the instructor will read. Other forms of research, such as surveys and questionnaires that you design and distribute, can add interesting information as well. This type of research is time-consuming and requires knowledge of survey design and interpretation, but it has the advantage of being original, unique, and current.

Selecting the Best Information

After you have gathered all the information you think you will need for your paper, the next step is to assess the quality of your information. If you have done your research thoroughly, you will have discovered much more about the subject than will be usable in your paper. It's time to analyze the information and select your best and most relevant material.

To test your information for usefulness, you must ask three questions.

---

1. Is the information relevant to the topic?

Sometimes, when you are researching, you can get sidetracked by information that is interesting but not relevant. Don't let this information distract you from your topic; focus on the information that supports your subject directly.

---

2. Is the information up-to-date?

Whether you need current information depends on the subject itself. If you are researching a field of knowledge that is changing quickly, then you need the most recent information available. For example, if you are writing a paper on computers, material from the 1950s would be useful only for giving a historical perspective; it would have no place in a discussion of current computer technology.

Your most up-to-date information will come from your own research—the surveys or interviews you conduct yourself. Your next most up-to-date source of information is periodicals. To check for currency, look at the date an article was published. Generally, the more recent the publication date, the more current the source of the information. The time between the writing of an article and its publication in a periodical is shorter than it is for books. Even recently published books may contain information that is out of date by the time the books are released.

---

3. Is the information from a reliable source?

Some sources of information affect the credibility of what is said. For example, most readers trust information taken from a city newspaper more than they trust the information in a tabloid such as *The National Enquirer.* When you need reliable information, use sources that represent the recognized experts in the field.

Taking Good Research Notes

As you do your research, remember that it is critical to identify the exact source of each piece of information or quotation. Good research notes will help you to keep track of the different ideas you find for your paper and the data that identify your sources. In addition to the information your source yields about your subject, you will need information about the source itself. For each published source that you will use in your paper, you will need to know

- the title and edition
- the author and/or editor
- the publisher, the place of publication, and the date of publication
- the volume number of the journal or magazine
- the page(s) from which the quotation (or the material you have paraphrased or summarized) was taken.

Some researchers keep every different piece of information on a separate index card; they include all of the information needed for the documentation. Other writers keep their notes on sheets of paper, clearly separating their own ideas from the ideas and words taken from sources. Using different colours of ink will help you to distinguish at a glance your words and ideas and those from a book or article. Technology has improved the way notes can be kept. Computers allow researchers to separate information through the creation of a database, and photocopiers, usually available in libraries, allow researchers to copy relevant pages of sources for later use. *Whatever system you use, it is very important to separate clearly one source from another and to keep track of the documentation information.* A little time spent on this step will save you hours of frustrating backtracking later on.

Avoiding Plagiarism

If you don't take clear and complete research notes, you'll easily get one source confused with another. The result of this confusion could be inaccurate documentation in your final paper. You must **credit** your sources; that is, you need to identify them for your readers. (The next chapter will show you, in detail, how to document your sources of information.) If you don't give adequate credit to the source of your information, your readers can become confused and may assume that everything in the paper is based on your own ideas. Readers who are confused about your sources may challenge you to identify where your information originated. If your readers are led to believe that all the ideas are yours and then find out that the ideas came from somewhere else, they may feel as though you have tried to deceive them. Whether you have deliberately or naïvely left your sources unidentified, the result is called plagiarism.

Plagiarism is a very serious offence. When college students commit it, the penalty varies from school to school, but it is usually severe. *Plagiarism means taking someone else's words or ideas without giving credit to the author of those words or ideas. Even if you paraphrase the original words or ideas, it is still considered plagiarism unless you identify your source.*

Intentionally trying to pass off someone else's work as your own is a form of cheating. Doing it unintentionally is unacceptably sloppy. What makes your paper unique is your interpretation of your research in relation to your subject. Your readers want to know not only what information you've found but also what you think of it and how you interpret it. It's *your* paper, after all. Here's how you can avoid plagiarism.

---

1. Keep good research notes.

Keep track of the documentation information you'll need for every idea or passage you take from your sources. As you are researching, ideas or interpretations that are not covered in the source material may occur to you. Note these ideas as your own, so that you can use them in the paper as well.

---

2. Organize your paper carefully.

If your paper is merely a collection of ideas from sources, it won't convey a clear message to your readers. Develop a good blueprint before you begin to write, and make sure that your source material is *supporting* your main points, not substituting for them.

---

3. Acknowledge all of your sources.

If you know where you got a fact or piece of information, give the source—even if you think the information is common knowledge. It's safer to give the source than it is to assume that "everybody knows that." Statistics should always have references because, as you know, the significance of numbers tends to change, depending on who is using them or who gathered the data.

> 4. If in doubt, ask your instructor.

If you aren't sure what to document, take your research notes and your blueprint for your paper to your instructor and ask. It's better to ask before the essay is submitted than to try to explain a problem after the paper is graded. Asking also saves you time.

CHAPTER 24

Documenting Your Research

As we have seen, in a research paper or report you bring together information on a subject from several different sources. You interpret it, organize it, and work it into a coherent presentation, part of which is your own and part of which is taken from your sources. Whether you are quoting, paraphrasing, or summarizing (see Chapter 21), you must acknowledge your sources to let your readers know exactly where you found your quotations and any borrowed ideas. Acknowledging your sources is called **documentation.**

When you give credit to your sources within your research paper, you need to follow a system of documentation. There are many different systems of documentation, but one of the most widely used is the Modern Language Association (MLA) system. Most instructors in English and the humanities will expect your papers to conform to the principles of format and documentation that are outlined in this chapter. If you are assigned a paper in the social sciences, you may be expected to use the *Publication Manual of the American Psychological Association* (3rd ed.) (APA style). For research essays in the biological sciences, your teacher may insist on the format in the *CBE* [Council of Biology Editors] *Style Manual: A Guide for Authors, Editors, and Publishers in the Biological Sciences* (CBE style).

If you learn the principles set forth in the following pages, which conform to the style recommended by the Modern Language Association (MLA style), you will be able to convert the format of your documentation to that of other systems with little difficulty. The manuals containing these other systems are available in college and university libraries and in most bookstores.

Acknowledging Your Sources

Whenever you include information from a source in your writing, you need to identify (in parentheses) that source within your paper. You also need to list that source among your "Works Cited" or "Works Consulted" at the end of your paper. The way the information is given both in the parenthetical reference and in the Works Cited is determined by the MLA (or another) style, and the style—including the order of information, capitalization, and punctuation—must be followed exactly. Not all sources are the same, and there is a specific format for every type of source you might need to use for your paper. Examples of the most common types of citations are given in this chapter; for more information, consult Joseph Gibaldi and Walter S. Achtert, *MLA Handbook for Writers of Research Papers,* 3rd ed. (New York: Modern Language Association, 1988).

Using References within Your Paper

Quotations, paraphrases, and summaries should be woven smoothly into your paper, not just strung together without commentary. Use your own introduction to a quotation to tie the source material to your discussion, and follow the quotation with an observation about its significance, as in this example:

> Word-processing programs make writing easier by allowing mistakes to be corrected instantly: "When a writer isn't worried about spoiling a page, it is possible to try ideas and see how they look before deciding to keep the text" (Smith 3). Reducing anxiety makes writing a more pleasant experience and also improves the quality of the writing. Writers are free to experiment with sentences and keep the best of what they produce.

Your quotations should be similarly introduced and discussed. Putting quotations in a context of your own will create coherence within your research papers.

If you are using a short quotation, identify the source in parentheses after the quotation marks but before the final period, as in this example:

> "Computers are essential to increasing productivity and improving recordkeeping systems" (Wood 12).

If your quotation is longer than four typed lines, place the source information in parentheses at the end of the quotation, after the period.

Wood observes that

> Computers are essential to increasing productivity and
> improving recordkeeping systems. When the initial cost
> of the system is measured against the benefits of
> improved efficiency, computers are not a luxury in the
> modern office. Computers are vital to the success of
> the organization. (12)

As we saw in Chapter 21, you don't always have to use a direct quotation from your source. You can summarize a paragraph or an entire book by using your own words to give the ideas. However, when you summarize, you must still identify the original source. Consider this example:

> In <u>Computer Crime</u>, J. B. Shaw describes the problems computers
> create for security. He explains that, despite the complex system
> of passwords and codes, computers are still susceptible to criminal
> activity.

You'll notice that the summary does not require a page reference. Page references are given only for direct quotations and paraphrases.

Citing Parenthetically within Your Paper

Every time you use information from a source that is not identified within your paragraph, you must identify it in parentheses immediately following the sentence or paragraph containing the information. (In the past, footnotes were used to identify the sources within a paper. Now, footnotes are used only to give additional explanation of a term or idea.) The parenthetical reference gives your readers only enough information to find the full listing of the source in your Works Cited or Works Consulted list.

Use parenthetical references to identify the sources of all quotations, paraphrases, summaries, facts, and ideas you have found in your research and used in your paper. Your parenthetical references should be clear, accurate, and as brief as possible. Normally, the author's surname and the exact page number(s) are all you need.

As a general rule, you need to include a piece of source information only once; don't repeat information unnecessarily. For example, if you've already mentioned the author's name in your paragraph, you need give only the page reference in your parentheses.

An excerpt from a research paper is reproduced below. Notice how the writer uses quotations and summary to introduce the results of the research. The excerpt also shows you the correct way to leave out a word or words from a passage you're quoting, using ellipses, and how to add a word or words to a quotation for readability, using square brackets.

Between 1980 and 1982, unemployment rates in Canada rose by almost 50 per cent. The people hardest hit by this phenomenal increase were the "chronically unemployed, [those who] experience frequent bouts of unemployment of relatively long durations" (Shaw 144). Six separate groups, distinguished from each other and from the working population by such factors as occupation, sex, age, geographic location, ethnic origin, and level of education, make up the chronically unemployed in our society (Shaw 143–44).

Workers in primary industries such as fishing, logging, or construction suffer unemployment more often and for longer periods than people in managerial, clerical, or sales jobs:

> In 1982 unemployment rates ranged from 3.7 percent for managers and administrators to 89 percent for sales and clerical workers and 12.6 percent for service workers. This compares to 19 percent for construction workers and 32 percent for workers in forestry and logging. ("Selected Indicators" 134)

In <u>A Longitudinal Analysis of the Canadian Labour Market</u>, Robertson reported that periods of unemployment for primary-industry workers last, on average, more than twice as long as the periods of unemployment experienced by managers or professionals (10).

Of all the chronically unemployed, women with dependent children suffer the greatest financial burden. In 1982, there were approximately 67,000 unemployed women living in households in which no one had a job. Of these, "about 57 per cent maintain[ed] the family . . . as single, separated, divorced, or widowed family heads" (Shaw 150).

Study the way the writer of this excerpt has used parenthetical references to identify information sources. The introductory paragraph contains a short quotation and a paraphrase. For both, a parenthetical reference identifies the author of the article from which the information was taken (because the author's name does not appear in the paragraph) and shows the page or pages on which it was found. For complete information about the article, readers would turn to the Works Cited list at the end of the paper. Under "Shaw," listed in alphabetical order, should be a standard entry for a periodical article. The entry would include the author's full name, the title of the article, the name of the journal, the publication date, and inclusive page numbers for the whole article:

Shaw, R. Paul. "The Burden of Unemployment in Canada."
   Canadian Public Policy/Analyse de Politiques 11.2 (1985):
   143–60.

In the second paragraph, the writer includes a block quotation. The parenthetical reference includes the shortened title of an **unsigned article**— no author is identified in the source—and the page on which the quotation was found. Complete information about the source would appear in the end-of-paper alphabetical list, under "Selected Indicators":

"Selected Indicators of Unemployment by Occupation." The Labour
   Force Dec. 1982: 130–34.

In the third paragraph, the writer's parenthetical reference gives only the page on which the information was found, because the author and title are included in the paragraph. Complete information about the source would appear in the alphabetical list of Works Cited or Works Consulted, under "Robertson":

Robertson, M. J. A Longitudinal Analysis of the Canadian Labour
   Market. Ottawa: Canadian Employment and Immigration
   Commission, 1982.

Sample Parenthetical References

Here are some typical examples of parenthetical references. Titles of whole publications (books, magazines, pamphlets, and similar entities) are underlined (printed in *italics*); titles of parts of publications (single chapters, articles, essays, poems, and so on) are placed in quotation marks.

1. Simple page reference, with the author's name given in your paragraph:

   Leo Panitch says that Canadians are deeply entrenched in the American empire "as their hewers of wood, drawers of water and drillers for oil" (14).

2. Identification of author, with the author's name not given in your paragraph:

   "Only a perspective which . . . recognizes the rights of Palestinians to demand and secure for themselves an escape from homelessness on a substantial part of their own land and in their own state and with equal prerogatives and obligations can help to avoid the mutual tragedy that is engulfing both peoples" (Panitch 35).

3. Identification of one of several titles by the same author, with the author's name given in your paragraph:

   Pierre Berton suggests a unique approach to divorce: "The ritual . . . should be held in a church and it ought to be presided over, whenever possible, by the same minister who forged the original bonds of matrimony" ("A Modest Proposal" 73).

   Whenever you are listing more than one work by the same author (under Works Cited or Works Consulted), you must give the work's title as well as the page reference in each parenthetical reference, to let your readers know from which work each quotation was taken.

4. Identification of author and of one of several titles by the same author:

   The entire ceremony is turned around in order to poke fun at both marriage and divorce; the little people on the divorce cake are "facing resolutely away from each other" (Berton, "A Modest Proposal" 74).

When you refer in your paper to several articles or books by the same writer, your parenthetical reference for each quotation or summary should identify the author and include the title as well as the page reference, so your readers know which work is your source.

5. Reference to one of several volumes:

> Only once in his two-volume work does Erickson suggest
>
> conspiracy (2: 184).

The number before the colon identifies the volume and the number(s) after the colon identify the page(s) you are referring to.

6. References to a literary classic or to the Bible:

> In Shakespeare's play, the duke's threat to give "measure for
>
> measure" (5.1.414) echoes the familiar passage in the Bible
>
> (Matthew 7.1–2).

Use Arabic numerals separated by periods for act, scene, and lines from a play, or to identify a biblical chapter and verse.

The List of Works Cited or Works Consulted

The final page in your research paper will be a list of **Works Cited** (only those sources from which you have quoted in your paper) or of **Works Consulted** (all the sources you found useful in preparing your paper). The list, together with the parenthetical references within your paper, provides your readers with all of the necessary information about the sources you used in preparing your paper: who wrote them, who published them, and where and when they were published. *By acknowledging and crediting your sources in these ways, you avoid plagiarism.*

Your final list of Works Cited or Works Consulted should be arranged alphabetically. Each item in this list gives your readers answers to the following questions:

> *For Books, Pamphlets, and Government Publications*
> Who wrote (or edited) it?
> What is the full title?
> What edition was used (if relevant)?
> Where was it published?
> Who was the publisher?
> When was it published?

For Articles
Who wrote it?
What is the full title?
What is the name of the periodical it appeared in?
What is the volume number of the periodical (if applicable)?
When was it published?
On what page(s) does the article appear?

In a list of Works Consulted, you may also wish to include information obtained from a lecture, a film, a TV show, or another nonprint source. The information required in these entries varies considerably, depending on the type of source you are documenting. Examples are provided below.

Once you have sorted your sources into alphabetical order (if there is no author, use the first word of the title—excluding *A, An,* and *The*—to alphabetize an entry), you are ready to confirm that all necessary information has been gathered and is listed in the proper style. Centre your heading, Works Consulted or Works Cited, double-space throughout the list, and indent the second and subsequent lines of each entry. The following examples will guide you in listing different types of sources.

Books, Pamphlets, and Government Publications

1. Book by one author:

Barnard, Sandie. <u>Speaking Our Minds</u>. Scarborough, Ontario:

Prentice-Hall, 1990.

Note that the publisher is usually identified by a short form of the company's full name: for example, Holt, Rinehart and Winston, Inc. is identified as Holt; University of Toronto Press becomes U of T Press; Prentice-Hall Canada, Ltd. becomes Prentice-Hall.

2. Book by more than one author:

Matte, Jacqueline, and Phyllis A. Richard. <u>Allons Bi-Bi</u>. Toronto:

Centennial, 1974.

Pyle, William W., Kermit D. Laison, and Michael Zin.

<u>Fundamental Accounting Principles</u>. Homewood, IL: Irwin,

1984.

3. Book edited by someone other than author:

> Hookey, Robert, Murray McArthur, and Joan Pilz, eds. <u>Contest:</u>
>
> > <u>Essays by Canadian Students</u>. 2nd ed. Toronto: Holt, 1994.
>
> Waldman, Nell, and Sarah Norton, eds. <u>Canadian Content</u>. 3rd
>
> > ed. Toronto: Harcourt Brace, 1996.
>
> Wilkinson, Anne. <u>The Collected Poems</u>. Ed. A. J. M. Smith.
>
> > Toronto: Macmillan, 1968.

4. Work in several volumes:

> Erickson, Edward W., and Leonard Waverman, eds. <u>The Energy</u>
>
> > <u>Question: An International Failure of Policy</u>. 2 vols.
> >
> > Toronto: U of T Press, 1974.

5. Article, essay, chapter, story, or poem in a collection:

> Trudeau, Pierre Elliott. "The Ascetic in a Canoe." <u>Canadian</u>
>
> > <u>Content</u>. Eds. Sarah Norton and Nell Waldman. Toronto:
> >
> > Holt, 1988. 27174.

6. Encyclopedia reference:

> "Prospecting." <u>Encyclopedia Canadiana</u>. 1970 ed.
>
> Swinton, George. "Inuit Art." <u>Canadian Encyclopedia</u>. 1988 ed.

7. Book by corporate author (company, commission, agency):

> Apple Computer, Inc. <u>Apple Computer Annual Report 1994</u>.
>
> > Cupertino, CA: Apple Computer, Inc., 1994.
>
> Carnegie Council on Policy Studies in Higher Education. <u>Giving</u>
>
> > <u>Youth a Better Chance: Options for Education, Work and</u>
> >
> > <u>Service</u>. San Francisco: Jossey, 1980.

8. Pamphlet:

Use the same form as for books.

> <u>Home Insurance Explained</u>. Toronto: Insurance Bureau of
>
> > Canada, 1994.
>
> Irwin, Michael. <u>What Do We Know about Allergies?</u> New York:
>
> > Public Affairs Committee, 1992.

9. Government publication:

If the author of the document is not named, identify the government first, then the agency, then the title, and so on.

Government of Canada. Ministry of Labour. <u>Establishment and</u>

<u>Operation of Safety and Health Committees</u>. Ottawa:

Minister of Supply and Services, 1984.

Province of Ontario. Ministry of Education. <u>Language across the</u>

<u>Curriculum</u>. Toronto: Ministry of Education, 1978.

Articles

1. Magazine or journal article with new page numbers starting for each issue:

Booth, David. "Distributorless Ignition Systems." <u>Canadian</u>

<u>Automotive Technician</u> April 1990: 17–22.

Hibler, Michelle. "Strollers." <u>Canadian Consumer</u> 20.2 (1990):

16–21.

Canadian Consumer is an example of a periodical that publishes a number of "issues" each year, making up an annual "volume." Identify the volume number (here, 20) right after the periodical title, add a period, and then give the issue number (here, 2) immediately before the year (1990).

2. Magazine or journal article with page numbers continuing through all the issues of an annual volume:

Denker, Debra. "Along Afghanistan's War-Torn Frontier."

<u>National Geographic</u> 167 (June 1985): 772–97.

Kemper, S. L., and O. Fennema. "Water Vapor Permeability of

Edible Bilayer Films." <u>Journal of Food Science</u> 49

(Nov.–Dec. 1984): 1478–81.

3. Newspaper article, signed or with byline:

Immen, Wallace. "It Came from beneath the Sea." <u>Globe & Mail</u>

8 Oct. 1994: D8.

4. Newspaper article, unsigned:

Alphabetize under first word of the title, excluding *A, An,* or *The.*

"Ontario Francophones Seek Roots in Quebec." <u>Toronto Star</u> 12
June 1995: A10.

5. Editorial in magazine or newspaper:

"Sacrificing people to fight inflation." Editorial. <u>Toronto Star</u> 8
May 1994: A18.

"Town named Soo." Editorial. <u>Our Times</u> 9.2 (April 1995): 4.

6. Review of book, film, concert, or theatrical performance:

Harris, Christopher. "Not the Flight We Expect from Imax." Rev.
of <u>Destiny in Space</u>, prod. Grame Ferguson. <u>Globe & Mail</u>
8 Oct. 1994: C15.

Low, Simone. "Rhymes on Fire." Rev. of <u>Fabulous Rhyming</u>
<u>Dictionary</u> by Gary Barwin. <u>Journal of Wild Culture</u> 1.4
(Winter 1988/89): 24.

Other Media

1. Computer software:

Chiu, Ken Kung Keung, et al. <u>Quicken</u>. Vers. 7. Computer
software. Intuit, 1993. DOS 3.0, 640 KB, disk.

Clarence, Paula. <u>The Business Writer</u>. Computer software. IPCF,
1984. TRS-80, cartridge.

2. Information from a computer service:

Flannery, Dana. "The Business of Beauty." <u>Working Women</u> Oct.
1994: 74–82. Dialog file 15, item HE 022979.

3. Interview:

Potvin, Felix. Interview. 9 Jan. 1995.

van Vogt, A. E. Interview. <u>Dream Makers: The Uncommon People</u>
<u>Who Write Science Fiction</u>. Ed. Charles Platt. New York:
Berkeley, 1980.

4. Radio or TV program:

(Include the title of the program, network, local station, city, and date of broadcast.)

Atom Egoyan: The Man behind the Mask. Prod. Dora Hencz and

Jon Steinberg. CBC. CBLT, Toronto. 7 July 1994.

Interview with Lorne Rubenstein. Conducted by Peter Gzowski.

Morningside. CBC. CBLT, Toronto. 13 Jan. 1995.

5. Recordings:

Fowke, Edith. Sally Go Round the Sun: Songs and Games of

Canadian Children. RCA, T-56666, n.d.

Handel, George Frederick. Messiah. With Elsie Morison, Marjorie

Thomas, Richard Lewis, and James Milligan. Huddersfield

Choral Soc. and Royal Liverpool Philharmonic Orch. Cond.

Sir Malcolm Sargent. Audiotape. Seraphim, 4X3G-6056,

1982.

Reservoir Dogs: Original Motion Picture Soundtrack. Music sup.

Karen Rachtman. Compact disc. MCA Records. MCAD-10541,

1992.

6. Film, filmstrip, or video cassette:

Include the title, director, distributor (if known), and year. You may include the writer, performers, and producer after the title. The size and length of a film are included after the date.

French Canadians. Filmstrip. Moreland-Latchford, Toronto, n.d.

73 fr., 35 mm.

Handling Complaints and Grievances. Film. American

Management Association, 1967. 16 mm, 17 min.

Lasers. Videotape. Ontario Educational Communications

Authority, 1980. 1/2 in., 30 min.

The Last Frontier: Oceans. Sound filmstrip. Global Productions,

1992. 12 min.

Rashomon. Film. Dir. Akira Kurosawa. With Toshiro Mifune and

Machiko Kyo. Daiei, 1950.

7. Lectures, speeches, addresses:

> Hume, Michael. "Gender Distinctions in Canadian Sitcoms." EN
>
> 180 lecture. Centennial College. Scarborough, Ontario. 23
>
> March 1995.
>
> Warberg, Carolyn. "Aggressive Play Behaviour in Young
>
> Children." Paper presented to the Early Childhood
>
> Educators, British Columbia. Vancouver, BC. 4 May 1990.

The preceding examples show you the formats you are most likely to need in preparing a research paper. Other questions may arise as you grapple with the task of documenting all your sources accurately. Check these more unusual formats before you panic.

1. More than one book by an author:

Substitute a line of three hyphens for the author's name in the second and any additional entries.

> Colombo, John Robert. <u>Canadian Literary Landmarks</u>. Toronto:
>
> Hounslow, 1984.
>
> - - -, ed. <u>Colombo's All-Time Great Canadian Quotations</u>. Toronto:
>
> Stoddart, 1994.

2. Book with a subtitle:

Put a colon after the title; then add the subtitle.

> Karpinski, Eva C., and Ian Lea. <u>Pens of Many Colours: A</u>
>
> <u>Canadian Reader</u>. Toronto: Harcourt Brace, 1993.

3. New edition of an older book:

Give the edition number and the date of the source you used.

> Waldman, Nell, and Sarah Norton, eds. <u>Canadian Content</u>. 3rd
>
> ed. Toronto: Harcourt Brace, 1996.

4. Paperback edition of a previously published book:

Put the date the book was originally published before the publication date of the edition you consulted.

> Laurence, Margaret. <u>The Stone Angel</u>. 1964. Toronto:
>
> McClelland, 1986.

5. More than three authors or editors:

Give the name of the first author or editor listed on the title page and add "et al."

Baugh, Albert C., et al. <u>A Literary History of England</u>. New

York: Appleton, 1948.

6. Publishing information not given:

Use "N.p." for "no place"; "n.p." for "no publisher"; "n.d." for "no date"; and "n. pag." for "no page numbers."

Bank of Montreal. <u>The Mortgage Control Handbook</u>. N.p.: n.p.,

n.d., n. pag.

7. Source not formally published

Harris, Jim. "So You Think You Had a Bad Day." <u>Dove</u> (John

Howard Society of Metropolitan Toronto) January 1990:

n. pag.

Norton, Sarah. "General Education and Generic Skills: Ontario's

Emperor Has No Clothes." Review of a review. 5 June 1995.

See the next page for a sample list of Works Consulted that shows what your final page should look like.

Works Consulted

Balkaran, Romani. "Consider Your Audience." Teaching-Learning Series workshop. Scarborough College. Scarborough, Ontario, 11 March 1994.

"Electronic Shopping." Consumer Reports 59 (Oct. 1994), 623.

Fine, Sean. "Has the Highest Court Lost Touch with Reality?" Globe & Mail 8 Oct. 1994: D2.

Mirvish, Ed. Personal interview. 15 March 1994.

Norton, Sarah, and Brian Green. The Bare Essentials, Form B. 3rd ed. Toronto: Harcourt, 1993.

Ricard, François. "This Little Hippie Went to Market." Saturday Night Oct. 1994: 44–48.

Sunbeam Corporation (Canada) Ltd. Solaray Ultrasonic Cool Mist Humidifier Model 456: Use and Care Instruction Manual. N.p.: n. p., n. d., n. pag.

Works Consulted if all works you looked at are included; Works Cited if only works quoted from are included.

Lecture, speech, or other spoken presentation.

Magazine article, unsigned; pages numbered continuously throughout an annual volume.

Newspaper article, signed; includes section as well as page number where necessary.

Personal interview.

Book with more than one author and in a second or later edition.

Magazine article, signed; each issue is renumbered starting at page 1.

Pamphlet by corporate author such as a business company; publishing information (publisher's city name, date) missing; no page numbers provided.

CHAPTER 25

Formatting a Research Paper

Although an old saying says "You can't judge a book by its cover," the way a book looks often influences your decision to read it or pass it by. Similarly, your research report should present a positive image. Its appearance should reflect all of the effort you put into its preparation. Otherwise, your reader may be turned off even before beginning to read.

Find out whether your instructor has any special requirements for the format of your research assignment. If so, follow them carefully. Otherwise, use the recommendations in this chapter, which includes an example of what a completed research paper looks like.

Paper

Type or computer-print your final draft on plain white letter-size $8^1/_2$" by 11" or 21.5 cm × 28 cm paper. Be sure to use a good ribbon on your typewriter or printer. If your instructor will accept a handwritten assignment, use blue or black ink and write neatly on one side of the paper only. *Always keep a copy of your paper.* (Instructors have occasionally been known to lose things.)

Spacing and Margins

Double-space throughout your assignment, including the title, quotations, and list of sources. If your paper is handwritten, write on every other line.

Leave a 2.5-cm (1-inch) margin all around the page. Indent paragraphs five spaces from the left margin. Indent long quotations (more than four typed lines) ten spaces from the left margin.

Page Numbers

Beginning with page 1, number *all* pages of your paper, including the list of sources. Put the numbers in the upper right corner of the page, 1.25 cm ($^1/_2$ inch) from the top edge and 2.5 cm (1 inch) from the right edge. (You may want to include your surname just before the number.)

Heading and Title

You do not need a separate title page for short papers. Beginning at the left margin, 2.5 cm (1 inch) from the top of the page, type on separate lines your name, your instructor's name, your course number, and the date. Then double-space and centre your title. Leave a double space between the title and the first line of your paper.

Presenting Source Titles

If you are not working on a word processor that allows you to use italics for titles, present the titles of complete works (books, magazines, tapes, programs, pamphlets, and so on) with underlining (for example, <u>The Best Short Stories of the Modern Age</u>). Put the titles of parts of whole works (a chapter in a book, an article in a periodical, an essay in a collection, an interview on a television program) in quotation marks (for example, "The Lottery" in <u>The Best Short Stories of the Modern Age</u>).

Projecting an Image

Your research paper should demonstrate your understanding of the subject, your research and writing skills, and your ability to follow specific requirements of documentation and format. Meeting the submission requirements is as important as any other aspect of the preparation of your paper. It may be the last stage of your writing task, but it is the first impression that your readers will have of your work.

The model shown here is a "live" paper, properly formatted; its author is Marty Chan, a University of Alberta student.

Study first the blueprint Marty prepared before writing his research paper. Notice how he included in his outline some notes on the sources he wanted to quote or paraphrase in each section. This technique saves hours of paper shuffling when you sit down to write.

Professor Pac-Man:

What Do Children Learn from Video Games?

Grabber: Debate about the pros and cons of video games is probably irrelevant. Children will continue to zap, blast, leap, and steer their way to video victory whether we approve or not.

Preview: A review of the pros and cons may help us guard against the negative effects and develop the positive educational values; we will consider escapism, interactivity, and reinforcement.

I. Escapism is the primary attraction.

A Critics suggest violent themes may promote real-life aggression. (Anderson and Ford)

B. The appeal of fantasy can make the games a powerful teaching tool. (Greenfield; Meer; Loftus and Loftus)

II. Interaction is a second attraction.

A. Video games demand active involvement of the player.

B. Critics are concerned that video games are replacing social interaction. (Greenfield; Scheibe and Erwin)

C. Video games can have positive, practical applications. (Loftus and Loftus)

III. Reinforcement accounts for much of the games' appeal.

A. Negative implications include "addiction." (Greenfield; Needham)

  B. Positive effects include motivating children to learn. (Loftus

    and Loftus; Malone)

Summary: Fantasy, interaction, and reinforcement give video games

    both positive and negative power over children. (Liss)

Clincher: Assessment of the effects of video games on children will

    eventually fall somewhere between the extremes.

1.25 cm. (¹/₂")

Chan 1

2.5 cm.

2.5 cm. (1 inch)

2.5 cm. Marty Chan

Professor G. Saywell

English 200

1 March 1991

Professor Pac-Man:

What Do Children Learn from Video Games?

Any debate about the pros and cons of video games is probably irrelevant; children will continue to zap, blast, leap, and steer their way to video victory regardless of our apprehension or approbation. Nevertheless, it is instructive to review the debate that pits those who fear the influence of the games against those who claim that playing them has value for young minds. Examining the evidence may enable us to guard against the negative social and psychological effects while recognizing and developing the positive educational values of the Mario Brothers and their ilk.

Video games owe their popularity to many factors. Escaping to a fantasy world where issues are straightforward and goals are clear is a major appeal. Another feature that draws players to the games is their interactivity; the passivity of the television viewer gives way to the excited participation of the role player in a personal adventure. Third, a clear and immediate reward for achievement in the games provides irresistible reinforcement and inducement to carry on through increasingly difficult skill levels.

Escapism is the primary attraction of video games. Whether controlling a dot-munching Pac-Man or donning the trunks of a

Chan 2

diminutive boxer named Little Mac, the players live for a time in a synthetic world. As long as they can compete with the machine, they will live happily in videoland—for good or ill.

Because the majority of popular video games draw on violent themes for their fantasies, critics suggest that there is a potentially dangerous carryover of aggression into real life. Craig A. Anderson and Catherine M. Ford concluded from experiments with college students that "aggressive video games [such as Zaxxon and Centipede] can have short-term negative effects on the game-player's emotional state. . . . The highly aggressive game [leads] to increased hostility and anxiety . . . " (398).

On the other hand, the producers of <u>Sesame Street</u>, the Children's Television Workshop, have proved that video games can present their action-oriented fantasy with positive, nonviolent themes (Greenfield 106). Regardless of the theme, UCLA psychology professor Seymour Feshbach asserts that fantasy is vital to child development (Meer 12). And, in an educational setting, learning can be enhanced by video games that use fantasy to "provide or provoke vivid images related to the material to be learned" (Loftus and Loftus 129). Children's literature from the Brothers Grimm to Dr. Seuss is rooted in fantasy. Should video games be censured for presenting the same themes electronically?

Another attraction of video games is interaction. Rather than passively watching the action, players participate in it. Typically, the player takes on the role of the main character in the video adventure, and it is this character whom the player manipulates and controls with joystick, keypad, or power glove. The concentration required for success at most games and the absorbing nature of the interactive involvement lead to the undivided focus on the screen observed in many regular players.

The value of the interactivity of video games is a heated issue among critics. Because the player deals solely with the machine in most applications, worried parents fear that video games will replace social interaction. Combine this isolation with violent themes and the consequences could be dire:

> It may be that the most harmful aspect of the violent video games is that they are solitary in nature. A two-person aggressive game seems to provide a cathartic or releasing effect for aggression, while a solitary aggressive game (such as Space Invaders) may stimulate further aggression. (Greenfield 104)

Although crowds of teenagers gather in arcades, they rarely socialize with each other; the solitary nature of the games discourages human contact. The degree to which video interaction replaces social interaction among players was remarked upon in a study in which players were found to be talking to the machines as if they were human (Scheibe and Erwin 1979).

Video interaction can have positive applications, however. Besides increasing powers of concentration and honing motor skills, video games can be unequalled teachers. Video educational software can do something a teacher can't: provide prolonged individual attention to the student. Interactivity of this nature is illustrated in a hypothetical video game described by Loftus and Loftus (133). The player learns Newton's law of motion by bombing ground targets from an airplane. Initially, the learning player drops the bomb when the plane is directly over the target, and the bomb overshoots the mark. After repeated tries, players eventually teach themselves to release the bomb at the precise point when its forward motion will combine with gravity to carry it to the target. Without direct instruction, the player has learned to apply Newton's law of motion.

The effectiveness of the bomber game described above derives not only from the role playing of bombardier, nor only from the compelling interactivity of the game, but also from the instantaneous reward for a successful performance: an exploding target. Reinforcement is an integral part of the lure of video games. A rescued princess, an extra life, a defeated enemy: these are a few of the many forms of rewards provided. As long as the game encourages players by reinforcing a successful effort, they will continue to play.

Like video fantasy and interaction, continual reinforcement is not necessarily positive. Researchers have shown that it can foster addiction. Game designers produce increasingly complex games: "The existence of multiple levels [is] also responsible for the addictive properties of the games. . . . A video game player makes visible progress in the form of improved score and reaching the next level. Yet there is always another level to master" (Greenfield 122). The addiction produced by these never-ending challenges can "spawn social problems such as gambling, vandalism, panhandling (for quarters), loan sharking, diversion of lunch money, and theft" (Needham 1983).

As any parent or teacher knows, reinforcement can be applied productively as well. For example, a spelling program rewards success by presenting a game of Asteroids on the screen (Loftus and Loftus 140). Once the students have finished playing the video game, the spelling program resumes. Knowledge that the game will reappear if they satisfy the program's spelling requirements motivates the players, providing them with a goal to work towards. In an experiment by Thomas Malone (1980), students learning about fractions were rewarded when their correct answers exploded balloons in a simulated darts game. A circus song trumpeted the players' success on popping three balloons. Visual and auditory rewards, instantaneously applied, encouraged success in learning fractions.

It is possible that the fantasy, interaction, and reinforcement that give video games their incredible power over children can have positive educational outcomes. At present, it must be admitted, the positive is largely potential, while escapism and (often violent) entertainment are currently the chief attractions of the games. This may be changing, however, as companies like Nintendo, the giant in home video systems, begin exploring educational applications. Nintendo recently donated $3 million to the Massachusetts Institute of Technology's Media Laboratory to develop educational software (Liss 71). Their goal is to develop programs that exploit the powerful features of video games to make learning more effective and more fun.

Chan 6

What are our children learning from video games? At worst, they may be encouraged to violence, socially inhibited, and dangerously obsessed by their electronic fantasy worlds. At best, they may be stimulating their imaginations, learning their school lessons more effectively than ever before, and enjoying their video education. The dire predictions made about the destructive effects of rock 'n' roll music, television, and even books have proven over time to be exaggerated. The wonderful educational potential predicted for new technologies has never fully materialized, either. Undoubtedly, the effects of video games on children will eventually fall somewhere between the extremes.

Works Consulted

Anderson, C. A., and C. M. Ford. "Affect of the Game Player: Short-term Effects of Highly and Mildly Aggressive Video Games." Personality and Social Psychology Bulletin 12.4 (1986): 390–402.

Greenfield, P. M. Mind and Media: The Effects of Television, Video Games, and Computers. Cambridge: Harvard University Press, 1984.

Liss, S. "Dr. Nintendo." Time 28 (May 1990): 71.

Loftus, G. R., and E. F. Loftus. Mind at Play: The Psychology of Video Games. New York: Basic Books, 1983.

Malone, T. W. What Makes Things Fun to Learn? A Study of Intrinsically Motivating Computer Games. Palo Alto: Xerox, 1980.

McDonald, M. C. "Video Games to Spot Problems." Psychology Today (September 1983): 12.

Meer, J. "Mickey Mouse vs. Donkey Kong." Psychology Today (September 1983): 12.

Needham, N. R. "The Impact of Video Games on American Youth." Education Digest 68.6 (1983): 40–42.

Rossel, R. D. "Addictive Video Games." Psychology Today May 1983: 87.

Scheibe, K. E., and M. Erwin. "The Computer as Altar." Journal of Social Psychology 108 (1979): 103–109.

Sentence Structure

CHAPTER 26

Cracking the Sentence Code

There is nothing really mysterious or difficult about sentences; you've been speaking them successfully since you were two. The difficulty arises when you try to write—not sentences, oddly enough, but paragraphs. Almost all college students, if asked to write ten sentences on ten different topics, could do so without an error. But when those same students write paragraphs, sentence fragments and run-on sentences—errors that confuse or annoy readers—tend to creep in.

The solution to fragment and run-on problems has two parts:

Be sure every sentence you write

1. sounds right, and
2. has a subject and a verb.

Your ear is the best instrument with which to test your sentences. If you read your sentences aloud, you'll probably be able to tell by the sound whether they are complete, clear, and satisfactory. A complete sentence is one that makes sense by itself.

Read these sentences aloud:

College is almost as interesting as television.

Although college is almost as interesting as television.

The second "sentence" doesn't sound right, does it? It does not make sense on its own and is in fact a sentence fragment.

Testing your sentences by reading them aloud won't work if you read your paragraphs straight through from beginning to end. The trick is to read from end to beginning. That is, read your last sentence aloud, and *listen* to it. If it sounds all right, then read aloud the next-to-last sentence, and so on, until you have worked your way back to the first sentence you wrote.

Now, what do you do with the ones that "sound funny"? Before you can fix them, you need to be able to "decode" each sentence to find out whether it has a subject and a verb. The subject and the verb are the bare essentials of the sentence; every sentence you write must have both. (The only exception is the **command,** in which the subject is understood rather than expressed. Consider this command: "Sign here." The subject *you* is understood.)

Finding Subjects and Verbs

A sentence is about *someone* or *something.* That someone or something is the **subject.** The word (or words) that tells what the subject *is* or *does* is the **verb.** The verb will express some sort of action, or condition, or occurrence.

Find the verb first. One way is by finding the word or group of words whose form can be changed to indicate a change in time. In the sentence

The prime minister has called an election.

has called (in the past) can be changed to *is calling* (present) or *will call* (future), so *has called* is the verb.

Once you have found the verb, find the subject by asking *whom* or *what* the verb is referring to.

Look at the following examples. We have underlined the subjects once and the verbs twice.

My aunt hired me for the summer.
(Hired expresses an action and is the verb.
Who or what hired [me]? My aunt hired me, so aunt is the subject.)

Canada has been described as "the land God gave to Cain."
(Has been described expresses an occurrence and is the verb.
Who or what has been described? Canada.)

Finding verbs seems not too difficult.
(Seems expresses a condition and is the verb.
Who or what seems [not too difficult]?
Finding, which is the subject.)

Now try your hand at finding subjects and verbs. Throughout Units Six to Ten, for exercises marked with an asterisk (*), you can compare your answers with those given in Appendix C.

EXERCISE 26.1*

Find the subject and the verb in each of the following sentences. Underline the subject with one line and the verb with two. Check your answers, and if you made even one mistake, carefully reread the section "Finding Subjects and Verbs." Be sure you understand this material thoroughly before you go on.

1. Algy met a bear.
2. A bear met Algy.
3. The bear was bulgy.
4. Sad to say, the bulge was Algy.
5. Grizzlies are famous for their unpredictability.
6. Meeting bears unexpectedly is clearly risky.
7. According to an old myth, bears never run downhill.
8. Take it from me. They do.
9. Females with cubs are especially dangerous.
10. Defending oneself presents a real problem.

Usually the subject comes before the verb in a sentence, but not always. Occasionally we find it after the verb:

> Into the back seat of the newly washed car <u>climbed</u> the eager <u>children</u>, happily clutching their ice-cream cones.

> At the bottom of the page, in red ink, <u>was</u> my <u>grade</u>.
> (Who or what <u>was</u>? My <u>grade</u>.)

In sentences beginning with *There* + some form of the verb *to be*, or with *Here* + some form of the verb *to be*, the subject is always found after the verb.

> There <u>are</u> few <u>temptations</u> I can resist.
> (Who or what <u>are</u>? <u>Temptations</u>.)

> There <u>will be</u> a <u>test</u> next week.
> (Who or what <u>will be</u>? A <u>test</u>.)

> Here <u>are</u> the <u>solutions</u> to last week's problem set.
> (Who or what <u>are</u>? <u>Solutions</u>.)

In questions, the subject often follows the verb:

> <u>Are</u> <u>we</u> safe here?   <u>Is</u> <u>he</u> late again?
> (Who or what <u>are</u>? <u>We</u>.)   (Who or what <u>is</u>? <u>He</u>.)

But notice that, in questions beginning with *who, whose, what,* or *which,* the subject and verb are in "normal" order:

<u>Who</u> <u>ordered</u> the pizza?   <u>What</u> <u>happened</u> last night?

<u>Whose</u> <u>turn</u> <u>is</u> it to pay?   <u>Which</u> <u>team</u> <u>won</u>?

To practise your skills, try the following exercises, underlining the subject in each sentence with one line, the verb with two. Check your answers to each set before you go on.

EXERCISE 26.2*

1. Here is an idea to consider.
2. Lucy Maud Montgomery lived in Ontario's Durham County before Confederation.
3. Who wants the last piece?
4. Eat slowly.
5. Exercise builds strong bodies and healthy minds.
6. Keep your body fit.
7. Far behind the Liberals and New Democrats trailed the Conservatives, bringing up the rear.
8. Pride goes before a fall.
9. Only in Canada is a so-called lack of national identity a distinctive national characteristic.
10. Only Irish whiskey contains ingredients from all four of the essential food groups: caffeine, fat, sugar, and alcohol.

EXERCISE 26.3*

1. Vancouver is a metropolitan centre with scores of distinct neighbourhoods.
2. The word "Toronto" is the Anglicization of the Native term for "meeting place."
3. The Salt Spring Islands were originally a part of the B.C. mainland.
4. Are you a year-round island resident?
5. At a joint meeting of the band councils, the chiefs opposed increased logging in Clayoquot Sound.
6. No evictions occurred last year.
7. The islanders' cohesiveness is the product of genuine neighbourliness and common community concerns.
8. There is surprisingly little vandalism, the plague of downtown areas.
9. For the average visitor to the islands, the combination of private and public properties is acceptable and even enjoyable.
10. Minutes from the middle of the city nestles my sunny, serene island retreat.

More about Verbs

The verb in a sentence may be a single word, as in most of the exercises you've just done, or it may be a group of words. **Helping verbs** are often added to main verbs so that an idea can be expressed precisely. The words *shall, should, may, might, can, could, must, ought, will, would, have, do,* and *be* are helping verbs.

> The complete verb in a sentence consists of the main verb together with any helping verbs.

Here are a few of the forms of the verb *write*. Notice that in questions the subject may come between the helping verb and the main verb.

You <u>may write</u> now.   He <u>had written</u> his apology.
He certainly <u>can write</u>!   You <u>ought</u> to write to him.
We <u>should write</u> home more often. We <u>will have written</u> by then.
I <u>shall write</u> tomorrow.   I <u>will write</u> to the editor.
He <u>could have written</u> yesterday. The proposal <u>has been written</u>.
She <u>is writing</u> her memoirs.   Orders <u>should have been written</u>.
<u>Did</u> he <u>write</u> to you?   <u>Could</u> you <u>have written</u> it in French?

One verb form, in particular, always takes a helping verb. Here is the rule:

> A verb ending in *-ing* MUST have a helping verb (or verbs) before it.

Here are a few of the forms an *-ing* verb can take:

I <u>am writing</u> the report.   She <u>must have been writing</u> all night.
You <u>will be writing</u> a report. You <u>are writing</u> illegibly.
He <u>should have been writing</u> it. I <u>was writing</u> neatly.
<u>Is</u> she <u>writing</u> the paper for him? <u>Have</u> you <u>been writing</u> on the wall?

Beware of certain words that are often confused with helping verbs:

> Words such as *not, only, always, sometimes, never, ever,* and *just* are NOT part of the verb.

These words sometimes appear in the middle of a complete verb, but they are modifiers, not verbs. Do not underline them:

I have just won the lottery!
He is almost always chosen first.
Most people do not welcome unasked-for advice.

Test yourself with Exercises 26.4 and 26.5. Underline the subject once and the complete verb twice. Check your answers to each set before you go on to the next.

EXERCISE 26.4*

1. He has talked nonstop for three hours.
2. She should have been examining each package.
3. Could they return the goods tomorrow?
4. In the winter, the car starts more easily inside the garage than outside.
5. Where is the nearest gas station?
6. He is not going to drive.
7. Which one does she prefer?
8. Parents will always perceive their offspring as small children.
9. The barometer has just fallen alarmingly.
10. Patiently and painstakingly, against all odds, struggled the little army.

EXERCISE 26.5*

1. In a couple of years, you will be a professional dancer.
2. By noon, he will have been sleeping for eighteen hours.
3. How are the club members identified?
4. The police will certainly stop all yellow cars on the road tonight.
5. How should the committee present this concept?
6. To some small degree at least, personal opinion is often presented as fact.
7. My boss does not understand me; neither does my husband.
8. Have you ever been to the Zanzibar tavern?
9. Little is known about his past, except that he visited Calgary twice.
10. Isn't she going home now?

More about Subjects

Very often, groups of words called **prepositional phrases** come before the subject in a sentence, or between the subject and the verb. When you're

looking for the subject in a sentence, prepositional phrases can trip you up
unless you know this rule:

> The subject of a sentence is never in a prepositional phrase.

You have to be able to identify prepositional phrases so that you will
know where *not* to look for the subject. A prepositional phrase is a group
of words that begins with a preposition and ends with the name of something or someone (a noun or a pronoun). Often a prepositional phrase will
indicate the direction or location of something. Here are some prepositional
phrases (the italicized words are prepositions):

about the book	*behind* the desk	*from* the office
above the desk	*below* the window	*in* the book
according to the book	*beside* the book	*in* front of the door
after the meeting	*between* the desks	*inside* the office
against the wall	*by* the book	*into* the elevator
along the hall	*concerning* the memo	*like* the book
among the books	*despite* the book	*near* the wall
among them	*down* the hall	*of* the typist
around the office	*except* the staff	*on* the desk
before lunch	*for* the manager	*onto* the floor
over a door	*under* the book	*with* a book
to the staff	*until* the meeting	*without* the book
through the window	*up* the hall	*without* them

When you're looking for the subject in a sentence, you can make the task
easier by crossing out any prepositional phrases. For example,

> The keyboard ~~of your computer~~ should be cleaned occasionally.
> What <u>should be cleaned</u>? The <u>keyboard</u> (not the computer).
>
> ~~In case of an emergency~~, one ~~of the group~~ should go ~~to the nearest~~
> ~~ranger station for help.~~
>
> Who <u>should go</u>? <u>One</u> (not the group).

In the two exercises that follow, first cross out the prepositional phrase(s)
in each sentence. Then underline the subject once and the verb twice.
Check your answers to each set before going on.

EXERCISE 26.6*

1. According to the old proverb, a stitch in time saves nine.
2. I have had a stitch in my side, and I have often been in stitches.

3. Stitching, in my opinion, is best left to tailors and surgeons.
4. For today's prices, clothing manufacturers should be sewing triple seams in their clothing, all by hand.
5. From the beginning, each item of clothing should be separately designed.
6. After that, every pattern piece should be cut by hand.
7. Each piece of cloth should then be sewn with great care to the other appropriate pieces, by one person.
8. The same craftsperson should then pay attention to double seaming and to details of hand finishing.
9. Items of clothing produced in this way might justify today's high prices.
10. In this kind of manufacturing procedure, the individual maker of the item should receive a specified percentage of the wholesale price.

EXERCISE 26.7*

1. In the next twenty years, the average age of the Canadian population will increase significantly.
2. For those of us now in our forties, this trend is good news.
3. For those in their teens, however, the news is not so good. They will have to carry the burden of caring for the increasing numbers of elderly persons in society.
4. On the positive side, the leaders of tomorrow will have the experience and wisdom of a large segment of the population to draw on in their planning and decision making.
5. Throughout history, cultures around the world have traditionally associated age with wisdom.
6. Ironically, however, this assumption is not always supported by the evidence.
7. There are many examples from the past and in the present of young leaders with more wisdom and maturity than their aged counterparts.
8. Consider, for example, Alexander the Great. He had conquered the known world by the age of 19.
9. For a contemporary example, consider the success stories of youthful entrepreneurs like Bill Gates. Many young people, just out of college, have launched hi-tech ventures to compete with old, established companies.
10. Over the next two decades, with the maturing of the "baby boomers," Canadians will encounter changes in lifestyle, in political focus, and in cultural attitudes towards the "young" and the "old."

EXERCISE 26.8

Write ten sentences of your own. Cross out all the prepositional phrases, and underline the subject once and the complete verb twice.

Multiple Subjects and Verbs

So far you have been working with sentences containing only one complete subject and one complete verb. Sentences can, however, have more than one subject and verb. Multiple subjects are called **compound subjects;** multiple verbs are **compound verbs.** Here is a sentence with a compound subject:

> Esquimault and Oak Bay border the city of Victoria.

This sentence has a compound verb:

> She groped and stumbled her way down the dark aisle of the movie theatre.

And this sentence has a compound subject and a compound verb:

> The detective and the police sergeant leaped from their car and seized the suspect.

The elements of a compound subject or verb are usually joined by *and* (but sometimes by *or*). Compound subjects and verbs may contain more than two elements, as in the following sentences:

> Careful planning, organization, and conscientious revision are the keys to good essay writing.

> I finished my paper, put the cat outside, took the phone off the hook, and crawled into bed.

EXERCISE 26.9*

In the following sentences, underline the subjects once and the verbs twice. Be sure to underline all the elements in a compound subject or verb.

1. The prime minister and the provincial premiers met at Harrison Lake.
2. They debated and drafted amendments to the unemployment insurance program.
3. The anesthetist and the surgeon scrubbed for surgery and hurried to the operating room.
4. Blue spruce and hemlock are both northern imports to Southern Ontario.
5. I tried and failed once, and then later tried again and succeeded.
6. My son or my daughter will drive me home.
7. The two dogs and the cat travelled a thousand miles in three months.

8. My retired father reads, travels, golfs, walks the dog, and loves all these activities.
9. Knock three times and ask for Joe.
10. Sight reading and improvising are necessary skills of the small-band musician.

EXERCISE 26.10

This exercise is a review. In the following sentences, find and underline the subjects once and the verbs twice. Be sure to underline all the elements in a compound subject or verb.

1. Consider the lilies of the field.
2. Melanie and Morris adjusted their chains, checked their earrings, and patted their spiked hair into place before stomping off to their job interviews.
3. I asked the necessary questions and recorded the householders' answers but was puzzled by one most unusual response.
4. In my house live my wife and I, our two teenagers, two dogs, one cat, and one ghost.
5. No other researcher got such a startling answer or finished a questionnaire so quickly.
6. On King Street, between St. Andrew's Church on the east and assorted small buildings on the west, lies Roy Thomson Hall.
7. Ragweed, goldenrod, and twitch grass formed the essential elements in the bouquet for his English teacher.
8. He spun around the corner, whirled into a doorway, and careened up the stairs, with the police in hot pursuit.
9. Today's artists must mirror the real world rather than create an ideal one.
10. This theory of art produces "slice-of-life" drama, encourages representational painting and visual art, engenders atonal music, and sells computers.

CHAPTER 27

Solving Sentence-Fragment Problems

Any group of words that is punctuated as a sentence but that does not have a subject or a complete verb is a **sentence fragment.** Fragments are perfectly appropriate in conversation and in some kinds of writing, but normally they are unacceptable in college, technical, and business writing. You've already learned how to spot a sentence fragment: read the words aloud, and check to see whether the subject or the verb (or both) is missing. Let's look at a few examples:

Now, as always, is greatly influenced by its willful neighbour.
(Who or what <u>is influenced</u>? The sentence doesn't tell you. The subject is missing.)

The argument being over whose turn it was to pay.
(The verb is missing.)

Historians attempting to analyze Canada's role in WW II.
(Part of the verb is missing. Remember that a verb ending in -*ing* must have a helping verb in front of it.)

For the computers in every lab but this one.
(Subject and verb are both missing.)

Regarding the student we discussed last week.
(Subject and verb are both missing.)

Now, what do you do with the fragments you've found?

> To change a sentence fragment into a complete sentence, add whatever is missing: a subject, a verb, or both.

You may need to add a subject:

Now, as always, <u>Canada</u> is greatly influenced by its willful neighbour.

You may need to add a verb:

The argument <u>was</u> over whose turn it was to pay.

You may need to add part of a verb:

Historians <u>are attempting</u> to analyze Canada's role in WW II.

You may need to add both a subject and a verb:

A <u>server</u> <u>is provided</u> for the computers in every lab but this one.

Sometimes you need to add more than just a subject and a verb:

<u>I</u> <u>have written</u> to the registrar regarding the student we discussed last week.

Don't let the length of a fragment fool you. Students often think that if a string of words is long it must be a sentence. Not so. No matter how long the string of words is, if it doesn't have both a subject and a verb, it is not a sentence. Here is an example, taken from "The Men of Moosomin," by Sara Jeannette Duncan:

Here and there a ruddy little pond, like a pocket looking glass dropped on the prairie, with a score or so of wild ducks swimming in it, or a slight round hollow where a pond used to be, with the wild ducks flying high.

Do you know what's missing? Can you change the fragment into a sentence? Work through the exercises below to develop your sentence-recognition skills.

In Exercises 27.1 through 27.3, read each "sentence" aloud. Put an *S* before each complete sentence and an *F* before each sentence fragment. Make each fragment into a complete sentence by adding whatever is missing: a subject, a verb, or both.

EXERCISE 27.1*

1. ____ Regarding myths and fairy tales.

2. ____ To decide on the basis of rumour, not facts.

3. ____ Trying to be helpful, I offered to check the files.

4. ____ Grading exams all evening after working all day.

5. ____ The party members gathering in the campaign office.

6. ____ We win.

7. ____ Hands over your head.

8. ____ Studying without my CD player.

9. ____ Having worked outdoors all his life.

10. ____ Wanting to please them, she had coffee ready on their arrival.

EXERCISE 27.2*

1. ____ Without any idea how to go about it.

2. ____ Hyperbole is an extravagant exaggeration used as a figure of speech.

3. ____ Exaggerating his own influence being of great importance to him.

4. ____ Knowing the truth.

5. ____ The result of poor planning and unclear goals.

6. ____ A disaster just waiting to happen.

7. ____ Let's hear it.

8. ____ Realizing their incredulity, she stopped speaking.

9. ____ The directions printed in the booklet included in the package.

10. ____ Does she really believe what she's saying?

EXERCISE 27.3*

1. ____ Unless he knows someone in the field.

2. ____ She is educated and intelligent but no social graces.

3. ____ The sweet smell of success is often mixed with less desirable aromas.

4. ____ Peter Pocklington speaking on financial success.

5. ____ Because financial gain is, for most people, synonymous with success.

6. ____ The saying "Nothing succeeds like success."

7. ____ For the moment, not looking at the money and power aspects of the question.

8. ____ To bring to actualization the best human instincts in oneself and others?

9. ____ The more personal aspects usually not considered when the topic comes up in ordinary conversation.

10. ____ In our culture, the tendency to equate financial worth with personal success.

Independent and Dependent Clauses

A group of words containing a subject and a verb is a **clause.** There are two kinds of clauses. An **independent clause** is one that makes complete sense on its own. It can stand alone, as a sentence. A **dependent clause,** as its name suggests, cannot stand alone as a sentence; it *depends* on another clause to make complete sense.

Dependent clauses are easy to recognize, because they begin with words such as these:

Dependent-Clause Cues

after	if	until
although	in order that	what, whatever
as, as if	provided that	when, whenever
as long as	since	where, wherever, whereas
as soon as	so that	whether
because	that	which, whichever
before	though	while
even if, even though	unless	who, whom, whose

Whenever a clause begins with one of these words or phrases, it is dependent.

> A dependent clause must be attached to an independent clause. If it stands alone, it is a sentence fragment.

Here is an independent clause:

I am a poor speller.

If we put one of the dependent-clause cues in front of it, it can no longer stand alone:

Because I am a poor speller.

We can correct this kind of fragment by attaching it to an independent clause:

Because I am a poor speller, I have chained my dictionary to my wrist.

EXERCISE 27.4*

Put an *S* before each clause that is independent and therefore a sentence. Put an *F* before each clause that is dependent and therefore a sentence fragment. Underline the dependent-clause cue in each sentence fragment.

1. _____ What parents don't know.

2. _____ As she was led to believe.

3. _____ Where three roads meet.

4. _____ If he decides on that basis.

5. _____ So that the children could see the performance with no difficulty.

6. _____ Although she practised it constantly.

7. _____ Since the horse stepped on her.

8. _____ As soon as the troops arrived, the fighting stopped.

9. _____ Whichever route the bikers choose.

10. _____ Before Rudolf bought his Harley.

In Exercises 27.5 and 27.6, identify the sentence fragments by underlining the dependent-clause cue in each fragment you find.

EXERCISE 27.5*

Before the curtain went up on the lavishly decorated and beautifully lit set. The actor playing Frankie could be seen pacing up and down nervously. Although he was a veteran of many stage performances and several popular movies and was accustomed to appearing before large audiences. Which made it very strange that he would demonstrate the symptoms of stage fright so clearly. Looking closely, a careful observer might have noticed, however, that he wasn't studying his lines or rehearsing his role. In fact, unless one were right beside him and watching very closely. The real purpose of his pacing could easily be missed. Although he appeared to be alone. He was, in reality, exercising his pet cockroach.

EXERCISE 27.6*

I am not a fashionable dresser. Although I enjoy going out to restaurants and theatres and other places where the fashion-conscious tend to congregate. I am sometimes regarded as an object of curiosity. While I find my hiking boots very comfortable and my Newfoundland sweater very cosy. The patrons of the ballet to which I wore them last month seemed critical. As if, unaccountably, they disapproved of my wardrobe selection. So, in order not to attract quite so much attention and to blend in a little better with the opera crowd. In preparation for last week's premiere performance, I bought a tie. Even though it cost me almost 10 dollars. Then I began to notice something rather odd. Ever since I splurged on this purchase, a truly beautiful abstract print in iridescent yellows, greens, and blues. Which is a neckwear item that definitely commands attention. Wherever I wear it. Whether I am dressed in my blue work shirt or my red plaid. The attention my tie attracts seems to be overwhelmingly favourable. Since everyone who sees it smiles. I assume they approve; perhaps they're even envious. This response is quite unlike the reaction I used to receive. When dressed in my former, tie-less, best. I have now graduated from gauche to gorgeous, according to my girlfriend. Who knows about these things.

Most sentence fragments are dependent clauses punctuated as sentences. Fortunately, this is the easiest kind of fragment to recognize and fix. All you need to do is join the dependent clause either to the sentence that comes before it or to the one that comes after it—whichever linkage makes better sense.

One final point: if you join your sentence fragment to the independent clause that follows it, you must separate the two clauses with a comma (see Chapter 37, p. 357).

Read the following example to yourself; then read it aloud (remember, last sentence first).

> Montreal is a sequence of ghettos. Although I was born and brought up there. My experience of French was a pathetically limited and distorted one.

The second "sentence" sounds incomplete, and the dependent-clause cue at the beginning of it is the clue you need to identify it as a sentence fragment. You could join the fragment to the sentence before it, but then you would get "Montreal is a sequence of ghettos, although I was born and brought up there," which doesn't make sense. Clearly the fragment should be linked to the sentence that follows it, like this:

Montreal is a sequence of ghettos. Although I was born and brought up there, my experience of French was a pathetically limited and distorted one.

(from Mordecai Richler, "Quebec Oui, Ottawa Non!")

EXERCISE 27.7*

The following paragraph contains both independent clauses and dependent clauses (fragments), all punctuated as if they were complete sentences. Letting meaning be your guide, join each fragment to the most appropriate independent clause. Remember to punctuate correctly. Then turn to the answer section to compare your sentences with the author's. (Excerpt from Pierre Berton's introduction to *The New City: A Prejudiced View of Toronto* by Henri Rossier and Pierre Berton, Toronto: Macmillan, 1961; 1961, cited in Alan Dawe, *Profile of a Nation,* Toronto: Macmillan, 1969. Adapted with permission of the author.)

The attitude to Toronto takes two forms. There is first the attitude of the non-Torontonians. Who live in places like St. John's, Maple Creek, and Vancouver. Then there is the attitude of the Torontonians themselves.

The attitude of the outsider is compounded of envy, malice and pity. In about equal quantities. It is admitted that Torontonians make large sums of money. But not much else. Certainly they never have any fun. There is none of the leisurely gracious living that is to be found in Montreal, say. Or Halifax, or Okotoks, Alberta. When a young man sets out for Toronto. He is surrounded by a covey of friends, all commiserating with him and whispering to him. To look about for a job for them in the big city. It is generally acknowledged that the bereaved young man will return, but he rarely does. If he sees his friends again, he sees them in Toronto. Where they all have a good cry and talk over the grand old days. When they were poor in Pelvis or West Webfoot.

The attitude of the Torontonians is that they simply do not care. What people think of them. They live in Toronto and that is good enough for them. For years a host of magazine articles, newspaper editorials, and commentators have baited Toronto. Toronto refuses to swallow the bait. One mayor tried to launch a campaign. To make the city popular but it fizzled out after a few days. Torontonians do not really care about being popular; in fact, about half the criticism about the city comes from its own people. Nobody baits Toronto quite as much as those who live there.

EXERCISE 27.8

Make each clause below into a dependent clause by adding one of the dependent-clause cues. Then add an independent clause to make a complete sentence.

Example: He felt very nervous.
             Although he felt very nervous (dependent-clause cue added).
             Although he felt very nervous, *he gave a good speech* (independent clause added).

1. They are hopeful.
2. He ate the cold leftover pizza.
3. She won't know immediately.
4. I want to see the new house.
5. There are eleven now.
6. Nothing ever goes right.
7. He is usually more careful.
8. She washed it thoroughly.
9. According to those in the media, the parties' opinions vary greatly.
10. Everyone knows something about computers' probable impact on future work.

EXERCISE 27.9

Using the following dependent-clause cues, write dependent clauses of your own. Then make each into a complete sentence by adding an independent clause. Watch your punctuation!

1. as long as
2. even though
3. until
4. in order that
5. whatever

6. though
7. whether
8. whom
9. which
10. after

EXERCISE 27.10

As a final test of your skill in correcting sentence fragments, try this exercise. Put an *S* before each complete sentence and an *F* before each sentence fragment. Make each fragment into a complete sentence.

1. _____ Although the class was long, boring, and frustrating for me because I hadn't read the assignment and couldn't understand the discussion.

2. _____ Pierre Berton's famous definition of a Canadian: "Someone who knows how to make love in a canoe."

3. _____ The point being that hard work, intelligence, and dedication are not always rewarded.

4. _____ Getting promoted is often a matter of knowing the right people and of being in the right place at the right time.

5. _____ Probably the fastest growing but least publicized of modern crimes being data theft, sometimes known as computer tapping.

6. _____ Help me figure this one out, would you please?

7. _____ As long as I've known you, an honest, patient, loyal friend.

8. _____ There are several things you should think about first.

9. _____ Goodman Ace's famous quip that television was called a "medium" because things on it were rarely well done.

10. _____ The problem resulting from our stumbling blindly into the future, ignorant of the harm technological advances can bring.

CHAPTER 28

Solving Run-On Problems

Just as a sentence can lack certain elements and thus be a fragment, so can it contain too many elements. A sentence with too much in it or with inadequate punctuation between clauses is a **run-on.** Run-ons occur most often when you write in a hurry or when you're disorganized and not thinking clearly. If you think about what you want to say and punctuate carefully, you shouldn't have any problems with them.

There are three kinds of run-on sentences: the comma splice, the fused sentence, and the true run-on.

Comma Splices and Fused Sentences

As its name suggests, the **comma splice** occurs when two complete sentences (independent clauses) are joined together with only a comma between them. Here's an example:

I was up all night, I'm exhausted.

A **fused sentence** occurs when two complete sentences are joined together with no punctuation at all:

I was up all night I'm exhausted.

> 1. The easiest way to fix a comma splice or a fused sentence is to join the independent clauses with a semicolon.

I was up all night; I'm exhausted.

To be sure you understand how to use semicolons correctly, read Chapter 38.

> 2. Another way to fix a comma splice or a fused sentence is to add an appropriate linking word between the two clauses.

Two types of linking words will work.

1. You can insert one of the following words: *and, but, or, nor, for, so,* or *yet.* These words should be preceded by a comma.

    I was up all night, and I'm exhausted.

2. You can insert one of the dependent-clause cues listed in Chapter 27, on p. 261.

    Because I was up all night, I'm exhausted.

> 3. The third way to fix a comma splice or a fused sentence is to make the independent clauses into separate sentences.

I was up all night. I'm exhausted.

All three solutions to the problem require that you use a word or punctuation mark strong enough to come between two independent clauses.

The sentences in the following exercises will give you practice in fixing comma splices and fused sentences. Correct the sentences where necessary, and then check your answers. (Since there are three ways to fix these errors, your answers may differ somewhat from our suggestions.) If you find that you're confused about when to use a semicolon and when to use a period, be sure to read p. 361 before going on.

EXERCISE 28.1*

1. The teacher's late, let's go!
2. Just let me do the talking, you'll get us a ticket if you open your mouth.
3. I keep buying lottery tickets, but I've won only once.

4. Hitting a golf ball may look easy, but it's not.
5. As long as you smile when you speak, you can say almost anything.
6. Montreal used to be called Ville Ste. Marie, I think, but before that it had a Native name.
7. Students today need summer jobs, tuition and living costs are too much for most families.
8. Bryan will be going to college if he is accepted, his parents have lots of money.
9. My word processor makes writing much easier, though it doesn't seem to spell any better than I do.
10. I am seeking a hero after whom I can model my life, so far I've rejected Sly Stallone, Madonna, and Hulk Hogan.

EXERCISE 28.2*

1. The comma splice gets its name from the film splice, two pieces of film are taped, or spliced, together.
2. Old movies are sometimes choppy and disconnected, they have been spliced badly or too often.
3. Two sentences cannot be spliced together with a comma, you need to use a semicolon or a period or a linking word between them.
4. You should be particularly careful when using linking words like "however," "consequently," "therefore," and "moreover," these words need a semicolon before them and a comma after when they join two independent clauses.
5. This isn't a very difficult rule, in fact, it's one of the easiest rules to learn because it has no exceptions.
6. The fused sentence is named after a melting process fusing is joining two things together that ordinarily are not connected.
7. Two independent clauses cannot be fused together with no punctuation you need a linking word, or a semicolon, or a period to join them.
8. What a sneaky way of reinforcing the lesson, it's almost diabolical.
9. Please don't put your feet on the table just because your mother isn't around to yell at you doesn't mean you can behave like a boor, other people have to use the table too.
10. There is not much future in typewriter repair, it has gone the way of blacksmithing and tobacco farming.

EXERCISE 28.3*

1. A Canadian who speaks three languages is called multilingual, one who speaks two languages is called bilingual, one who speaks only one language is called an English Canadian.
2. I'm sure the job couldn't have been as bad as he claims, maybe he just didn't try hard enough.

3. Meetings such as this are fine for small groups, large groups have to be handled in a different way.
4. I'll be glad to help you out, when you need me just call, I'll be here all day.
5. In Canada, winter is more than a season, it's a bad joke.
6. Perfection is probably impossible to achieve, but that doesn't mean you should stop trying.
7. It may seem foolish, especially after all the wrangling over our new constitution, but I still believe in a unified Canada, I believe in one nation extending from sea to sea. The Fathers of Confederation were right, a federation of provinces can work.
8. Career opportunities appear very good for students in a wide range of technical programs, however most employers are looking for people with experience as well as training.
9. People with high-technology skills are urgently required in several fields, plastics processing, mould-making, and tool- and die-making are three examples.
10. For college students in technology programs, then, the future looks bright, however a diploma does not necessarily guarantee job security.

The Run-On Sentence

In the true **run-on sentence,** too many ideas are crowded into one sentence. In general, a sentence should convey no more than two ideas. There is no hard-and-fast rule about how many clauses you may have in a sentence, but more than two independent clauses can result in a sentence that's hard to read and even harder to understand.

> When I first started living away from home on my own, I decided I would like to have some company in my tiny apartment, so I bought three fish together with a bowl that very soon proved to be too small as the fish grew and grew, quadrupling in size in only a few short months, but since I couldn't really afford one of the monster aquariums recommended by the local pet store in my neighbourhood, I traded my fish together with their bowl to a friend who lived on the other side of town for a kitten his female cat had recently produced, and that is how I came to own Max, my best and truest friend and constant companion.

It's obvious that the writer who created this monster got carried away with enthusiasm for the tale and just scribbled down everything that came to mind. If you take your time, keep your readers in mind, and revise conscientiously, you won't make this sort of error. When you find run-ons in your writing, you can fix them by following two steps:

> 1. Cut out all unnecessary words.
> 2. Apply the three solutions for comma splices and fused sentences: semicolons, linking words, and sentence breaks.

Here's how you can turn a monster sentence into a clear, correct one:

First, read through your sentence carefully and identify any words or phrases that are not absolutely essential to your meaning:

> When I *first* started living *away from home* on my own, I decided I would like to have some company *in my tiny apartment,* so I bought three fish together with a bowl that *very* soon proved to be too small *as the fish grew and grew, quadrupling in size in only a few short months,* but since I couldn't *really* afford one of the monster aquariums recommended by the local pet store *in my neighbourhood,* I traded my fish *together with their bowl* to a friend *who lived on the other side of town* for a kitten *his female cat had recently produced,* and that is how I came to own Max, my best *and* and truest friend and constant companion.

Run-on sentences are often plagued by **wordiness.** (See Chapter 47 for hints on how to eliminate unnecessary words from your writing.) In this example, the words in italics are unnecessary, redundant, or padding, and should be eliminated. Here's how the sentence reads without them:

> When I started living on my own, I decided I would like to have some company, so I bought three fish together with a bowl that soon proved to be too small, but since I couldn't afford one of the monster aquariums recommended by the local pet store, I traded my fish to a friend for a kitten, and that is how I came to own Max, my truest friend and constant companion.

This version is an improvement, but it still contains too many ideas for one sentence. Let's apply step 2.

> When I started living on my own, I decided I would like to have some company. I bought three fish together with a bowl that soon proved to be too small. Since I couldn't afford one of the monster aquariums recommended by the local pet store, I traded my fish to a friend for a kitten. That is how I came to own Max, my truest friend and constant companion.

This version is clear, concise, and easy to read.

EXERCISE 28.4*

Using the four types of corrections you've learned in this chapter, make the following sentences easier to read. There is more than one right way of fixing each sentence; just be sure your corrected sentences make sense and are easy to read. The answers we've provided are only suggestions.

1. I personally think that people talk too much, if they listened to themselves more closely, they would probably talk less.

2. Learning to ride a horse all by yourself without instruction or lessons is very difficult I have a friend who taught himself to ride by watching old Clint Eastwood films, he should be out of traction in a couple of weeks from now.

3. Arnold Schwarzenegger will most probably not be remembered as one of the world's truly great actors, his movies are far too popular to qualify as great classics, however, he will be remembered as someone who definitely made the most of his talents.

4. According to her friends, Sabina's homemade wine is really quite drinkable despite some unfortunate harshness, the colour is quite good, the bouquet is really excellent, the afterburn is pretty impressive too.

5. Going bald isn't so bad now that many men and even some women are shaving their heads these days as a fashion statement, in fact, baldness is a real advantage sometimes I don't have to spend time fussing with my hair in the morning and high winds never bother me in the slightest.

6. Having inherited her great-aunt's millions, Drusilla has become a complete hypocrite, insisting with every other breath that she hasn't

changed a bit, she drives a Rolls flaunts furs and drips with bunches of diamonds but do you think she ever offers to buy lunch?

7. Beagles, dogs which are a kind of small hound dog, make really excellent pets because of their happy, cheerful, affectionate nature and the reason I know is that I personally have owned five of them over the past few years.

8. When I woke up this morning, I had a hard time getting up out of bed because I knew I ought to eat some breakfast but I didn't have time and then realized I had to finish an essay for a 9:00 class, and because of the cold I suspected my car probably wouldn't start and I wouldn't likely be able to get to school on time anyway, and so I just decided to stay in bed.

9. Canada's eternal squabbling about French versus English may soon be irrelevant since linguistic analysts predict that Mandarin and Spanish will be the languages spoken by the majority of the world's population within a few years and several Canadian school systems are already offering these two languages in their curricula to give their students an extra added advantage when they graduate into a world of international free trade.

10. The United Nations must consider the circumstances very carefully before sending peacekeeping troops to a war-torn nation to keep the peace, unless the situation is a threat to world peace or is so completely out of control that innocent people and children are being killed the

United Nations must remain neutral if it does not it runs the risk of help-

ing one political faction to gain dominance over another by interfering.

EXERCISE 28.5*

Correct the run-ons in the following passage. Try to use a variety of ways to revise them into clear, concise, easy-to-read sentences. Our answers are suggestions.

On opening night of our school play, I was more nervous than I have

ever been in my life before or have ever been since, because, while I knew

the lines for my rather insignificant part in the plot, I also knew that our

crew was under-rehearsed and really not ready to go before a live audience

with this play and I was terrified that something would go wrong while I

was on stage and I would be made to look like a fool in front of all my

family and friends, who, of course, had front-row seats. As it turned out

my fears were justified, the performance was a complete disaster.

Within ten minutes of the curtain going up, a sound cue was missed

and the whole cast, myself included, stood around helplessly waiting for

the phone to ring so that the heroine could answer it, as was called for in

the script but finally after what seemed like an eternity the sound person

woke up and started the sound tape but unfortunately she was so

flustered she hit the wrong cue and instead of the telephone ring, we

heard the noise of a gunshot. After a short pause while we looked at each

other in panic, the heroine muttered something about the servants

shooting mice in the basement and picked up the phone which still had

not rung, and there was a stir in the audience they were stifling giggles.

It got worse, much worse, in the second act, when the killer tried to escape with the actor playing the role of the detective right behind him, the door through which he was supposed to make his exit stuck shut and trying to jerk the door open, the villain pulled half the set down on top of both of them. At least this allowed him to escape the audience was now laughing loudly as the second-act curtain fell.

In the dramatic third and final act, the hero was supposed to shoot the villain just as he was poised about to stab the poor helpless heroine but when the hero aimed his pistol and pulled the trigger of course the phone rang. Completely undone, the actor playing the villain had a sudden inspiration, he got the brilliant idea of pretending to die of a heart attack and keeled over. By this time, the audience were no longer able to contain their waves of laughter that washed over us, they were practically in hysterics as we took our bows, but all was not completely lost. They called us back repeatedly, again and again, for curtain calls and even stood to cheer as the curtains parted for the fourth time apparently they had mistaken our tragic drama of death and revenge for a slapstick comedy. I enjoyed the applause and the congratulations afterwards but it took two days for my tension headache to subside, I never went on stage again.

EXERCISE 28.6

As a final test of your ability to identify and correct sentence errors, supply the appropriate sentence breaks to make this garble into a grammatically correct paragraph.

Gordon is convinced that he is a great musician all that he requires is to discover the instrument on which his genius can flower in the course of trying to make this discovery, he has tried the alto recorder, the B flat clarinet, the Spanish guitar, and the five-string banjo each of these instruments was taken up with enthusiasm and devotion, but each was cast aside within a few months as it revealed that it could not bring forth Gordon's hidden musical talents several suggestions were made at about this time in his musical career, the most memorable by his parents who had to endure the loud learning process on each instrument, but Gordon was certain of success and deaf to any hint that his lack of musicianship was due to anything but his bad luck in not being able to discover his proper medium his parents gave up his friends deserted him but still he persisted his refusal to quit was finally rewarded and now he may be heard recorded on several albums and live with his group at many music festivals after about twelve frustrating years of experimentation Gordon discovered the instrument that best expresses his talent: the kazoo.

CHAPTER 29

Solving Modifier Problems

Felix was complimented on a great game and a fine job of goaltending *by his mother.*

Snarling furiously and baring his teeth, Maurice crawled through a basement window only to confront an angry watchdog.

When she was a first-year student, the English professor told Mara she could *almost* write all her assignments on computer.

These sentences show what can happen to your writing if you aren't sure how to use modifiers. A **modifier** is a word or group of words that adds information about another word in a sentence. In the examples above, the italicized words are modifiers. Used correctly, modifiers describe, explain, or limit another word, making its meaning more precise. Used carelessly, however, modifiers can cause confusion or, even worse, amusement. Few things are more embarrassing than being laughed at when you didn't mean to be funny.

You need to be able to recognize and solve two kinds of modifier problems: misplaced modifiers and dangling modifiers.

Misplaced Modifiers

Modifiers must be as close as possible to the words they apply to. Usually, readers will assume that a modifier modifies whatever it's next to. It's important to remember this, because, as the following examples show, changing the position of a modifier can change the meaning of your sentence.

Ahmed walked (only) as far as the corner store. (He didn't walk any farther.)

Ahmed (only) walked as far as the corner store. (He didn't ride or fly.)

(Only) Ahmed walked as far as the corner store. (No one else went.)

Ahmed walked as far as the (only) corner store. (There were no other corner stores.)

> To make sure a modifier is in the right place, ask yourself, "What does it apply to?" and put it beside that word or words.

When a modifier is not close enough to the word(s) it refers to, it is said to be misplaced. A **misplaced modifier** can be *a single word in the wrong place:*

The supervisor told me they needed someone who could use both Excel and WordPerfect (badly.)

Is some company really hiring people to do poor work? Or does the company urgently need someone familiar with spreadsheets and word processing? Obviously, the modifier *badly* belongs next to *needed:*

The supervisor told me they (badly) needed someone who could use both Excel and WordPerfect.

> Be especially careful with these words: *almost, nearly, just, only, even, hardly, merely, scarcely.* Put them right before the words they modify.

Misplaced: She (nearly) answered every question.
Correctly placed: She answered (nearly) every question.

Misplaced: After driving all night, we (almost) arrived at 7:00 A.M.
Correctly placed: After driving all night, we arrived at (almost) 7:00 A.M.

A misplaced modifier can also be *a group of words in the wrong place:*

(Bundled up in down clothing to keep warm,) the dog team waited for the driver.

The modifier, *bundled up in down clothing,* is too far away from the word it is supposed to modify, *driver.* In fact, it seems to modify *dog team,* making the sentence ridiculous. We need to rewrite the sentence:

The dog team waited for the driver, bundled up in down clothing to keep warm.

Look at this one:

I drove to Saskatoon, where my aunt lives in a rental car.

In a rental car applies to *drove* and should be closer to it:

I drove in a rental car to Saskatoon, where my aunt lives.

Notice that a modifier need not always go right next to what it modifies; it should, however, be as close as possible to it.

Occasionally, as in the examples above, the modifier is obviously out of place. The writer's intention is clear, and the sentences are easy to correct. But sometimes modifiers are misplaced in such a way that the meaning is not clear, as in the following example:

Raj said after the game that he wanted to talk to the press.

Did Raj *say* it after the game? Or is he going to *talk to the press* after the game? To avoid confusion, we must move the modifier and, depending on which meaning we want, write either

After the game, Raj said he wanted to talk to the press.

or

Raj said he wanted to talk to the press after the game.

Now try your hand at relocating modifiers. In Exercises 29.1 and 29.2, rewrite the sentences that contain misplaced modifiers, positioning the modifiers correctly. Check your answers to the first set before continuing.

EXERCISE 29.1*

1. Trevor left the can of Pet Grrmet out for the dog that he had opened.

2. Our supervisor told us on the first day no one takes coffee breaks.

3. We only made a real effort when the score got close.

4. Professor Green told us in September he thought our class was a hopeless case.

5. We almost enjoyed the whole movie; only the ending was a disappointment.

6. Matt and Christie found an apartment in a highrise within walking distance of the campus with two bedrooms and a sunken living room.

7. There just are enough pieces to go around.

8. It seems there is almost a game every day during baseball season.

9. A charming, intelligent companion is sought by a vertically challenged but wealthy gentleman who looks good in evening gowns and diamonds.

10. One of us could only go because there was enough money just to buy one ticket.

EXERCISE 29.2*

1. One finds the best Chinese food in those restaurants where the Chinese eat usually.

2. He caught sight of a canary and several finches using his new binoculars.

3. Juan had played ball professionally before coming to the Blue Jays for several major American teams.

4. The football practices have been organized for players who are not with a team in the summertime as a keep-fit measure.

5. Vancouver is a wonderful city for anyone who likes rain and fog to live in.

6. Some games are less demanding in terms of time and equipment, such as tiddlywinks.

7. The Human Rights Code prohibits discrimination against anyone who is applying for a job on the basis of race, sex, or age.

8. I was able to loosen the clamp that held the broken cable in place with a screwdriver.

9. They waited breathlessly under the trees for the return of their dog, which had been sprayed by a skunk with an open can of tomato juice.

10. Tonight Sue Johanson will lead a panel discussion on relaxation, including how to tone and stretch muscles, how to relieve tension, and even how to sleep through sex.

Dangling Modifiers

A **dangling modifier** occurs when there is *no appropriate word in the sentence for the modifier to apply to.* Or, a modifier is said to be "dangling" when the sentence does not contain a *specific word* or *idea* to which the modifier could sensibly refer. With no appropriate word to modify, the modifier *seems* to apply to whatever it's next to, often with ridiculous results:

After a good night's sleep, my teachers were impressed with my unusual alertness.
(This sentence seems to say that the teachers had a good night's sleep.)
Trying desperately to finish an essay, my room-mate's stereo made it impossible to concentrate.
(The *stereo* was writing an essay?)

Dangling modifiers are trickier to fix than misplaced ones; you can't simply move danglers to another spot in the sentence. There are, however, two ways in which you can fix them. One way requires that you remember this rule:

> When a modifier comes at the beginning of a sentence, it modifies the subject of the sentence.

(The rule has exceptions called adverbial modifiers, but they won't give you any trouble. Example: Quickly she did as she was told.)

This rule means that you can avoid dangling modifiers by choosing the subjects of your sentences carefully. All you have to do is make sure the subject is an appropriate one for the modifier to apply to. Using this method, we can rewrite our two examples by changing the subjects:

After a good night's sleep, I impressed my teachers with my unusual alertness.

Trying desperately to finish an essay, I found it impossible to concentrate because of my room-mate's stereo.

Another way to correct a dangling modifier is by changing it into a dependent clause:

After I had had a good night's sleep, my teachers were impressed with my unusual alertness.

When I was trying desperately to finish an essay, my room-mate's stereo made it impossible to concentrate.

Sometimes a dangling modifier comes at the end of a sentence:

A Neon is the car to buy, looking for power, style, and an affordable price.

Can you correct this sentence? Try it; then look at the suggestions at the foot of the page.

Here are two suggestions:
1. *Add a subject:* Looking for power, style, and an affordable price, I decided a Neon was the car to buy.
2. *Change the dangler to a dependent clause:* A Neon is the car to buy, since I am looking for power, style, and an affordable price.

Here is a summary of the steps to follow in solving modifier problems:

---

1. Ask "What does the modifier apply to?"
2. Be sure there is a word or group of words *in the sentence* for the modifier to apply to.
3. Put the modifier as close as possible to the word or word group it applies to.

EXERCISE 29.3*

Most of the following sentences contain dangling modifiers. Make corrections by changing the subject of the sentence to one the modifier can appropriately apply to. There is no one "right" way to correct each sentence; our answers are only suggestions.

1. Driving recklessly and without lights, the police stopped Gina at a road block.
2. My supervisor gave me a lecture about punctuality after being late twice in one week.
3. After criticizing both my work and my attitude, I was fired.
4. Standing a full 2.5 m tall and weighing about 300 kg, Patricia decided not to antagonize the bear.
5. After scoring the winning goal in overtime, a huge celebration wound through the city.
6. As a conscientious and dedicated teacher, the workload sometimes seems overwhelming to Nina.
7. In less than a minute after applying the ointment, the pain began to ease.
8. Falling in love with a new man every week, Amy is an enthusiastic fan of the afternoon soap *Trouble, Tears, and Tragedy.*
9. Whistling loudly, the graveyard didn't seem like such a frightening place.
10. It was a great moment: after making the speech of a lifetime, the delegates chose her to lead the party into the next election.

EXERCISE 29.4*

Correct the dangling modifiers in Exercise 29.3 by changing them into dependent clauses.

EXERCISE 29.5*

In the following sentences, correct the misplaced and dangling modifiers in any way you choose. Our answers are only suggestions.

1. Only she was the baker's daughter, but she could loaf all day.
2. Being horribly hung over, the only problem with a free bar is knowing when to quit.
3. Plump, round, and purple, the judges were impressed by Sandor's turnips.
4. In a hurry to get to the interview on time, my résumé was left lying on my desk at home.
5. As a college student constantly faced with new assignments, the pressure is sometimes intolerable.
6. Reading the national edition of *The Globe & Mail*, the provincial premiers plan to meet with the prime minister next week in Calgary.
7. After looking at the half-price raincoat all week, they sold it before I got to the store on payday.
8. The Canadian Brass receives enthusiastic acclaim for its witty presentation, its wide repertoire, and its clarity of tone from Vancouver to St. John's.
9. Rolling on her back, eager to have her tummy scratched, Queen Elizabeth couldn't resist the little Corgi puppy.
10. Deeply concerned about the spread of AIDS and wanting to do something to prevent more deaths in the community, volunteers to mount an awareness campaign were solicited.

EXERCISE 29.6

Correct the misplaced and dangling modifiers in the sentences below, using any solution you choose.

1. Obviously having drunk too much, I drove poor Tanya to her apartment, made her a pot of coffee, and called her mother.

2. When trying for your Red Cross bronze medal, your examiner will consider speed, endurance, and resuscitation techniques.

3. The University of Alberta's research in heart disease this month will be summarized in a special issue of the *Canadian Medical Journal*.

4. Trapped under a delicate crystal wine glass on the elegantly set table, his guests observed that most despised of uninvited dinner guests, a cockroach.

5. Not being reliable about arriving on time, I can't hire her to supervise others who are punctual.

6. The parks superintendent explained that reforestation was urgent in British Columbia's northernmost provincial parks on Friday at the Victoria conference.

7. A worm-eating warbler was spotted by Hazel Miller while walking along the branch of a tree and singing.

8. The only used motorcycles we could find had been ridden by bikers which were in pretty bad shape.

9. We always pay our respects to our friends and relatives when they have passed on in a funeral parlour.

10. "This bus has a seating capacity of 56 passengers with a maximum height of 14 feet, 6 inches." (Sign on a double-decker bus in Charlottetown, P.E.I.)

CHAPTER 30

The Parallelism Principle

When writing about items in a series—such as main points in a preview statement, for example—you must be sure all the items are **parallel;** that is, they must be written in the same grammatical form.

> Krystal likes biking, shopping, and to sleep.

The items in this list are not parallel. Two ending in *-ing,* but the third *(to hike)* is the infinitive form of the verb. To correct the sentence, you must make all the items in the list take the same grammatical form—either

> Krystal likes to bike, to shop, and to sleep.

or

> Krystal likes biking, shopping, and sleeping.

Correct faulty parallelism by giving the items in a series the same grammatical form.

One way to tell whether all the items in a list are parallel is to picture (or actually write) the items in list form, one below the other, aligning the similar elements. That way, you can make sure that all the elements are the same—that they are all words, or phrases, or clauses.

NOT PARALLEL	PARALLEL

Amin is kind,
        considerate, and
    likes to help.
	Amin is kind,
	        considerate, and
	    helpful.

NOT PARALLEL	PARALLEL
I support myself by tending bar, piano, and shooting pool.	I support myself by tending bar, playing piano, and shooting pool.
Her upbringing made her neat, polite, and an obnoxious person.	Her upbringing made her neat, polite, and obnoxious.
Gordon tries to do what is right, different things, and make a profit.	Gordon tries to do what is right, what is different, and what is profitable.
With his sharp mind, by having the boss as his uncle, and few enemies, he'll go far.	With his sharp mind, the boss as his uncle, and few enemies, he'll go far.

or

Having a sharp mind,
   the boss as his uncle, and
   few enemies,
      he'll go far.

As you can see, achieving parallelism is partly a matter of developing an ear for the sound of a correct list. Practice, and the exercises in this chapter, will help. As you work through the exercises, try to spot faulty parallelism from the *sound* of the sentences, before you examine them closely to correct their mistakes. Check your answers to each set before going on. There are several ways to correct parallelism problems; our answers are only suggestions.

EXERCISE 30.1*

1. This program is easy to understand and using it is not difficult, either.

2. We were told that we would have to leave and to take nothing with us.

3. We organized our findings, wrote the report, and our presentation was made.

4. Today's personal computers are fast, high-powered, and compact in size.

5. Rudolf's doctor advised that he should be careful with his back and not to strain his mind.

6. The company is looking for an employee who has a car and knowing the city would be a help.

7. To me, winter means driving in dangerous conditions, bulky clothing, and huge heating bills.

8. Although he refused to get into high boots or wearing a toque, Bruce did accept my offer of a down-filled jacket.

9. We noticed with approval the in-ground pool, the trout pond, which was spring-fed, and the tennis court that could be used in all weather conditions.

10. If it is to be useful, your report must be organized clearly, the writing must be good, and your research should be thorough.

EXERCISE 30.2*

1. Bodybuilding has made me what I am today: physically perfect, very prosperous financially, and practically friendless.

2. If there is no heaven, then hell can't exist either.

3. In my tiny home town, two significantly related crimes prevail: vandalism, and there is a lot of drug trafficking.

4. I'd like to help, but I'm too tired, I'm too poor, and my time is already taken up with other things.

5. I wanted either a Mother's pizza or I wanted a Big Mac from McDonald's.

6. Garfield understands pretty clearly what he can get away with and what he can't.

7. My sister, who's trying to teach me to play tennis, says that my forehand and serve are all right, but to work on strengthening my backhand.

8. The two factors thought to be most important in a long-lasting marriage are how committed each partner is to the marriage and the willingness to compromise.

9. Yuri claimed that, through repetition and being firm, he had trained his guppy to be obedient, quiet, and show loyalty.

10. The new budget must deal with several major problems, two of them being the devalued Canadian dollar and the fact that the inflation rate rose so high.

EXERCISE 30.3*

Make the following lists parallel. In each case there's more than one way to do it, because you can make your items parallel with any item in the list. Therefore, your answers may differ from ours. Here's an example:

Wrong: Stick handling   score a goal

Right: Stick handling   goal scoring
Also right: handle the stick   score a goal

1. *Wrong:* wine   women   singing
   Right:

2. *Wrong:* privately   in public
   Right:

3. *Wrong:* employers   those working for
                              the employer
   Right:

4. *Wrong:* lying about all   to do whatever I
           morning   please
   Right:

5. *Wrong:* individually   as a group
   Right:

6. *Wrong:* happy   healthy   wisdom
   Right:

7. *Wrong:* doing your best   don't give up
   Right:

8. *Wrong:* information   education   entertaining
   Right:

9. *Wrong:* insufficient time   too little money   not enough staff
   Right:

10. *Wrong:* French is the   English is the best   Profanity is best
            language of   language for   in German
            love   business
    Right:

EXERCISE 30.4*

As a test of your mastery of parallel structure, try correcting these sentences.

1. In order to succeed in this economy, small businesses must be creative, look forward, and show innovation and flexibility.
2. Not being able to speak the language causes confusion, is frustrating, and it's embarrassing.
3. Although the first candidate we interviewed seemed frightened and to be shy, the second was a composed person and showed an outgoing personality.
4. Trying your best and success are not always the same thing, but of the two, the former is the more important.
5. Our chances of a long-term relationship are slim since getting dressed up is something you enjoy, you love to dance, and you like crowds: three things that I consider torture.
6. Lowering our profit margin, prices will be raised, and two management layoffs will enable us to meet our budget.
7. To lick one's fingers and picking one's teeth in a sophisticated dining room is bound to attract criticism and perhaps even being invited to leave.

8. New potatoes out of the garden, vine-ripened beefsteak tomatoes, and freestone peaches picked by hand from our tree: these are my favourite summer foods.
9. After an enjoyable dinner, I like to drink a cappuccino, a dark-chocolate mint, and, occasionally, a good cigar.
10. Influential factors in any nation's economic regression are bad management of natural resources, policies regarding national debt might be unwise, and workers' demands may be inflationary.

EXERCISE 30.5

Correct the faulty parallelism in the following paragraph.

The dictionary can be both a useful resource and an educational entertainment. Everyone knows that its three chief functions are to check spelling, for finding out the meanings of words, and what the correct pronunciation is. Few people, however, use the dictionary for discovery and learning. There are several methods of using the dictionary as an aid to discovery. One is randomly looking at words, another is to read a page or two thoroughly, and still another is by skimming through words until you find an unfamiliar one. It is by this latter method that I discovered the word "steatopygous," a term I now try to use at least once a day. You can increase your vocabulary significantly by using the dictionary, and of course a large and varied vocabulary can be used to baffle your colleagues, employers will be impressed, and your English teacher will be surprised.

CHAPTER 31

Refining by Combining

To reinforce what you've learned so far about sentence structure, try your voice and your hand (preferably with a pencil in it) at sentence combining. You've freed your writing of fragments; you've cast out demon comma splices; you're riding herd on run-ons. You may find, however, that your sentences, although technically correct, are choppy or repetitious. And you may be bored with conveying the same idea in the same old way. Sentence combining will not only test your mastery of sentence structure but also enable you to polish and refine your writing.

What is sentence combining? Sometimes called sentence generating, sentence building, sentence revising, or embedding, **sentence combining** is a technique that enables you to avoid a choppy, monotonous style while at the same time producing correct sentences. You can combine sentences in three ways:

> 1. Link two or more short sentences into a longer one using a connecting word such as *and, or,* or *but.*
> 2. Merge two or more short sentences into a longer one using dependent-clause cues (see Chapter 27).
> 3. Combine clusters of related sentences into paragraphs.

Let's look at an example of two short, technically correct sentences that could be combined:

The paperboy collects on Fridays.

The paperboy delivers *The Winnipeg Free Press* on Saturdays.

There are several ways of combining these two statements into a single smooth sentence:

The paperboy delivers *The Winnipeg Free Press* on Saturdays and collects on Fridays.

The paperboy, who delivers *The Winnipeg Free Press* on Saturdays, collects on Fridays.

On Fridays, the paperboy collects for *The Winnipeg Free Press*, which he delivers on Saturdays.

The aim of sentence combining is to make good sentences, not long ones. Don't forget that clarity is essential and that brevity has force. By rearranging words, changing their form, deleting repetitious or unnecessary words or phrases, and adding clear connectives, you can combine a number of short statements into several acceptable sentences.

Here's an example:

1. Correct but stilted sentences conveying an idea:

    Pierre Trudeau was an influence.

    He influenced Canadian politics.

    His influence was strong in the 1970s.

2. Correct and smooth sentences conveying the same idea:

    Pierre Trudeau had a strong influence on Canadian politics in the 1970s.

    Pierre Trudeau strongly influenced Canadian politics in the 1970s.

    In the 1970s, Canadian politics was strongly influenced by Pierre Trudeau.

The skills that you learn by combining sentences identify you as a perceptive and sensitive writer. They are useful not only in writing and speaking, but also in reading, listening, and problem solving.

In the following exercises, make sure you rehearse your solutions *orally* before you write them. You may also want to refer to Chapters 39 and 40 for advice on using the comma and the semicolon, respectively.

EXERCISE 31.1*

Combine the following sentences, using the connecting word *and, but, or, nor, for, so,* or *yet*.

1. The Beatles are a musical institution.
   Their music appeals to every generation.

2. Kate Bush does not give live performances.
   She does not tour with her music.

3. Janet Jackson has a famous brother.
   She had to work hard to create a unique sound.

4. Van Halen is a progressive-rock group.
   They take offence at being labelled "heavy-metal."

5. You can read about Michael Jackson's skin-bleaching routine in medical journals.
   You can listen to "Black or White."

6. The Rolling Stones originated in the 1960s.
   They are still performing now, in the 1990s.

7. Madonna is considered a controversial artist.
   She has made several sexually explicit videos.

8. Phil Collins is a popular contemporary solo artist.
   His roots go back to Genesis.

9. Bryan Adams is to be commended for his work on "All for One."
   Rod Stewart and Sting contributed to making the song a success.

10. Jethro Tull is unusual among popular rock groups.
    They occasionally feature classical instruments such as the flute.

EXERCISE 31.2*

Using dependent-clause cues (see Chapter 27, p. 261), combine the following sentences into longer, more interesting units.

1. The Calgary Flames have been a mainstay in the NHL.
   The team moved from Atlanta.

2. Fred McGriff has a devastating swing.
   He is one of the most feared hitters in the National League.

3. Roberto Alomar of the Toronto Blue Jays won a "gold glove."
   It was in recognition of his outstanding defensive skills.

4. Deion Sanders is a talented athlete.
   He is playing baseball for the Atlanta Braves or football for the Atlanta Falcons.

5. The Blue Jays always seem to win.
   The SkyDome roof is closed.

6. The Vancouver Canucks are now acknowledged as a team to be reckoned with.
   They struggled for years to improve.

7. The Montreal Expos draw impressive crowds to Olympic Stadium.
   They are winning.

8. The Montreal Canadiens have won many Stanley Cups.
   The Quebec Nordiques have yet to win even one.

9. Wayne Gretzky is an exceptional hockey player.
   Some sports writers consider him a defensive liability.

10. Tony Fernandez is an important role model for his team.
    He is a bigger role model for children in the Dominican Republic.
    Tony Fernandez comes from the Dominican Republic.

EXERCISE 31.3*

Combine the following sentences, using the connecting words listed in Exercise 31.1 and the dependent-clause cues listed in Chapter 27 (p. 261).

1. Rudolf loses a girlfriend.
   He goes shopping for new clothes.

2. Failure breeds fatigue, according to Mortimer Adler.
   There is nothing more energizing than success.

3. Love one another.
   Make not a bond of love.

4. You must learn to love yourself.
   You can truly love someone else.

5. Marriage is for serious people.
   I have not considered it an option.

6. Divorce is an an acknowledgement.
   There was not a true commitment in the first place.
   Some people still believe this.

7. Twenty percent of adults in America are illiterate.
   Fifty percent of the adults who *can* read say they never read books.
   This is an astonishing fact.

8. Canada is a relatively rich country.
   Most of us brush up against hunger and homelessness almost daily.
   We encounter men and, less often, women begging.
   They are on downtown streetcorners.

9. In his essay "A Modest Proposal for a Divorce Ceremony," Pierre Berton proposed that Canada institute a formal divorce ceremony.
   The divorce ceremony would be like a formal wedding ceremony.
   All the symbolism would be reversed.

10. The bride, for example, would wear black.
    Immediately after the ceremony, the newly divorced couple would go into the vestry.
    They would scratch their names off the marriage register.

After you have combined a number of sentences, you can evaluate your work. Read your sentences out loud. How they *sound* is important. Test your work against these six characteristics of successful sentences:

1.	Meaning	Have you conveyed the idea you intend?
2.	Clarity	Is your sentence clear? Can it be understood on the first reading?
3.	Coherence	Do the various parts of the sentence fit together logically and smoothly?
4.	Emphasis	Are the most important ideas and phrases either at the end or at the beginning of the sentence?
5.	Conciseness	Is the sentence wordy? Have you cut out all redundant or repetitious words?
6.	Rhythm	Does the sentence flow smoothly? Are there any interruptions in the development of the key idea(s)? Do the interruptions help to emphasize important points, or do they merely distract the reader?

If your sentences pass all six tests of successful sentence style, you may be confident that they are both technically correct and pleasing to the ear. No reader could ask for more.

Grammar

CHAPTER 32

Mastering Subject–Verb Agreement

Errors in grammar are like flies in soup: most of them don't affect meaning any more than flies affect flavour. But they *are* both distracting and irritating. They must be eliminated from your writing if you want your readers to pay attention to what you say rather than to how you say it.

One of the most common grammatical errors is failure to make the subject and verb in a sentence agree with each other. Here is the rule for subject–verb agreement:

> Singular subjects take singular verbs.
> Plural subjects take plural verbs.

Singular and Plural

Here's an example of the singular and plural forms of a regular verb (*print*) in the present tense:

	SINGULAR	PLURAL
First person	I print	we print
Second person	you print	you print
Third person	*she (he, it, the writer) prints	*they (the writers) print

You can figure out from this example what the term **person** means. We have asterisked the third person forms of the verb because these are the only forms likely to cause you trouble.[1] In the third person, the endings of verbs and their subjects do not match. Singular verbs regularly end in "s" (*prints*), but singular subjects do not (*writer*). Plural subjects regularly end in "s" (*writers*), but plural verbs do not (*print*). When you are using a regular verb in the third person, remember that *either* the subject *or* the verb ends in "s," but not both.

Remember that *singular* words concern *one* person or thing . . .

The smoke <u>alarm</u> <u>rings</u>. <u>Geoff</u> <u>watches</u> TV.

. . . while *plural* words (and compound subjects) concern *more than one* person or thing:

The smoke <u>alarms</u> <u>ring</u>. <u>Geoff and Tina</u> <u>watch</u> TV.

The rule for subject–verb agreement will cause you no problem as long as you make sure that the word the verb agrees with is really the subject of the sentence. To see how a problem can arise, look at this example:

One of the boys write graffiti.

The writer of this sentence forgot that the subject of a sentence is *never* in a prepositional phrase. The verb needs to be changed to agree with the true subject, "One":

<u>One</u> of the boys <u>writes</u> graffiti.

If you're careful about identifying the subject of your sentence, you'll have no trouble with subject–verb agreement. To sharpen your subject-finding ability, review Chapter 26, "Cracking the Sentence Code." Then do the following exercises.

EXERCISE 32.1*

Rewrite each of the following sentences, using the alternative beginning shown.

Example: <u>She</u> <u>wants</u> to learn desktop publishing.
        <u>They</u> <u>want</u> to learn desktop publishing.

1. He sells used essays to other students.
   They

---

[1]All verbs in the present tense have an *-s* form in the third person singular. The only verb that has an *-s* form in the past tense is the verb *to be:* he (she, it) *was.*

2. The woman maintains that her boss has been ogling her.
   The women
3. That new computer affects the entire office procedure.
   Those
4. Everyone who shops at Pimrock's receives a free can of tuna.
   All those
5. That girl's father is looking for a rich husband for her.
   Those

E X E R C I S E 3 2 . 2 *

Rewrite each sentence, switching the position of its two main elements.

Example: <u>Chocolate milkshakes</u> <u>are</u> my weakness.
             My <u>weakness</u> <u>is</u> chocolate milkshakes.

1. What Marcia spends most of her time on is movies.
   Movies

2. Frequent nights of debauchery were the cause of his downfall.

3. What kept Superman strong was clean living and Lois Lane.

4. Something that I didn't understand was accounting procedures.

5. Your stunning good looks are the reason for your success in the aluminum-siding business.

So far, so good. You can find the subject, even when it's hiding on the far side of the verb or nearly buried under a load of prepositional phrases. You can match up singular subjects with singular verbs, and plural subjects with plural verbs. Now let's take a look at a few of the complications that make subject–verb agreement into such a disagreeable problem.

Six Special Cases

Some subjects are tricky. They look singular but are actually plural, or they look plural when they're really singular. There are six kinds of these slippery subjects, all of them common, and all of them likely to trip up the unwary writer.

> 1. Compound subjects joined by *or; either . . . or; neither . . . nor;* or *not . . . but*

All the compound subjects we've dealt with so far have been joined by *and* and have required plural verbs, so agreement hasn't been a problem. But watch out when the two or more elements of a compound subject are joined by *or; either . . . or; neither . . . nor;* or *not . . . but.* In these cases, the verb agrees in number with the nearest subject. That is, if the subject closest to the verb is singular, the verb will be singular; if the subject closest to the verb is plural, the verb must be plural, too.

Neither <u>the coach</u> nor <u>the players</u> <u>are</u> ready to quit.

Neither <u>the players</u> nor <u>the coach</u> <u>is</u> ready to quit.

EXERCISE 32.3*

Circle the correct verb in each of the following sentences.

1. Neither the man nor his previous wives (know knows) who buried the treasure in the orchard.
2. Not high interest rates but high unemployment (is are) Canadians' first concern.
3. The college has decided that neither final marks nor a diploma (is are) to be issued to students owing library fines.
4. Either your job performance or your school assignments (is are) going to suffer if you continue your frantic lifestyle.
5. According to my guidebook entitled *Sightseeing in Transylvania*, not sharp stakes but garlic cloves (repel repels) the dreaded vampires.

> 2. Subjects that look like compound subjects but really aren't.

Don't be fooled by phrases beginning with such words as *with, like, as well as, together with, in addition to,* or *including.* These phrases are *not* part of the subject of the sentence. Mentally cross them out; they do not affect the verb.

Dwight's <u>brother</u>, ~~together with three of his buddies~~, <u>is</u> going to the Yukon to look for work.

Obviously four people are looking for work. Nevertheless, the subject (<u>brother</u>) is singular, and so the verb must be singular (<u>is going</u>).

All my <u>courses</u>, ~~except economics~~, <u>are</u> easier this term.

If you mentally cross out the phrase "except economics," you can easily see that the verb (<u>are</u>) must be plural to agree with the plural subject (<u>courses</u>).

EXERCISE 32.4*

Circle the correct verb in each of the following sentences.

1. Many Canadians, including the prime minister, (is are) fluent in both English and French.
2. Our city, along with many other North American urban centres, (register registers) a dangerous level of carbon monoxide pollution in the summer months.
3. Tonya Harding, like Elizabeth Manley and Katarina Witt, (is are) a legendary skating figure, although the reasons for their fame are very different.
4. Darryl's parole officer, together with the police and his wife, (keep keeps) a close eye on him.
5. My English instructor, in addition to my math, biology, and even my learning skills instructor, (inflict inflicts) a lot of pressure on me.

---

3. Words that end in *-one*, *-thing*, or *-body*

When used as subjects, the following words are always singular, and they require the singular form of the verb:

everyone	everything	everybody
anyone	anything	anybody
someone	something	somebody
no one	nothing	nobody

The last part of the word is the tip-off here: every*one*, any*thing*, no*body*. If you focus on this last part, you'll remember to use a singular verb with these subjects. For the most part, these words cause trouble only when modifiers crop up between them and their verbs. For example, no one would write "Everyone are here." The trouble starts when you sandwich a bunch of words in between the subject and the verb. You might, if you weren't on your toes, write this: "Everyone involved in implementing the company's new policies and procedures are here." Obviously the meaning is plural: several people are present. But the subject (every*one*) is singular, so the verb must be *is*.

EXERCISE 32.5*

Circle the correct verb in each of the following sentences.

1. Nobody, according to hundreds of recording artists, (love loves) you when you're down and out.

2. Everybody who ever owned a Volkswagen Bug (know knows) how much fun driving can be.
3. Anyone in the final year of school who (want wants) credit cards can get them simply by applying.
4. Everything I could ever want on a canoe trip (is are) available at Campers' Co-op.
5. Nothing that we have seen so far, except perhaps the Ferrari, (interest interests) us.

---

4. *Each, either (of), neither (of)*

Used as subjects, these take singular verbs.

> <u>Either</u> <u>is</u> acceptable to me.

> <u>Each</u> <u>wants</u> desperately to win.

> <u>Neither</u> of the stores <u>is</u> open after six o'clock. (Remember, the subject is never in a prepositional phrase.)

EXERCISE 32.6*

Circle the correct verb in each of the following sentences.

1. Unless we hear from the coach, neither of those team members (is are) playing this evening.
2. Either of those courses (involve involves) field placement.
3. You will be pleased to hear that neither (has have) the measles.
4. Each of the women (want wants) to win the Ms. Oshawa bodybuilding competition.
5. Strict discipline is what each of those teachers (believe believes) in.

---

5. Collective nouns

A **collective noun** is a word that names a group. Some examples are *company, class, committee, team, crowd, band, family, audience, public,* and *majority.* When you are referring to the group acting as a *unit,* use a *singular* verb. When you are referring to the *members* of the group acting *individually,* use a *plural* verb.

> The <u>team</u> <u>is</u> sure to win tomorrow's game. (Here *team* refers to the group acting as a whole.)

> The <u>team</u> <u>are</u> getting into their uniforms now. (The separate members of the team are acting individually.)

EXERCISE 32.7*

Circle the correct verb in each of the following sentences.

1. The whole gang (plan plans) to attend the bikers' rally.
2. The wolf pack (has have) been practically wiped out by local ranchers.
3. By noon on Friday, the whole dorm (has have) left their rooms and headed for the local pubs and coffee houses.
4. After only two hours' discussion, the committee (was were) able to reach consensus.
5. The majority of Canadians, according to a recent survey, (is are) not so conservative about sex and morality as we had assumed.

> 6. Units of money, time, mass, length, and distance

When being used as subjects, these all require singular verbs.

> Four kilometres is too far to walk in this weather.

> Remember that 2.2 pounds equals a kilogram.

> Three weeks is a long time to wait to get our papers back.

EXERCISE 32.8*

Circle the correct verb in each of the following sentences.

1. No wonder you are suspicious if 70 dollars (was were) what you paid for last night's pizza.
2. Tim told his girlfriend that nine years (seem seems) like a long time to wait.
3. Forty hours of classes (is are) too much in one week.
4. When you are anxiously awaiting the next gas station, 30 kilometres (is are) a long distance.
5. Seventy-five cents (seems seem) a fair price for a slightly tattered Kelly Gruber card.

In Exercises 32.9 through 32.11, correct the errors in subject–verb agreement. Check your answers to each exercise before going on.

EXERCISE 32.9*

1. My sense of the schools are that none of them are any good.

2. Neither of us remember who ran against Ralph Klein for premier of

   Alberta.

3. Every one of the SUNshine Boys appeal to my sense of the sublime.

4. My whole family, with the exception of the cat, dislike anchovies on pizza.

5. Popular belief notwithstanding, quicksand do not suck you under or pull you down.

6. It is the suction created by the victims that are responsible for the pulling effect.

7. Neither age nor illness prevents Uncle Alf from pinching the nurses.

8. Eight hundred dollars per term, all students agree, are too much to pay for their education.

9. The birth of quintuplets were too much for the mother to cope with.

10. Everything that we agreed to last night seem silly this morning.

EXERCISE 32.10*

Quebec City, along with Montreal, Toronto, and Vancouver, are among Canada's great gourmet centres. While Toronto is a relative latecomer to this list, neither Quebec City nor Montreal are strangers to those who seeks fine dining. Indeed, travel and food magazines have long affirmed that the inclusion of these two cities in a Quebec vacation are a "must." Montreal is perhaps more international in its offerings, but Quebec City provides exquisite proof that French-Canadian cuisine and hospitality is second to none in the world. Amid the old-world charm of the lower city is to be found some of the quaintest and most enjoyable traditional restaurants; the newer sections of town boasts equally fine dining in more contemporary surroundings. The combination of the wonderful food and the city's fascinating charms are sure to make any visitor return frequently. Either the summer, when the city blooms and outdoor cafés abound, or the winter, when Carnaval turns the streets into hundreds of connecting parties, are wonderful times to visit one of Canada's oldest and most interesting cities.

EXERCISE 32.11*

The interest in wrestlers and their managers, fans, and friends are fascinating proof that our society needs cheap thrills. The concept of good and evil fighting it out in epic battles are an enduring one. In simpler times, everyone who felt the need to witness such struggles were able to watch westerns on TV and see the Bad Guy (wearing the black hat) gunned down at high noon by the reluctant Good Guy (wearing the white hat). The complexity of our society, where good and evil is constantly redefined, mean that we seldom get a clear decision in the battles we see each day on the news, let alone witness the triumph of good over evil. Into this frustrating world comes Rowdy Roddy Piper, Hulk Hogan, the Junk Yard Dog, and King Kong Bundy. The variety of names, personalities, and "show-biz" tricks are bewildering. Though the staging of the various moves and even the outcomes of the matches are obvious, the immense popularity of the matches, both on television and in the arenas, are undeniable. Like Rambo and Dirty Harry, the

professional wrestler cuts through frustrating complexity and represents

good or evil in its simplest, most dramatic form. To a great many people,

wrestling—not to mention wrestlers—are irresistible.

EXERCISE 32.12

As a final check of your mastery of subject–verb agreement, correct the
following sentences as necessary.

1. In my opinion, neither of the lead singers are any good.
2. The faculty, with the full support of the college administration, treats plagiarism as a serious offence.
3. Either good looks or intelligence run in our family, but never at the same time.
4. No one, believe it or not, look forward to the end of term more than the maintenance staff.
5. Finding my skis after a year away were difficult, but remembering how to use them after all these months are going to be an even greater challenge.
6. The number of layoffs reported in the headlines seem to be increasing monthly.
7. We couldn't help noticing that the orchestra are playing better now that the conductor is sober.
8. With cutbacks at every level of government, it is no longer true that every Canadian who need medical services have access to immediate treatment.
9. Our cafeteria, with its dreary salad bar, greasy chips, and soggy sandwiches, completely take away my appetite.
10. Canada's aboriginal population are thought to have come to this continent from Asia thousands of years before the Europeans arrived in North America.

CHAPTER 33

Using Verbs Effectively

Now that you've conquered subject–verb agreement, it's time to turn to the three remaining essentials of correct verb use: **form, consistency,** and **voice.** These terms may not mean much to you at this point, but don't let them intimidate you. You'll probably discover that you know more about them than you think. You'll also find that using verbs effectively will noticeably improve your writing. Good writers pay especially careful attention to verbs. A verb is to a sentence what an engine is to a car: it's the source of power—and it can also be a source of trouble.

Choosing the Correct Verb Form

Every verb has four forms:

1. the **base form:** used by itself or with *can, may, might, shall, will, could, would, should,* or *must;*
2. the **past tense** form: used by itself;
3. the *-ing* **form:** used with *am, is, are, was,* or *were;* and
4. the **past participle** form: used with *have, has,* or *had.*

These forms are the principal parts of a verb. Here are some examples:

BASE	PAST TENSE	*-ING* FORM	PAST PARTICIPLE
walk	walked	walking	walked
learn	learned	learning	learned
seem	seemed	seeming	seemed
enjoy	enjoyed	enjoying	enjoyed

To use verbs correctly, you must know their principal parts. Knowing two facts will help you. First, your dictionary will give you the principal parts of certain verbs (the irregular ones). Just look up the base form, and you'll find the past tense and the past participle beside it, usually in parentheses. If the past tense and the past participle are *not* given, the verb is **regular.** So, the second thing you need to know is how to form the past tense and the past participle of regular verbs: by adding *-ed* to the base form. The examples listed above—*walk, learn, seem,* and *enjoy*—are regular verbs.

Many of the most common verbs are **irregular.** Their past tense and past participle are formed in a variety of ways. Following is a list of the principal parts of some of the most common irregular verbs. (We have not included the *-ing* form, because it never causes any difficulty. It is always made up of the base form + *-ing.*)

The Principal Parts of Common Irregular Verbs

BASE (Use with *can, may, might, shall, will, could, would, should, must.*)	PAST TENSE	PAST PARTICIPLE (Use with *have, has, had.*)
be (am, is, are)	was, were	been
bear	bore	borne
become	became	become
begin	began	begun
bid (offer to pay)	bid	bid
bite	bit	bitten
blow	blew	blown
break	broke	broken
bring	brought	brought
build	built	built
burst	burst	burst
buy	bought	bought
catch	caught	caught
choose	chose	chosen
come	came	come
cost	cost	cost
deal	dealt	dealt
dive	dived/dove	dived
do	did	done
draw	drew	drawn
drink	drank	drunk
drive	drove	driven

BASE	PAST TENSE	PAST PARTICIPLE
eat	ate	eaten
fall	fell	fallen
feel	felt	felt
fight	fought	fought
find	found	found
fling	flung	flung
fly	flew	flown
forget	forgot	forgotten/forgot
forgive	forgave	forgiven
freeze	froze	frozen
get	got	got/gotten
give	gave	given
go	went	gone (*not* went)
grow	grew	grown
hang (suspend)	hung	hung
hang (put to death)	hanged	hanged
have	had	had
hear	heard	heard
hide	hid	hidden
hit	hit	hit
hold	held	held
hurt	hurt	hurt
keep	kept	kept
know	knew	known
lay (put or place)	laid	laid
lead	led	led
leave	left	left
lend	lent	lent
lie (recline)	lay	lain
lose	lost	lost
make	made	made
mean	meant	meant
meet	met	met
pay	paid	paid
put	put	put
ride	rode	ridden
ring	rang	rung
rise	rose	risen
run	ran	run
say	said	said
see	saw (*not* seen)	seen
sell	sold	sold
set	set	set
shake	shook	shaken

BASE	PAST TENSE	PAST PARTICIPLE
shine	shone	shone
sing	sang	sung
sit	sat	sat
sleep	slept	slept
slide	slid	slid
speak	spoke	spoken
speed	sped	sped
spend	spent	spent
stand	stood	stood
steal	stole	stolen
strike	struck	struck
swear	swore	sworn
swim	swam	swum
swing	swung	swung
take	took	taken
teach	taught	taught
tear	tore	torn
tell	told	told
think	thought	thought
throw	threw	thrown
wear	wore	worn
win	won	won
wind	wound	wound
write	wrote	written

EXERCISE 33.1*

In each of the following sentences, write on the blank line the correct form (either the past tense or the past participle) of the verb shown to the left of the sentence. Do not add or remove helping verbs.

1. come   Down from the high mountain that lay beyond the little town _____ the strangest creature they had ever seen.

2. spend   Appearing in the town square in the morning, he had apparently _____ the night crouched in a handy tree.

3. make   Odd-looking, but not frightening or ugly, he _____ even the early-morning dogs look his way.

4. be   He could have _____ a Hobbit, so much like Frodo did he look.

5. lose   Apparently he had _____ his way while picnicking with his friends in the foothills.

6. speak   The children from Miss Bundy's Nursery School
   find   _____ to him first and _____ him friendly and intelligent.

7. know   The townspeople all _____ the legend of a mountain kingdom of little people.

8. have   Now they _____ evidence before their eyes for the truth of the story.

9. choose   They could have _____ to ignore or do away with the friendly little fellow.

10. tell   Instead, he stayed and _____ them more about the
    lead   mountain kingdom and eventually _____ them there to see it for themselves.

EXERCISE 33.2*

The following sentences require both the past tense and the past participle of the verb shown at the left. Write the required form in each blank. Do not add or remove helping verbs.

1. win   Tom had _____ the long-distance run many times before he _____ his first sprint.

2. wear   The shabby tuxedo had been _____ many times by Tom's father, but at yesterday's presentation Tom _____ it with pride.

3. do   Tom _____ what he had never _____ before: he made a speech.

4. forget   It was amazing: all his notes were _____ and he even _____ to be nervous.

5. become   Tom _____ quite good at speech making on behalf of the fitness cause; having _____ proficient, he was asked to speak at many other meetings and banquets.

6. see   Having been _____ and mobbed on the street outside, Tom then _____ that he would have to avoid recognition.

7. set   Having _____ a world record for the mile when he was 20, Tom _____ another one for the decathlon when he was 25.

8. fall   Tom had _____ and broken an ankle when he was 12; he _____ again and broke his arm a year later.

9. meet   I was _____ at the door by this medical and athletic miracle; he surely _____ all my expectations.

10. keep   Now 60, he had _____ himself in top condition over the years and still _____ up a daily exercise routine.

EXERCISE 33.3*

Find and correct the verb errors in the following sentences.

1. I would have wrote more often if I had knowed you cared.
2. The telephone rung and rung, but no one answered because everyone had went out for pizza.
3. I never seen a person who done nothing but lay around the house as much as she does.
4. The whole family was shook up when they learned Gerald had stole Dad's car and took off for Seattle.
5. "Strike three!" yelled the umpire as soon as I swang the bat, but I run around the bases anyway.
6. Orville's pumpkins would have growed twice as big if they hadn't froze in the cold snap.
7. If Rudolph and Dwight had known what was good for them, they would have switch to pop after they had drank the entire contents of the beer keg.
8. Anna should have stole second base; she should not have ran for home.
9. The boys have went out to get more beer since they've already drank the two cases I brung.
10. After the neighbourhood bully had deliberately busted my daughter's balloon, she layed on the ground and sobbed.

EXERCISE 33.4

As a final test of your mastery of verb forms, correct the errors in the following sentences.

1. The wind had blew the roof off the house and drove a hole into the side of the barn.
2. The stars shined like diamonds the night I told Emmy-Lou how I feeled about her and gave her the ring that costed me a week's pay.
3. Dan had drove very slowly on the gravel road, but once he reached the highway, he speeded away into the darkness.
4. They had all wore yellow ribbons to show they hadn't forgot him.
5. The gypsy fortuneteller had spoke, but she didn't tell us anything that we hadn't knew before.
6. The church bells rung out the news that a great battle had been fought, and a great victory had been won.
7. That teached us a lesson that we have keeped all these years.
8. After the band had sang "The Lion Sleeps Tonight" seven times, we realized they had been payed too much, because they only knowed four tunes.
9. The priest has spoke with the condemned man who will be hung in the morning unless the governor gives him a stay of execution.
10. When he slided into third base after he had stole second and the throw had went into centre field, he had tore a big hole in his pants and had to leave the game.

Keeping Your Tenses Consistent

Verbs are time markers. The different tenses are used to express changes in time:

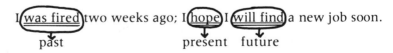

I was fired two weeks ago; I hope I will find a new job soon.
     past   present future

Sometimes, as in the sentence above, it is necessary to use several different tenses in a single sentence to get the meaning across. But usually, whether you're writing a sentence, a paragraph, an essay, or a report, you will *use one tense throughout*. Normally you will choose either the past or the present tense. Here is the rule to follow:

> Don't change tense unless meaning requires it.

Readers like and expect consistency. If you begin a sentence with "I worried and fretted and delayed," your readers will tune in to the past-tense verbs and expect any other verbs in the sentence to be in the past tense, too. Therefore, if you finish the sentence with ". . . and then I decide to give it a try," your readers will be jolted abruptly out of one time frame and into another. This sort of jolting is uncomfortable, and readers don't like it.

Shifting tenses is like shifting gears: it should be done smoothly and when necessary—never abruptly, out of carelessness, or on a whim. Avoid causing verbal whiplash: keep your tenses consistent.

> *Wrong:* Monika starts the car and revved the engine.
> *Right:* Monika started the car and revved the engine.
> *Also right:* Monika starts the car and revs the engine.

> *Wrong:* Krystal flounces into the room and sat down. Everyone stares.
> *Right:* Krystal flounced into the room and sat down. Everyone stared.
> *Also right:* Krystal flounces into the room and sits down. Everyone stares.

In Exercises 33.5 and 33.6, most of the sentences contain unnecessary tense shifts. Use the first verb in each sentence as your time marker, and change the tense(s) of the other verb(s) in the sentence to agree with it.

EXERCISE 33.5*

1. Rolly goes home and kicked his cat.

2. Hank Aaron broke Babe Ruth's record of 714 home runs in a lifetime when he hits number 715 in 1974.

3. Children are quite perceptive and will know when you are lying to them.

4. We had just finished painting the floor when the dog runs through.

5. When Knowlton Nash walked into the room, the ladies go crazy.

6. You ought not to venture into that place until the police arrive.

7. Tim walked into the room, took one look at Lefty, and smashes him right through the wall.

8. First you will greet the guests; then you show them to their rooms.

9. The largest cheese ever produced took 43 hours to make and weighs a whopping 15 723 kilograms.

10. He watches television until he finally went to sleep.

EXERCISE 33.6*

1. Murphy's Law states that everything that can go wrong will.

2. I tried to warn him about her evil ways, and what thanks do I get?

3. The embarrassed girl didn't say anything. She just blushes and runs from the room.

4. Before Roger noticed the snowstorm, he's already up and dressed.

5. They agreed to our living here after we offer them a substantial bribe.

6. In the interests of good community relations and to prevent them from blowing up our house, I vote that we will pay what they asked for.

7. Drusilla looks like a sweet young thing; when she spoke, however, the toughest truck drivers blush.

8. Whenever I skip chemistry, it seemed old Mr. Bunsen was lurking in the hall to catch me.

9. The goons in hockey keep ruining the sport for those who want to play it the way it is intended to be played.

10. We attempted to change Rudolf's mind all day, but we didn't know he's already voted.

EXERCISE 33.7*

Correct the faulty tense shifts in this passage.

For some reason when mistakes or accidents happened in radio or television, they were often hilariously funny. If, in the course of a conversation, someone said, "Here come the Duck and Doochess of Kent," listeners would probably be mildly amused. But many years ago, when an announcer makes that slip on a live radio broadcast, it becomes one of the most famous blunders in radio history. Tapes of the slip will be filed in "bloopers" libraries all over the world. This heightened sense of hilarity is the reason that so many people who worked in radio dedicated their creativity to making the on-air announcer laugh while reading the news. To take one example, Lorne Greene's is the deeply serious voice that is heard on the CBC news during World War II. He is the victim of all kinds of pranks aimed at getting him to break up while reading the dark, often tragic, news of the combat overseas. The pages of his news script are set on fire while he reads. He is even stripped naked as he reads, calmly, and apparently without strain. Lorne Greene is a true professional. Many other newscasters, however, have proved to be highly susceptible to falling apart on air at the slightest provocation. And there will always be people around a radio station who could not resist giving them that little push.

EXERCISE 33.8

To test and reinforce your mastery of correct verb forms and tense consistency, correct the errors in the following paragraph. Use the italicized verb as your time marker.

The art of writing *is* not dead. Thanks to the increasing use of computers in homes and businesses, it will now be more important than ever to be able to write competently. Not everyone will agree with this statement. Many people will continue to think that electronic technology has eliminated the need for learning how to write, but it will be clear that reports of the death of the written word were premature. The widespread use of computer networking, bulletin boards, e-mail, and electronic forums made it more important than ever to write well. In the past, when letters were written on paper, writers could have checked their messages over very carefully to ensure there were no errors or potentially embarrassing miscommunications before sealing the envelope and putting it in the mail. Now, however, communication is instantaneous, and any writing faults will be immediately apparent. The exposure of writing flaws, however, is not the only reason electronic communication links require the ability to write clear, precise, unambiguous prose. Paper letters were normally mailed to a few people, at most. Electronic mail, on the other hand, will often be sent to dozens, even hundreds, of receivers; therefore, the message will need to be especially carefully crafted if all recipients are to understand precisely what the writer intended. In the world of electronic communication, good writing skills will be even more important than ever before.

Choosing between Active and Passive Verbs

In addition to their principal parts and tenses, verbs can be classified according to **voice:** they can be either **active** or **passive.** Think back to Chapter 26, where you learned how to identify the subject and verb in a sentence. You will recall that *the verb is the word or word group that expresses an action, a condition, or an occurrence,* and that you can always identify the verb because it is the only *word or word group whose form can be changed to indicate a change in time: past, present, or future.* These two conditions always hold, whether the verb is active or passive. If you want your writing to be effective, you need to understand the distinction between active and passive verbs. Here is the rule to follow:

> Always use an active verb *unless* you have a specific reason to choose a passive one.

You probably use the passive voice far more often than you think you do, and you probably use it unconsciously. To be a better writer, you need to know the distinction between active and passive, to understand their different effects on the reader, and to use the passive voice only when it is appropriate to your meaning.

When the subject of a sentence *performs the action of the verb,* the verb is in the active voice. When the subject of a sentence isn't actually doing anything but instead *is being acted upon,* the verb is in the passive voice. The difference will become clear if you study the following examples carefully.

ACTIVE VERB	PASSIVE VERB
<u>Dwight</u> <u>bought</u> the last round.	The last <u>round</u> <u>was bought</u> by Dwight.
Our sociology <u>instructor</u> <u>cancelled</u> class again today.	Our sociology <u>class</u> <u>was cancelled</u> by our instructor again today.
The <u>counsellor</u> <u>will see</u> you now.	<u>You</u> <u>will be seen</u> by the counsellor now.
The <u>president</u> <u>has called</u> an all-staff meeting for Thursday.	An all-staff <u>meeting</u> <u>has been called</u> by the president for Thursday.
After <u>Cara</u> <u>had read</u> the report, the <u>committee</u> <u>recommended</u> its adoption.	After the <u>report</u> <u>had been read</u> by Cara, its <u>adoption</u> <u>was recommended</u> by the committee.

Notice that the sentences with passive verbs have two things in common. First, their verbs consist of some form of "to be" (*am, is, are, was, were, will be, has been*, etc.) plus the past participle of the verb that expresses the action, condition, or occurrence that is at the heart of the sentence: "was bought"; "was cancelled"; "will be seen"; "has been called"; "had been read"; and "was recommended." Second, the sentences with passive verbs are longer than those with active verbs.

Because they lead to wordy sentences, you should avoid passive verbs unless you have a special reason for using them.

There are three good reasons for choosing a passive verb rather than an active one.

1. *When the person or agent that performed the action is not known.*

    My books <u>were stolen</u> from my locker this morning.

    Giovanna's father <u>was killed</u> in Bosnia.

    Unlike the streets of a typical prairie city, which <u>are laid out</u> on a grid, Vancouver's streets <u>are laid out</u> to follow the curves and bends of the harbour and the Fraser River.

2. *When you want to place the emphasis on the person, place, or object that was acted upon* rather than on the subject that performed the action:

    Early this morning, the Bank of Montreal at 16th and Granville <u>was robbed</u> by four men wearing nylon stockings over their heads and carrying shotguns.

This sentence focusses the reader's attention on the bank, rather than on the four men. A quite different effect is produced when the sentence is reconstructed in the active voice:

    Four men wearing nylon stockings over their heads and carrying shotguns <u>robbed</u> the Bank of Montreal at 16th and Granville early this morning.

3. *When you are writing a technical or scientific report or a legal document.* Passive verbs are the appropriate choice when the focus is on the facts, methods, and procedures involved, rather than on who discovered or performed them. Passive verbs also tend to establish an impersonal tone that is appropriate in these kinds of writing. Contrast the emphasis and tone of the following sentence pairs:

    Passive: The heat <u>was increased</u> to 200°C and <u>was allowed</u> to remain at that temperature.
    Active: My lab partners and I <u>increased</u> the heat to 200°C and <u>allowed</u> it to remain at that temperature.

> *Passive:* Having been found guilty, the accused <u>was sentenced</u> to
>   two years.
> *Active:* The jury <u>found</u> the accused guilty, and the judge <u>sentenced</u>
>   him to two years.

In general, because active verbs are more concise and forceful than passive verbs, they add vigour and impact to your writing. The distinction between active and passive is not something you should worry about during the drafting stage, however. The time to focus on verbs and decide whether active or passive would best serve your purpose is during revision. When you find a passive verb in your draft, think about who is doing what. Ask yourself *why* the "who" is not the subject of the sentence. If there's a good reason, then use the passive verb. Otherwise, choose an active verb.

EXERCISE 33.9*

Rewrite the sentences below, changing their verbs from passive to active. Note that you may have to add a word or word group to identify the "doer" of the action of the verb.

Example: Matt's two front teeth <u>were knocked out</u> by Clark's shot.
    Clark's shot <u>knocked out</u> Matt's two front teeth.

 1. The espresso will be made by the server in a few minutes.
 2. "Brothers in Arms" was recorded by Dire Straits.
 3. When it gets cold, the block heater is plugged in overnight.
 4. For many years, steroids have been used by professional athletes to improve speed and endurance.
 5. The dough must not be kneaded, or your pastry will be tough.
 6. *Do-It-Yourself Surgery,* which is the current best-seller, was written by Dr. Lance Boyles.
 7. Four of Dwight's buddies were arrested during a routine check of Barry's Bingo Bistro.
 8. While our neighbours were vacationing in the Caribbean, their house was broken into by thieves.
 9. The latest multimedia technology will be displayed and demonstrated in the graphics lab by technicians from Apple, Dell, and IBM.
10. The Red Sox and the White Sox have finally been replaced as the stupidest team names in sports by the Mighty Ducks.

EXERCISE 33.10*

Rewrite each of the sentences below, changing the active verbs to passive ones (or vice versa), and then decide which sentence is more effective.

 1. k.d. lang won another Juno.
 2. Rudolf spiked the ball, giving us the winning point.

3. City council passed a law forbidding smoking in burning buildings.
4. As the storm clouds gathered, we pedalled our bicycles faster and faster.
5. Forty-eight hours later, 2 ml of sterile water was added to the culture in the Petri dish.
6. By standing in line all night, Krystal managed to get four tickets for the concert.
7. The 10:00 news revealed the truth behind the famous Doobie Brothers scandal.
8. The judgement was finally announced today, almost a year after the environmental hearings were concluded.
9. An unbelievable run of luck saved us from bankruptcy.
10. After a long debate, the committee finally agreed to endorse Yasmin's fundraising proposal.

EXERCISE 33.11*

Rewrite the following paragraph, changing passive verbs to active where appropriate.

The person they most admired was identified recently by Russian women between the ages of 16 and 25 as Madonna. This startling fact was revealed in an article in a popular magazine after more than 3000 subscribers had been surveyed by them. In order of popularity, Michael Jackson, the Beatles, and Queen Elizabeth were also admired by the young women. Russian men's tastes in popular entertainment were also reported. The people they most admired were named by males between 16 and 25 as Depeche Mode and the Beatles. This age group's favourite leisure activities were also identified by the survey. Movies, drawing and painting, dancing, needlework, and pop music were favoured by the women, while music videos, art, electronics, painting, and guitar playing were enjoyed by the men. When the respondents were asked to list, in order of priority, the countries where a pen pal would be most likely to be sought by them, Canada was ranked third by both sexes. In first place

was placed the United States, followed by England. Australia and

Germany were tied for fourth place.

EXERCISE 33.12

This exercise is a review. It will test and reinforce your understanding of verb forms, tense, and voice. Revise the following passage to eliminate all incorrect or inappropriate verb choices.

In the past few years, the global economy has been heard about a great

deal. We became aware that international trade will be the trend of the

future, and goods sold abroad by Canadians would pay for the many

things that will be imported by us. As trade barriers go down, freer trade

between nations will mean a better life for all of us, here and abroad.

This sounded like an ideal world, with products whisking back and forth

to the benefit of everyone. But as I think about this wonderful future, I

begun to realize that in many ways it's already here. A German car is

driven by me, and an Australian jacket worn. Many of my shirts were

made in Asia, and the whiskey I drink is made in Scotland. My computer

is American, my coffee Colombian, my stereo Japanese, and my boots

Brazilian. Foods cooked with products from Thailand, India, the West

Indies, China, and Lebanon are enjoyed by me and most of my friends.

Many Canadian products, foods, items of clothing, and beverages will be

found in my home, to be sure, but products from every corner of the

globe will be found beside them. Canada have always been a trading

nation. When a global economy is talked about, people are really talking about a system that has been enjoyed by Canadians for years. While some trade barriers did still exist, for the most part our economy is a huge bazaar. Our marketplace is filled with the products of the world. At the same time, the products and raw materials, the talents and services of Canadians are sought by virtually all the nations on earth. For Canada at least, the global economy is nothing new. It has been lived in by us for years.

CHAPTER 34

Solving Pronoun Problems

Look at these sentences. Can you tell what's wrong with them?

"Dwight must choose between you and I," Krystal said.

When you are on a diet, it is a good idea for one to avoid Bagel World.

We had invited everybody to come with their partner, so we were a little surprised when Marcel showed up with his Doberman.

Everyone is expected to do their duty.

Rudolf's nose was badly sunburned, but it has now completely disappeared.

Most of the students that were protesting tuition increases were ones which had been elected to council.

These sentences all contain pronoun errors. After verbs, pronouns are the class of words most likely to cause problems for writers. In this chapter we will look at the three aspects of pronoun usage that can trip you up if you're not careful: pronoun form, agreement, and consistency. We'll also look at the special problems of usage that can lead to sexist language.

1. Choosing the Correct Pronoun Form

First you need to be sure you are using the "right" pronouns—that is, the correct pronoun forms—in your sentences. Here are some examples of incorrect pronoun usage:

Her and me can't agree on anything.

The reason for the quarrel is a personal matter between she and I.

How do you know which form of a pronoun to use? The answer depends on the pronoun's place and function in your sentence.

There are two forms of personal pronoun: one is used for subjects and the other is used for objects. Pronoun errors occur when you confuse the two. In Chapter 26, you learned to identify the subject of a sentence. Keep that information in mind as you learn this basic rule:

> When a subject is (or is referred to by) a pronoun, that pronoun must be in **subject form;** otherwise, use the **object form.**

SUBJECT PRONOUNS

Singular	*Plural*
I	we
you	you
he, she, it, one	they

She and *I* tied for first place. (The pronouns are the subject of the sentence.)

The lucky winners of the all-expenses-paid weekend in Boston Bar are *they.* (The pronoun refers to the subject of the sentence, "winners.")

The student who regularly asks for extra help is *he.* (The pronoun refers to the subject of the sentence, "student.")

We serious bikers prefer Harleys to Hondas. (The pronoun refers to the subject of the sentence, "bikers.")

OBJECT PRONOUNS

Singular	*Plural*
me	us
you	you
him, her, it, one	them

Between you and *me,* I think he's cute. ("Me" is not the subject of the sentence; it is one of the objects of the preposition "between.")

Omar asked *him* and *me* for help. ("Him" and "me" are not the subject of the verb "asked"; "Omar" is, so the pronouns need to be in the object form.)

The police are always suspicious of *us* bikers. ("Us" does not refer to the sentence's subject, "police"; it refers to "bikers," the object of the preposition "of.")

Be especially careful when using pronouns in compound subjects or after prepositions. If you can remember these two tips, you'll be able to eliminate most potential errors:

1. A pronoun that is part of a compound subject is *always* in subject form.
2. A pronoun that follows a preposition is *always* in object form.

Examples:

> *She* and *I* had tickets to Rush. (The pronouns are used as a compound subject.)

> It is up to *you* and *her* to pay for the damage. (The pronouns follow the preposition "to.")

Here's a practically foolproof way to figure out which pronoun form you need. When you have a pair of pronouns to deal with, mentally cross out one at a time. Applying this technique to the first example above, you get "*She* had tickets" and "*I* had tickets," both of which sound right and are correct. In the second sentence, if you try the pronouns separately, you get "It is up to *you*" and "It is up to *her*." Again, you know by the sound that these are the correct forms. (You would never say, "*Her* had tickets," "*Me* had tickets," or "It is up to *she*.") If you deal with paired pronouns one at a time, you are unlikely to choose the wrong form.

EXERCISE 34.1*

Correct the pronouns in these sentences as necessary.

1. No one except you and I would go camping in this weather.
2. Him and I can't figure out this problem set any better than you and her could.
3. Dwight and him fell asleep in class, as usual.
4. It is hard to believe that anyone could snore as loudly as them.
5. We can use the film passes all week, and you and her can use them on the weekend, when Biff and me are going skiing.
6. Thanks to the recommendations provided by your math instructor and I, you and her got the tutorial jobs.
7. As we were going to class, Karl and me heard that there had been an explosion in the lab.
8. If it hadn't been for Hassan and he, the only ones to show up would have been you and I.

9. Eugene and him agreed to split the price of a case with Stan and I.
10. Only two students passed the midterm: Nadia and me.

Choosing the correct pronoun form is more than just a matter of not wanting to appear ignorant or careless. Sometimes the form you use determines the meaning of your sentence. Consider these two sentences:

Dwight is more interested in his new car than *I.*
Dwight is more interested in his new car than *me.*

There's a world of difference between the meaning of the subject form ("Dwight is more interested in his new car than *I* [am]") and the object form ("Dwight is more interested in his new car than [in] *me*").

When using a pronoun after *than, as well as,* or *as,* decide whether you mean to contrast the pronoun with the subject of the sentence. If you do, use the subject form of the pronoun. If not, use the object form.

Example: Rudolf would rather watch television than I. (*I* is contrasted with *Rudolf.*)

Rudolf would rather watch television than me. (*Me* is contrasted with *television.*)

EXERCISE 34.2*

Correct the following sentences where necessary.

1. At fourteen, my younger brother is already taller than me.
2. No one likes partying more than him and Krystal.
3. Would you like to join Dwight and I for dinner and a movie?
4. Only one person in this firm could manage the department as well as him.
5. At last I have met someone who enjoys grilled liver as much as me!
6. We can skate as well as them, but they are much better at shooting and defending than us.
7. More than me, Serge uses the computer to draft and revise his papers.

EXERCISE 34.3*

Revise the following paragraph to correct all errors in pronoun form.

(1) My boyfriend and me have different opinions when it comes to food. (2) I like fast food better than him. (3) He likes vegetables better than me. (4) In fact, between you and I, he is a vegetarian, though he

would deny it. (5) When we go out with friends, it is difficult for they to know where to take him and I since our tastes are so different. (6) The only type of restaurant where us and them can all have what we like is Italian. (7) There, him and his friends can sample pasta primavera and eggplant parmigiana, while my friends and me tuck into spaghetti and meatballs and pepperoni pizza. (8) We are probably not as healthy as them, but they don't seem to enjoy their food as much as us.

Now that you know how to choose the correct form of pronouns within a sentence, let's turn to the problems of using pronouns consistently throughout a sentence and a paragraph.

2. Pronoun–Antecedent Agreement

The name given to this pronoun problem may sound formidable, but the idea is very simple. Pronouns are words that substitute for or refer to the name of a person, place, or thing mentioned elsewhere in your sentence or in your paragraph. The word or word group that a pronoun substitutes for or refers to is called the **antecedent.**

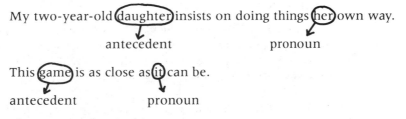

My two-year-old daughter insists on doing things her own way.

             antecedent   pronoun

This game is as close as it can be.

antecedent   pronoun

The rule to remember is this:

> A pronoun must agree with its antecedent.

You probably follow this rule most of the time without even realizing that you know it. For example, you would never write

My two-year-old daughter insists on doing things *its* own way.
   or
This game is as close as *she* can be.

because you know that these pronouns don't agree with their antecedents.

There are three kinds of pronoun–antecedent problem, however, that you need to watch out for: relative pronouns; pronouns ending in *-one, -body,* or *-thing;* and vague references.

2.1 Relative Pronouns

The first potential difficulty with pronoun–antecedent agreement is how to use the relative pronouns—*who/whoever, whom/whomever, which,* and *that.* Relative pronouns can be used for only one purpose: to refer to someone or something specifically mentioned in the sentence or paragraph. Here is the guideline to follow:

> *Who, whom, whoever,* and *whomever* refer to people.
> *That* and *which* refer to everything else.

The student *who* won the Governor General's medal decided to go to Dalhousie.

The women *who* were present vetoed the proposal.

The moose *that* I met looked hostile.

Her car, *which* is imported, is smaller than cars *that* are built here.

Hints

1. Whether you need *who* or *whom, whoever* or *whomever,* depends on the pronoun's place and function in your sentence. Apply the basic rule of pronoun usage: if the pronoun is acting as, or refers to, the subject, use *who/whoever.* Otherwise, use *whom/whomever.*

My husband was the idiot *who* entered a contest to win a trip to Moose Factory. (The pronoun refers to the subject of the sentence, "husband.")

The trip's promoters were willing to settle for *whomever* they could get. (The pronoun does not refer to the sentence's subject, "promoters"; it is the object of the preposition "for.")

An even simpler solution to this problem is to rewrite the sentence so you don't need either *who* or *whom:*

My husband entered a contest to win a trip to Moose Factory.

The trip's promoters were willing to settle for anyone they could get.

2. *That* is required more often than *which.* You should use *which* only in a clause that is separated from the rest of the sentence by commas.

> The moose *that* I met looked hostile.

> The moose, *which* was standing right in front of my car, looked hostile.

EXERCISE 34.4*

Correct the following sentences where necessary.

1. For two weeks, the pitcher that gave up the winning run had to live in hiding.
2. I am a long-time fan of David Cronenberg, a film director that began his career in Canada.
3. The vacuum-cleaner salesperson which came to our door was the sort of person that won't take no for an answer.
4. We are often attracted to people which are completely opposite to us.
5. The roast, which had been in the oven for three hours, was dried out by the time the last of the people that we had invited finally arrived.
6. Meat Loaf, which is the star headlining tonight's show, is responsible for two albums which have been nominated for Juno awards.
7. Rudolf's grandmother always told him that people that couldn't fly should stay out of airplanes.
8. Yesterday we took our ancient Lada, which we had bought from a friend that had lost his licence, to a scrap yard who paid us $50 for it.
9. People that take afternoon naps often pay a penalty: they are also people that suffer from insomnia.
10. The math problems which we worked out last night would have stymied anyone that hadn't done all the problem sets.

2.2 Pronouns Ending in *-one, -body,* or *-thing*

The second tricky aspect of pronoun–antecedent agreement involves these pronouns:

anyone	anybody	anything
everyone	everybody	everything
no one	nobody	nothing
someone	somebody	something
each (one)		

In Chapter 32 you learned that when these words are used as subjects, they are singular and take singular verbs. So it makes sense that the pronouns that stand for or refer to them must also be singular.

> Antecedents ending in *-one, -body,* or *-thing* are singular and must be referred to by singular pronouns: *he, she, it; his, her, its.*

Please put everything back in *its* place.
Anybody can retire comfortably if *he* or *she* begins planning now.
Everyone is expected to do *his* duty.
No one in *his* right mind would claim *he* enjoys living in this climate.

But take another look at the last two sentences. Until about twenty years ago, the pronouns *he, him,* and *his* were used with singular antecedents and were considered to refer to both men and women. Now, however, many readers are sensitive to gender bias in writing and feel that the masculine pronoun is inappropriate when referring to both sexes. As a writer, you should be aware of this sensitivity. If you want to appeal to the broadest possible audience, you should avoid what may be seen as sexist language.

In speech it has become acceptable to use plural pronouns with *-one, -body,* or *-thing* antecedents. Although these antecedents are grammatically singular and take singular verbs, they are often plural in meaning, and in conversation we find ourselves saying

Everybody clapped *their* hands and cheered.
No one has to stay if *they* don't want to.

This usage is acceptable only in speech; it is not acceptable in Standard Written English. Errors in pronoun–antecedent agreement are sometimes made because people are attempting to write gender-free language—that is, to write without indicating whether the person referred to is male or female.

A sentence like "Everyone is required to do *their* oral presentation" is incorrect, as we have seen; however, it does avoid making "everyone" male. It also avoids the awkwardness of "Everyone is expected to do *his* or *her* oral presentation."

There are two better ways to solve this problem.

1. Revise the sentence to leave the pronoun out.

An oral presentation is required of everyone.
     or
Everyone is required to deliver an oral presentation.

Such creative avoidance of gender-specific or incorrect constructions can be an interesting challenge. The results often sound a little artificial, however. The second method is easier to accomplish.

2. Revise the sentence to make both the antecedent and the pronoun plural.

> You are all required to deliver your oral presentations.
> *or*
> All students are required to deliver their oral presentations.

Here are a couple of examples for you to study:

> *Problem:* Each of the workers has his or her assignment.
> *Revision 1:* Each of the workers has an assignment.
> *Revision 2:* All of the workers have their assignments.

> *Problem:* Everyone will enjoy seeing his or her school friends again.
> *Revision 1:* Everyone will enjoy seeing school friends again.
> *Revision 2:* All graduates will enjoy seeing their school friends again.

EXERCISE 34.5*

In the following sentences, choose the correct word from the pairs in parentheses. Check your answers carefully before continuing.

1. Everyone who enjoys a thrilling match will reserve (his their) seat for today's chess club meeting.
2. Despite the inconvenience, everyone climbed to the fourth floor to hand in (her their) course evaluations.
3. Each of her sons has successfully completed (his their) diploma.
4. Someone with lots of money left (her their) purse in the washroom.
5. Every reporter must decide for (himself themselves) how far (he they) will go in pursuit of a story.

EXERCISE 34.6*

Rewrite the sentences in Exercise 34.5 to eliminate gender-specific language.

EXERCISE 34.7*

Correct the following sentences where necessary, being careful to avoid awkward repetition and gender-specific language.

1. Virginia claims that every one of her male friends has a room of their own.
2. Almost everyone I know is worried about whether he or she will find a job that will be suitable for him or her.
3. Anybody who applies for a job with this institution can expect to spend a lot of their time in selection committee interviews.

4. Taking a picture of someone when they are not looking can produce interesting results.

5. Nearly every man who can cook will tell you that they enjoy preparing food.

2.3 Vague References

Avoiding the third difficulty with pronoun–antecedent agreement depends on your common sense and your ability to think of your readers. If you try to look at your writing from your readers' point of view, it is unlikely that you will break this rule:

> A pronoun must *clearly* refer to the correct antecedent.

The mistake that occurs when you fail to follow this rule is called a **vague reference:**

> Ari told his brother that he was losing his hair.

Who is going bald? Here's another:

> The faculty are demanding higher salaries and fewer teaching hours, but the administration does not support them.

What does the administration not favour: higher salaries, fewer classes, or the faculty themselves?

In sentences like these, you can only guess the meaning because you don't know who or what is being referred to by the pronouns. You can make such sentences less confusing by using either more names or other nouns, and by using fewer pronouns. For example:

> Ari told his brother Sam that Sam was losing his hair.

> The faculty are demanding higher salaries and fewer teaching hours, but the administration does not support their demands.

Another type of vague reference occurs when there is no antecedent at all in the sentence for the pronoun to refer to.

> I sold my skis last year and can't even remember how to do it anymore. (Do what?)

> Reading is Sophia's passion, but she says she doesn't have a favourite. (A favourite what?)

How would you revise these sentences?

Be sure that every pronoun has a clear antecedent with which it agrees in number. Both must be singular, or both must be plural. Once you have mastered this principle, you'll have no trouble with pronoun–antecedent agreement.

EXERCISE 34.8*

Correct the following sentences where necessary. Some perfectly correct answers of yours may differ from the answers we've given. That's because the reference is so vague that the sentence can be understood in more than one way.

1. The gorilla was mean and thirsty because he had finished it all in the morning.
2. If your pet rat won't eat its food, feed it to the kitty.
3. Chuck told Rocco his teeth were falling out.
4. Whenever Stefan and Matt played poker, he stacked the deck.
5. I know that smoking is bad for me and everyone else, but I can't give them up.
6. Madonna has transformed herself at least three times in her career, which few other performers can claim.
7. Daphne backed her car into a garbage truck and dented it.
8. Rocco was suspicious of handgun control because he thought everyone should have one for late-night subway rides.
9. Rushing out the door, Rhonda slammed into a woman fixing her make-up; unfortunately, the force of the blow jammed a tube of lipstick up the poor woman's nose, breaking it.
10. If Preston and Lucien begin to argue, he'll tell him that he's never had any use for him and that he ought to keep his crazy ideas to himself.

EXERCISE 34.9

Correct the following sentences where necessary.

1. Each of her suitors had their own faults, but Drusilla decided to choose the one that had the most money.

2. Embezzling is what he does best, but he hasn't been able to pull one off lately.

3. Everyone may pick up their exams after Tuesday.

4. Our instructor said that passing grades would be given to those that successfully completed their field placement.

5. Each candidate must submit their portfolio, their résumé, and a neatly folded 50-dollar bill in order to be granted an interview.

6. Farida said to Myra that she had no idea how she felt when Alan broke up with her.

7. Everyone but me said that they would like to work for the company who gave me the job.

8. All of the girls are looked on as a sister here at Camp Kitsch-i-koo-mee.

9. Liz and Larry are a couple that don't have to worry where its next dollar is coming from.

10. Before a Canadian votes, it is their responsibility to make themselves familiar with the issues and the candidates.

3. Person Agreement

So far we have focussed on using pronouns correctly and clearly within a sentence. Now let's turn to the problem of **person agreement,** which means using pronouns consistently throughout a paragraph. Just like verbs, pronouns have three categories of "person" that we can use when we write or speak:

> **first person:** I, we
> **second person:** you (singular and plural)
> **third person:** he, she, *-one, -thing,* or *-body* pronouns; one; they

Here is the rule for person agreement:

Do not mix "persons" unless meaning requires it.

In other words, you must be consistent: if you begin a discussion in second person, you must use second person all the way through. Look at this sentence:

If *you* wish to succeed, *one* must work hard.

This is the most common error—mixing second-person *you* with third-person *one*. Here's another example:

> *One* can live happily in Inuvik only if *you* have a very warm coat.

We can correct this error by using the second person throughout:

- *You* can live happily in Inuvik if *you* have a very warm coat.

or by using the third person throughout:

- *One* can live happily in Inuvik if *one* has a very warm coat.
  or
- *People* can live happily in Inuvik only if *they* have very warm coats.

The bulleted sentences raise two points of style that you should be aware of:

1. Don't overuse *one*. Although all three versions are correct, they sound somewhat different from one another. The sentence in the second person sounds the most informal and natural—like something you would say. The second sentence, which uses *one* twice, sounds the most formal—even a little stilted. The third sentence falls between the other two in formality and is the one you'd be most likely to use in writing for school or business.
2. Don't overuse *he* or *she*. This construction is clumsy if it occurs too frequently.

> A student can easily pass this course if he or she applies himself or herself to his or her studies.

You can fix sentences like these by switching the whole sentence to the plural:

> Students can easily pass this course if they apply themselves to their studies.

EXERCISE 34.10*

In each of the following sentences, select the correct word from the choices given in parentheses. Check your answers before continuing.

1. If you want to make good egg rolls, I advise (them her you) to buy the ready-made wrappings.
2. If you win tonight's lottery, will (one he you) tell (one's his your) friends?
3. Even young children can learn to swim if (one they she) have a good instructor and apply (oneself themselves herself).

4. Every person working in this office should know that (they she) helped finish an important project.
5. When we toured the House of Commons, (you we he one) didn't see a single MP.

EXERCISE 34.11*

Correct the following sentences where necessary.

1. After the unfortunate brawl, Biff learned that if a person stomps on police officers, they can expect to end up in jail.

2. Everyone can expect to experience the horrors of nuclear war unless they raise their voices against nuclear proliferation.

3. If one leaves garbage at one's campsite, you may well have bears as midnight callers.

4. I knew she wasn't the woman for me when she asked me if Wayne Gretzky was the leader of Solidarity.

5. One will always think about the opportunities he's missed, even if you're happy with what you have.

6. Canadians who worry about street violence should keep in mind that, in comparison with New York, you are safe in downtown Kapuskasing after dark.

7. You should always wear garlic around the neck if one fears vampires.

8. Any woman who wears garlic won't have to worry about men harassing them, either.

9. Can one really know another person if you have never been to their home?

10. A sure way to lose one's friends is to eat all the Baskin Robbins ice

cream yourself.

EXERCISE 34.12

In the following passage, choose the right word from those in parentheses, keeping the person and number of the pronouns in agreement with the italicized word in the first sentence of each paragraph.

(1) When *people* see a dreadful occurrence, such as a war, an earthquake, or mass starvation, on television, it does not always affect (you one them). (2) It is one thing for people to see the ravages of war (yourself oneself themselves) and another thing to see a three-minute newsclip of the same battle, neatly edited by the CBC. (3) Even the horrible effects of natural catastrophes that wipe out whole populations are somehow minimized or trivialized when (we people you) see them on TV. (4) And while people may be shocked and horrified by the gaunt faces of starving children on the screen, (you one they) can easily escape into (our your their) familiar world of Egg McMuffins, Shake'n Bake, and Sara Lee Cheesecakes that is portrayed in commercial messages.

(5) Thus, the impact of television on *us* is a mixed one. (6) It is true that (you we they) are shown events, tragic and otherwise, that (you we they) could not possibly have seen before television. (7) In this way (our their your) world is drawn together more closely. (8) However, the risk in creating this immediacy, and perhaps the most tragic consequence of all, is that (we people you) may become desensitized and cease to feel or care about (your our their) fellow human beings.

EXERCISE 34.13*

Correct all pronoun errors in the following paragraph.

(1) There is a new winter sport that those of you who love the cold

and the snow should try. (2) One doesn't need as much money or skill

as one does for downhill skiing, and the equipment is much less trouble.

(3) When you take all the factors into consideration, snowboarding is

really the best way to enjoy winter. (4) First, we don't need to take out a

loan for the equipment; one can buy a decent snowboard and boots for less than half the price of most alpine ski outfits. (5) Second, we don't

need lessons to begin. (6) If you have ever skateboarded, then

snowboarding is easy. (7) Even if one is a complete novice, it doesn't

take long to become expert with a board. (8) Third, you don't have all

the hassle of changing outfits whenever we want to go out to the slopes.

(9) You can't walk in alpine ski boots, and skis are awkward to carry.

(10) But boarding boots are comfortable, and the board is easily tucked

under one's arm. (11) The only problems with snowboarding are that

skiers sometimes make your life difficult on the hill because they are

jealous of our mobility and freedom, and ski lifts are not designed to get

one safely to the top of a hill with a snowboard. (12) Despite these two

minor difficulties, snowboarding is gaining in popularity because it is an

easy and inexpensive winter sport.

EXERCISE 34.14

This exercise will test and reinforce your understanding of pronoun form, agreement, and consistency. Revise the following passage, correcting all pronoun errors.

(1) Getting engaged is the worst mistake I ever made. (2) My

girlfriend and me should have eloped or just started living together

instead of going through the process which has dominated our lives for

the past year. (3) Vera wanted a big wedding more than me, but one

does what one thinks is necessary, and so I went along with her plans.

(4) This meant one had to set the date well in advance so that the

photographer, the caterer, and the hall, not to mention your family and friends, could be alerted to keep the day free. (5) Setting the date meant an official engagement, and since Vera wanted one, we went off to the jeweller's. (6) Most of the rings were obviously intended for people much richer than us, but for a mere six weeks' salary, I was able to purchase the smallest one Vera would accept.

(7) Anyone that has gone through this process knows that their whole life is now centred on The Day. (8) One's life is consumed with choosing invitations and menus, with assembling the guest list, with choosing attendants, and with getting fitted for clothes you will probably never wear again. (9) Vera and her parents fretted over the tiniest details. (10) Her mother, Violet, is someone that is so generous she almost smothers you. (11) The salesperson in the bridal salon told her she would look good in a simple dress that cost only as much as a compact car. (12) Vera liked it less than her mother, but since it reminded her of her own wedding dress, it was the one she had to have. (13) Violet and Murray, her father, ended up making all the decisions that Vera and me should have been making, but us and them would have been arguing all the time if we hadn't just given in.

(14) Meanwhile, Vera's friends were having a wonderful time, enjoying every second of the planning and preparations. (15) You would have thought it was them that were getting married, not Vera and me. (16) One friend was baking the cake. (17) Another was getting their husband to chauffeur us in his 1966 Dodge. (18) The only part of the

prenuptial preparations that interested my friends was planning a stag party for the groom: poor, miserable, embarrassed I.

(19) After a couple of months of this activity, getting married began to seem more trouble than it was worth, but since everyone now expected it, we had no choice but to go ahead and have one. (20) Every man that has gone through this experience even once in their life knows the feeling of helplessness as they are swept along in the current of the event. (21) All they can do is pray to keep one's sanity, one's cool, and one's solvency. (22) After the agonies of an engagement, marriage is a piece of cake.

Punctuation

CHAPTER 35

Question and Exclamation Marks

The Question Mark

Everyone knows that a question mark follows an interrogative, or asking, sentence, but we all sometimes forget to include it. Let this chapter serve as a reminder not to forget!

> The **question mark** is the end punctuation for all interrogative sentences.

The question mark gives your readers an important clue to the meaning of your sentence. "There's more?" is vastly different in meaning from "There's more!" and that difference is communicated to readers by the punctuation alone.

The only time you don't end a question with a question mark is when the question is part of a statement.

Is anyone there? (question)
I asked if anyone was there. (statement)
Do you understand? (question)
I wonder whether you understand. (statement)

EXERCISE 35.1*

Supply the correct end punctuation for the following sentences. Then check your answers.

1. Did you ever think that the Canadian dollar would drop below the U.S. 70-cents mark
2. Our trip to the States this summer is going to be very expensive, isn't it
3. I cannot believe that you would question my integrity
4. I wonder if my apartment will ever be the same after their visit
5. How can you just stand there while a woman is being beaten
6. If we can't finish the project on time, will we lose the contract
7. Finish your nice liver casserole, children, or you won't get any dessert
8. Did you know there are only 18 000 elephants in all of India
9. We have no answer to the question why we hired an unqualified, inexperienced person for such a sensitive position
10. Did you know that Harpo Marx was just as capable of talking as his brothers Groucho, Chico, Gummo, and Zeppo

The Exclamation Mark

The exclamation mark is a useful piece of punctuation for conveying your tone of voice to your readers. There is a distinct difference in tone between these two sentences:

> There's a man behind you.

> There's a man behind you!

In the first sentence, information is being supplied, perhaps about the line-up at a grocery-store check-out counter. The second sentence might be a shouted warning about a mugger.

Use an **exclamation mark** as end punctuation in sentences requiring extreme emphasis or dramatic effect.

Please note that the exclamation mark will have "punch" or drama only if you use it sparingly. If you use an exclamation mark after every third sentence, how will your readers know when you really mean to indicate excitement? The overuse of the exclamation mark is a technique employed in comic books. The writers of comics use an exclamation mark after every sentence to try to heighten the impact of their characters' words. Instead, they rob their exclamation marks of all meaning.

Practically any sentence could end with an exclamation mark, but remember that the punctuation changes the meaning of the sentence. Read each of the following sentences with and without an exclamation mark, and picture the situation that would call for each reading.

He's gone   Don't touch that button

The room was empty   There she goes again

EXERCISE 35.2*

Supply the correct end punctuation for each of the following sentences. In many cases, the punctuation you use will depend on how you want the sentence to be read. Notice the extent to which different punctuation can change the meaning of a sentence.

1. You must be kidding

2. Turn left Now

3. I can't believe I actually passed

4. Oh, great We're moving to Backwater, Ontario

5. Run It's right behind you

6. I'm freezing Turn the heat up

7. "Workers of the world, unite" (Karl Marx)

8. Finally Someone is coming to take our order

9. For the last time, leave me alone

10. Get lost I can manage perfectly well by myself

EXERCISE 35.3

Supply correct end punctuation for these sentences.

1. We aren't sure if we're getting paid this week or not
2. Reginald wanted his broker to tell him whether pork bellies would be a good investment
3. Where in the world are you going with your hair dyed green and that safety pin in your nose
4. Arthur asked Catherine where she was going

5. Would you believe that the heaviest world-champion boxer, Primo Carnera, weighed in at 123 kg in a 1933 fight
6. That's one king-size heavyweight
7. Do you mean to tell me that your lovely necklace is made of shellacked moose-droppings
8. You must be kidding
9. Dr. and Mr. Widget arrived at the reception in their new Rolls-Royce
10. Hooray This chapter is finished

CHAPTER 36

Quotation Marks

Quotation marks (" ") are used to set off direct speech (dialogue), short passages of quoted material, and some titles. Quotation marks come in pairs; there must be a set to show where the dialogue, quotation, or title begins and a set to show where it ends. You must be absolutely sure that whatever you put between them is stated *exactly* as it is in the source you are using. The only other thing you need to know about quotation marks is how to punctuate what comes between them.

Dialogue

When you quote direct speech, include normal sentence punctuation. If the speaker's name is included in your own sentence, set it off with commas. A comma or the end punctuation mark that is part of the quotation comes *inside* the final set of quotation marks. An end punctuation mark that is not part of the quotation goes outside the final set of quotation marks.

"Did you," Rick asked in a rage, "drink all of my Brador?"

"No, there are a couple of swigs left," I said.

Can you believe that Krystal actually said to Dwight, "Get lost!"?

Be careful to put quotation marks only around direct speech (someone's exact words). Don't use quotation marks with indirect speech:

In a rage, Rick asked me if I had drunk all his Brador. (These are not Rick's exact words, nor is the sentence a question.)

I can't believe that Krystal actually told Dwight to get lost. (These are not the speaker's exact words, and the sentence is a statement, not a question.)

A quotation *within* a quotation is punctuated by single quotation marks:

"If you really expect me to go out with you again," Lori told her date, "you'll stop calling me 'Babe.'"

Quoted Material

When you quote a *short* written passage, you can work it into your own sentence. Again, include normal sentence punctuation within the quotation marks. (See Chapter 21 for more specific instructions, examples, and exercises.)

"Marriage," wrote Dr. Samuel Johnson, "has many pains, but celibacy has no pleasures."

"The medium is the message," observed Marshall McLuhan in his book *Understanding Media*.

According to Rudolph, who is Canada's champion couch potato, "Death is Nature's way of telling you to slow down."

If your own introductory words form a complete sentence, use a colon:

Dr. Samuel Johnson is famous for his remark on wedded life: "Marriage has many pains, but celibacy has no pleasures."

Marshall McLuhan captured the imagination of a generation brought up on television: "The medium is the message."

Rudolf, Canada's champion couch potato, summed up Generation X's attitude to exercise as follows: "Death is Nature's way of telling you to slow down."

All the lines of a *long* quoted passage (more than four lines of print) should be indented ten spaces from the left margin so that the quotation stands apart from your own text. An indented quotation is not enclosed in quotation marks. You will find examples of long quotations on pp. 197–98 and p. 223.

Titles

Unless you are using a word processor that prints out italics, titles of whole books or volumes should be *underlined;* titles of parts of those books or volumes should be placed in quotation marks. Thus, titles of books, magazines, pamphlets, newspapers, plays, and films should be italicized or underlined. Titles of single articles, essays, stories, or poems should be placed in quotation marks.

> "The Bear on the Delhi Road," a poem by Earle Birney, appears in <u>Fifteen Canadian Poets</u>.

> "I Am Jane's Pancreas," in <u>Reader's Digest</u>, makes fascinating reading.

Note: In printed works—such as this text—titles of books are printed in *italics,* not underlined.

EXERCISE 36.1*

Place the quotation marks correctly and insert the necessary punctuation in the following sentences.

1. Pardon me, boys, is this the Transylvania Station? asked the man in the black cape.
2. The child asked when his mother would call.
3. This film exclaimed Granny is more explicit than *National Geographic!*
4. As *The Globe & Mail* put it The Canadian dollar went on a roller-coaster ride yesterday.
5. It was the philosopher Ludwig Feuerbach who first said man is what he eats, and we here at Big Boy restaurants certainly agree with that.
6. Raoul claimed that he was deathly afraid of airplanes.
7. Your every whim will be catered to promised the Sybaritic Spas brochure.
8. I wondered whether they would peel grapes for me and find slaves to perform lomi-lomi on my aching muscles.
9. If not I asked my friend why should we spend $800 for a weekend in Collingwood?
10. The Guinness Book of Records claims that the oldest living thing is the California bristlecone pine tree which is almost 5000 years old.

EXERCISE 36.2*

Place the quotation marks and punctuation correctly in these sentences. Check your answers before going on to the next exercise.

1. Did you see the strange look on his face asked Roderick.
2. Frank asked Reva if she would like to play bridge.

3. Of course she answered, usually willing to oblige.
4. Have you read my essay, Dreaming Your Way to an Energized Future Dr. Piffle asked his numbed audience. It's in my new book, entitled Upscale Networking in a Self-Actualized Cosmos.
5. The fellow to my left hissed I'd sooner be horsewhipped; where do they find these guys?
6. I forget whether it was John Paul Jones or George Chuvalo who said I have not yet begun to fight.
7. The vice-president had bad news for the staff Due to lower-than-expected profits from the bookstore and excessive vandalism at the parking gates, you're all terminated.
8. The book claims that someday we will get injections of our own white blood cells taken during our youth; these injections will ward off infections and ageing.
9. Wasn't it Irving Layton who described ageing as the inescapable lousiness of growing old?
10. Pierre Trudeau once told Canadians that the state had no business in the nation's bedrooms.

EXERCISE 36.3

Now test your understanding of quotation marks and the punctuation that goes with them.

1. How could you possibly have got through twelve or more years of school, fumed Professor Green, and not know the first thing about punctuating direct speech, quotations from printed material, or titles of published works
2. Cinderella had a few choice words for her fairy godmother How do you expect me to walk, let alone dance, in glass slippers, anyway
3. Would you rather the fairy replied go to the ball in your Reeboks
4. Essay Essentials deserves to be a best-seller, said Professor Browning. The chapter entitled Quotation Marks alone is worth the price of the book.
5. He shoots! He scores! was the trademark exclamation of Foster Hewitt, Canada's hockey broadcast pioneer.
6. There is a tide in the affairs of men, began the actor, and half the audience murmured the words of the famous soliloquy along with him.
7. Listen Krystal said Dwight. They're playing our song, Muskrat Love.
8. The Golden Rule for the 1990s seems to be that those who have the gold, rule.
9. If it's all right with you, Bruce said to his mother gently, I'd really rather that you and Dad didn't come along on my first date.
10. When she returned our tests, Miss Grundy said she was amazed we had mastered the mysteries of quotation marks so quickly.

CHAPTER 37

The Comma

The **comma** is the most frequently used—and misused—punctuation mark in English. Leaving out a necessary comma can distort the meaning of a sentence. Unnecessary commas can distract your readers and give your sentences a jerky quality. Perhaps nothing is so sure a sign of a competent writer as the correct use of commas, so it is very important that you master them. This chapter presents four rules that will give you a good indication of when you should use a comma. If the sentence you are writing is not covered by one of these four rules, remember this:

When in doubt, leave the comma out!

Four Comma Rules

In this section we present the four essential rules that cover most instances in which you need to use a comma.

1. Use commas to separate items in a series of three or more.

Required subjects are math, English, bookkeeping, and business law.

Hold down the shift key, press the Control key, and touch F1 to start the program.

Our dog is at the vet's, the cat is pregnant, the kids have the flu, my husband is having a nervous breakdown, and tomorrow my in-laws arrive for a two-week visit.

The comma before the *and* at the end of the list is optional; use it or leave it out, but be consistent.

EXERCISE 37.1*

Insert commas where necessary in the following sentences.

1. Philosophy and sociology are the two subjects I am finding most difficult.
2. *Germinal The Trial* and *Middlemarch* are three of my favourite novels.
3. Be sure to pick up gin tonic limes and ice.
4. All we need now is gift wrap ribbon tape a card and a bow.
5. Rudolf stomped into the room threw himself into a chair drained a six-pack of Blue and crushed the cans against his forehead.

> 2. Use comma(s) to separate from the rest of the sentence any word or expression that is *not essential* to the sentence's meaning or that means the same as something else in the sentence.

Three tests in one week are too many, in my opinion.

The phrase "in my opinion" is not essential to the meaning of the sentence, so it's separated from the rest of the sentence by a comma.

Stephen Leacock, one of the world's great humorists, was a professor of economics at McGill.

The phrase "one of the world's great humorists" means the same as "Stephen Leacock." The two expressions refer to the same person, so the second is set off by commas. When a nonessential word or phrase occurs in the middle of a sentence, rather than at the beginning or the end, be sure to put commas *both* before and after it.

If it were up to me, Selena, I'd hire you right now.

The word "Selena," the name of the person being spoken to, is not essential to the meaning of the sentence, so it's set off by commas.

EXERCISE 37.2*

Insert commas where necessary in the following sentences. Check your answers before going on.

1. The cheetah is of course the fastest animal on earth.
2. Everyone who sees the movie will be shocked.
3. Malcolm Lowry an alcoholic British expatriate wrote *Under the Volcano* perhaps the finest novel ever written in Canada.
4. Many children in this school it seems are arriving in the morning without having had an adequate breakfast.
5. The lead singer in a bid for notoriety bit the head off a bat during the performance.

---

3. Place a comma between independent clauses when they are joined by these transition words:

and	nor	for
or	but	yet
so		

We enjoyed the concert, but it was expensive.

It's cold in this classroom, so I'm going to wear my toque.

I just can't seem to make it to class on time, yet I feel I should go.

I didn't win the bet, for our team lost in overtime.

Be sure that the sentence contains two independent clauses rather than a single subject and a compound verb.

They fought hard for change and finally won the election. (Here They is the subject and there are two verbs, fought and won. No comma is needed between two verbs that share one subject.)

They fought hard for change, and they finally won the election. (This sentence has two independent clauses—They fought and they won— joined by "and." The comma is required here.)

EXERCISE 37.3*

Insert commas where necessary in the following sentences. Check your answers before continuing.

1. I refuse to wear that turkey costume to the party nor will I go as a horse's rear end.

2. Yesterday he broke up with her but today he is begging for forgiveness.
3. We loved the book but hated the movie.
4. The boss told him to stop leering at the female staff members or she would fire him.
5. Waving a red flag in front of a bull is supposed to enrage him yet experiments have shown that bulls are colour-blind.

---

4. Put a comma after any word or group of words that comes immediately before an independent clause.

Rudolf, you aren't paying attention. (The second rule applies here, too.)

Though almost 40, he still considers himself one of the boys.

Despite the fact that we lost, it was a good game.

If the mountain won't come to us, we'll have to go to the mountain.

EXERCISE 37.4*

Write out the four comma rules on a sheet of paper. Then insert commas where necessary in the following sentences. Check your answers when you're done.

1. Third insert your finger into the electrical socket.
2. Overwhelmed by the generous offer we spent the evening watching Paul's home movies.
3. If you work for an airline company policy states you are entitled to one free trip a year.
4. In addition your next of kin is entitled to reduced fares.
5. Unless you learn to use commas properly your writing will lack sophistication and polish.

One final note about the comma before you try the review exercises: *never* place a *single* comma between a subject and its verb:

Right: Adam and Celene are going into business.

Never: Adam and Celene, are going into business.

However, two commas between a subject and its verb are all right *if* the commas are setting off nonessential material:

Adam and Celene, both recent graduates, are going into business.

Insert commas where necessary in Exercises 37.5 through 37.8. Check your answers to each set, and make sure you understand any mistakes before you go on to the next exercise.

EXERCISE 37.5*

1. Pinot noir which is a type of grape grown in California Oregon British Columbia and Ontario produces a delicious red wine.
2. There are I am told people who don't like garlic but you won't find any of them eating at Freddy's.
3. I use e-mail to communicate with my colleagues a fax machine to keep in touch with clients and Canada Post to send greetings to my friends
4. Canada Post which often takes four days to deliver a letter within a city is known in our office as "snail mail."
5. "You must agree Ms. Petrarch that my poems are classics."
6. According to G.K. Chesterton "If a thing is worth doing it is worth doing badly."
7. Looking for a competent computer technologist we interviewed tested investigated and rejected 30 applicants.
8. How you choose to phrase your resignation is up to you but I expect to have it on my desk by morning.
9. Rudolf's beard which looks ragged and moth-eaten could hardly be described as a fashion statement.
10. Canada a country known internationally for beautiful scenery peaceful intentions and violent hockey always places near the top of the United Nations' list of desirable places to live.

EXERCISE 37.6*

1. Fascinating challenging high-paying jobs are available to the people who transfer to our exciting Beirut branch office.
2. Oswald your lawyers agreed to work with you not against you didn't they?
3. Our guard dog a Rottweiler caught an intruder and maimed him for life.
4. Unfortunately my Uncle Ladislaw was the intruder and he intends to sue us for every penny we have.
5. The year 1945 marked the end of World War II and the beginning of assistance to war-torn nations.
6. All warm-blooded animals that give live birth and suckle their young are classified as mammals but no one knows how to classify the warm-blooded egg-laying chick-nursing platypus.
7. We are pleased with your résumé and we are offering you an interview this week.
8. We are pleased with your résumé and are offering you an interview this week.

9. Although Biff begged Drusilla refused to wear a tattooed heart with his name in the middle.
10. Igor asked "May I show you to your quarters or would you prefer to spend the night in the dungeon?"

EXERCISE 37.7*

I sometimes wonder what our ancestors, were they able to observe us now would think of some of the activities we take for granted. I'm sure that rollerblading would seem peculiar to them as would surfing water-skiing and hang-gliding. However I suspect that our forebears would find even those strange activities understandable perhaps even enjoyable compared with jogging. The sight of otherwise perfectly reasonable people decked out in various types of colourful underwear doggedly puffing and sweating along every pathway road and trail would I am convinced put The Fear into Great-Grandad and send him scurrying back whence he had come.

All kinds of people jog: there are short joggers tall joggers fat joggers thin joggers; serious joggers light-hearted joggers fashionable joggers and practical joggers; joggers with outfits of every hue from black to white and every shade in between. In fact there may be more people who jog than people who don't!

I gave up on jogging some years ago with the excuse that although I adored distance running an old basketball injury prevented me from measuring up to my own expectations. This pitiful story together with a wistful sigh for lost youth usually gets me off the hook. While my friends claim to be fit and keen I take satisfaction in quoting Satchel Paige the famous baseball player who at age 60 pitched three scoreless innings in the major leagues. In his "Six Rules for a Long Life," Satch warns "On no account run." This is sound advice and I intend to live by this sensible and energy-efficient rule.

EXERCISE 37.8

To test your mastery of commas, provide the necessary punctuation for the following sentences.

1. There seems to be a feeling among this year's crop of students unexpressed but nevertheless sincerely believed that it is not possible to fail a college course.
2. The source of this belief in my opinion is the students' high-school experience but it could also stem from the fact that they haven't yet had any assignments returned.
3. Samuel de Champlain Jacques Cartier and Étienne Brûlé were among the first Europeans to explore what is now Canada.
4. Murray Porter one of an increasing number of Canadian aboriginal singers is the author of "1492: Who Found Who" a song about Christopher Columbus.
5. Angered by her refusal hurt by her tone and humiliated by her friends Wayne returned to his table and vowed he would never again ask Sparkle to dance with him.
6. Having forgotten their keys Dwight and Rudolf tried to force the door open but eventually had to break it down.
7. While the Superbowl tradition goes back about three decades the Grey Cup has a history that stretches back into the last century.
8. One could in fact make a case that honesty integrity and forthrightness are liabilities to anyone who seeks to succeed in politics.
9. The partners in our company which produces and tests software include a civil servant from Newfoundland a technologist from Quebec a teacher from Manitoba and a rancher from Alberta.
10. It took Gordie Howe 26 years to set the NHL record for career goals 801 but it took Wayne Gretzky only 15 years in the league to tie Howe's goal record.

CHAPTER 38

The Semicolon

The colon and **semicolon** are often confused and used as if they were interchangeable. They serve very different functions, however, and their correct use can dramatically improve your readers' understanding of your writing. Here is one function of the semicolon:

> The semicolon can replace the period; in other words, it can appear between two independent clauses.

You should use the semicolon when the two clauses (sentences) you are joining are closely connected in meaning or when there is a cause-and-effect relationship between them.

I'm too tired; I can't stay awake any longer.

There's a good movie on tonight; it's a Canadian film called *Léolo*.

A period could have been used instead of the semicolon in either of these sentences, but the close connection between the clauses prompted the writer to use a semicolon.

Certain connecting or transition words are sometimes put between independent clauses to show cause and effect or continuation of an idea. Words used in this way must be preceded by a semicolon and followed by a comma.

> Put a semicolon in front of these words and a comma after:
>
> | | | |
> |---|---|---|
> | ; i.e., | ; nevertheless, | ; then, |
> | ; e.g., | ; otherwise, | ; in addition, |
> | ; consequently, | ; furthermore, | ; on the other hand, |
> | ; however, | ; in fact, | ; instead, |
> | ; therefore, | ; thus, | ; finally, |
> | ; moreover, | ; that is, | ; also, |
> | ; besides, | ; as a result, | |
> | ; for example, | ; next, | |

I've spent nearly three years here; nevertheless, I'm thinking of transferring to another college.

The interviewer told me, "Your qualifications are inadequate; furthermore, your letter of application and your résumé are a mess."

For once, I started my term paper when it was assigned; consequently, I expect to finish it well before the deadline.

Note, however, that when the words listed in the box are used as nonessential expressions rather than as connecting words, they are separated from the rest of the sentence by commas (rule 2 in Chapter 37).

However hard I try, I just can't seem to please Professor Gradgrind.

Two minutes later, however, she contradicted her earlier instructions.

Sometimes semicolons should be used in a list instead of commas:

> To make a *complex* list easier to read and understand, put semicolons between the items instead of commas.

Here's an example:

We need to take several items: matches to start a fire; an axe or hatchet to cut wood; cooking utensils and eating implements; and, of course, food.

EXERCISE 38.1*

Put a checkmark next to the sentences that are correctly punctuated. Check your answers before continuing.

1. _____ We've eaten all the goodies, it's time to go home.

2. _____ Many doctors claim weather affects our health; in fact, barometric pressure has a direct effect on arthritis.

3. _____ Your instructor would like to see you pass, however, there may be a small fee involved.

4. _____ Florence is going to Hollywood, she wants to appear on *Let's Make a Deal.*

5. _____ We knew that the party was a huge success: Uncle Morty tap-danced across the top of the piano Aunt Madeline did her Big Bird imitation and Biff wrestled two of his cousins.

6. _____ Many people dislike hockey; because some of the players act like goons rather than athletes.

7. _____ Orville tried and tried; but he couldn't get the teacher's attention.

8. _____ He dangled one of his classmates from a window; that caught the teacher's eye immediately.

9. _____ First we'll have a cool drink then we'll see if we can find a way to start this car.

10. _____ Dudley left his clothes by the pool; so it's no wonder people in the lounge are looking at him strangely.

EXERCISE 38.2*

Correct the faulty punctuation in Exercise 38.1.

EXERCISE 38.3*

Correct the faulty punctuation.

1. When you consider the consequences; cheating on your income tax is probably not a good idea.
2. A decade ago, distinct computer languages were used for specific purposes, for example; COBOL was used in business, whereas FORTRAN was used in the sciences.
3. Today however most programs are written in C++ or in high-level Unix.
4. There are many Canadians who are famous abroad but virtually unknown at home, one example is Norman Bethune.

5. My telephone is not working. The silence is wonderful thus I have decided not to get it fixed.

EXERCISE 38.4*

Insert commas and semicolons where necessary in these sentences. Then check your answers.

1. A day without puns is like a day without sunshine, it leaves gloom for improvement.
2. We must organize our finances otherwise we'll be broke before April.
3. We had all hoped you would be able to join us, however, since you have a previous engagement we'll just have to carry on without you.
4. As a dog lover in general and an Afghan owner in particular I have to take a lot of abuse, for example my wife gave me a book rating the intelligence of various breeds of dog and the Afghan ranked 79th out of 79 breeds tested.
5. It is not very difficult to become wealthy if you're in your early twenties all you need to do is put the price of a pack of cigarettes a day into an RSP each year and you'll be a millionaire by the time you retire.
6. Foolishly, I chose to write my essay about NAFTA, I thought it was a new football league.
7. We decided to go to a nearby restaurant for pizza, that is we would have gone but Norm insisted on waiting for Mairi and by the time we got there it was closed.
8. The entire town is in an uproar it seems Rudolf has been missing since yesterday.
9. There is one person however who does not seem to be distressed and that is Rudolf's mother.
10. According to a recent *Gourmet Magazine* poll four of the top ten restaurants in the world are in Paris, three those ranking eighth ninth and tenth are in the United States and two are in Tokyo. One is in Thailand.

EXERCISE 38.5*

Correct the punctuation in these sentences by changing commas to semicolons or colons where necessary. (Lewis Thomas, excerpt from "Notes on Punctuation," in *The Medusa and the Snail* by Lewis Thomas, New York: Viking Press, 1979, pp. 126–27.)

1. I have grown fond of semicolons in recent years. The semicolon tells you that there is still some question about the preceding full sentence, something needs to be added.
2. It is almost always a greater pleasure to come across a semicolon than a period. The period tells you that that is that, if you didn't get all the meaning you wanted or expected, you got all the writer intended to parcel out and now you have to move along.

3. But with a semicolon there, you get a pleasant little feeling of expectancy, there is more to come, read on, it will get clearer.

4. Colons are a lot less attractive, for several reasons, firstly, they give you the feeling of being rather ordered around, or at least having your nose pointed in a direction you might not be inclined to take if left to yourself, and, secondly, you suspect you're in for one of those sentences that will be labelling the points to be made, firstly, secondly, and so forth, with the implication that you haven't enough sense to keep track of a sequence of notions without having them numbered.

5. Also, many writers use this system loosely and incompletely, starting out with number one and number two as though counting off on their fingers but then going on and on without the succession of labels you've been led to expect, leaving you floundering about searching for the ninthly or seventeenthly that ought to be there but isn't.

EXERCISE 38.6

Test your mastery of the semicolons and commas by correcting the punctuation in these sentences.

1. Growing old has never really bothered me in fact I consider ageing a huge improvement over the alternative.

2. There's someone at the door I think she wants to speak to you about the rent.

3. The construction was way behind schedule consequently we lost our performance bonus.

4. Among many products being standardized by the European Community is the condom however a number of nations have complained that the standard size is too small.

5. Failing to stop at the light was in fact the least of his offences the police were much more interested in his expired driver's licence.

6. The prospect of having to cope with the much-publicized "information highway" or "info-bahn" terrifies me I was destined to be a pedestrian on the highway of technological life.

7. I suggest you offer me a 15 percent increase in salary otherwise there will be no reason for me to take on this extra responsibility.

8. A practice that works well in one country may not work in another for example every man in Switzerland is required to own a rifle. The United States might be able to adopt this practice quite comfortably however Canada could not.

9. There are no frozen pizzas no Buffalo-style chicken wings and no ice cream left in the freezer; so we might as well eat out tonight.

10. To use or not to use a semicolon is often a matter of the writer's choice nevertheless there are some instances in which it is required.

CHAPTER 39

The Colon

The **colon** functions as an "introducer." When a statement is followed by a list or by one or more examples, the colon between the statement and what follows alerts the readers to what is coming.

Penny's personality is characterized by two dominant traits: tenacity and viciousness.

There are three things I can't stand: brussels sprouts, cats, and Leslie Nielsen's films.

Only one person can cure your TV addiction: you.

The statement that precedes the colon must be a complete sentence (an independent clause). Therefore, a colon can never come after *is* or *are*. For example,

Two things I cannot stand are: cats and brussels sprouts.

This is incorrect because the statement before the colon is not a complete sentence.

The colon, then, follows a complete statement and introduces a list or example that defines or amplifies something in the statement. The information after the colon often answers the question "what?" or "who?"

There is a single barrier to the achievement of worldwide peace: [what?] human nature.

He peered into the clear water to see his favourite friend: [who?] himself.

The colon is also used after a complete sentence introducing a quotation.

Irving Layton is not fond of academic critics: "There hasn't been a writer of power and originality during the past century who hasn't had to fight his way to acceptance against the educated pipsqueaks hibernating in universities." (Layton, in a letter to *The Montreal Star*)

The uses of the colon can be summed up as follows:

> The colon follows an independent clause and introduces one of three things: an example, a list, or a quotation.

EXERCISE 39.1*

Put a checkmark next to the sentences that are correctly punctuated. Check your answers before going on.

1. ____ Believe it or not, the country that produces the most films every year is: India.

2. ____ In drafting the budget, we must be careful to avoid the one technique the president has said she will not entertain deficit financing.

3. ✓ I have a hard time choosing between my two favourite teams, which are the Nordiques and the Canucks.

4. ____ According to Roderick, who is several decades out of date, the only important things in life are: sex, drugs, and rock 'n' roll.

5. ____ Sebastian's room-mates are trying to encourage him to: move with the times.

6. ✓ One topic has dominated the health concerns of the world throughout the 1990s: AIDS.

7. ✓ Two of Canada's highest awards in professional sports are the Stanley Cup and the Grey Cup.

8. ____ All most students ask is that their teachers treat them with: courtesy, fairness, and respect.

9. ____ Of course, there are always a few students who demand what no true professional will provide special treatment.

10. ✓ Jordan wants to go home to be comforted by the only person in the world who truly understands him: his mother.

EXERCISE 39.2*

Insert colons in the following sentences where necessary, and then check your answers. If you find you've made any mistakes, review the chapter, study the examples, and be sure you understand why your answers were wrong before going on.

1. I have set myself three goals this year to achieve an 80 percent average, to get a good summer job, and to buy a car.
2. Right after we moved in, we discovered we had a problem termites.
3. Our credit card consultant asked us an important question after our bankruptcy "Why don't you cut up your credit cards?"
4. Several Canadian writers are even better known abroad than they are at home Carol Shields, Neil Bissoondath, and Michael Ondaatje are three examples.
5. There are a number of inexpensive activities that will improve physical fitness; swimming, tennis, jogging, even brisk walking.
6. Jocelyn is trying very hard to accomplish two mutually contradictory things a significant weight loss and success as a restaurant critic.
7. Several of the animals on the international list of endangered species are native to Canada; the wood bison, the Northern kit fox, and the whooping crane.
8. We'll finish the assignment by tomorrow only if we stay up all night and consume vast quantities of pizza and black coffee.
9. The majority of Canada's population is worn out and exhausted at the end of a long, hard winter, but most people are able to console themselves with one comforting thought, spring will arrive sometime in May or June.
10. There are several troublesome implications of biological engineering, but one in particular is frightening to most people the cloning of human beings.

EXERCISE 39.3*

Correct the incorrectly punctuated sentences in Exercise 39.1.

EXERCISE 39.4

To test your knowledge of colons, put a check mark beside the sentences that are correctly punctuated.

1. ____ There aren't many people I look up to, but one of them is: Shaquille O'Neal.

2. ____ The TV is always asking me challenging questions "It's 11:05. Do you know where your children are?"

3. ____ You have all the qualities of a Doberman: except one, loyalty.

4. ____ For my birthday, my sister gave me: a pair of hand-knitted socks (I'm allergic to wool), a box of chocolates (I'm on a diet), and a coffee mug with the Petro-Canada logo on it.

5. ____ For a number of reasons, my favourite relative is not: my sister

6. ____ In spite of his ineptitude, he won a prize; the slow-but-steady-progress award.

7. ____ He wants to apologize to you: but he's afraid you won't talk to him.

8. ____ Several names are not on my list of possible names for our new son: including Rex, Nero, Attila, and Leaf.

9. ____ The guitar riff in this tune is great but has one serious drawback: I can't play it.

10. ____ I have a meeting this afternoon, but I don't want to go; I know it will be: boring and useless.

EXERCISE 39.5

Correct the incorrectly punctuated sentences in Exercise 39.4.

CHAPTER 40

Dashes and Parentheses

When you are talking with someone, you use your voice and your delivery to punctuate: you pause for a short time (commas) or for a longer time (semicolons and periods); you shout (exclamation marks); or you query (question marks). When you write, your punctuation substitutes for your body language: it helps you make sure your writing will make sense to your readers.

One of the stylistic devices you can use to add variety and flexibility to your writing is the insertion into your sentences of words or phrases that add to but are *not essential* to the sentence's meaning. That is, the word or phrase could be omitted and the sentence would still be complete and would still make sense. It might, however, lack grace or interest.

You can use four punctuation marks to add nonessential material to your sentences: quotation marks, commas, dashes, and parentheses. You are already familiar with the first two. Here is your opportunity to master the last two: the **dash**—which looks like this—and **parentheses** (round brackets). (If you are typing, the dash is two hyphens with no space on either side.)

Dashes

Dashes are used to mark a break in thought or an abrupt shift in emphasis.

> 1. Use a dash to introduce a word, phrase, or clause that summarizes or restates what came just before.

I still love dried apricots and pickled beets—foods my mother gave me as treats when I was a child.

Perseverance, spirit, and skill—these three qualities ensure a good game.

Atwood, Ondaatje, Laurence, Mowat, Clarke, and Richler—for a country with a relatively small population, Canada has produced an extraordinary number of internationally acclaimed novelists.

---

2. Use a pair of dashes to enclose a series of items separated by commas.

Four of the managers—Olive, Muhsin, Luis, and Neville—are new to the McDonald's franchise at the zoo.

Because they were afraid of the police, my so-called friends—Roman, Faye, and Luba—all betrayed me.

The apartment he showed me would have been fine, had it not been for the tenants—moths, cockroaches, and silverfish—already making it their home.

---

3. Use a dash or a pair of dashes to set off from the rest of the sentence a climactic or emphatic comment.

I expect—and I always will—that students at this level should be self-motivated.

Our neighbour—the accused murderer—is hanging out rabbit pelts to dry.

If you really want to go—even though you haven't been invited—I'll take you.

Note that dashes set off material that is not grammatically part of the sentence. If you were to omit the words set off by dashes, the sentence would still make sense.

Dashes can be misused if you use them too frequently. Unless you are writing very informally—in a personal letter, for instance—save dashes for the very occasional phrase to which you want to draw emphatic attention.

EXERCISE 40.1*

Add dashes where they are appropriate.

1. The aboriginal tribes of England I've forgotten their name painted themselves blue.
2. My purpose in moving from Vancouver to Hope like that of hundreds of people before me was to find affordable housing.
3. We shall have to start without her again!
4. Skiing and skating if you like these sports, you'll love Quebec.
5. Tending to his garden, writing his memoirs, and dining with friends these were the pleasures Arnold looked forward to in retirement.
6. What is missing in his life is obvious rest and relaxation!
7. Zoe should do well in fact, I'm sure she will in the engineering program.
8. Rudolf was amazed positively thunderstruck when he learned Uncle Vladimir had won a million dollars.
9. Historians, diarists, and chroniclers these are the recorders of our past.
10. Dashes allow you to insert with a kind of shout the occasional exclamation into your sentences.

Parentheses

Like dashes, parentheses are used to enclose an interruption to a sentence. The difference between them is a matter of tone: dashes SHOUT—they serve to draw the reader's attention to the material they enclose—but parentheses (which should be used sparingly) "whisper." Parentheses are similar to theatrical asides; they are subordinate to the main narrative or action but are not to be missed.

---

1. Use parentheses to enclose extra information that is not emphasized.

Giselle's teaching schedule (she is in class seven hours a day) gives her little time to meet with students individually.

They brought me to their village and presented me to their chief (who was a woman) and to the tribal councillors.

Note the difference in tone your choice of punctuation makes. Compare the example above with this version:

They brought me to their village and presented me to their chief—who was a woman—and to the tribal councillors.

> 2. Use parentheses to enclose explanatory material that is not part of the main sentence.

"Lightweight Lit." (an essay presented earlier) was written by an English teacher who prefers to remain anonymous.

The Malagasy (people of Madagascar) like to eat a kapoaka of rice (enough to fill a condensed-milk can) three times a day.

> 3. Parentheses are used to enclose reference data in a research paper. (See Chapter 24.)

EXERCISE 40.2*

Add parentheses where they are appropriate.

1. Five of the students I was asked not to name them have volunteered to be peer tutors.
2. The apostrophe is explained in the unit on spelling pp. 376–414.
3. Jason complained that being a manager he became one in March was like being a cop.
4. I have enclosed a cheque for one hundred and fifty dollars $150.00.
5. More members of the Canadian armed forces died in World War I 1914–1918 than in any war before or since.
6. Although Mozart lived a relatively short time he died when he was 36, he composed hundreds of musical masterpieces.
7. As news of his "miracle cures" spread patients began to come to him from all over the province, the country doctor had to move his clinic to a more central location.
8. The new contract provided improved working conditions, a raise in salary 5 percent, and a new dental plan.
9. After years of producing undrinkable wine, Ontario now boasts a few very good wineries Inniskillin and Hillebrand are two that come to mind.
10. "One of the most important tools for making paper speak in your own voice is punctuation; it plays the role of body language; it helps readers hear you the way you want to be heard" Baker, "How to Punctuate," 48–49.

EXERCISE 40.3*

Add dashes and parentheses where appropriate in the following sentences.

1. The function of parentheses see the explanation on p. 372 is to set apart material that interrupts the main idea of the sentence and that the writer does not want to emphasize.
2. Dashes, on the other hand I love dashes are used to set off a dramatic or emphatic interruption.
3. My English instructor who appears not to have read the information on pp. 370–71 ruthlessly strikes out all my dashes, complaining that my penchant for this piece of punctuation makes my sentences sound breathless and incoherent.
4. This club plays jazz mostly Dixieland jazz nightly from 10 until 2.
5. On their first date, Rupert took Freda bowling she hates bowling; I doubt that they will see each other again.
6. The case of beer if you can believe Rudolf was finished off by three unknown intruders who then disappeared.
7. We should we must find a way to cut our expenses by at least 10 percent.
8. Years ago, Victor Borge invented a system of oral punctuation that assigned sounds some of them hilarious to each piece of punctuation, supposedly to give listeners the same benefits readers have in understanding the precise meaning of a message.
9. Obnoxious people Rudolf and Dwight come to mind light up the room when they leave.
10. Canadian hockey broadcaster Foster Hewitt created a sports catch-phrase "He shoots! He scores!" during overtime coverage of a hockey match between the New York Rangers and the Toronto Maple Leafs on April 4, 1933. The Rangers won.

Spelling

CHAPTER 41

Three Suggestions for Quick Improvement

Of all the errors you might make in writing, spelling is the one that is noticed by everyone, not just English teachers. No piece of writing that is full of misspellings can be classified as good. Misspellings can cause misunderstanding, as when an English teacher promised his students a course with "a strong *vacational* emphasis." (Those students who weren't misled wondered what he was doing teaching English.)

Sometimes misspellings cause confusion. Take this sentence, for example:

Mouse is a desert with a base of wiped cream.

It takes a few seconds to "translate" the sentence into a definition of *mousse*, a *dessert* made with *whipped* cream.

Most often, though, misspellings are misleading in the sense that they spoil the image you want to present. You want, naturally, to be seen as intelligent, careful, and conscientious. But if your writing is riddled with spelling errors, your readers will think you are careless, uneducated, or even stupid. It is not true, by the way, that intelligence and the ability to spell go hand in hand. It *is* true, though, that people generally think they do. So, to prevent both confusion and embarrassment, it is essential that you spell correctly.

There are three things you can do to improve your spelling almost instantly:

> 1. Buy and use a good dictionary.

A good dictionary is an indispensable tool for any writer. You will need it *every time* you write. Most of your doubts about spelling can be answered if you take the time to check in your dictionary. The time you spend looking up words will not be wasted; your rewards will be the increased accuracy of your writing and the increased respect of your readers. Useful dictionaries are the *Gage Canadian Dictionary* (a Canadian reference, ideal for use at home or in the office), and the *Merriam-Webster Unabridged Dictionary*. The standard reference tool is the *Oxford English Dictionary*, now available on CD-ROM. While it is the authoritative English language dictionary, it has one drawback for student writers: it does not indicate syllable breaks.

If you wonder how it's possible to look up a word that you can't spell, look at the dictionaries we've recommended. At the front of each is a "Guide to the Dictionary," and in the Guide is a chart showing the common spellings for all the sounds in the English language. If you know only how to pronounce a word, the chart will help you find its spelling. Another way to find a word you can't spell is to look up a **synonym**—a word that means the same thing. In the dictionary entry for the synonym, you'll probably find the word you're looking for.

Another useful tool, if you're writing your essay on a word processor, is a spell-check program. These aren't foolproof, though—as we'll see later—so don't count on your computer to solve *all* your spelling problems.

> 2. Ask a good speller.

Some people seem to have been born with the ability to spell. Such people are more reliable than a computer program. Often they are secretly proud of their talent and pleased to demonstrate it, so don't be afraid to ask. They probably aren't as good at something else as you are; you may have a talent they could use in exchange.

> 3. Learn three basic spelling rules.

English spelling is frustratingly irregular, and no rule holds true in *all* cases. But there are three simple rules that do hold for most words, and mastering these rules will help you avoid many common errors.

Before learning the three rules, you need to know the difference between **vowels** and **consonants**. The vowels are **a, e, i, o,** and **u** (and sometimes **y**). All the other letters are consonants.

Rule 1: Dropping the Final *e*

The first rule tells you when to drop the final, silent *e* when adding an ending to a word.

Drop the final, silent *e* when adding an ending that begins with a vowel.

Keep the final, silent *e* when adding an ending that begins with a consonant.

Keeping this rule in mind, look at these examples:

ENDINGS THAT BEGIN WITH A VOWEL	ENDINGS THAT BEGIN WITH A CONSONANT
-ing: amuse + ing = amusing	*-ment:* amuse + ment = amusement
-ed: live + ed = lived	*-ly:* live + ly = lively
-able: like + able = likable	*-ness:* like + ness = likeness
-ible: force + ible = forcible	*-ful:* force + ful = forceful
-er: use + er = user	*-less:* use + less = useless

In Exercises 41.1 and 41.2, combine each word with the ending to form a new word. When you have finished each set, check your answers.

EXERCISE 41.1*

1. desperate + ly =

2. crackle + ing =

3. generate + or =

4. atone + ment =

5. mate + ing =

6. rare + ly =

7. elevate + or =

8. emerge + ing =

9. positive + ly =

10. apologize + ing =

EXERCISE 41.2*

1. excite + ment =

2. interfere + ence =

3. desire + able =

4. continue + ance =

5. abridge + ing =

6. remove + able =

7. dissolute + ly =

8. acquire + ing =

9. shake + able =

10. aerate + ing =

EXERCISE 41.3*

Add *e* in the blank space wherever it's needed to complete the spelling of these words. If no *e* is needed, leave the space blank.

1. apologiz_____ing

2. encourag_____ment

3. nois_____y

4. issu_____able

5. fam_____ous

6. abridg_____ment

7. mov_____able

8. officiat_____ing

9. valu_____ation

10. realiz_____ing

Exceptions to Rule 1

Three common words do not follow the rule:

argue + ment = argument
nine + th = ninth
true + ly = truly

There is one more exception to Rule 1: after soft *c* (as in *notice*) and soft *g* (as in *change*), keep the final, silent *e* when adding an ending beginning with *a* or *o*. Here are two examples:

notice + able = noticeable
outrage + ous = outrageous

Rule 2: Doubling the Final Consonant

The second rule tells you when to double the final consonant, when adding an ending to a word.

> When adding an ending that begins with a vowel (such as *-able, -ing, -ed,* or *-er*), double the final consonant of the root word if the word
> 1. ends with a *single* consonant preceded by a *single* vowel *and*
> 2. is stressed on the last syllable.

Notice that a word must have *both* characteristics for the rule to apply. Let's look at a few examples:

begin + er	ends with a single consonant (*n*) preceded by a single vowel (*i*) and is stressed on the last syllable (*begín*), so the rule applies, and we double the final consonant:	beginner
control + ed	ends with a single consonant (*l*) preceded by a single vowel (*o*) and is stressed on the last syllable (*contról*), so the rule applies:	controlled
drop + ing	ends with a single consonant (*p*) preceded by a single vowel (*o*) and is stressed on the last syllable (there is only one: *dróp*), so the rule applies:	dropping
appear + ing	ends with a single consonant (*r*) preceded by *two* vowels (*ea*), so the rule does not apply, and we do not double the final consonant:	appearing
turn + ed	ends with *two* consonants (*rn*), so the rule does not apply:	turned
open + er	ends with a single consonant (*n*) preceded by a single vowel (*e*) but is *not* stressed on the last syllable (*ópen*), so the rule does not apply:	opener

In words such as *equip, quit,* and *quiz,* the *u* should be considered part of the *q* and not a vowel. These words then follow the rule: *equipping, quitter,* and *quizzed.*

(*Note:* There is a group of words ending in l, t, or s, that, according to our rule, do not need a double consonant before the ending. Some examples are label, counsel, focus, and format. You will sometimes see this consonant doubled—labelled, counselled, focussed, formatting—this spelling is also correct. For these words, it doesn't matter which spelling you choose; what matters is that you use one spelling or the other consistently!)

Exercises 41.4 through 41.7 require you to combine each word with the ending to form a new word. Check your answers to each set before going on.

EXERCISE 41.4*

1. blot + ing =

2. span + ing =

3. submit + ed =

4. fail + ing =

5. blur + ed =

6. regret + able =

7. admit + ing =

8. bat + ing =

9. beg + ing =

10. entail + ed =

EXERCISE 41.5*

1. forget + ing =

2. confer + ed =

3. refer + ing =

4. strip + ed =

5. shoot + ing =

6. expel + ing =

7. grab + ed =

8. jar + ing =

9. knit + ing =

10. hinder + ed =

EXERCISE 41.6*

1. defer + ing =

2. remit + ance =

3. regret + ful =

4. cuddle + ed =

5. acquit + al =

6. concur + ed =

7. flag + ing =

8. pin + ing =

9. bar + ed =

10. refer + ed =

EXERCISE 41.7*

1. occur + ence =

2. persist + ence =

3. emerge + ence =

4. recur + ence =

5. persevere + ance =

6. consist + ency =

7. suffer + ance =

8. resist + ance =

9. concur + ence =

10. deter + ence =

When it comes to adding *-ence*, three words are especially troublesome. *Prefer, refer,* and *confer* all appear to require a double final consonant. But they don't, because when you add *-ence*, the stress shifts to the *first* syllable of the word. So you write:

prefér	preférring	preférred	*but*	préference
refér	reférring	reférred	*but*	réference
confér	conférring	conférred	*but*	cónference

Rule 3: Words Containing *ie* or *ei*

There are almost a thousand common English words containing *ie* or *ei*, so remembering the rule that governs them is worthwhile. It helps to keep in mind that *ie* occurs roughly twice as often as *ei*.

The old rhyme tells you most of what you need to know to spell these words:

> Write *i* before *e*, except after *c*
> Or when sounded like *ā*, as in *neighbour* and *weigh*.

If you remember this rhyme, you'll have no difficulty in spelling words like *belief, piece, ceiling, receive,* and *freight.*

Unfortunately, the rhyme covers only two of the cases in which we write *e* before *i*: after *c*, and when the syllable is pronounced with a long *ā* sound. So an addition to the rule is necessary:

> If short *ĕ* or long *ī* is the sound that is right,
> Write *e* before *i*, as in *their* or in *height.*

This rule covers words such as *Fahrenheit, seismic, heir,* and *leisure* (pronounce it to rhyme with *pleasure*). *Either* and *neither* can be pronounced "eye-ther" and "nye-ther," so they too require *ei*.

There are, of course, exceptions. This silly sentence contains the most common ones:

A *weird species* of *sheik seized caffeine, codeine,* and *protein.*

Exercises 41.8 through 41.10 will help you to pin down *ie* versus *ei*. Fill in the blanks with *ie* or *ei*. After you finish each set, check your answers.

EXERCISE 41.8*

1. br_____f
2. fr_____ndly
3. f_____lding
4. ach_____ve
5. rel_____ve
6. retr_____val
7. dec_____ve
8. l_____sure
9. rec_____pt
10. gr_____ve

EXERCISE 41.9*

1. p_____r
2. hyg_____ne
3. h_____rarchy
4. dec_____t
5. f_____rce
6. p_____ced
7. for_____gn
8. w_____ght
9. rec_____ve
10. spec_____s

EXERCISE 41.10*

1. Can we really trust _____ther of them, when we know th_____r

   bel_____fs to be so similar?

2. After all, anyone who thinks that we are dec_____ved by everything

   we perc_____ve must be a few grams short of a full kilo.

3. If we can't trust our own senses, what conc_____vable information is

   there that we can rec_____ve with confidence?

4. Frankly, it would be a great rel_____f if n_____ther of them ever

   appeared in my life again.

5. My n_____ghbour is so conc_____ted, she speaks to no one on our

   block. The children think she's w_____rd.

There are three or four more spelling rules we could explain here, but we won't—for two reasons. First, there are many exceptions to the remaining "rules" for English spelling. And second you don't need to memorize more rules *if you use your dictionary*. Now is the time to read the "Guide to the Dictionary" at the front of your dictionary. Reading it won't be very entertaining, but it will be well worth your while.

The Guide outlines the kinds of information given for each word in your dictionary and explains the abbreviations and symbols that are used. You will discover, for example, that you don't need to memorize long lists of irregular plurals: your dictionary provides the irregular plurals of the words you look up. It also gives the irregular forms of verbs, adjectives, and adverbs. (If you've forgotten how *regular* plurals, verb forms, adjectives, and adverbs are formed, the Guide will remind you.) Most dictionaries will also tell you how to add various endings to root words and even where you can divide a word when you need to hyphenate it at the end of a line. Take half an hour to read the Guide in your dictionary; then do Exercises 41.11 and 41.12.

EXERCISE 41.11*

Write the plural form of each word listed below. Use your dictionary, and check your answers before continuing.
1. hero
2. history
3. criterion
4. ghetto
5. personnel
6. crisis
7. data
8. phenomenon
9. nucleus
10. appendix

EXERCISE 41.12*

Combine each of the following root words with the ending given. Again, use your dictionary and check your answers.

1. lonely + ness =
2. copy + ed =
3. crazy + ness =
4. easy + er =
5. pretty + est =
6. reply + s =
7. reply + ing =
8. thirty + eth =
9. unnecessary + ly =
10. traffic + ing =

CHAPTER 42

Sound-Alikes, Look-Alikes, and Spoilers

Using a dictionary, asking a good speller for help, and applying the three spelling rules will make an immediate improvement in your spelling. By following two additional suggestions you will further increase your spelling accuracy, but the skills involved will take longer to master. First, learn to tell apart words that are often confused because they sound or look alike. Second, learn to spell the words that most people find difficult—words we call Spelling Spoilers. Don't try to master all of these words at once. Instead, memorize a few each week, and review them frequently. In two or three months, you could be one of the people poor spellers turn to for help!

Sound-Alikes and Look-Alikes

Some of your spelling troubles are probably caused by your using words that either sound or look like the words you really want. A computer spell-check program cannot help you with these words because, if you're like most people, you don't misspell them. What makes the spelling "wrong" is the sense of the sentence in which you've used them. *Hear, our, meat,* and *have* are, as isolated words, correctly spelled. But if you combine them into a "sentence"—*Meat me hear in have an our*—you end up with a tangle of misspellings no computer can unravel.

Careful pronunciation sometimes helps to correct this problem. For example, if you pronounce the words *accept* and *except* differently, you'll be less likely to confuse them in your writing. It is also useful to make up memory aids to help yourself remember the difference between words that sound alike but have very different meanings. We have included in this list a few pairs of words that do not look or sound alike, but that are commonly confused.

accept **except**	**A**ccept means "**ta**ke." It is always a verb. **Ex**cept means "**ex**cluding."
	Everyone *except* Brian *accepted* my explanation.
advice **advise**	The difference in pronunciation makes the difference in meaning clear. *Advise* (rhymes with *wise*) is a verb. *Advice* (rhymes with *nice*) is a noun.
	I *advise* you not to listen to free *advice*.
affect **effect**	*Affect* as a verb means "influence." As a noun, it means "a strong feeling." *Effect* is a noun meaning "result." If you can substitute *result*, then *effect* is the word you need. (Occasionally *effect* can be a verb—meaning "bring about"—but you probably won't need to use it that way.)
	Learning about the *effects* of caffeine *affected* my coffee-drinking habits. Most disturbed people display inappropriate *affect*.
a lot **allot**	*A lot* (often misspelled *alot*) should be avoided. Use *many* or *much* instead. *Allot* means "distribute" or "assign."
	He still has a̶ ̶l̶o̶t̶ ̶o̶f̶ *many* problems, but he's coping a̶ ̶l̶o̶t̶ *much* better. The teacher will *allot* the assignments according to the students' interests.
amount **number**	*Amount* is used with uncountable things; *number* is used with countable things.
	You may have a large *number* of jelly beans in a jar, but a small *amount* of candy. (Jelly beans are countable; candy is not.)
are **our**	*Are* is a verb. *Our* shows ownership.
	Marie-Claire Blais and Margaret Atwood *are* two of Canada's best-known writers. Canada is *our* home and native land.

assure
ensure
insure

Assure means "state with confidence; pledge or promise."

She *assured* him she would keep his letters always.
The prime minister *assured* the Inuit their concerns would be addressed in the near future.

Ensure means "make certain of something."

The extra 20 dollars will *ensure* your getting a good seat.
No number of promises can *ensure* that love will last.

Insure means "guarantee against financial loss." We *insure* lives and property.

Kevin *insured* the book before he sent it airmail.
We have *insured* both our home and our car against fire and theft.

choose
chose

Pronunciation gives the clue here. *Choose* rhymes with *booze* and means "select." *Chose* rhymes with *rose* and means "selected."

Please *choose* a topic.
I *chose* film making.

cite
sight
site

To *cite* is to quote or mention. A lawyer *cites* precedents. Writers *cite* their sources in research papers. You might *cite* a comedian for her wit, or a politician for his honesty. A *site* is a place.

The Plains of Abraham is the *site* of a famous battle.
Tiananmen Square is the *site* of the massacre.
Pape and Mortimer is the *site* of our new industrial design centre.

A *sight* is something you see.

With her spiked hair and seven earrings, she was a *sight* to behold.

coarse
course

Coarse means "rough, unrefined." (Remember: the word **arse** is co**arse**.) For all other meanings, use *course*.

That sandpaper is too *coarse*.
You'll enjoy the photography *course*.
Of *course* you'll do well.

complement   A *complement* completes something. A *compliment* is a gift of
compliment   praise.

> A glass of wine would be the perfect *complement* to the
> meal.
> Some people are embarrassed by *compliments*.

conscience   Your *conscience* is your sense of right and wrong. *Conscious*
conscious   means "aware" or "awake"—able to feel and think.

> After Katy cheated on the test, her *conscience* bothered
> her.
> Katy was *conscious* of having done wrong.
> The injured man was *unconscious* for an hour.

consul   A *consul* is a government official stationed in another coun-
council   try. A *council* is an assembly or official group. Members of a
counsel   council are *councilors*. *Counsel* can be used to mean both
  "advice" and "to advise."

> The Canadian *consul* in Mexico was very helpful.
> The Women's Advisory *Council* meets next month.
> Maria gave me good *counsel*.
> She *counselled* me to hire a lawyer.

continual   *Continual* refers to an action that goes on regularly, but with
continuous   interruptions. *Continuous* refers to an action that goes on
  without interruption.

> The student *continually* tried to interrupt the lecturer,
> but his voice went on in a *continuous* drone.
> There is a *continuous* flow of traffic during rush hour.

credible   *Credible* refers to a story; *credulous* describes the person who
credulous   believes an incredible story.
creditable

> Nell was fortunate that the police found her story
> *credible*.
> My brother is so *credulous*, we call him Gullible Gus.

Creditable means "worthy of reward or praise."

> After two semesters, Eva has finally begun to produce
> *creditable* work.

desert
dessert

A *désert* is a dry, barren place. As a verb, *desért* means "leave behind." *Dessért* is "double good," the kind of food you'd like two servings of, so give it two *s*'s.

> The tundra is Canada's only *desert* region.
> My neighbour *deserted* her husband and children.
> *Dessert* is my favourite part of the meal.

dining
dinning

You'll spell *dining* correctly if you remember the phrase "wining and dining." You'll probably never use *dinning*. It means "making a loud noise."

> The children are in the *dining* room.
> We are *dining* out tonight.
> The noise from the bar was *dinning* in our ears.

disburse
disperse

Disburse means "to pay out money;" that is what **burs**ars do. *Disperse* means "to break up"; crowds are sometimes *dispersed* by the police.

> The college's financial-aid officer will *disburse* the students' loans at the end of this week.
> The students gathered in Tiananmen Square were *dispersed* by the army.

does
dose

Pronunciation provides the clue. *Does* rhymes with *buzz* and is a verb. *Dose* rhymes with *gross* and refers to a quantity of medicine.

> John *does* drive fast, *doesn't* he?
> My grandmother gave me a *dose* of cod liver oil.

farther
further

You'll have no trouble distinguishing between these two if you associate *farther* with *distance* and *further* with *time*.

> Dana wanted me to walk a little *farther* so we could discuss our relationship *further*.

faze
phase

Fazed usually has a *not* before it; to be *not fazed* means to be not disturbed, or concerned, or taken aback. *Phase* means "stage of development or process."

> Unfortunately, Theo was not the least bit *fazed* by his disastrous grade report.
> Since Meiling works full-time, she has decided to complete her degree in *phases*.

fewer
less

Fewer is used with countable things; *less,* with uncountable things.

> In May, there are *fewer* students in the college, so there is *less* work for the faculty to do.
> The *fewer* attempts you make, the *less* your chance of success.

With units of money or measurement, however, you use *less:*

> I have *less* than 20 dollars in my wallet.
> Walter's house is on a lot that is *less* than four metres wide.

forth
fourth

Forth means "**for**ward" or "onward." ***Fourth*** contains the number **four,** which gives it its meaning.

> Please stop pacing back and *forth.*
> The B.C. Lions lost their *fourth* game in a row.

hear
here

Hear is what you do with your **ear**s. *Here* is used for all other meanings.

> Now *hear* this!
> Ray isn't *here.*
> *Here* is your assignment.

imply
infer

A speaker or writer *implies;* a listener or reader *infers.* To *imply* is to hint, or to say something indirectly. To *infer* is to draw a conclusion from what is stated or hinted at.

> I *inferred* from his sarcastic remarks that he was not very fond of Sheila.
> In her introduction of Rami, Sheila *implied* that she greatly admired him.

it's
its

It's is a shortened form of *it is.* The apostrophe takes the place of the *i* in *is.* If you can substitute *it is,* then *it's* is the form you need. If you can't substitute *it is,* then *its* is the correct word.

> *It's* really not difficult. (*It is* really not difficult.)
> The book has lost *its* cover. ("The book has lost *it is* cover" makes no sense, so you need its.)

It's is also commonly used as the shortened form of *it has.* In this case, the apostrophe takes the place of the *h* and the *a.*

> *It's* been a good year for us.

later **latter**	*Later* refers to time and has the word **late** in it. *Latter* means "the second of two" and has two *t*'s. It is the opposite of *former*.

> It is *later* than you think.
> You take the former, and I'll take the *latter*.

loose **lose**	Pronunciation is the key to these words. *Loose* rhymes with *goose* and means "not tight." *Lose* rhymes with *ooze* and means "misplace" or "be defeated."

> A *loose* electrical connection is dangerous.
> Some are born to win, some to *lose*.

miner **minor**	A *miner* works in a **mine**. *Minor* means "lesser" or "not important." For example, a *minor* is a person of less than legal age.

> Liquor can be served to *miners*, but not if they are *minors*.
> For me, spelling is a *minor* problem.

moral **morale**	Again, pronunciation provides the clue you need. *Móral* refers to the understanding of what is right and wrong. *Morále* refers to the spirit or mental condition of a person or group.

> People often have to make *moral* decisions.
> The low *morale* of the workers prompted the strike.

peace **piece**	*Peace* is what we want on **ea**rth. *Piece* means "a part or portion of something," as in "a **pie**ce of **pie**."

> Everyone hopes for *peace* in Bosnia.
> A *piece* of the puzzle is missing.

personal **personnel**	*Personal* means "private." *Personnel* refers to the group of people working for a particular employer or to the office responsible for maintaining employees' records.

> The letter was marked "*Personal* and Confidential."
> We are fortunate in having hired highly qualified *personnel*.
> Fatima works in the *Personnel* Office.

principal **principle**	*Principal* means "main." A *principle* is a ru**le**.

> A *principal* is the main administrator of a school.
> Oil is Alberta's *principal* industry.
> I make it a *principle* to submit my essays on time.

quiet
quite

If you pronounce these words carefully, you won't confuse them. *Quiet* has two syllables; *quite* has only one.

The librarian asked us to be *quiet*.
We had not *quite* finished our homework.

stationary
stationery

Stationary means "fixed in pl**a**ce." *Stationery* is writing pap**er**.

Did you want a portable or a *stationary* computer?
Please order a new supply of *stationery*.

than
then

Than is used in comp**a**risons. Pronounce it to rhyme with *can*. *Then* refers to time and rhymes with *when*.

Rudi is a better speller *than* I.
He made his decision *then*.
Eva withdrew from the competition; *then* she realized the consequences.

their
there
they're

Their indicates ownership. *There* points out something or indicates place. It includes the word **here,** which also indicates place. *They're* is a shortened form of *they are*. (The apostrophe replaces the *a* in *are*.)

It was *their* fault.
There are two weeks left in the term.
You should look over *there*.
They're late, as usual.

too
two
to

The *too* with an extra *o* in it means "more than enough" or "also." *Two* is the number after one. For all other meanings, use *to*.

He thinks he's been working *too* hard. She thinks so, *too*.
There are *two* sides *to* every argument.
The *two* women knew *too* much about each other *to* be friends.

weather
whether
wether

Whether means "which of the two" and is used in all cases when you aren't referring to the climatic conditions outside (*weather*). A *wether* is a castrated ram, so that word's uses are limited.

were
where
we're

If you pronounce these three carefully, you won't confuse them. *Were* rhymes with *fur* and is a verb. *Where* is pronounced "hwear," includes the word **here,** and indicates place. *We're* is a shortened form of *we are* and is pronounced "weer."

> You *were* joking, *weren't* you?
> *Where* did you want to meet?
> *We're* on our way.

who's
whose

Who's is a shortened form of *who is* or *who has.* If you can substitute *who is* or *who has* for the *who's* in your sentence, then you are using the right spelling. Otherwise, use *whose.*

> *Who's* coming to dinner? (*Who is* coming to dinner?)
> *Who's* been sleeping in my bed? (*Who has* been sleeping in my bed?)
> *Whose* calculator is this? ("*Who is* calculator" makes no sense, so you need *whose.*)

woman
women

Confusing these two is guaranteed to irritate your women readers. *Woman* is the singular form; compare **man.** *Women* is the plural form; compare **men.**

> A *woman's* place is wherever she chooses to be.
> The *women's* movement promotes equality between *women* and men.

you're
your

You're is a shortened form of *you are.* If you can substitute *you are* for the *you're* in your sentence, then you're using the correct form. If you can't substitute *you are,* use *your.*

> *You're* welcome. (*You are* welcome.)
> Unfortunately, *your* hamburger got burned. ("*You are* hamburger" makes no sense, so *your* is the word you want.)

In Exercises 42.1 through 42.4, choose the correct word from those in parentheses. If you don't know an answer, go back and reread the explanation. Check your answers after each set.

EXERCISE 42.1*

1. Limiting (coarse course) selection so drastically will (affect effect) students' academic development and subsequent job opportunities.

2. (Are Our) you going to (accept except) the offer?
3. Eat your vegetables; (than then) you can have your (desert dessert).
4. If (your you're) overweight by 50 pounds, (loosing losing) the excess will be a long-term proposition.
5. It's (quiet quite) true that they did not get (hear here) until two in the morning.
6. Ironically, it is the saint, not the sinner, (who's whose) (conscience conscious) troubles him.
7. He (assured ensured insured) me he would keep the (amount number) of changes to a minimum.
8. (Its It's) hard to tell the dog from (its it's) owner.
9. To (choose chose) a (coarse course) of action contrary to your lawyer's (advice advise) would be foolish.
10. Constant (dining dinning) out (does dose) become boring after a while.

EXERCISE 42.2*

1. It is (incredible incredulous) to me that our society's (morals morales) have declined so drastically over the last twenty years.
2. After the accident, the (moral morale) of the (miners minors) did not recover for many months, but the owners appeared not to be (fazed phased) by this sad fact.
3. The chief librarian did not mean to (infer imply) that (farther further) cuts to services were being considered.
4. The (affect effect) of trying to (disburse disperse) the angry crowd was to cause a near riot.
5. (Who's Whose) (principals principles) are so strong that they wouldn't pay (fewer less) taxes if they could get away with it?
6. The (forth fourth) reason Akbar (cited sighted sited) for his absence was the inclement (weather whether wether).
7. It's (your you're) fault that we are (continually continuously) harassed by door-to-door salespeople; your welcoming smile (assures ensures insures) that they'll return again and again.
8. Try to remain (conscience conscious) through today's class, because I plan to take my critique of the Young Offenders Act (a lot allot much) (farther further), and this material will be on the test.
9. Ranjan could not (accept except) the fact that the (councillors counsellors) rejected her plan to (faze phase) out parking in the downtown core.
10. Canadian (woman's women's) pay, on average, is 30 percent less than that of men; this statistic is a(n) (amount number) that should cause our politicians serious concern.

EXERCISE 42.3*

1. Bartender, do you (hear here)? Over (hear here), we want beer.
2. (To Too Two) be (stationary stationery) for that long is to be dead.

3. (Loosing Losing) or winning is not important in the early stages of learning a sport; (its it's) the development of skills and attitudes that really matters.
4. Olerud, (your you're) being sent to the (miner minor) leagues!
5. He served her a (peace piece) of rhubarb pie; (latter later), she (complemented complimented) him on his perfect crust.
6. The (weather whether) will have a major influence on (weather whether) we are able to land at Goose Bay.
7. He is handsome, clever, and talented, but his (coarse course) language entirely spoils the (affect effect) at his interviews.
8. The fact that I have (fewer less) friends than you do doesn't (faze phase) me.
9. (Woman Women) working in traditionally male areas of employment are the ones (who's whose) competence is most often questioned.
10. Clarence (choose chose) to (accept except) the (principal's principle's) apology.

EXERCISE 42.4*

(Their They're There) must be a better way to cope with house renovations. If I were to describe my (personal personnel) agony during the months it took for the construction workers and contractors to (acheive achieve) their final (affect effect), (you're your) heart would bleed. Plaster dust was the worst problem, because it gets into everything, making even (dinning dining) an uncomfortable experience. As the walls were torn (lose loose) and the house was gradually reduced to (it's its) skeleton, plaster dust found (its it's) way into every crack and corner. The noise and confusion (affected effected) my (moral morale), and I became inclined to use (course coarse) language, particularly with those who insisted on giving me (advice advise). (Later Latter), when my (conscience conscious) got the better of me, my feeble attempts at apology (were we're) not (accepted excepted). In the end, the renovations cost me my (peace piece) of mind, my (friends freinds), and more money (than then) I dreamed possible.

EXERCISE 42.5

Now test your mastery of sound-alikes and look-alikes by correcting the errors in the following paragraph.

I would advice anyone who's schedule seems to be to full to try the solution I came up with fewer than three weeks ago. I pulled the plug on my TV set. Overwhelmed with assignments and unable to chose among priorities, I realized that one of my problems was the huge number of hours I was spending in front of the tube. I stopped to consider: how were my viewing habits effecting me? Had my knowledge been farther increased after I had watched television continually for four or five hours? I decided I should be spending less hours glued to the tube and more time on my coarses. I also decided not to faze in the process, but to quit cold turkey. My decision to give up TV was not a matter of principal with me, and I don't want to imply that I am anti-entertainment. It was simply a question of making a conscience choice wether I wished to spend more time on laughing or on learning. To assure that I wouldn't continuously be tempted by the site of it, I put the set in a closet. The results have been more dramatic then I thought possible. With the noise of the tube no longer dining in my ears, my apartment is a haven of peace and quite. Some of my assignments are actually completed before there due, and, for the first time in my life, I have been getting complements on my work. You can imagine the affect this has had on my morale! Except for the occasional twinge of regret that I have lost track of whose doing what to whom in my favourite soap opera, I am much happier for choosing to loose the tube.

Spelling Spoilers

Here is a list of words that are frequently misspelled. Have someone dictate the list to you. Circle the ones you misspell, and memorize them, a few at a time. Try to learn ten each week. Review your list often, until you have mastered every word. Making up memory aids for especially troublesome words will help you conquer them. Here are some examples to get you started:

accommodate: It means "make room for," and the word itself makes room for two *c*'s and two *m*'s.

business: Bu**sin**ess is no **sin**.

environment: The word *environ*ment, like the earth, has **iron** in it.

friend: He is a fri**end** to the **end**.

grammar: Poor gram**mar** will **mar** your writing.

absence	forty	proceed
accommodate	friend	professor
achievement	gauge	psychology
acknowledge	government	recommend
across	grammar	relevant
adolescence	guarantee	repetition
among	guidance	restaurant
answer	height	rhythm
argument	hoping	ridiculous
beginning	hypocrisy	safety
buiness	immediately	schedule
careful	independent	separate
category	laboratory	shining
clothes	license (*or* licence)	similar
committee	likely	somewhat
conscious	loneliness	speech
convenience	lonely	studying
criticism	maintenance	succeed
definitely	marriage	superintendent
dependent	mentally	supersede
desperate	necessary	surprise
disappear	ninety	technique
disappoint	ninth	thorough
discipline	occasionally	tragedy
dissatisfied	omission	truly
doesn't	opinion	unnecessary
eighth	opportunity	until
embarrassed	paid	unusual
environment	parallel	usually
exercise	perform	vacuum
existence	planned	vicious
explanation	possess	Wednesday
extremely	prejudice	writing
familiar	privilege	written
February	probably	
finally	procedure	

EXERCISE 42.6

Make up sentences containing the words you misspelled when the list of Spelling Spoilers was dictated. Underline the Spelling Spoiler(s) in each sentence. (If you do this exercise once a week, you will master the list very quickly.)

One final suggestion. You may find that, despite all your efforts, there are a few words you just cannot spell correctly. The solution? Either write them out on the inside cover of your dictionary or, even simpler, don't use them. Look in your dictionary or thesaurus to find synonyms (different words with the same or similar meanings), and use those instead. Two thesauruses are available in inexpensive paperback editions: *Roget's Thesaurus* and Soule's *Dictionary of English Synonyms.*

CHAPTER 43

Capital Letters

Capital letters should be used in a few specific places and nowhere else. Some people seem to have "capitalitis": they put capital letters on words randomly, regardless of whether the words are nouns, adjectives, or verbs. Like "exclamatosis," "capitalitis" is a disease communicated by comic books, which capitalize every word.

Not very many people have this problem. If you, like most people, generally use capitals correctly, skip this chapter and go on to the next one. If you are puzzled about capital letters, though, or have readers who are puzzled by your use of them, read on.

Capitalize the first letters of words that fit these descriptions:

1. the first word in a sentence and the first word in a direct quotation:

   Put out the garbage.
   "Would you please take out the garbage?" she asked.

2. the names of specific persons:

   Anne Murray   Mordecai Richler

   the names of specific places:

   Alberta   Elm Street
   Mars   Morocco
   Oz   Sept-Îles

   and the names of specific things:

   Camosun College
   Labatt's Blue

CN Tower
Lake Titicaca

3. the days of the week, the months of the year, and specific holidays (but not the seasons or geographic directions):

Monday	July	north
Friday	summer	southwest
October	winter	Canada Day

4. the titles of specific people (but not the names of their positions), books, films, and courses (but not subject names, unless they're languages):

Governor General Romeo LeBlanc   *but* the governor
                                              general
Pope John Paul II   *but* the pope
Mr. and Ms. O'Connor
Essay Essentials
Teenage Mutant Ninja Turtles
Mathematics 101   *but* the subject of mathematics
English 101   *but* the English language

5. the names of specific companies, businesses, organizations, and departments:

Chateau Gai	Liberal Party
Arc Industries	Personnel Department
Winnipeg Rotary Club	Vancouver City College

EXERCISE 43.1*

Correct the capitalization in the following sentences.

1. why in the World would you buy a toyota?
2. We need to get rid of some of our High-School habits when we start College.
3. have you read dr. Ernie l. Twaddle's new book, *I'm OK—You're Fat: A Self-Help guide to fitness fascism*?
4. The loyalists were considered Patriots by the inhabitants of upper Canada but Traitors by people in the united states.
5. I didn't do very well in my Fluid Power Course; maybe I'd better switch to Culinary Arts.
6. well, look who's here; it's mr. olympics.
7. Take a right at Yonge Street, a left at lawrence avenue, and a right at Avenue road.
8. My english teacher also teaches french to asian Immigrants.
9. Asha's Father, being Conservative in his tastes, disapproved of Karim's leather jacket and harley-davidson 750.

10. Neither was he amused when asha ran off with Karim's Rock Group, the stoned angels.

EXERCISE 43.2*

1. Several Psychiatrists in california are developing Computer Programs to treat patients with mild forms of Depression or Neurosis.
2. They envision Computer Therapy Programs within the next fifteen years that will diagnose the Patient's problem (To be confirmed by a Psychiatrist) and select a Treatment Program.
3. The Computer would interact with the Patients and switch to various Subprograms to analyze their mental problems.
4. A tv camera could view the Patients to see if they exhibit signs of Stress, Nervousness, or Lying.
5. Thus, a computer with a sophisticated psychiatric program could appear to understand and empathize with a troubled patient.
6. Most psychiatrists are against such Unorthodox Treatment Methods, but proponents of Computer Therapy argue that it has many advantages.
7. These advantages include low cost and convenience: the Computer would function as a cheap Psychiatrist, available on Weekends and Holidays, Summer or Winter.
8. Other advantages are the long-term total Memory of the Computer and its appearance of honesty and objectivity.
9. Personally, I am surprised that anyone in the Medical Profession takes such a proposal seriously; treatment of complex Human Problems by machine seems perverse to me.
10. Taking my own personal depressions, fears, and phobias to a vdt would be likely to trigger a massive Anxiety Attack.

EXERCISE 43.3

Correct the capitalization in the following sentences.

1. If today were saturday, I'd have to go home for my Father's Birthday.
2. Failing Sociology is like eating soup with a fork: It's difficult, but you can do it if you really try.
3. July First is canada day, when we celebrate the anniversary of confederation, which occurred in 1867.
4. Although Ms. Lau is a member of the new democratic party, she is quite conservative in her thinking on Economics and social issues.
5. A complex program like microsoft's excel takes up a large amount of computer memory.
6. Trying to learn english as quickly as possible, Wong Bao Lin took two Night School classes a week and listened to audio tapes several hours every day.

7. The caribe is the name of the sailboat my french Professor bought for touring the caribbean islands in the Winter.

8. If I drop Math and Accounting, I will be able to concentrate on English and marketing, but it will mean adding a semester to my Program.

9. My German Shepherd's name, Layla, comes from an Eric Clapton song about the former wife of one of the beatles.

10. Rudolf and Dwight are packing away the essentials, cigarettes, doritos, and Beer, in preparation for the end of the World, which they are convinced will occur on december 31, a.d. 1999.

CHAPTER 44

The Apostrophe

We have chosen to deal with apostrophes and hyphens (to be discussed in Chapter 45) in this unit because, unlike other punctuation marks, they do not indicate the relationship among the elements of a sentence or a paragraph. Instead, when used correctly, apostrophes and hyphens indicate a relationship between the elements of a word.

Although it isn't hard to use them correctly, apostrophes are often misused. Sometimes you need an apostrophe so that the reader can understand what you're trying to say. Consider the difference in meaning between these two sentences:

The teacher began class by calling the students names.

The teacher began class by calling the students' names.

In most cases, however, a misused apostrophe doesn't confuse readers; it merely irritates or amuses them:

Seasons Greetings from the Simpson's.

Its time to give the fish it's food.

New potato's for sale.

The apostrophe is used for two distinct purposes: to indicate contraction and to indicate possession.

Contraction

The rule about where to put apostrophes in contractions is one of the rare rules to which there are no exceptions. It *always* holds.

> When two words are shortened into one, and a letter (or letters) is left out, the apostrophe goes in the place of the missing letter(s).

cannot → can't   we are → we're
is not → isn't   we will → we'll
it is, it has → it's   who is, who has → who's
there is → there's   will not → won't (Note the slight
                                                          spelling variation here.)
they are → they're   you would → you'd

EXERCISE 44.1*

Make these sets of words into contractions.

1. he will   _____
2. you have _____
3. I am   _____
4. do not   _____
5. who has   _____

6. would not _____
7. we are   _____
8. who will _____
9. you will _____
10. did not _____

EXERCISE 44.2*

Place apostrophes correctly in these words.

1. cant   _____
2. youre   _____
3. theyre   _____
4. shouldnt _____
5. wholl   _____

6. dont   _____
7. youll   _____
8. were   _____
9. theyve   _____
10. itll   _____

EXERCISE 44.3*

Correct these sentences by placing apostrophes where needed.

1. Yes, its a long way from Halifax to Vancouver, but weve been in training for three months.
2. Were taking the train to Antigonish and were biking to Halifax; then well begin the big trip west.

3. There isnt a dry eye in the theatre when Spielbergs film reaches its climax.
4. Those two havent made it through a meeting since the college adopted its No Smoking policy.
5. Wasnt it Mark Twain who said, "Its easy to stop smoking; Ive done it dozens of times"?

Possession

The apostrophe also shows ownership or possession. Here's the rule that applies in most circumstances:

> 1. Add *'s* to the word that indicates the *owner*.
> 2. If the resulting word ends in a double or triple *s*, erase the last one, leaving the apostrophe in place.

Examples:

person	+ 's = person's	clerk	+ 's = clerk's
people	+ 's = people's	Pamela	+ 's = Pamela's
women	+ 's = women's	Marx	+ 's = Marx's
sisters	+ 's = sisters'ȿ	mother-in-law	+ 's = mother-in-law's
teacher	+ 's = teacher's	teachers	+ 's = teachers'ȿ
Archimedes	+ 's = Archimedes'ȿ	goodness	+ 's = goodness'ȿ

When you're forming possessives, you must be careful to determine first whether the *owner* is singular or plural. For example:

the student's names (The names belong to a *student*.)

the students' names (The names belong to two or more *students*.)

If you remember that possession indicates belonging to, you can figure out where to put the apostrophe by "translating" your sentence like this:

Incorrect:	The police officer asked Elmo for his drivers licence.
	1. Translation: the licence belongs to a *driver*.
	2. Add *'s*.
Correct:	The police officer asked Elmo for his driver's licence.

Incorrect:	The college finally met the librarians demands.
	1. Translation: the demands belong to the *librarian*? or the *librarians*? Here's where you have to decide whether *one* or *more than one* is involved.
	2. Add *'s*.
Correct:	The college finally met the librarian's demands. (Only one librarian was involved.)
Also correct:	The college finally met the librarians' demands. (More than one librarian was involved.)

Possession does not have to be literal. The owner does not have to be a person or thing. Ideas or concepts can be "owners," too:

day's work = the work of, or belonging to, a day

arm's length = the length of, or belonging to, an arm

You should know that there are alternatives to the second part of the apostrophe rule for possessives given in the box above. Many writers prefer to keep the final *s* when forming possessives of one-syllable words ending in *s* and of some proper names. In these words, the *'s* represents a pronounced sound, and the *s* after the apostrophe is retained to reflect that sound. Here are some examples:

boss's temper	class's decision
Brutus's betrayal	Yeats's poem

Note that the following words, called **possessive pronouns**, are already possessive in form and do not take the *'s*:

my/mine	its
your/yours	our/ours
her/hers	their/theirs
his	whose

Four possessive pronouns are often confused with contractions that sound like them. When you need to decide which word to use, you can separate the contraction into its two root words and try them out in the sentence. If the sentence makes sense, then the contraction is the word you need. If not, use the possessive. Better yet, you can memorize these words:

POSSESSIVES		CONTRACTIONS	
their:	they own something	they're	= they are
your:	you own something	you're	= you are
whose:	"who" owns something	who's	= who is, who has
its:	it owns something	it's	= it is, it has

Examples: They're going to try *their* luck at cards.
You're losing *your* hair.
Who's been sleeping in *whose* bed?
It's obvious the car has a hole in *its* muffler.

EXERCISE 44.4*

Make the following words possessive.

1. their
2. Chris
3. her
4. gentlemen
5. strawberries

6. mystery
7. one
8. Burgess
9. chairmen
10. ladies

EXERCISE 44.5*

In the sentences below, make the words in parentheses possessive.

1. One (week) work under (he) supervision is enough.
2. By the (day) end, our (dogs) coats of fur were matted with burrs.
3. That (church) contributions to the Relief Fund were very generous, thanks to (it) (minister) hard work.
4. The (children) temperaments are not like (he); they're like (their) (mother).
5. (Today) television stars seem unable to resist (producers) temptations to make them into (tomorrows) film idols.

EXERCISE 44.6*

Correct the following sentences by adding apostrophes where necessary.

1. A floppy disks quality is measured by its ability to store information without error.
2. Diplomatic ambassadors wives or husbands are often as important to a missions success as the ambassadors themselves.
3. Near Chicoutimi is one of the countrys most beautiful parks, where the skills of canoeists, fishermen, and wildlife photographers can all be put to the test on a summers day.
4. The Leafs forward and the Oilers defenceman were exchanged during the last days trading at the NHL meetings.
5. Maviss career got its start when she sang seafarers songs in the yacht clubs dining lounge.

Exercises 44.7 through 44.8 will test and reinforce your understanding of both contraction and possession.

EXERCISE 44.7*

In each of the sentences below, choose the correct word from those in parentheses. Check your answers before going on.

1. (Its It's) going to run (its it's) laps faster than yours, but I bet my (turtles turtle's) legs are shorter than your (turtles turtle's) legs.
2. (Its It's) strange what creatures people choose to race; (their there they're) going to have the national championship cricket race in Japan next week.
3. Where (your you're) going, (your you're) biggest problem will be maintaining (your you're) health.
4. (Joan's Joans') career goals involve the Humane (Society's Societies) plan to extend this (provinces province's) lost-animal services into their Manitoba and Saskatchewan facilities.
5. (Someones Someone's) got to take responsibility for the large numbers of domestic animals (whose who's) owners have abandoned them.
6. (Their There They're) isn't much chance that the (Jones's Jones' Joneses') animals will find (their there they're) way home, since (its it's) 500 desolate miles from Moose Factory to Cochrane.
7. (Countries Country's Countries') that maintain (their there they're) neutrality find (their there they're) under pressure from super (power's powers powers') delegations.
8. The Ringling (Brothers Brother's Brothers') circus animals were well cared for compared with the animals of (todays today's todays') circuses.
9. My (fathers father's fathers') (uncles uncle's) hound could scent a (foxes fox's) ten-day-old trail even in dense (woods woods') teeming with other wildlife.
10. Contrary to some (people's peoples) opinions, postal (workers worker's workers') contracts are most often settled by both (sides side's sides') willingness to bend long before a (strikes strike's) necessary.

EXERCISE 44.8

Test your mastery of apostrophes by correcting the errors in the following paragraph.

Mens hair seems to get an undue amount of peoples attention. The length of a mans hair often causes more comment and criticism than his politics, his religion, or even the sports team he roots for. Recently, for example, a national columnists entire article was devoted to an attack on men who wear their hair in a ponytail. When short hair is in fashion, as it has been for most of the last 75 years, those who dare to allow their locks' to curl over their collars invite stares and ridicule. Even during the sixties' and seventies', when long hair was considered stylish, many young men who grew their hair to their shoulders may have won their friend's approval, but those long locks were an object of their mother's criticism and their father's scorn. Yet historys lesson is that fashion is cyclical, and it wasnt that long ago that any man who appeared in public without his hair pulled back into a ponytail or covered by a long wig was considered "not a gentleman." Short hairs supporters were rebels and nonconformists. Its difficult to imagine, but probably true, that 100 years' ago young men were criticized by their parents for their cropped heads. "If youre going to live under my roof," Father would declare, "youll have to let your hair grow to you're shoulders!" Today, short hair is again the favoured fashion statement, but a cut thats too short raises suspicions' about the wearers' possibly radical politics. Hairs ability to create an image isn't surprising: after all, its immediately visible. But it's ability to excite observers interest, fear, anger, or even outrage, is remarkable.

CHAPTER 45

The Hyphen

A **hyphen (-)** is required in three distinct writing situations: as part of the correct spelling of a word (e.g., mother-in-law, self-esteem); to divide a word at the end of a line; and to separate or join two or more words or parts of words. There are five rules to follow.

> 1. Use a hyphen to divide a word at the end of a written or typed line.

Your dictionary shows where words can be divided. Most dictionaries mark the syllables of a word with a dot: syl·lables = syl-lables. Never divide a word of only one or two syllables; reserve the hyphen at the end of a line for words of three or more syllables (e.g., commu-nity). If the word is already hyphen-ated (e.g., self-reliance, ex-president), break it after the hyphen.

> 2. Use a hyphen to separate a prefix from the main word when two of the same vowels come together.

Examples: pre-empted, co-operate, re-elected, re-enter. When the two vowels are different, however, no hyphen is required: semiautomatic, realign, preamble.

> 3. Use a hyphen with compound numbers from twenty-one to ninety-nine, with fractions, and with dimensions.

Examples: forty-six, one-eighth, ninety-eight, six-by-eight.

> 4. Use a hyphen to join two or more words that serve as an adjective *before* a noun.

Examples: The first-born child is often the best loved.

Word-of-mouth advertising is very effective.

A good writer has a well-thumbed, up-to-date dictionary.

> 5. Use a hyphen to avoid ambiguity.

Examples: The contractor re-covered the roof with asphalt shingles.

The contractor recovered his money.

The government's plan provided for nursing-home care. (care in a nursing home)

The government's plan provided for nursing home-care. (care at home by nurses)

The prime minister will address small business owners. (Do you really want to say he will talk only to short people?)

The prime minister will address small-business owners. (These people are owners of small businesses.)

EXERCISE 45.1*

Each of the following sentences requires one or more hyphens. Review the rules in the boxes above; then try your hand at correcting these sentences.

1. Mei decided to sublet her fifth floor apartment.
2. Anwar claims he is allergic to classical music but addicted to new wave music.
3. Chrétien won most of the ethnic vote, which gave him a two thirds majority in a hard fought contest.
4. Hand knitted sweaters are usually more expensive than factory produced ones.
5. In 1950, at the age of forty seven, George Orwell died of tuberculosis.
6. For months after Nicolae Ceauşescu was overthrown, the world was shocked by revelations of the repression suffered by the Rumanian people.

7. Would you relay this message to Mr. Chan: the masons would like to re lay the bricks this evening?
8. Our next door neighbour teaches in a high school but does not like to be known as a high school teacher.
9. A face to face meeting with an anti intellectual always gets my adrenalin going.
10. Because Angela was an attorney at law and had once been an all Canadian athlete, her forty five year old former coach was not surprised when she became Minister of Recreation.

The Finishing Touches

CHAPTER 46

Avoiding Inappropriate Language

Clichés

A **cliché** is an expression that was created long ago and that has been used and overused ever since. Cliché-filled writing will bore your readers. Worse, it may cause them to miss the seriousness of your message and find it funny.

Spoken English is full of clichés. In the rush to express an idea, we often take the easy way, using ready-made expressions to put our thoughts into words. There is less excuse to *write* in clichés. Writers have time to think through carefully what it is they want to say, and to revise and edit what they've said. Taking the time to find appropriate words and interesting phrases demonstrates courtesy and concern for your readers.

> He was sick as a dog, but we got him to the hospital in the nick of time.

"Sick as a dog" and "nick of time" are clichés. Readers know more or less what these phrases mean, but they are tired, worn-out ways of expressing that meaning. It is difficult to get rid of *all* clichés in your writing, but you can be aware of them and try to use them as seldom as possible.

If you are a native speaker of English, it is easy to recognize a cliché. When you can read the first few words of a phrase and fill in the rest automatically, the phrase is a cliché. Here are some examples: free as a _____; a pain in the _____; it goes without _____; last but not _____. The endings are so predictable, readers can skip over them. And they do. Such phrases give the impression that there's nothing new in your writing, that it's all been said before.

The solution to a cliché problem is simple: don't write automatically. Think about what you want to say; then say it in your own words, not everyone else's.

As you read through Exercise 46.1, notice how hard it is to form a mental picture of what the sentences are saying and how hard it is to remember what you've read—even when you've just finished reading it. Clichés are like Teflon cookware: the meaning, like the food, doesn't stick.

EXERCISE 46.1

Rewrite these sentences, expressing the ideas in your own words.

1. As luck would have it, I was rewarded for not throwing in the sponge. Like a bolt from the blue, the announcement came; the announcer did not cut corners: "Ms. LaFortune, you are the lucky winner of $2000, cold, hard cash."

2. When you are playing poker, it is good to keep your cool; otherwise, you can lose your shirt. If you hang in there, you can make your day.

3. By and large, the research team left no stone unturned. To cut a long story short, funds were eventually few and far between.

4. The customer is always right, say the managers. It doesn't matter that you are bone-tired, work till the wee small hours, or get falsely accused of giving someone the short end of the stick. To coin a phrase, you end up a sadder but wiser salesperson.

5. She worked like a beaver all day, sorting out her things. At the stroke of midnight, she hit the hay but tossed and turned all night long. Her better half, however, told her she had slept like a log.

6. Sick and tired of the gossip of her guests, Sara decided to catch 40 winks. Early in the game, she had lost the thread of the conversation and decided to give up the ghost.

7. It is clear as crystal that she has a heart as big as all outdoors. Good as gold, gentle as a lamb, and quick as greased lightning would describe her general disposition. In the foreseeable future, she will in all likelihood take the manager's job—lock, stock, and barrel.

8. I liked the schedule in no way, shape, or form, so I gave advance warning of my intention to walk off the job. This drastic action, needless to say, was interpreted as a knee-jerk response. When all is said and done, the powers that be should see this serious crisis in terms of a moment of truth.

9. It was a dark and stormy night, raining cats and dogs. Merv stopped dead in his tracks, went pale as a ghost, and fainted dead away. When he came to, to his surprise, not only had his pockets been picked to the bone, but also his clothes had been ripped to shreds.

10. Karim was feeling like a million bucks. Little did he know that at that very moment, just around the corner, a group of desperate thieves was conspiring to take the wind out of his sails by leaving him high and dry without two cents to rub together.

Broadcasting is one of the chief refuges of the cliché. It's a rare newscast that doesn't include the expression "informed sources" or "claimed the life" or "skyrocketing inflation." Listening carefully for such overworked phrases on the radio and TV will make you more aware of them in your own writing and perhaps less likely to use them.

Jargon

Jargon, a special breed of cliché, is made up of technical words or phrases used in science, the trades, sports, or the professions. Sometimes "shop talk" or "trade language" enters the everyday language we use outside our jobs. The sailing world, for example, has a highly developed jargon: "making headway," "being taken aback," "taking another tack," and "battening down the hatches" are all nautical terms. Many of these expressions have found their way into everyday colloquial usage. The jargon of some professions is so highly technical and specialized it amounts almost to a private language. Those in the profession are familiar with it and use it to communicate; those not in the profession are "outsiders" to whom the technical language is incomprehensible. Although jargon is useful, even necessary, in the context of the job, it is inappropriate in most writing because *it does not communicate.* Unless your reader shares your private language, your message will be lost.

As a writer, you need to be sensitive to the fact that your vocabulary—even the content of your language—is shaped and influenced by your experiences and the contexts within which you live and work.

Consider this example from *The Book of Jargon* by D.E. Miller:

> A group of people witness a car accident. What each person sees, and how he or she describes it, is determined to a large extent by the language each one normally uses. A doctor or nurse would see and describe contusions, lacerations, fractures, and hemorrhages. A lawyer would think in terms of civil liabilities and criminal negligence. A mechanic would see crushed fenders, bent axles, and damaged chassis. A psychologist would be concerned about stress reactions, trauma, and guilt. You or I might see and describe the pain and injury caused by a driver's error in judgment or lapse of skill.

The existence of jargon, then, is not the problem; the abuse of jargon is the problem. It limits your audience to those who have the same specialized vocabulary you do. To the rest of the world, your writing will be difficult to understand or even meaningless. You can't expect to communicate with a general reader in sentences like this: "The professor tried to segue into a piece on business letters, but the tally light didn't come on, so he did a jump cut back to grammar before fading to black." This may be a colourful way to describe what happened in a writing class, but it will be understood only by readers familiar with the specialized vocabulary of television broadcasting.

Be especially careful to avoid jargon that *imitates* a specialized vocabulary. Writers who are a little unsure of their subject matter or their audience sometimes try to impress their readers with jargon. Writing that has chains of abstract words and long, complicated sentences is sound without meaning, as the following sentence illustrates:

> **Thus the meaningful verbalization of conceptual improvisation at the interpersonal interface is contraindicated by frustrations arising from idiosyncratic linguistic actualization, in terms of vocabulary, so that the verbalized formulations of the initiating consciousness actuate latent rejection mechanisms.**

Who knows what this means? More important, who cares? Very few readers would have the patience to go through this passage, dictionary in hand, trying vainly to translate its tortured prose into plain English. The cure for this kind of jargon is consideration for your readers. If you really want to get your message across, write plainly and clearly in language your readers can be expected to understand.

EXERCISE 46.2

Write as many examples of jargon as you can identify for each of the following occupations:

1. computer technologist: LAN, bus, platform . . .
2. television broadcaster: voice-over, spot, fade . . .
3. sports enthusiast: low blow, at the post, on deck . . .
4. marketing manager: focus group, bait-and-switch, push strategy . . .
5. your own career field:

Slang

Slang is nonstandard language that signifies an informal and close relationship among those who speak it to each other. There are innumerable examples of slang, from *A-OK* to *zowie*. Slang changes rapidly, and even dictionaries don't attempt to keep up with all the terms. Like jargon, slang serves to identify and reinforce membership in particular subgroups in society—students, the armed forces, the police, criminals, or members of a trade or profession, for example. Unlike jargon, slang is highly colourful, nontechnical language, but it is often short-lived. On the street, you may be called "thick" ("stupid"), and outside of class, you may be known as a "grind" (hard-working student); for those in the military, "R and R" means "rest and relaxation," but to a mechanic it means "removed and replaced (or repaired)." Computer operators love slang: when a piece of computer equipment (especially software) ceases to function properly, it is said to "bomb" or "hang." A "bug" is a hitch, a fault, a problem. A "glitch" is the source of a malfunction: it is usually unexpected and can be anything from a loose wire to a power failure. "Wetware" is the human brain.

Slang can limit or even block your communication with your readers. It is the most quickly dated type of language: what is "in" today may well be laughed at in a few months. ("Right on, man. What a groovy scene. Far out!") The good news is that yesterday's slang may be today's **colloquialism** (highly informal, casual language) and tomorrow's standard English. It may surprise you to learn that the following words were once considered slang: fireworks, dwindle, clumsy, boardwalk, movies, blurb, stunt, fan, absurd, nice, awful, sneak, fake.

Because slang dates so quickly, and because it is understood by a limited group of people, you should avoid it in your writing. Unless you are quoting someone who has used slang, use Standard Written English. If you're in doubt as to the status of a word, check your dictionary. The notation *sl.* or *slang* appears after slang words or after a slang meaning of a word. (Some words, such as *neat* and *chick* and *hammered,* have both a general meaning and a slang meaning.) Taking the time to choose words and expressions appropriate to standard written English increases your chance of successful communication and demonstrates your concern for and courtesy to your readers.

EXERCISE 46.3

The following are slang terms in current use. "Translate" them into general-level English words that could be appropriately used in writing.

bad	crib	filthy	humongous	sick
bomb	down	fresh	mad	stoked
crazy	dweeb	ho	nerd	wannabe

Abusages

Some words and expressions that appear in writing are simply incorrect. We've named these misused, misspelled, or nonstandard expressions **abusages.** Usage mistakes occur when bad speech habits spill over into writing. Their use makes the writer appear ignorant to anyone who knows anything about the English language. Abusages are never good English, even in speech; however, we hear them so often in daily conversation that, after a while, they become so familiar they sound right. They aren't, and you need to be aware of the ones that are most likely to trip you up. The list of abusages that follows includes some of the worst offenders. You should add to it the abusages your instructors hate most. Go through the list carefully and mark the expressions that sound all right to you. Then memorize the Standard Written English equivalent beside each one. These are the expressions you will need to look out for when you edit your writing.

"alot"	There is no such word. Use *many* or *much*.
"alright"	This is a misspelling of *all right*.
"anyways"	Also, "anywheres" and "a long ways." There is no *s* on any of these words.
"between you and I"	A commonly misused expression for *between you and me*.
"could of"	Also, "would of," "should of," and so on. The helping verb is *have: could have*.
"didn't do nothing"	This, along with all other double negatives ("couldn't get nowhere," "wouldn't talk to nobody," and so on), is wrong. Write *didn't do anything* or *did nothing*.
"irregardless"	There is no such word. Use *regardless*.
"irrevelant"	This is a misspelling. Spell the word *irrelevant*.
"media" used as singular word	The word *media* is plural. The singular is *medium*. Write "TV is a mass medium. Print and radio are also examples of mass media."
"off of"	Use *off* alone: "I fell off the wagon."
"prejudice" used as an adjective	It is wrong to write "She is prejudice against men." Use *prejudiced*.
"prejudism"	There is no such word. Use *prejudice:* "He should show no prejudice to either side."
"real" used as an adverb	"Real sad," "real swell," and "real nice" are wrong. Use *really* or *very*.
"reason is because"	Use *the reason is that:* "The reason is that I don't use a deodorant."
"suppose to"	Also, "use to." Use *supposed to* and *used to*.
"themself"	Also, "theirself," "ourselfs," "yourselfs," and "themselfs." The plural of *self* is *selves: themselves, ourselves,* and so on. Don't use "theirselves," though; there's no such word.

"youse"   There is no such word. "You" is used for both singular and plural. When waiting on tables, don't say "May I help youse?" to a group of English instructors if you want a tip.

EXERCISE 46.4

Correct the following sentences where necessary.

1. Alot of young people today are trying to fight prejudism not only in society but also within themselfs.
2. I'm suppose to ask youse if the reason for the delay is because it's raining.
3. It's unresponsible of us to blame television or any other media for causing violence.
4. Television is responsible, however, for the fact that alot of ungrammatical expressions sound alright to us.
5. Between you and I, the reason I didn't talk to nobody about Dwight's cheating on the test was because he would of broke my arm.

CHAPTER 47

Eliminating Wordiness

Wordiness is a problem that may develop if you try too hard to impress a reader with your use of words. Keep in mind that no reader wants to read "fill" or "padding." All writing should be as concise as it can be while still conveying your message clearly. Even authors like Dickens and Michener, who have written vast quantities, chose their language carefully, trying not to waste their readers' time with unnecessary words.

Here's an example of what can happen when, in trying to impress, you lose sight of the need to communicate. Do you recognize your writing style in this?

> In my own opinion, I feel very strongly indeed that the government of this Dominion of Canada is basically in need of an additional amount of meaningful input from its electors, the people of this country, at this point in time, frankly speaking. For too long a period of time, the leaders of this nation in Ottawa have, rightly or wrongly, gone heedlessly off on their own particular course of action without the benefit of consultation or dialogue with the people, who, it stands to reason, are most willing and able to provide, clearly and without doubt, a distinct and clear path to follow into the future world of tomorrow.

By eliminating wordiness, you could make this into a clear statement.

The following are some of the worst offenders we have collected from student writing. In some cases, many words are used when one or two would do; in others, the wording is **redundant** (it says the same thing twice).

WORDY	ACCEPTABLE
absolutely complete	complete
absolutely nothing	nothing
actual fact	fact
at that point in time	then
basic fundamentals	fundamentals
circled around	circled
collect together	collect
completely free	free
continue on	continue
could possibly (*also* may possibly *and* might possibly)	could (*or* may *or* might)
dead bodies	corpses
disappear from view	disappear
entirely eliminated	eliminated
equally as good	as good
essential prerequisite	prerequisite
exactly identical	identical
few and far between	rare
final conclusion	conclusion
green in colour	green
having the same thing in common	having in common
I personally feel	I feel
in my opinion, I think	in my opinion
in this day and age	now
new innovation	innovation
personal friend	friend
proceed ahead	proceed
real, genuine leather	genuine leather
repeat again	repeat
repeat the same	repeat
seven AM in the morning	seven AM
small in size	small
such as, for example	such as
surround on all sides	surround
taking active steps	taking steps
true fact	fact
very (most, quite, rather) unique	unique

To avoid wordiness, eliminate clichés, repetition, redundancy, and unnecessary jargon.

EXERCISE 47.1

Revise these sentences to make them as concise as possible.

1. I myself personally feel that there is absolutely no basis in fact for the idea that UFOs exist.

2. Getting up at 5 AM in the morning and repeating the exact same daily routine every day for three weeks wore me out and exhausted me.

3. Although we did see the first No Trespassing sign, which was bright yellow in colour and very large, we went on further ahead, regardless, until we came to the second sign, which was exactly identical to the first.

4. In my opinion, I believe that my essay is equally as good as Krystal's and deserves equally as good a mark, which it would have got if it weren't for the actual fact that the professor hates me.

5. Friends are few and far between when you have absolutely nothing in your pocket and are surrounded on all sides by creditors who are threatening to go to the police and proceed with criminal charges unless you come up with the money you owe them.

6. My sister and I share quite a few physical characteristics in common, such as, for example, exactly identical curly hair and a quite unique eye colour.

7. In my view, I feel that an English program that teaches the basic fundamentals is an essential prerequisite before a person can succeed in college, the business world, or the community at large.

8. On February 14, for Valentine's Day, Rudolf gave Krystal, who is his closest, most intimate friend, a uniquely unusual genuine gold ring with a tiny little diamond.

9. "As a new beginning teacher," we told our English instructor, "you should try to recognize the utter impossibility of gaining and holding the respect of your students so long as you are so completely and totally devoted to insisting that we follow grammar rules and regulations that entirely eliminate the creativity from our writing."

10. 'Twas the nocturnal segment of the diurnal period preceding the annual Yuletide celebration, and throughout our structure of domestic residence, kinetic activity was not in evidence among the possessors of this potential, including that species of domestic rodent, *Mus musculus.*

On-Screen Writing

Word processors are common equipment in writing labs and are increasingly available to students both at school and at home. Different writers are comfortable with different tools; for some, the pen is really the most effective implement. If you write best with pen in hand, continue to use pen and paper for your writing until you have completed a first draft. At that point, however, you will find it worthwhile to transfer your thoughts to a screen for revising, editing, proofreading, and printing.

If you can use a word processor during all the steps in the writing process, the machine can improve your writing in many significant ways. However, a word processor demands two skills of you that the pen does not: reasonable keyboarding skill and a ready knowledge of the functions of the word-processing program. Without these two skills, word processing can be a time-consuming and frustrating experience.

Some people like to use the word processor for freewriting or brainstorming. They key in words as fast as they can type, with no concern for spelling, organization, style, or structure. In this way, all the ideas they can think of are stored in the processor for recall on the screen. As they write draft after draft, revising and shaping, they can roll back to their original list to be sure no points have been omitted. Revisions are easy to enter, paragraphs can be relocated, and the latest draft is available for another reading.

By taking advantage of these capacities of a word processor, you can save time and effort and have an attractive final product. We suggest the following approach to creating essays on the word processor.

Organizing

1. Enter the subject of your paper in capital letters at the top of the page. If you've been assigned a specific subject, this step is easy. If you are making up your own subject, or working with vague subject guidelines, enter a **working title**, one that serves to identify your paper but will probably be replaced later. Do you think you have enough to say on the subject? Should you do some research first, and begin work when you have notes in front of you? The guidelines in Chapter 2 for choosing a subject will lead you through this critical process.

2. Begin writing your main points, using a new line for each main point. Don't worry about writing complete sentences, or developing your ideas, or even spelling your words correctly. Get down as many points about your subject as you can think of.

3. Sit back and examine your main points critically. Delete those that overlap with other points, those that don't relate directly to the subject, and those that are so weak you have nothing significant to say about them. Split up any entries that cover two or three points. Reduce your list to three or four solid main points. The more time and effort you spend here, the less you will need for drafting and revising.

4. Under each main point, write as much as you can on how you will develop or expand that point. Don't worry about keeping your supporting ideas in order, or about composing complete sentences, correcting your spelling, or following a particular organization.

5. When you have written everything you can in rough form about each main point, use the block-move function on your word processor to arrange your points in the order you feel is most appropriate. See Chapter 3 for information on effective ordering of main points.

Save your file. (It's a good idea to save a backup file, too.)

Writing

1. Print out the work you have produced so far.

2. Keep the printout close by, for reference, and write a paragraph for each of the main points. Remember to include a topic sentence, appropriate development of ideas, and a concluding sentence.

Save your file.

3. Read over your paragraphs. Is each one well developed? Is the order of the paragraphs appropriate? Taken together, do they deal adequately with your subject? This is the time to weave in more information, add or change main points, or rearrange the order of your statements.

4. Write your introductory and concluding paragraphs. Test each for effectiveness by reviewing the tips in Chapter 10. Writing your introduction and conclusion after you write the body of your essay is easier than doing the paragraphs in sequence. When you've finished the body, you know what you've said and how you've said it; you can then introduce and conclude your subject more effectively and in less time.

Save your file.

Revising

1. Some writers like to print out their work at this point, do their revising on paper, and then make changes on the screen. If you do a printout, you'll be able to see your essay as a whole, rather than one screen at a time, and your review of your work will be more effective. If you're impatient, though, or pressed for time, you can revise on-screen.

2. Read your essay slowly and critically. Use the Guide to Revision on the inside front cover to help you.

3. Enlist your word processor's functions to help you eliminate errors. Use the spelling checker if your program has one (if it doesn't, consider getting one that "stands alone" or works outside the word processor), but remember that a spelling checker is not foolproof. It can tell you that you have spelled *it's* or *accept* or *effect* correctly, but it doesn't know whether you have used them correctly in your sentence. The "find" function is useful for correcting a repeated error. Tell the program to find each appearance of *it's*, for example, and read carefully to make sure you have used it correctly. Some programs also have a grammar checker, which can help you locate some errors in sentence structure, grammar, and word choice so you can make corrections.

4. Replace or rewrite any awkward words, phrases, or sentences. If something doesn't sound quite right to you, don't be satisfied until it does. Polish and revise until every sentence is as clear and well expressed as you can possibly make it. The "thesaurus" function can be helpful, but don't use its most complex expressions in the hope of impressing your readers.

Save your file.

Printing

1. If you have not already done so, set your program to print "double space." Double spacing is a courtesy to your readers, helps you to spot errors much more easily, and is also required by most English teachers.

2. Set your printer to the setting that will produce the darkest, clearest type. Don't make your readers strain their eyes to read faint print. Avoid the hard-to-read "draft" setting.

3. Print out your essay.

4. Finally, proofread your work to make sure you haven't missed an error. If you can, put the essay aside for a few days and then reread it with a clear mind and a fresh point of view. One of the word processor's chief advantages is that if you spot an error that must be corrected or an improvement that should be made, it's simple and painless to do so and then print out a fresh copy. Whiteout and messy pen insertions are considered relics of the past. Every paper you hand in can be clean, neat, and error-free.

List of Grammatical Terms

adjectives   Words that modify (describe, restrict, relate to, make more precise) nouns and pronouns. They answer the questions *What kind? How many? Which?*—e.g., the *competent* student; *five* home runs; my *last* class.

adverbs   Words that modify verbs, adjectives, and other adverbs. They answer the questions *When? How? Where? Why? How much?*—e.g., Nino talks *fast* (fast modifies the verb *talks*); he is a *very* fast talker (*very* modifies the adjective *fast*); he talks *really* fast (*really* modifies the adverb *fast*). Adverbs often—but not always—end in *-ly*.

antecedent   The word that a pronoun refers to or stands for. Literally, it means "going before, preceding." The antecedent usually comes before the pronoun that refers to it—e.g., *Karyn* believes *she* is possessed. (*Karyn* is the antecedent to which the pronoun *she* refers.)

clause   A group of words that contains a subject and a verb. If the group of words can stand by itself and make complete sense, it is called an **independent clause** (or **principal clause** or **main clause**). If the group of words does not make complete sense on its own but is linked to another clause (depends on another clause for its meaning), it is called a **dependent** or **subordinate clause.** E.g., *The porch collapsed.* This group of words can stand by itself, so it is an independent clause.
But consider another word group: *When Kalim removed the railing with his tractor.* This group of words has a subject,

Kalim, and a verb, *removed,* but it does not make complete sense on its own. It depends for its meaning on *The porch collapsed;* therefore, it is a dependent clause.

colloquialism A word or group of words that we use in casual conversation or in informal writing.

> Steve *flunked* his accounting exam.
> *Did* you *get* what the teacher said about job placement?
> I can't believe that *guy* is serious about learning.

comma splice The error that results when the writer joins two independent clauses with a comma—e.g., *The comma splice is an error, it is a kind of run-on sentence.* (See Chapter 37.)

dependent-clause cue A word or phrase that introduces a dependent clause—e.g., *when, because, in order that, as soon as.*

modifier A word or group of words that adds information about another word (or phrase or clause) in a sentence. See **adjective, adverb, dependent clause,** and Chapter 29.

nouns Words that name persons, places, and things and have the grammatical capability of being possessive. There are **concrete** nouns that are **proper** (*Calgary, Beijing, Gaza, January, Sharon*); **common** (*woman, man, city, car, animal*); and **collective** (*group, audience, swarm, jury, committee*). There are also **abstract** nouns (*truth, softness, pride, confidence*). Unlike their concrete cousins, abstract nouns refer to concepts, ideas, characteristics—things we know or experience through our intellect rather than through our senses.

object The "receiving" part of a sentence. The **direct object** is a noun or noun substitute (pronoun, phrase, or clause) that is the target or receiver of the action expressed by the verb in a sentence. It answers the question *what?* or *whom?* of the verb—e.g., Denis threw the *ball.* (Denis threw *what?*)

> He wondered *where the money went.* (He wondered *what?*)
> Munira loves *Abdul.* (Munira loves *whom?*)

The **indirect object** is a noun or pronoun that is the indirect target or receiver of the action expressed by the verb in a sentence. It is *always* placed in front of the direct object. It answers the question *to whom?* or *to what?*

> Doug threw me the ball. (Doug threw *to whom?*)
> Lisa gave her composition a title. (Gave *to what?*)

The **object of a preposition** is a noun or noun substitute (pronoun, phrase, or clause) that follows a preposition—e.g., after the *storm* (*storm* is a noun, object of the preposition *after*); before *signing the lease* (*signing the lease* is a phrase, object of the preposition *before*); he thought about *what he wanted to do* (*what he wanted to do* is a clause, object of the preposition *about*).

Notice that what follows a preposition is always its object; that is why the subject of a sentence or clause can never be found in a prepositional phrase.

participle	Form of a verb that can be used as an adjective (the *completed* work, the *weeping* willows) or as part of a verb phrase (am *succeeding*, have *rented*).

The **present participle** of a verb ends in *-ing*.
The **past participle** of a regular verb ends in *-d* or *-ed*.
For the past participles of common **irregular verbs,** see pp. 311–13 and a dictionary.

person	A category of pronouns and verbs. **First person** refers to the person who is speaking (*I, we*). **Second person** refers to the person being spoken to (*you*). **Third person** is the person or thing being spoken about (*he, she, it, they,* and any noun or pronoun that may substitute for one of these).

phrase	A group of meaning-related words that acts as a noun, a verb, an adjective, or an adverb within a sentence. Phrases do not make complete sense on their own because they do not contain both a subject and a verb.

Please order *legal-size manila file folders.* (phrase acting as a noun)
I *must have been sleeping* when you called. (verb phrase)
Sightseeing in Ottawa, we photographed the monuments *on Parliament Hill.* (phrases acting as adjectives)
Portaging a canoe *in this weather* is no fun. (phrase acting as an adverb)

prefix	A meaningful letter or group of letters added to the beginning of a word (1) to change its meaning or (2) to change its word class.

1. *a* + moral = amoral
   contra + indication = contraindication
   an + hydrous = anhydrous
   a + sexual = asexual
   dis + establish = disestablish
2. *de* + nude (adjective) = denude (verb)
   in + dent (noun) = indent (verb)
   in + put (verb) = input (noun)
   a + maze (noun) = amaze (verb)

Some prefixes require a hyphen:

anti-welfare reform
all-Canadian
mid-February
de-emphasize
re-establish

preposition	A word that connects a noun, pronoun, or phrase to some other word(s) in a sentence. The noun, pronoun, or phrase is the *object* of the preposition. (That is why the **subject** of a sentence is never found in a prepositional phrase.)

I prepared the minutes *of the union meeting.* (of relates *meeting* to *minutes*)

One *of the parents* checks the children every half hour. (*of* relates parents to *One*)

prepositional phrase	A group of grammatically related words having the function of a noun, an adjective, or an adverb and beginning with a preposition. See the list on p. 254.
pronouns	Words that are noun-like. They usually substitute for nouns, but sometimes they substitute for other pronouns.

He will market *anything that* brings in money.
Everyone must earn *her* badges.

There are several kinds of pronouns:

> **personal:** I, we, you, he, she, it, they, me, us, him, her, them
> **possessive:** my, our, your, his, her, its, their
> **demonstrative:** this, these, that, those
> **relative:** who, which, that, whom, whose
> **interrogative:** who? whose? whom? which? what?
> **indefinite:** all *"-one, -thing,* or *-body"* pronouns (such as *everyone, something,* and *anybody*); *each; neither; either; few; none; several.*

subject	In a sentence, the person, thing, or concept that the sentence is about—the topic of the sentence (see Chapter 26). In a paper, what the essay is about—the topic of the paper (see Chapter 3).
suffix	A letter or group of letters that is added to the end of a word (1) to change its meaning, (2) to change its grammatical role, or (3) to change its word class.

1. king + *dom* = kingdom
   tooth + *less* = toothless
   few + *er* = fewer
   home + *less* = homeless
2. love (base form) + *s* = loves (third person singular, present tense)
   student + *'s* = student's (possessive singular)
   eat (base form) + *en* = eaten (past participle)
   teacher + *s* = teachers (plural)
3. your (adjective) + *s* = yours (pronoun)
   happy (adjective) + *ily* = happily (adverb)
   act (verb) + *ive* = active (adjective)
   activate (verb) + *ion* = activation (noun)

With the help of a dictionary, identify the prefixes and suffixes in *antidisestablishmentarianism.* How many are there?

tenses	Verbs indicate past, present, or future time. The different forms of the verb used to indicate time are called *tenses.* The verb ending (e.g., play*s*, play*ing*, play*ed*) and any helping verbs associated with the main verb (*will* play, *has* played, *had* played, *will have* played) show the tense of the verb.

There are simple tenses:

present: ask, asks
past: asked
future: will ask

and perfect tenses:

present: have (has) asked
past: had asked
future: will (shall) have asked

The simple, perfect, and future tenses can also be **progressive:** am asking, have been asking, will be asking, etc.

transitions Words or phrases that help readers follow the text smoothly from one sentence to the next or from one paragraph to another. See Chapters 9 and 12, and p. 356.

verbs Words that say something about a person, place, or thing and whose form may be changed to indicate tense. They may make a statement, ask a question, or give commands. They may express action (physical or mental), occurrence, or condition (mode of being).

Roberto *hit* an inside curve for a home run. (physical action)
Laurence *believed* the Blue Jays would win. (mental action)
Father's Day *falls* on the first Sunday of June. (occurrence)
Mildred eventually *became* interested in English. (condition)

Some verbs are called **linking verbs:** they help to make a statement by linking the subject to a word that describes or explains it.

William Hubbard *was* Toronto's first black mayor. (*was* links *William Hubbard* to *mayor*)
Mohammed *looks* tired. (*looks* links *Mohammed* and *tired*)

In addition to *am, is, are, was, were,* and *been,* some common linking verbs are *appear, become, feel, grow, look, taste, remain, seem, smell, sound.*

Another class of verbs is called **helping verbs.** They show the time of a verb as future or past (*will* go, *has* gone), or as a continuing action (*is* reading); and they show the passive voice (*was* completed).

voice Verbs may be **active** or **passive,** depending on whether the subject of the verb is *acting* (active voice) or *being acted upon* (passive voice).

In 1988, the Conservative government *introduced* another set of tax reforms. (active)
Another set of tax reforms *was introduced* in 1988. (passive)

Answers to Selected Exercises

UNIT SIX: Sentence Structure

Chapter 26: Cracking the Sentence Code (pp. 248–57)

EXERCISE 26.1

1. <u>Algy</u> <u>met</u> a bear.
2. A <u>bear</u> <u>met</u> Algy.
3. The <u>bear</u> <u>was</u> bulgy.
4. Sad to say, the <u>bulge</u> <u>was</u> Algy.
5. <u>Grizzlies</u> <u>are</u> famous for their unpredictability.
6. <u>Meeting</u> bears unexpectedly <u>is</u> clearly risky.
7. According to an old myth, <u>bears</u> never <u>run</u> downhill.
8. <u>(You)</u> <u>Take</u> it from me. <u>They</u> <u>do</u>.
9. <u>Females</u> with cubs <u>are</u> especially dangerous.
10. <u>Defending</u> oneself <u>presents</u> a real problem.

EXERCISE 26.2

1. Here <u>is</u> an <u>idea</u> to consider.
2. <u>Lucy Maud Montgomery</u> <u>lived</u> in Ontario's Durham County before Confederation.
3. <u>Who</u> <u>wants</u> the last piece?
4. <u>(You)</u> <u>Eat</u> slowly.
5. <u>Exercise</u> <u>builds</u> strong bodies and healthy minds.
6. <u>(You)</u> <u>Keep</u> your body fit.

7. Far behind the Liberals and New Democrats <u>trailed</u> the <u>Conservatives</u>, bringing up the rear.
8. <u>Pride</u> <u>goes</u> before a fall.
9. Only in Canada <u>is</u> a so-called <u>lack</u> of national identity a distinctive national characteristic.
10. Only Irish <u>whiskey</u> <u>contains</u> ingredients from all four of the essential food groups: caffeine, fat, sugar, and alcohol.

EXERCISE 26.3

1. <u>Vancouver</u> <u>is</u> a metropolitan centre with scores of distinct neighbourhoods.
2. The <u>word</u> "Toronto" <u>is</u> the Anglicization of the Native term for "meeting place."
3. The <u>Salt Spring Islands</u> <u>were</u> originally a part of the B.C. mainland.
4. <u>Are</u> <u>you</u> a year-round island resident?
5. At a joint meeting of the band councils, the <u>chiefs</u> <u>opposed</u> increased logging in Clayoquot Sound.
6. No <u>evictions</u> <u>occurred</u> last year.
7. The islanders' <u>cohesiveness</u> <u>is</u> the product of genuine neighbourliness and common community concerns.
8. There <u>is</u> surprisingly little <u>vandalism</u>, the plague of downtown areas.
9. For the average visitor to the islands, the <u>combination</u> of private and public properties <u>is</u> acceptable and even enjoyable.
10. Minutes from the middle of the city <u>nestles</u> my sunny, serene island <u>retreat</u>.

EXERCISE 26.4

1. <u>He</u> <u>has talked</u> nonstop for three hours.
2. <u>She</u> <u>should have been examining</u> each package.
3. <u>Could</u> <u>they</u> <u>return</u> the goods tomorrow?
4. In the winter, the <u>car</u> <u>starts</u> more easily inside the garage than outside.
5. Where <u>is</u> the nearest gas <u>station</u>?
6. <u>He</u> <u>is</u> not <u>going</u> to drive.
7. Which one <u>does</u> <u>she</u> <u>prefer</u>?
8. <u>Parents</u> <u>will</u> always <u>perceive</u> their offspring as small children.
9. The <u>barometer</u> <u>has</u> just <u>fallen</u> alarmingly.
10. Patiently and painstakingly, against all odds, <u>struggled</u> the little <u>army</u>.

EXERCISE 26.5

1. In a couple of years, <u>you</u> <u>will be</u> a professional dancer.
2. By noon, <u>he</u> <u>will have been sleeping</u> for eighteen hours.
3. How <u>are</u> the club <u>members</u> <u>identified</u>?
4. The <u>police</u> <u>will</u> certainly <u>stop</u> all yellow cars on the road tonight.
5. How <u>should</u> the <u>committee</u> <u>present</u> this concept?
6. To some small degree at least, personal <u>opinion</u> <u>is</u> often <u>presented</u> as fact.
7. My <u>boss</u> <u>does</u> not <u>understand</u> me; neither <u>does</u> my <u>husband</u> (<u>understand</u> me).
8. <u>Have</u> <u>you</u> ever <u>been</u> to the Zanzibar tavern?
9. <u>Little</u> <u>is known</u> about his past, except that <u>he</u> <u>visited</u> Calgary twice.
10. <u>Isn't</u> <u>she</u> <u>going</u> home now?

EXERCISE 26.6

1. ~~According to the old proverb~~, a stitch ~~in time~~ saves nine.
2. I have had a stitch ~~in my side~~, and I have often been ~~in stitches~~.
3. Stitching, ~~in my opinion~~, is best left ~~to tailors and surgeons~~.
4. ~~For today's prices~~, clothing manufacturers should be sewing triple seams ~~in their clothing~~, all ~~by hand~~.
5. ~~From the beginning~~, each item ~~of clothing~~ should be separately designed.
6. ~~After that~~, every pattern piece should be cut by hand.
7. Each piece ~~of cloth~~ should then be sewn ~~with great care to the other appropriate pieces, by one person~~.
8. The same craftsperson should then pay attention ~~to double-seaming~~ and ~~to details of hand-finishing~~.
9. Items ~~of clothing~~ produced ~~in this way~~ might justify today's high prices.
10. ~~In this kind of manufacturing procedure~~, the individual maker ~~of the item~~ should receive a specified percentage ~~of the wholesale price~~.

EXERCISE 26.7

1. ~~In the next twenty years~~, the average age ~~of the Canadian population~~ will increase significantly.
2. ~~For those of us~~ now ~~in our forties~~, this trend is good news.
3. ~~For those in their teens~~, however, the news is not so good. They will have to carry the burden ~~of caring for the increasing numbers of elderly persons in society~~.
4. ~~On the positive side~~, the leaders ~~of tomorrow~~ will have the experience and wisdom ~~of a large segment of the population~~ to draw on ~~in their planning and decision-making~~.
5. ~~Throughout history~~, cultures ~~around the world~~ have traditionally associated age ~~with wisdom~~.
6. Ironically, however, this assumption is not always supported ~~by the evidence~~.
7. There are many examples ~~from the past~~ and ~~in the present of young leaders with more wisdom and maturity~~ than their aged counterparts.
8. (You) Consider, ~~for example~~, Alexander the Great. He had conquered the known world ~~by the age of 19~~.
9. ~~For a contemporary example~~, (you) consider the success stories ~~of youthful entrepreneurs like Bill Gates~~. Many young people, just ~~out of college~~, have launched hi-tech ventures to compete ~~with old, established companies~~.
10. ~~Over the next two decades, with the maturing of the "baby boom,"~~ Canadians will encounter changes ~~in lifestyle, in political focus,~~ and ~~in cultural attitudes toward the "young" and the "old."~~

EXERCISE 26.9

1. The prime minister and the provincial premiers met at Harrison Lake.
2. They debated and drafted amendments to the unemployment insurance program.
3. The anesthetist and the surgeon scrubbed for surgery and hurried to the operating room.
4. Blue spruce and hemlock are both northern imports to Southern Ontario.
5. I tried and failed once, and then later tried again and succeeded.
6. My son or my daughter will drive me home.

7. The two <u>dogs</u> and the <u>cat</u> <u>travelled</u> a thousand miles in three months.
8. My retired <u>father</u> <u>reads</u>, <u>travels</u>, <u>golfs</u>, <u>walks</u> the dog, and <u>loves</u> all these activities.
9. <u>(You)</u> <u>Knock</u> three times and <u>ask</u> for Joe.
10. <u>Sight reading</u> and <u>improvising</u> <u>are</u> necessary skills of the small-band musician.

Chapter 27: Solving Sentence-Fragment Problems (pp. 258–67)

We have made the sentence fragments into complete sentences only for the first two sets and only to give you an idea of how the sentences might be formed. Many different sentences can be made out of the fragments given; just be sure each of your sentences has a subject and a verb.

EXERCISE 27.1

1. F   <u>He</u> <u>is</u> the college's expert regarding myths and fairy tales.
2. F   <u>It</u> <u>is</u> silly to decide on the basis of rumour, not facts.
3. S
4. F   <u>Grading</u> exams all evening after working all day <u>exhausts</u> even the most enthusiastic teacher.
5. F   The party <u>members</u> gathering in the campaign office <u>called</u> for a recount of the ballots.
6. S
7. F   <u>(You)</u> <u>Put</u> your hands over your head.
8. F   <u>I</u> <u>am</u> incapable of studying without my CD player.
9. F   Having worked outdoors all his life, upon retirement <u>he</u> <u>spent</u> his time in his garden.
10. S

EXERCISE 27.2

1. F   Without any idea how to go about it, <u>we</u> <u>decided</u> to make a pie.
2. S
3. F   <u>Exaggerating</u> his own influence <u>is</u> of great importance to him.
4. F   Knowing the truth, <u>we</u> <u>paid</u> little attention to his stories.
5. F   Our <u>failure</u> <u>was</u> the result of poor planning and unclear goals.
6. F   This <u>experiment</u> <u>is</u> a disaster just waiting to happen.
7. S
8. S
9. F   <u>We</u> <u>followed</u> the directions printed in the booklet included in the package.
10. S

EXERCISE 27.3

1. F
2. F
3. S
4. F
5. F

6. F
7. F
8. F
9. F
10. F

EXERCISE 27.4

1. F What
2. F As
3. F Where
4. F If
5. F So that

6. F Although
7. F Since
8. S
9. F Whichever
10. F Before

EXERCISE 27.5

<u>Before</u> the curtain went up on the lavishly decorated and beautifully lit set. The actor playing Frankie could be seen pacing up and down nervously. <u>Although</u> he was a veteran of many stage performances and several popular movies and was accustomed to appearing before large audiences. <u>Which</u> made it very strange that he would demonstrate the symptoms of stage fright so clearly. Looking closely, a careful observer might have noticed, however, that he wasn't studying his lines or rehearsing his role. In fact, <u>unless</u> one were right beside him and watching very closely. The real purpose of his pacing could easily be missed. <u>Although</u> he appeared to be alone. He was, in reality, exercising his pet cockroach.

EXERCISE 27.6

I am not a fashionable dresser. <u>Although</u> I enjoy going out to restaurants and theatres and other places where the fashion-conscious tend to congregate. I am sometimes regarded as an object of curiosity. <u>While</u> I find my hiking boots very comfortable and my Newfoundland sweater very cosy. The patrons of the ballet to which I wore them last month seemed critical. <u>As if</u>, unaccountably, they disapproved of my wardrobe selection. So, <u>in order</u> not to attract quite so much attention and to blend in a little better with the opera crowd. In preparation for last week's premiere performance, I bought a tie. <u>Even though</u> it cost me almost 10 dollars. Then I began to notice something rather odd. Ever <u>since</u> I splurged on this purchase, a truly beautiful abstract print in iridescent yellows, greens, and blues. <u>Which</u> is a neckwear item that definitely commands attention. <u>Wherever</u> I wear it. <u>Whether</u> I am dressed in my blue work shirt or my red plaid. The attention my tie attracts seems to be overwhelmingly favourable. <u>Since</u> everyone who sees it smiles. I assume they approve; perhaps they're even envious. This response is quite unlike the reaction I used to receive. <u>When</u> dressed in my former, tie-less, best. I have now graduated from gauche to gorgeous, according to my girlfriend. <u>Who</u> knows about these things.

EXERCISE 27.7

The attitude to Toronto takes two forms. There is first the attitude of the non-Torontonians, **w**ho live in places like St. John's, Maple Creek, and Vancouver. Then there is the attitude of the Torontonians themselves.

The attitude of the outsider is compounded of envy, malice and pity **in** about equal quantities. It is admitted that Torontonians make large sums of money, **b**ut not much else. Certainly they never have any fun. There is none of the leisurely gracious living that is to be found in Montreal, say, **o**r Halifax, or Okotoks, Alberta. When a young man sets out for Toronto, **h**e is surrounded by a covey of friends, all commiserating with him and whispering to him **t**o look about for a job for them in the big city. It is generally acknowledged that the bereaved young man will return, but he rarely does. If he sees his friends again, he sees them in Toronto, **w**here they all have a good cry and talk over the grand old days **w**hen they were poor in Pelvis or West Webfoot.

The attitude of the Torontonians is that they simply do not care **w**hat people think of them. They live in Toronto and that is good enough for them. For years a host of magazine articles, newspaper editorials, and commentators have baited Toronto. Toronto refuses to swallow the bait. One mayor tried to launch a campaign **t**o make the city popular, but it fizzled out after a few days. Torontonians do not really care about being popular; in fact, about half the criticism about the city comes from its own people. Nobody baits Toronto quite as much as those who live there.

Chapter 28: Solving Run-On Problems (pp. 268–77)

EXERCISE 28.1

1. The teacher's late; let's go!
2. Just let me do the talking; you'll get us a ticket if you open your mouth.
3. correct
4. correct
5. correct
6. correct
7. Students today need summer jobs because tuition and living costs are too much for most families.
8. Bryan will be going to college if he is accepted; his parents have lots of money.
9. correct
10. I am seeking a hero after whom I can model my life. So far I've rejected Sly Stallone, Madonna, and Hulk Hogan.

EXERCISE 28.2

1. The comma splice gets its name from the film splice; two pieces of the film are taped, or spliced, together.
2. Old movies are sometimes choppy and disconnected **because** they have been spliced badly or too often.
3. Two sentences cannot be spliced together with a comma. **Y**ou need to use a semicolon, or a period, or a linking word between them.
4. You should be particularly careful when using linking words like "however," "consequently," "therefore," and "moreover." **T**hese words need a semicolon before them and a comma after when they join two independent clauses.
5. This isn't a very difficult rule; in fact, it's one of the easiest rules to learn because it has no exceptions.
6. The fused sentence is named after a melting process. **F**using is joining two things together that ordinarily are not connected.
7. Two independent clauses cannot be fused together with no punctuation; you need a linking word, or a semicolon, or a period to join them.
8. What a sneaky way of reinforcing the lesson; it's almost diabolical.

9. Please don't put your feet on the table. Just because your mother isn't around to yell at you doesn't mean you can behave like a boor, **for** other people have to use the table too.
10. There is not much future in typewriter repair; it has gone the way of blacksmithing and tobacco farming.

EXERCISE 28.3

1. A Canadian who speaks three languages is called multilingual; one who speaks two languages is called bilingual; and one who speaks only one language is called an English Canadian.
2. I'm sure the job couldn't have been as bad as he claims; maybe he just didn't try hard enough. *Or:* I'm sure the job couldn't have been as bad as he claims. **M**aybe he just didn't try hard enough.
3. Meetings such as this are fine for small groups, **but** large groups have to be handled in a different way.
4. I'll be glad to help you out. **W**hen you need me just call; I'll be here all day.
5. In Canada, winter is more than a season; it's a bad joke.
6. correct
7. It may seem foolish, especially after all the wrangling over our constitution, but I still believe in a unified Canada. I believe in one nation extending from sea to sea. The Fathers of Confederation were right; a federation of provinces can work.
8. Career opportunities appear very good for students in a wide range of technical programs; however, most employers are looking for people with experience as well as training.
9. People with high-technology skills are urgently required in several fields; plastics processing, mould-making, and tool- and die-making are three examples.
10. For college students in technology programs, then, the future looks bright; however, a diploma does not necessarily guarantee job security.

EXERCISE 28.4

1. I think people talk too much. If they listened to themselves more, they would talk less.
2. Learning to ride a horse without instruction is difficult. I have a friend who taught himself to ride by watching old Clint Eastwood films; he should be out of traction in a couple of weeks.
3. Arnold Schwarzenegger will probably not be remembered as one of the world's great actors. His movies are too popular to qualify as classics; however, he will be remembered as someone who made the most of his talents.
4. According to her friends, Sabina's homemade wine is quite drinkable. Despite some unfortunate harshness, the colour is good, the bouquet is excellent, and the afterburn is impressive too.
5. Going bald isn't so bad now that many men and even some women are shaving their heads as a fashion statement; in fact, baldness is an advantage sometimes. I don't have to spend time fussing with my hair, and high winds never bother me.

6. Having inherited her great-aunt's millions, Drusilla has become a hypocrite. Insisting she hasn't changed a bit, she drives a Rolls, flaunts furs, and drips with diamonds, but do you think she ever offers to buy lunch?

7. Beagles, a kind of small hound, make excellent pets because of their cheerful, affectionate nature. I know because I have owned five of them.

8. When I woke up this morning, I had a hard time getting up. I knew I ought to eat breakfast, but I didn't have time. Then I realized I had to finish an essay for a 9:00 class. Because of the cold, I suspected my car wouldn't start, and I wouldn't be able to get to school on time. So I decided to stay in bed.

9. Canada's eternal squabbling about French versus English may soon be irrelevant. Linguistic analysts predict that Mandarin and Spanish will be the languages spoken by the majority of the world's population within a few years. Several Canadian school systems already offer these languages to give their students an advantage when they graduate into a world of international free trade.

10. The United Nations must consider carefully before sending peacekeeping troops to a war-torn nation. Unless the situation is a threat to world peace or is so out of control that innocent people are being killed, the United Nations must remain neutral. If it does not, it risks helping one political faction gain dominance over another.

EXERCISE 28.5

On opening night of our school play, I was more nervous than I have ever been before or since. While I knew the lines for my rather insignificant part, I also knew that our crew was not ready to go before a live audience. I was terrified that something would go wrong while I was on stage, and I would be made to look like a fool in front of my family and friends, who, of course, had front-row seats. As it turned out, my fears were justified. The performance was a disaster.

Within ten minutes of the curtain going up, a sound cue was missed and the whole cast stood around helplessly waiting for the phone to ring so that the heroine could answer it, as was called for in the script. Finally the sound person woke up and started the sound tape, but she was so flustered she hit the wrong cue. Instead of the telephone ring, we heard the noise of a gunshot. After a short pause while we looked at each other in panic, the heroine muttered something about the servants shooting mice in the basement and picked up the phone, which still had not rung. There was a stir in the audience; they were stifling giggles.

It got worse, much worse. In the second act when the killer tried to escape with the detective right behind him, his exit door stuck shut. Trying to jerk the door open, the villain pulled half the set down on top of them. At least this allowed him to escape. The audience was laughing loudly as the curtain fell.

In the final act, the hero was supposed to shoot the villain just as he was poised to stab the helpless heroine. The hero aimed his pistol, pulled the trigger, and of course the phone rang. Completely undone, the actor playing the villain had the brilliant idea of pretending to die of a heart attack and keeled over. By this time, the audience were no longer able to contain their laughter. They were practically in hysterics as we took our bows. But all was not lost. They called us back repeatedly for curtain calls and even stood to cheer as the curtains parted for the fourth time. Apparently they had mistaken our tragic drama of death and revenge for a slapstick comedy. I enjoyed the applause and the congratulations, but it took two days for my tension headache to subside. I never went on stage again.

Chapter 29: Solving Modifier Problems (pp. 278–86)

EXERCISE 29.1

1. Trevor left out the can of Pet Grrmet he had opened for the dog.
2. On the first day, our supervisor told us no one takes coffee breaks. (*Or:* Our supervisor told us no one takes coffee breaks on the first day.)
3. We made a real effort only when the score got close.
4. In September, Professor Green told us he thought our class was a hopeless case. (*Or:* Professor Green told us he thought our class was a hopeless case in September.)
5. We enjoyed almost the whole movie; only the ending was a disappointment.
6. In a highrise within walking distance of the campus, Matt and Christie found an apartment with two bedrooms and a sunken living room.
7. There are just enough pieces to go around.
8. It seems there is a game almost every day during baseball season.
9. A charming, intelligent companion who looks good in evening gowns and diamonds is sought by a vertically challenged but wealthy gentleman.
10. Only one of us could go because there was enough money just to buy one ticket.

EXERCISE 29.2

1. One usually finds the best Chinese food in those restaurants where the Chinese eat.
2. Using his new binoculars, he caught sight of a canary and several finches.
3. Juan had played ball professionally for several major American teams before coming to the Blue Jays.
4. The football practices have been organized as a keep-fit measure for players who are not with a team in the summertime.
5. Vancouver is a wonderful city to live in for anyone who likes rain and fog.
6. Some games, such as tiddlywinks, are less demanding in terms of time and equipment.
7. The Human Rights Code prohibits discrimination on the basis of race, sex, or age against anyone who is applying for a job.
8. With a screwdriver, I was able to loosen the clamp that held the broken cable in place.
9. With an open can of tomato juice, they waited breathlessly under the trees for the return of their dog, which had been sprayed by a skunk.
10. Tonight Sue Johanson will lead a panel discussion on relaxation through sex, including how to tone and stretch muscles, how to relieve tension, and even how to sleep.

EXERCISE 29.3

1. Driving recklessly and without lights, Gina was stopped by the police at a road block.
2. After being late twice in one week, I was lectured by my supervisor about punctuality.
3. After criticizing both my work and my attitude, my supervisor fired me.

4. Standing a full 2.5 m tall and weighing about 300 kg, the bear made it easy for Patricia to decide not to antagonize it.
5. After scoring the winning goal in overtime, the team was carried in a huge celebration through the city.
6. As a conscientious and dedicated teacher, Nina finds the workload sometimes overwhelming.
7. In less than a minute after applying the ointment, I found the pain began to ease.
8. Falling in love with a new man every week, the star of the afternoon soap *Trouble, Tears, and Tragedy* has an enthusiastic fan in Amy.
9. Whistling loudly, the boys found that the graveyard didn't seem like such a frightening place.
10. It was a great moment: after making the speech of a lifetime, Catherine was chosen by the delegates to lead the party into the next election.

EXERCISE 29.4

1. Because she had been driving recklessly and without lights, the police stopped Gina at a road block.
2. After I had been late twice in one week, my supervisor gave me a lecture about punctuality.
3. After both my work and my attitude had been criticized, I was fired.
4. Patricia decided not to antagonize the bear, which stood a full 2.5 m tall and weighed about 300 kg.
5. After our team had scored the winning goal in overtime, a huge celebration wound through the city.
6. Because Nina is a conscientious and dedicated teacher, the workload sometimes seems overwhelming to her.
7. In less than a minute after I had applied the ointment, the pain began to ease.
8. Amy is an enthusiastic fan of the afternoon soap *Trouble, Tears, and Tragedy*, whose star falls in love with a new man every week.
9. When the boys began whistling loudly, the graveyard didn't seem like such a frightening place.
10. It was a great moment: after Catherine had made the speech of a lifetime, the delegates chose her to lead the party into the next election.

EXERCISE 29.5

1. She was the baker's only daughter, but she could loaf all day. (*Or:* She was only the baker's daughter but she could loaf all day.)
2. Being horribly hung over, I came to the realization that the only problem with a free bar is knowing when to quit.
3. The judges were impressed by Sandor's plump, round, purple turnips.
4. In a hurry to get to the interview on time, I left my résumé lying on my desk at home.
5. As a college student constantly faced with new assignments, I find the pressure is sometimes intolerable.
6. In the national edition of *The Globe & Mail*, I learned that the provincial premiers plan to meet with the prime minister in Calgary next week.
7. After I had been looking at the half-price raincoat all week, the store sold it before I got there on payday.

8. The Canadian Brass receives enthusiastic acclaim from Vancouver to St. John's for its witty presentation, its wide repertoire, and its clarity of tone.
9. Queen Elizabeth couldn't resist the little Corgi puppy, which was rolling on her back, eager to have her tummy scratched.
10. Deeply concerned about the spread of AIDS and wanting to do something to prevent more deaths in the community, the mayor solicited volunteers to mount an awareness campaign.

Chapter 30: The Parallelism Principle (pp. 287–92)

EXERCISE 30.1

1. This program is easy to understand and to use.
2. We were told that we would have to leave and that we could take nothing with us.
3. We organized our findings, wrote the report, and made our presentation.
4. Today's personal computers are fast, powerful, and compact.
5. Rudolf's doctor advised him not to strain his back or his mind.
6. The company is looking for an employee who has a car and who knows the city.
7. To me, winter means dangerous driving, bulky clothing, and huge heating bills.
8. Although he refused to get into high boots or wear a toque, Bruce did accept my offer of a down-filled jacket.
9. We noticed with approval the in-ground pool, the spring-fed trout pond, and the all-weather tennis court.
10. If it is to be useful, your report must be clearly organized, well written, and thoroughly researched.

EXERCISE 30.2

1. Bodybuilding has made me what I am today: physically perfect, financially prosperous, and practically friendless.
2. If there is no heaven, then there is no hell.
3. In my tiny home town, two significantly related crimes prevail: vandalism and drug trafficking.
4. I'd like to help, but I'm too tired, too poor, and too busy.
5. I wanted either a Mother's pizza or a McDonald's Big Mac.
6. correct
7. My sister, who's trying to teach me to play tennis, says that my forehand and serve are all right, but that my backhand needs strengthening.
8. The two factors thought to be most important in a long-lasting marriage are the commitment of each partner to the marriage and the willingness of each partner to compromise.
9. Yuri claimed that, through repetition and firmness, he had trained his guppy to be obedient, quiet, and loyal.
10. The new budget must deal with several major problems, two of them being the devalued Canadian dollar and the high rate of inflation.

EXERCISE 30.3

1. wine   women   song
2. privately   publicly
3. employers   employees
4. lying about all morning   doing whatever I please
5. as individuals   as a group
6. happy   healthy   wise
7. do your best   don't give up
8. information   education   entertainment
9. not enough time   not enough money   not enough staff
10. French is the language of love
    English is the language of business
    German is the language of profanity

EXERCISE 30.4

1. In order to succeed in this economy, small businesses must be creative, forward-looking, innovative, and flexible.
2. Not being able to speak the language is confusing, frustrating, and embarrassing.
3. Although the first candidate we interviewed seemed frightened and shy, the second was composed and outgoing.
4. Trying your best and succeeding are not always the same thing, but of the two, the former is the more important.
5. Our chances of a long-term relationship are slim since you enjoy getting dressed up, you love to dance, and you like crowds: three things that I consider torture.
6. Lowering our profit margin, raising our prices, and laying off two managers will enable us to meet our budget.
7. Licking one's fingers and picking one's teeth in a sophisticated dining room is bound to attract criticism and perhaps even an invitation to leave.
8. New potatoes dug from the garden, beefsteak tomatoes ripened on the vine, and freestone peaches hand-picked from our tree: these are my favourite summer foods.
9. After an enjoyable dinner, I like to drink a cappuccino, eat a dark-chocolate mint, and, occasionally, smoke a good cigar.
10. Influential factors in any nation's economic regression are bad management of natural resources, unwise policies regarding national debt, and inflationary demands of workers.

Chapter 31: Refining by Combining (pp. 293–97)

EXERCISE 31.1

1. The Beatles are a musical institution, for (*or* and) their music appeals to every generation.
2. Kate Bush does not give live performances, nor does she tour with her music.
3. Janet Jackson has a famous brother, so (*or* and) she had to work hard to create a unique sound.

4. Van Halen is a progressive-rock group, but they take offence at being labelled "heavy-metal."
5. You can read about Michael Jackson's skin-bleaching routine in medical journals, or you can listen to "Black or White."
6. The Rolling Stones originated in the 1960s, and (*or* yet) they are still performing now, in the 1990s.
7. Madonna is considered a controversial artist, for she has made several sexually explicit videos.
8. Phil Collins is a popular contemporary solo artist, but his roots go back to Genesis.
9. Bryan Adams is to be commended for his work on "All for One," but Rod Stewart and Sting contributed to making the song a success.
10. Jethro Tull is unusual among popular rock groups, for they occasionally feature classical instruments such as the flute.

EXERCISE 31.2

1. Since the team moved from Atlanta, the Calgary Flames have been a mainstay in the NHL.
2. Because Fred McGriff has a devastating swing, he is one of the most feared hitters in the National League.
3. Roberto Alomar of the Toronto Blue Jays won a "gold glove," which was in recognition of his outstanding defensive skills.
4. Deion Sanders is a talented athlete, whether he is playing baseball for the Atlanta Braves or football for the Atlanta Falcons.
5. The Blue Jays always seem to win when (*or* whenever) the SkyDome roof is closed.
6. After struggling for years, the Vancouver Canucks are so improved that they are now acknowledged as a team to be reckoned with.
7. The Montreal Expos draw impressive crowds to Olympic Stadium as long as they are winning.
8. The Montreal Canadiens have won many Stanley Cups, but the Quebec Nordiques have yet to win even one.
9. Wayne Gretzky is an exceptional hockey player, even if some sports writers consider him a defensive liability.
   or
   Although Wayne Gretzky is an exceptional hockey player, some sports writers consider him a defensive liability.
10. Although Tony Fernandez, who comes from the Dominican Republic, is an important role model for his team, he is a bigger role model for children in the Dominican Republic.

EXERCISE 31.3

1. Whenever Rudolf loses a girlfriend, he goes shopping for new clothes.
2. According to Mortimer Adler, failure breeds fatigue, and there is nothing more energizing than success.
3. Love one another, but make not a bond of love. (Kahlil Gibran)
4. You must learn to love yourself before you can truly love someone else.
5. Marriage is for serious people, so I have not considered it an option.
   or
   Because marriage is for serious people, I have not considered it an option.

6. Some people still believe that divorce is an acknowledgement that there was not a true commitment in the first place.
7. It is an astonishing fact that 20 percent of adults in America are illiterate, and 50 percent of the adults who *can* read say they never read books.
8. Although Canada is a relatively rich country, most of us brush up against hunger and homelessness almost daily, when we encounter men and, less often, women begging on downtown streetcorners.
9. In his essay "A Modest Proposal for a Divorce Ceremony," Pierre Berton proposed that Canada institute a formal divorce ceremony, which would be like a formal wedding ceremony, but all the symbolism would be reversed.
10. The bride, for example, would wear black, and immediately after the ceremony, the newly divorced couple would go into the vestry and scratch their names off the marriage register.

UNIT SEVEN: Grammar

Chapter 32: Mastering Subject–Verb Agreement (pp. 300–309)

EXERCISE 32.1

1. They sell used essays to other students.
2. The women maintain that their boss has been ogling them.
3. Those new computers affect the entire office procedure.
4. All those who shop at Pimrock's receive free cans of tuna.
5. Those girls' fathers are looking for rich husbands for them.

EXERCISE 32.2

1. Movies are what Marcia spends most of her time on.
2. The cause of his downfall was frequent nights of debauchery.
3. Clean living and Lois Lane were what kept Superman strong.
4. Accounting procedures were something that I didn't understand.
5. The reason for your success in the aluminum-siding business is your stunning good looks.

EXERCISE 32.3

1. know
2. is
3. is
4. are
5. repel

EXERCISE 32.4

1. are
2. registers
3. is
4. keeps
5. inflicts

EXERCISE 32.5

1. loves
2. knows
3. wants
4. is
5. interests

EXERCISE 32.6

1. is
2. involves
3. has
4. wants
5. believes

EXERCISE 32.7

1. plans
2. has
3. have
4. was
5. are

EXERCISE 32.8

1. was
2. seems
3. is
4. is
5. seems

EXERCISE 32.9

1. My sense of the schools *is* . . .
2. Neither of us *remembers* . . .
3. Every one of the SUNshine Boys *appeals* . . .
4. My whole family, with the exception of the cat, *dislikes* . . .
5. Popular belief notwithstanding, quicksand *does* . . .
6. It is the suction created by the victims that *is* . . .
7. correct
8. Eight hundred dollars per term, all students agree, *is* . . .
9. The birth of quintuplets *was* . . .
10. Everything that we agreed to last night *seems* . . .

EXERCISE 32.10

Quebec City, along with Montreal, Toronto, and Vancouver, *is* among Canada's great gourmet centres. While Toronto is a relative latecomer to this list, neither Quebec City nor Montreal *is a stranger* to those who *seek* fine dining. Indeed, travel and food magazines have long affirmed that the inclusion of these two cities in a

Quebec vacation *is* a "must." Montreal is perhaps more international in its offerings, but Quebec City provides exquisite proof that French-Canadian cuisine and hospitality *are* second to none in the world. Amid the old-world charm of the lower city *are* to be found some of the quaintest and most enjoyable traditional restaurants; the newer sections of town *boast* equally fine dining in more contemporary surroundings. The combination of the wonderful food and the city's fascinating charms *is* sure to make any visitor return frequently. Either the summer, when the city blooms and outdoor cafés abound, or the winter, when Carnaval turns the streets into hundreds of connecting parties, *is a* wonderful *time* to visit one of Canada's oldest and most interesting cities.

EXERCISE 32.11

The interest in wrestlers and their managers, fans, and friends *is* fascinating proof that our society needs cheap thrills. The concept of good and evil fighting it out in epic battles *is* an enduring one. In simpler times, everyone who felt the need to witness such struggles *was* able to watch westerns on TV and see the Bad Guy (wearing the black hat) gunned down at high noon by the reluctant Good Guy (wearing the white hat). The complexity of our society, where good and evil *are* constantly redefined, *means* that we seldom get a clear decision in the battles we see each day on the news, let alone witness the triumph of good over evil. Into this frustrating world *come* Rowdy Roddy Piper, Hulk Hogan, the Junk Yard Dog, and King Kong Bundy. The variety of names, personalities, and "show-biz" tricks *is* bewildering. Though the staging of the various moves and even the outcomes of the matches are obvious, the immense popularity of the matches, both on television and in the arenas, *is* undeniable. Like Rambo and Dirty Harry, the professional wrestler cuts through frustrating complexity and represents good or evil in its simplest, most dramatic form. To a great many people, wrestling—not to mention wrestlers—*is* irresistible.

Chapter 33: Using Verbs Effectively (pp. 310–26)

EXERCISE 33.1

1. came
2. spent
3. made
4. been
5. lost

6. spoke, found
7. knew
8. had
9. chosen
10. told, led

EXERCISE 33.2

1. won, won
2. worn, wore
3. did, done
4. forgotten, forgot
5. became, become

6. seen, saw
7. set, set
8. fallen, fell
9. met, met
10. kept, kept

EXERCISE 33.3

1. I would have written more often if I had *known* you cared.
2. The telephone *rang* and *rang*, but no one answered because everyone had *gone* out for pizza.
3. I never saw a person who did nothing but *lie* around the house as much as she does.
4. The whole family was *shaken* up when they learned Gerald had *stolen* Dad's car and taken off for Seattle.
5. "Strike three!" yelled the umpire as soon as I *swung* the bat, but I *ran* around the bases anyway.
6. Orville's pumpkins would have *grown* twice as big if they hadn't *frozen* in the cold snap.
7. If Rudolph and Dwight had *known* what was good for them, they would have switched to pop after they had *drunk* the entire contents of the beer keg.
8. Anna should have *stolen* second base; she should not have *run* for home.
9. The boys have *gone* out to get more beer since they've already *drunk* the two cases I brought.
10. After the neighbourhood bully had deliberately *burst* my daughter's balloon, she *lay* on the ground and sobbed.

EXERCISE 33.5

1. Rolly goes home and *kicks* his cat.
2. Hank Aaron broke Babe Ruth's record of 714 home runs in a lifetime when he *hit* number 715 in 1974.
3. Children are quite perceptive and *know* when you are lying to them.
4. We had just finished painting the floor when the dog *ran* through.
5. When Knowlton Nash walked into the room, the ladies *went* crazy.
6. correct
7. Tim walked into the room, took one look at Lefty, and *smashed* him right through the wall.
8. First you will greet the guests; then you *will show* them to their rooms.
9. The largest cheese ever produced took 43 hours to make and *weighed* a whopping 15 723 kilograms.
10. He watches television until he finally *goes* to sleep.

EXERCISE 33.6

1. correct
2. I tried to warn him about her evil ways, and what thanks *did* I get?
3. The embarrassed girl didn't say anything. She just *blushed* and *ran* from the room.
4. Before Roger noticed the snowstorm, he *was* already up and dressed.
5. They agreed to our living here after we *offered* them a substantial bribe.
6. In the interests of good community relations and to prevent them from blowing up our house, I vote that we *pay* what they asked for.
7. Drusilla looks like a sweet young thing; when she *speaks*, however, the toughest truck drivers blush.
8. Whenever I skip chemistry, it *seems* old Mr. Bunsen *is* lurking in the hall to catch me.
9. correct

10. We attempted to change Rudolf's mind all day, but we didn't know he *had* already voted.

EXERCISE 33.7

For some reason when mistakes or accidents *happen* in radio or television, they *are* often hilariously funny. If, in the course of a conversation, someone said, "Here come the Duck and Doochess of Kent," listeners would probably be mildly amused. But many years ago, when an announcer *made* that slip on a live radio broadcast, it *became* one of the most famous blunders in radio history. Tapes of the slip *are* filed in "bloopers" libraries all over the world. This heightened sense of hilarity is the reason that so many people who *work* in radio *dedicate* their creativity to making the on-air announcer laugh while reading the news. To take one example, Lorne Greene's *was* the deeply serious voice that *was* heard on the CBC news during World War II. He *was* the victim of all kinds of pranks aimed at getting him to break up while reading the dark, often tragic, news of the combat overseas. The pages of his news script *were* set on fire while he *read*. He *was* even stripped naked as he *read*, calmly, and apparently without strain. Lorne Greene *was* a true professional. Many other newscasters, however, have proved to be highly susceptible to falling apart on air at the slightest provocation. And there *have* always *been* people around a radio station who could not resist giving them that little push.

EXERCISE 33.9

1. The server will make espresso in a few minutes.
2. Dire Straits recorded "Brothers in Arms."
3. When it gets cold, we plug in the block heater overnight.
4. For many years, professional athletes have used steroids to improve speed and endurance.
5. You must not knead the dough, or your pastry will be tough.
6. Dr. Lance Boyles wrote *Do-It-Yourself Surgery*, which is the current best-seller.
7. The police arrested four of Dwight's buddies during a routine check of Barry's Bingo Bistro.
8. Thieves broke into our neighbours' house while they were vacationing in the Caribbean.
9. Technicians from Dell, IBM, and Apple will display and demonstrate the latest multimedia technology in the graphics lab.
10. The Mighty Ducks have finally replaced the Red Sox and the White Sox as the stupidest team name in sports.

EXERCISE 33.10

1. Another Juno was won by k.d. lang. (Active is more effective.)
2. The ball was spiked by Rudolf, giving us the winning point. (Active is more effective.)
3. A law forbidding smoking in burning buildings has been passed by city council. (Passive is more effective, because it focusses the readers' attention on the law rather than on who brought the law into being.)
4. As the storm clouds gathered, our bicycles were pedalled faster and faster. (Active is more effective.)

5. Forty-eight hours later, the technician added 2 ml of sterile water to the culture in the Petri dish. (Passive is more effective; it puts the focus on the procedure rather than on the person.)
6. Four tickets for the concert were got by Krystal after standing in line all night. (Active is more effective.)
7. The truth behind the famous Doobie Brothers scandal was revealed on the 10:00 news. (Passive is more effective; what was revealed is of more interest than who revealed it.)
8. The judge finally announced her judgement today, almost a year after the environmental hearings were concluded. (Passive is more effective, for the same reason as in sentence 7.)
9. We were saved from bankruptcy by an unbelievable run of luck. (Which form of the verb is more effective in this sentence depends on what you want to emphasize: being saved from bankruptcy or the run of luck.)
10. After a long debate, Yasmin's fundraising proposal was finally endorsed by the committee. (Passive is more effective, because it focusses attention on the individual proposal rather than on the anonymous committee.)

EXERCISE 33.11

Russian women who are between the ages of 16 and 25 recently *identified* Madonna as the person they most admired. This startling fact *appeared* in an article in a popular magazine that *had surveyed* more than 3000 subscribers. *The young women also admired,* in order of popularity, Michael Jackson, the Beatles, and Queen Elizabeth. Russian men's tastes in popular entertainment were also reported. Males between 16 and 25 *named* Depeche Mode and the Beatles as the people they most admired. The survey also *identified* this age group's favourite leisure activities. *The women favoured* movies, drawing and painting, dancing, needlework, and pop music, while *the men enjoyed* music videos, art, electronics, painting, and guitar playing. When the respondents were asked to list, in order of priority, the countries in which they would be most likely to seek a pen pal, Canada was ranked third by both sexes. The United States *came* first, followed by England. Australia and Germany *tied* for fourth place.

Chapter 34: Solving Pronoun Problems (pp. 327–44)

EXERCISE 34.1

1. No one except you and *me* . . .
2. *He* and I can't figure out this problem set any better than you and *she* could.
3. Dwight and *he* fell asleep . . .
4. It is hard to believe that anyone could snore as loudly as *they.*
5. We can use the film passes all week, and you and *she* can use them on the weekend when Biff and *I* are going skiing.
6. Thanks to the recommendations provided by your math instructor and *me,* you and *she* got the tutorial jobs.
7. As we were going to class, Karl and *I* heard . . .
8. If it hadn't been for Hassan and *him* . . .
9. Eugene and *he* agreed to split the price of a case with Stan and *me.*
10. Only two students passed the midterm: Nadia and *I.*

EXERCISE 34.2

1. At fourteen, my younger brother is already taller than *I*.
2. No one likes partying more than *he* and Krystal.
3. Would you like to join Dwight and *me*. . . ?
4. Only one person in this firm could manage the department as well as *he*.
5. At last I have met someone who enjoys grilled liver as much as *I*!
6. We can skate as well as *they*, but they are much better at shooting and defending than *we*.
7. More than *I*, Serge uses the computer. . . .

EXERCISE 34.3

1. My boyfriend and *I*. . . .
2. I like fast food better than *he*.
3. He likes vegetables better than *I*.
4. In fact, between you and *me*. . . .
5. . . . it is difficult for *them* to know where to take him and *me*. . . .
6. The only type of restaurant where *we* and *they* can all have what we like is Italian.
7. There, *he* and his friends. . . , while my friends and *I* tuck into spaghetti. . . .
8. We are probably not as healthy as *they*, but they don't seem to enjoy their food as much as *we*.

EXERCISE 34.4

1. For two weeks, the pitcher *who*. . . .
2. . . . a film director *who* began his career in Canada.
3. The vacuum-cleaner salesperson *who* came to our door was the sort of person *who*. . . .
4. We are often attracted to people *who*. . . .
5. . . . the last of the people *(whom)* we had invited finally arrived.
6. Meat Loaf, *who* is the star headlining tonight's show, is responsible for two albums *that*. . . .
7. Rudolf's grandmother always told him that people *who* couldn't fly. . . .
8. . . . which we had bought from a friend *who* had lost his licence, to a scrap yard *that* paid us $50 for it.
9. People *who* take afternoon naps often pay a penalty: they are also people *who*. . . .
10. The math problems *(that)* we worked out last night would have stymied anyone who. . . .

EXERCISE 34.5

1. his
2. her
3. his
4. her
5. himself, he

EXERCISE 34.6

1. Everyone who enjoys a thrilling match will reserve a seat. . . .
2. . . . everyone climbed to the fourth floor to hand in the course evaluations.
3. Each of her sons has successfully completed his diploma.
4. Someone with lots of money left a purse in the washroom.
5. All reporters must decide for themselves how far they will go. . . .

EXERCISE 34.7

1. Virginia claims that every one of her male friends has a room of his own.
2. Almost everyone I know is worried about finding a suitable job.
3. Anybody who applies for a job with this institution can expect to spend a lot of time in selection committee interviews.
4. Taking pictures of people when they are not looking can produce interesting results.
5. Nearly every man who can cook will tell you that he enjoys preparing food.

EXERCISE 34.8

1. The gorilla was mean and thirsty because he had finished all his food in the morning.
2. If your pet rat won't eat its food, feed the pellets to the kitty.
3. Chuck told Rocco Chuck's teeth were falling out.
4. Whenever Stefan and Matt played poker, Stefan stacked the deck.
5. I know that smoking is bad for me and everyone else, but I can't give up cigarettes.
6. Madonna has transformed herself at least three times in her career, which is a claim few other performers can make.
7. Daphne backed her car into a garbage truck and dented her fender.
8. Rocco was suspicious of handgun control because he thought everyone should have a gun for late-night subway rides.
9. Rushing out the door, Rhonda slammed into a woman fixing her make-up; unfortunately, the force of the blow jammed a tube of lipstick up the poor woman's nose and broke the lipstick.
10. If Preston and Lucien begin to argue, Lucien will tell Preston that he's never had any use for him and that he ought to keep his crazy ideas to himself.

EXERCISE 34.10

1. you
2. you, your
3. they, themselves
4. she
5. we

EXERCISE 34.11

1. After the unfortunate brawl, Biff learned that if a person stomps on police officers, he can expect to end up in jail.

2. People can expect to experience the horrors of nuclear war unless they raise their voices against nuclear proliferation.
3. If you leave garbage at your campsite, you may well have bears as midnight callers.
4. correct
5. You will always think about the opportunities you've missed, even if you're happy with what you have.
6. Canadians who worry about street violence should keep in mind that, in comparison with New York, they are safe in downtown Kapuskasing after dark.
7. You should always wear garlic around the neck if you fear vampires.
8. Any woman who wears garlic won't have to worry about men harassing her, either.
9. Can you really know another person if you have never been to his or her home?
10. A sure way to lose your friends is to eat all the Baskin Robbins ice cream yourself.

EXERCISE 34.13

1. correct
2. You don't need as much money or skill as you do for downhill skiing. . . .
3. correct
4. First, you don't need to take out a loan for the equipment; you can buy a decent snowboard. . . .
5. Second, you don't need lessons to begin.
6. correct
7. Even if you are a complete novice. . . .
8. Third, you don't have all the hassle of changing outfits whenever you want to. . . .
9. correct
10. But boarding boots are comfortable, and the board is easily tucked under your arm.
11. . . . because they are jealous of your mobility and freedom, and ski lifts are not designed to get you safely to the top of a hill with a snowboard.
12. correct

UNIT EIGHT: Punctuation

Chapter 35: Question and Exclamation Marks (pp. 346–49)

EXERCISE 35.1

1. question mark
2. question mark
3. period
4. period
5. question mark
6. question mark
7. period
8. question mark
9. period
10. question mark

EXERCISE 35.2

1. exclamation mark
2. exclamation mark, exclamation mark
3. exclamation mark
4. exclamation mark, exclamation mark (or period)
5. exclamation mark and period
6. two exclamation marks (or exclamation mark and period)
7. exclamation mark (inside final quotation mark)
8. exclamation mark, exclamation mark (or exclamation mark and period)
9. exclamation mark
10. exclamation mark, exclamation mark (or exclamation mark and period)

Chapter 36: Quotation Marks (pp. 350–53)

EXERCISE 36.1

1. "Pardon me, boys, is this the Transylvania Station?" asked the man in the black cape.
2. correct
3. "This film," exclaimed Granny, "is more explicit than *National Geographic!*"
4. As *The Globe & Mail* put it, "The Canadian dollar went on a roller-coaster ride yesterday."
5. It was the philosopher Ludwig Feuerbach who first said, "Man is what he eats," and we here at Big Boy restaurants certainly agree with that.
6. correct
7. "Your every whim will be catered to," promised the Sybaritic Spas brochure.
8. correct
9. "If not," I asked my friend, "why should we spend $800 for a weekend in Collingwood?"
10. *The Guinness Book of Records* claims that the oldest living thing is the California bristlecone pine tree, which is almost 5000 years old.

EXERCISE 36.2

1. "Did you see the strange look on his face?" asked Roderick.
2. correct
3. "Of course," she answered, usually willing to oblige.
4. "Have you read my essay, 'Dreaming Your Way to an Energized Future'?" Dr. Piffle asked his numbed audience. "It's in my new book entitled *Upscale Networking in a Self-Actualized Cosmos.*"
5. The fellow to my left hissed, "I'd sooner be horsewhipped; where do they find these guys?"
6. I forget whether it was John Paul Jones or George Chuvalo who said, "I have not yet begun to fight."
7. The vice-president had bad news for the staff: "Due to lower-than-expected profits from the bookstore and excessive vandalism at the parking gates, you're all terminated."
8. correct

9. Wasn't it Irving Layton who described ageing as "the inescapable lousiness of growing old"?
10. correct

Chapter 37: The Comma (pp. 354–60)

EXERCISE 37.1

1. correct
2. *Germinal, The Trial*(,) and *Middlemarch* are three of my favourite novels.
3. Be sure to pick up gin, tonic, limes(,) and ice.
4. All we need now is gift wrap, ribbon, tape, a card(,) and a bow.
5. Warren stomped into the room, threw himself into a chair, drained a six-pack of beer(,) and crushed the cans against his forehead.

EXERCISE 37.2

1. The cheetah is, of course, the fastest animal on earth.
2. correct
3. Malcolm Lowry, an alcoholic British expatriate, wrote *Under the Volcano*, perhaps the finest novel ever written in Canada.
4. Many children in this school, it seems, are arriving in the morning without having had an adequate breakfast.
5. The lead singer, in a bid for notoriety, bit the head off a bat during the performance.

EXERCISE 37.3

1. I refuse to wear that turkey costume to the party, nor will I go as a horse's rear end.
2. Yesterday he broke up with her, but today he is begging for forgiveness.
3. correct
4. The boss told him to stop leering at the female staff members, or she would fire him.
5. Waving a red flag in front of a bull is supposed to enrage him, yet experiments have shown that bulls are colour-blind.

EXERCISE 37.4

1. Third, insert your finger into the electrical socket.
2. Overwhelmed by the generous offer, we spent the evening watching Paul's home movies.
3. If you work for an airline, company policy states you are entitled to one free trip a year.
4. In addition, your next of kin is entitled to reduced fares.
5. Unless you learn to use commas properly, your writing will lack sophistication and polish.

EXERCISE 37.5

1. Pinot noir, which is a type of grape grown in California, Oregon, British Columbia(,) and Ontario, produces a delicious red wine.
2. There are, I am told, people who don't like garlic, but you won't find any of them eating at Freddy's.
3. I use e-mail to communicate with my colleagues, a fax machine to keep in touch with clients(,) and Canada Post to send greetings to my friends.
4. Canada Post, which often takes four days to deliver a letter within a city, is known in our office as "snail mail."
5. "You must agree, Ms. Petrarch, that my poems are classics."
6. According to G.K. Chesterton, "If a thing is worth doing, it is worth doing badly."
7. Looking for a competent computer technologist, we interviewed, tested, investigated(,) and rejected 30 applicants.
8. How you choose to phrase your resignation is up to you, but I expect to have it on my desk by morning.
9. Rudolf's beard, which looks ragged and moth-eaten, could hardly be described as a fashion statement.
10. Canada, a country known internationally for beautiful scenery, peaceful intentions(,) and violent hockey, always places near the top of the United Nations' list of desirable places to live.

EXERCISE 37.6

1. Fascinating, challenging, high-paying jobs are available to the people who transfer to our exciting Beirut branch office.
2. Oswald, your lawyers agreed to work with you, not against you, didn't they?
3. Our guard dog, a Rottweiler, caught an intruder and maimed him for life.
4. Unfortunately, my Uncle Ladislaw was the intruder, and he intends to sue us for every penny we have.
5. correct
6. All warm-blooded animals that give live birth and suckle their young are classified as mammals, but no one knows how to classify the warm-blooded, egg-laying, chick-nursing platypus.
7. We are pleased with your résumé, and we are offering you an interview this week.
8. correct
9. Although Biff begged and pleaded, Drusilla refused to wear a tattooed heart with his name in the middle.
10. Igor asked, "May I show you to your quarters, or would you prefer to spend the night in the dungeon?"

EXERCISE 37.7

I sometimes wonder what our ancestors, were they able to observe us now, would think of some of the activities we take for granted. I'm sure that rollerblading would seem peculiar to them, as would surfing, water-skiing(,) and hang-gliding. However, I suspect that our forebears would find even those strange activities understandable, perhaps even enjoyable, compared with jogging. The sight of otherwise perfectly reasonable people decked out in various types of colourful underwear, doggedly puffing and sweating along every pathway, road(,) and trail would, I am convinced, put The Fear into Great-Grandad and send him scurrying back whence he had come.

All kinds of people jog: there are short joggers, tall joggers, fat joggers, thin joggers; serious joggers, light-hearted joggers, fashionable joggers(,) and practical joggers; joggers with outfits of every hue from black to white and every shade in between. In fact, there may be more people who jog than people who don't!

I gave up jogging some years ago with the excuse that, although I adored distance running, an old basketball injury prevented me from measuring up to my own expectations. This pitiful story, together with a wistful sigh for lost youth, usually gets me off the hook. While my friends claim to be fit and keen, I take satisfaction in quoting Satchel Paige, the famous baseball player, who, at age 60, pitched three scoreless innings in the major leagues. In his "Six Rules for a Long Life," Satch warns, "On no account, run." This is sound advice, and I intend to live by this sensible and energy-efficient rule.

Chapter 38: The Semicolon (pp. 361–65)

EXERCISE 38.1

1. incorrect
2. correct
3. incorrect
4. incorrect
5. incorrect

6. incorrect
7. incorrect
8. correct
9. incorrect
10. incorrect

EXERCISE 38.2

1. We've eaten all the goodies; it's time to go home.
2. correct
3. Your instructor would like to see you pass; however, there may be a small fee involved.
4. Florence is going to Hollywood; she wants to appear on *Let's Make a Deal.*
5. We knew that the party was a huge success: Uncle Morty tap-danced across the top of the piano, Aunt Madeline did her Big Bird imitation, and Biff wrestled two of his cousins.
6. Many people dislike hockey because some of the players act like goons rather than athletes.
7. Orville tried and tried, but he couldn't get the teacher's attention.
8. correct
9. First, we'll have a cool drink; then we'll see if we can find a way to start this car.
10. Dudley left his clothes by the pool, so it's no wonder people in the lounge are looking at him strangely.

EXERCISE 38.3

1. When you consider the consequences, cheating on your income tax is probably not a good idea.
2. A decade ago, distinct computer languages were used for specific purposes; for example, COBOL was used in business, whereas FORTRAN was used in the sciences.

3. Today, however, most programs are written in C++ or in high-level Unix.
4. There are many Canadians who are famous abroad but virtually unknown at home; one example is Norman Bethune.
5. My telephone is not working. The silence is wonderful; thus, I have decided not to get it fixed.

EXERCISE 38.4

1. A day without puns is like a day without sunshine; it leaves gloom for improvement.
2. We must organize our finances; otherwise, we'll be broke before April.
3. We had all hoped you would be able to join us; however, since you have a previous engagement, we'll just have to carry on without you.
4. As a dog lover in general and an Afghan owner in particular, I have to take a lot of abuse; for example, my wife gave me a book rating the intelligence of various breeds of dog, and the Afghan ranked 79th out of 79 breeds tested.
5. It is not very difficult to become wealthy if you're in your early twenties; all you need to do is put the price of a pack of cigarettes a day into an RSP each year, and you'll be a millionaire by the time you retire.
6. Foolishly, I chose to write my essay about NAFTA; I thought it was a new football league.
7. We decided to go to a nearby restaurant for pizza; that is, we would have gone, but Norm insisted on waiting for Mairi, and by the time we got there, it was closed.
8. The entire town is in an uproar; it seems Rudolf has been missing since yesterday.
9. There is one person, however, who does not seem to be distressed, and that is Rudolf's mother.
10. According to a recent *Gourmet Magazine* poll, four of the top ten restaurants in the world are in Paris; three, those ranking eighth, ninth(,) and tenth, are in the United States; and two are in Tokyo. One is in Thailand.

EXERCISE 38.5

1. I have grown fond of semicolons in recent years. The semicolon tells me that there is still some question about the preceding full sentence; something needs to be added.
2. It is almost always a greater pleasure to come across a semicolon than a period. The period tells you that that is that; if you didn't get all the meaning you wanted or expected, you got all the writer intended to parcel out and now you have to move along.
3. But with a semicolon there, you get a pleasant little feeling of expectancy; there is more to come; read on; it will get clearer.
4. Colons are a lot less attractive, for several reasons: firstly, they give you the feeling of being rather ordered around, or at least having your nose pointed in a direction you might not be inclined to take if left to yourself, and, secondly, you suspect you're in for one of those sentences that will be labelling the points to be made: firstly, secondly, and so forth, with the implication that you haven't enough sense to keep track of a sequence of notions without having them numbered.
5. correct

Chapter 39: The Colon (pp. 366–69)

EXERCISE 39.1

1. incorrect		6. correct
2. incorrect		7. correct
3. correct		8. incorrect
4. incorrect		9. incorrect
5. incorrect		10. correct

EXERCISE 39.2

1. I have set myself three goals this year: to achieve an 80% average, to get a good summer job, and to buy a car.
2. Right after we moved in, we discovered we had a problem: termites.
3. Our credit card consultant asked us an important question after our bankruptcy: "Why don't you cut up your credit cards?"
4. Several Canadian writers are even better known abroad than they are at home: Carol Shields, Neil Bissoondath, and Michael Ondaatje are three examples.
5. There are a number of inexpensive activities that will improve physical fitness: swimming, tennis, jogging, even brisk walking.
6. Jocelyn is trying very hard to accomplish two mutually contradictory things: a significant weight loss and success as a restaurant critic.
7. Several of the animals on the international list of endangered species are native to Canada: the wood bison, the Northern kit fox, and the whooping crane.
8. correct
9. The majority of Canada's population is worn out and exhausted at the end of a long, hard winter, but most people are able to console themselves with one comforting thought: spring will arrive sometime in May or June.
10. There are several troublesome implications of biological engineering, but one in particular is frightening to most people: the cloning of human beings.

EXERCISE 39.3

1. Believe it or not, the country that produces the most films every year is India.
2. In drafting the budget, we must be careful to avoid the one technique the president has said she will not entertain: deficit financing.
3. correct
4. According to Roderick, who is several decades out of date, the only important things in life are sex, drugs, and rock 'n' roll.
5. Sebastian's room-mates are trying to encourage him to move with the times.
6. correct
7. correct
8. All most students ask is that their teachers treat them with courtesy, fairness, and respect.
9. Of course, there are always a few students who demand what no true professional will provide: special treatment.
10. correct

Chapter 40: Dashes and Parentheses (pp. 370–74)

EXERCISE 40.1

1. The aboriginal tribes of England—I've forgotten their name—painted themselves blue.
2. My purpose in moving from Vancouver to Hope—like that of hundreds of people before me—was to find affordable housing.
3. We shall have to start without her—again!
4. Skiing and skating—if you like these sports, you'll love Quebec.
5. Tending to his garden, writing his memoirs, and dining with friends—these were the pleasures Arnold looked forward to in retirement.
6. What is missing in his life is obvious—rest and relaxation!
7. Zoe should do well—in fact, I'm sure she will—in the engineering program.
8. Rudolf was amazed—positively thunderstruck—when he learned Uncle Vladimir had won a million dollars.
9. Historians, diarists, and chroniclers—these are the recorders of our past.
10. Dashes allow you to insert—with a kind of shout—the occasional exclamation into your sentences.

EXERCISE 40.2

1. Five of the students (I was asked not to name them) have volunteered to be peer tutors.
2. The apostrophe is explained in the unit on spelling (pp. 376–414).
3. Jason complained that being a manager (he became one in March) was like being a cop.
4. I have enclosed a cheque for one hundred and fifty dollars ($150.00).
5. More members of the Canadian armed forces died in World War I (1914–1918) than in any war before or since.
6. Although Mozart lived a relatively short time (he died when he was 36), he composed hundreds of musical masterpieces.
7. As news of his "miracle cures" spread (patients began to come to him from all over the province), the country doctor had to move his clinic to a more central location.
8. The new contract provided improved working conditions, a raise in salary (5 percent), and a new dental plan.
9. After years of producing undrinkable wine, Ontario now boasts a few very good wineries (Inniskillin and Hillebrand are two that come to mind).
10. "One of the most important tools for making paper speak in your own voice is punctuation; it plays the role of body language; it helps readers hear you the way you want to be heard" (Baker, "How to Punctuate," 48–49).

EXERCISE 40.3

1. The function of parentheses (see the explanation on p. 372) is to set apart material that interrupts the main idea of the sentence and that the writer does not want to emphasize.
2. Dashes, on the other hand—I love dashes—are used to set off a dramatic or emphatic interruption.
3. My English instructor (who appears not to have read the information on pp. 370–71) ruthlessly strikes out all my dashes, complaining that my

penchant for this piece of punctuation makes my sentences sound breathless and incoherent.

4. This club plays jazz—mostly Dixieland—nightly from 10 until 2.
5. On their first date, Rupert took Freda bowling (she hates bowling); I doubt that they will see each other again.
6. The case of beer—if you can believe Rudolf—was finished off by three unknown intruders who then disappeared.
7. We should—we must—find a way to cut our expenses by at least 10 percent.
8. Years ago, Victor Borge invented a system of oral punctuation that assigned sounds (some of them hilarious) to each piece of punctuation, supposedly to give listeners the same benefits readers have in understanding the precise meaning of a message.
9. Obnoxious people—Rudolf and Dwight come to mind—light up the room when they leave.
10. Canadian hockey broadcaster Foster Hewitt created a sports catchphrase—"He shoots! He scores!"—during overtime coverage of a hockey match between the New York Rangers and the Toronto Maple Leafs on April 4, 1933. (The Rangers won.)

UNIT NINE: Spelling

Chapter 41: Three Suggestions for Quick Improvement (pp. 376–86)

EXERCISE 41.1

1. desperately
2. crackling
3. generator
4. atonement
5. mating
6. rarely
7. elevator
8. emerging
9. positively
10. apologizing

EXERCISE 41.2

1. excitement
2. interference
3. desirable
4. continuance
5. abridging
6. removable
7. dissolutely
8. acquiring
9. shakable
10. aerating

EXERCISE 41.3

1. apologizing
2. encouragement
3. noisy
4. issuable
5. famous
6. abridgement
7. movable
8. officiating
9. valuation
10. realizing

EXERCISE 41.4

1. blotting
2. spanning
3. submitted
4. failing
5. blurred
6. regrettable
7. admitting
8. batting
9. begging
10. entailed

EXERCISE 41.5

1. forgetting
2. conferred
3. referring
4. stripped
5. shooting
6. expelling
7. grabbed
8. jarring
9. knitting
10. hindered

EXERCISE 41.6

1. deferring
2. remittance
3. regretful
4. cuddled
5. acquittal
6. concurred
7. flagging
8. pinning
9. barred
10. referred

EXERCISE 41.7

1. occurrence
2. persistence
3. emergence
4. recurrence
5. perseverance
6. consistency
7. sufferance
8. resistance
9. concurrence
10. deterrence

EXERCISE 41.8

1. brief
2. friendly
3. fielding
4. achieve
5. relieve
6. retrieval
7. deceive
8. leisure
9. receipt
10. grieve

EXERCISE 41.9

1. pier
2. hygiene
3. hierarchy
4. deceit
5. fierce
6. pieced
7. foreign
8. weight
9. receive
10. species

EXERCISE 41.10

1. either, their, beliefs
2. deceived, perceive
3. conceivable, receive
4. relief, neither
5. neighbour, conceited, weird

EXERCISE 41.11

1. heroes
2. histories
3. criteria
4. ghettos
5. personnel
6. crises
7. data
8. phenomena
9. nuclei (or nucleuses)
10. appendices (or appendixes)

EXERCISE 41.12

1. loneliness
2. copied
3. craziness
4. easier
5. prettiest
6. replies
7. replying
8. thirtieth
9. unnecessarily
10. trafficking

Chapter 42: Sound-Alikes, Look-Alikes, and Spoilers (pp. 387–400)

EXERCISE 42.1

1. course, affect
2. Are, accept
3. then, dessert
4. you're, losing
5. quite, here
6. whose, conscience
7. assured, number
8. It's, its
9. choose, course, advice
10. dining, does

EXERCISE 42.2

1. incredible, morals
2. morale, miners, fazed
3. imply, further
4. effect, disperse
5. Whose, principles, less
6. fourth, cited, weather
7. your, continually, ensures
8. conscious, much, further
9. accept, councillors, phase
10. women's, number

EXERCISE 42.3

1. hear, here
2. To, stationary
3. Losing, it's
4. you're, minor
5. piece, later, complimented
6. weather, whether
7. coarse, effect
8. fewer, faze
9. Women, whose
10. chose, accept, principal's

EXERCISE 42.4

There must be a better way to cope with house renovations. If I were to describe my *personal* agony during the months it took for the construction workers and contractors to *achieve* their final *effect, your* heart would bleed. Plaster dust was the worst problem, because it gets into everything, making even *dining* an uncomfortable experience. As the walls were torn *loose* and the house was gradually reduced to *its* skeleton, plaster dust found *its* way into every crack and corner. The noise and confusion *affected* my *morale,* and I became inclined to use *coarse* language, particularly with those who insisted on giving me *advice. Later,* when my *conscience* got the better of me, my feeble attempts at apology *were* not *accepted.* In the end, the renovations cost me my *peace* of mind, my *friends,* and more money *than* I dreamed possible.

Chapter 43: Capital Letters (pp. 401–404)

EXERCISE 43.1

1. Why in the world would you buy a Toyota?
2. We need to get rid of some of our high-school habits when we start college.
3. Have you read Dr. Ernie L. Twaddle's new book, *I'm OK—You're Fat: A Self-Help Guide to Fitness Fascism?*
4. The Loyalists were considered patriots by the inhabitants of Upper Canada but traitors by people in the United States.
5. I didn't do very well in my fluid power course; maybe I'd better switch to culinary arts.
6. Well, look who's here; it's Mr. Olympics.
7. Take a right at Yonge Street, a left at Lawrence Avenue, and a right at Avenue Road.
8. My English teacher also teaches French to Asian immigrants.
9. Asha's father, being conservative in his tastes, disapproved of Karim's leather jacket and Harley-Davidson 750.
10. Neither was he amused when Asha ran off with Karim's rock group, The Stoned Angels.

EXERCISE 43.2

1. Several psychiatrists in California are developing computer programs to treat patients with mild forms of depression or neurosis.
2. They envision computer therapy programs within the next fifteen years that will diagnose the patient's problem (to be confirmed by a psychiatrist) and select a treatment program.
3. The computer would interact with the patients and switch to various subprograms to analyze their mental problems.
4. A TV camera could view the patients to see if they exhibit signs of stress, nervousness, or lying.
5. correct
6. Most psychiatrists are against such unorthodox treatment methods, but proponents of computer therapy argue that it has many advantages.

7. These advantages include low cost and convenience: the computer would function as a cheap psychiatrist, available on weekends and holidays, summer or winter.
8. Other advantages are the long-term total memory of the computer and its appearance of honesty and objectivity.
9. Personally, I am surprised that anyone in the medical profession takes such a proposal seriously; treatment of complex human problems by machine seems perverse to me.
10. Taking my own personal depressions, fears, and phobias to a VDT would be likely to trigger a massive anxiety attack.

Chapter 44: The Apostrophe (pp. 405–11)

EXERCISE 44.1

1. he'll
2. you've
3. I'm
4. don't
5. who's
6. wouldn't
7. we're
8. who'll
9. you'll
10. didn't

EXERCISE 44.2

1. can't
2. you're
3. they're
4. shouldn't
5. who'll
6. don't
7. you'll
8. we're
9. they've
10. it'll

EXERCISE 44.3

1. Yes, it's a long way from Halifax to Vancouver, but we've been in training for three months.
2. We're taking the train to Antigonish and we're biking to Halifax; then we'll begin the big trip west.
3. There isn't a dry eye in the theatre when Spielberg's film reaches its climax.
4. Those two haven't made it through a meeting since the college adopted its No Smoking policy.
5. Wasn't it Mark Twain who said, "It's easy to stop smoking; I've done it dozens of times"?

EXERCISE 44.4

1. their
2. Chris's
3. her
4. gentlemen's
5. strawberries'
6. mystery's
7. one's
8. Burgess' *or* Burgess's
9. chairmen's
10. ladies'

EXERCISE 44.5

1. week's, his
2. day's, dogs'
3. church's, its, minister's
4. children's, his, their, mother's
5. Today's, producers', tomorrow's

EXERCISE 44.6

1. A floppy disk's quality is measured by its ability to store information without error.
2. Diplomatic ambassadors' wives or husbands are often as important to a mission's success as the ambassadors themselves.
3. Near Chicoutimi is one of the country's most beautiful parks, where the skills of canoeists, fishermen, and wildlife photographers can all be put to the test on a summer's day.
4. The Leafs' forward and the Oilers' defenceman were exchanged during the last day's trading at the NHL meetings.
5. Janis's career got its start when she sang seafarers' songs in the yacht club's dining lounge.

EXERCISE 44.7

1. It's, its, turtle's, turtle's
2. It's, they're
3. you're, your, your
4. Joan's, Society's, province's
5. Someone's, whose
6. There, Joneses', their, it's
7. Countries, their, they're, powers'
8. Brothers', today's
9. father's, uncle's, fox's, woods
10. people's, workers', sides', strike's

Chapter 45: The Hyphen (pp. 412–14)

EXERCISE 45.1

1. Mei decided to sublet her fifth-floor apartment.
2. Anwar claims he is allergic to classical music but addicted to new-wave music.
3. Chrétien won most of the ethnic vote, which gave him a two-thirds majority in a hard-fought contest.
4. Hand-knitted sweaters are usually more expensive than factory-produced ones.
5. In 1950, at the age of forty-seven, George Orwell died of tuberculosis.
6. For months after Nicolae Ceauşescu was overthrown, the world was shocked by revelations of the repression suffered by the Rumanian people.

7. Would you relay this message to Mr. Chan: the masons would like to re-lay the bricks this evening?
8. Our next-door neighbour teaches in a high school but does not like to be known as a high-school teacher.
9. A face-to-face meeting with an anti-intellectual always gets my adrenalin going.
10. Because Angela was an attorney-at-law and had once been an all-Canadian athlete, her forty-five-year-old former coach was not surprised when she became Minister of Recreation.

UNIT TEN: The Finishing Touches

Chapter 46: Avoiding Inappropriate Language (pp. 416–23)

EXERCISE 46.4

1. Many young people today are trying to fight prejudice not only in society but also within themselves.
2. I'm supposed to ask you if the rain is the reason for the delay.
3. It's irresponsible of us to blame television or any other medium for causing violence.
4. Television is responsible, however, for the fact that many ungrammatical expressions sound all right to us.
5. Between you and me, the reason I didn't talk to anybody about Dwight's cheating on the test was that he would have broken my arm.

READINGS

Heavenly Hostesses
Margaret Visser

1   There is an ancient insistence in our culture that women ought to be pure, and that this involves *not moving around*. Women stay home; they are there for roving males to return to. Mobility in women is therefore disconcerting and probably expressive of promiscuity. This bias is only one of the many difficulties which have bedevilled airline flight attendants throughout their short but variegated history.

2   Male couriers, literally "runners" — women were at first unthinkable in this role — first accompanied pilots when passengers became common in the air. Paying travellers in the 1920s had to be both rich and adventurous; there were trains and ships for the fainter-hearted. Being venturesome did not, however, preclude a need to be looked after by underlings: cosseted, comforted, fed.

3   Couriers helped people on with mufflers, foot-warmers, and overcoats (early planes were glacial), plugged ears with cotton batting, provided brown paper bags when needed, opened windows in flight, and then closed them on landing so that flying mud from a wet field would not enter the cabin. Passengers sat in cushioned wicker chairs, around tables set with linen cloths, china, silver cutlery, potted plants, and vases of cut flowers. As more space was provided, tables were placed along the windows as in a railway dining car. Conversation was limited to short cries and written notes, since the noise was tremendous. Mishaps with the crockery must have been frequent, because the vibration shook chairs across the floor and worked eyeglasses invariably down people's noses.

4   Meals were served, cold but magnificent and with many courses, by men in white jackets and gloves. When night flights began there were foldout beds with sheets, pillows, and blankets, and stewards woke passengers with china cups of tea. Bowls of soup as well as coffee and tea could be heated on a stove in the rear of the aircraft. This serving of meals and tea had changed the courier's name: he was now a steward, on an analogy with ocean liner staff. He was always male and white, in North America as well as in Europe.

5   In May 1930, the first six women began to serve customers on aircraft. It was an American idea, daring and brilliant. Who cared if women got mobile? Some could surely be found who were able to withstand the dangers and fight off the innuendoes of night stopovers, long distances away from home, and constant movement. There were other, more immediately convenient, myths to hand.

6   These women were welcoming *hostesses* (the new name doubtless helped), every one a registered nurse, capable, motherly, and understanding. They wore green suits on the ground but white nurses' attire, with capes and caps, on board. Their job was to comfort passengers, and give a good example by not, though women, showing fear.

7   They were strong too, even though they were unacceptable unless under 5 ft. 4 in. in height and weighing less than 120 lb. They carried luggage on board and unloaded the aircraft again at the end of the journey. They cleaned messes, dusted the plane inside and out, helped fuel it and mend punctures, and might even assist the pilot to push it into the hangar. They held passengers'

hands going up and down steps, hovered over the bilious, prevented visitors to the washroom from opening the exit door by mistake, and pointed out the places of interest passing below. If all seats were full the hostess would sit on the mailbag at the back of the plane.

8   Gradually, more and more women were accepted for work on aircraft both within the U.S. and elsewhere, but they really only "arrived" after the War. And immediately their job took on, along with nursing and waitressing, the third aspect: stewardesses were to be selected for looks. Besides having to be white, under twenty-five, and certifiably unmarried, they had to undergo cosmetic training, hairstyling, and lessons in how to charm male passengers. Rules for achieving this demanded relentless smiling and mandatory "eye contact," as well as cunning methods of walking and climbing steps.

9   The myth of the Swinging Stewardesses took off, at once empowered by ancient suspicions surrounding "unbridled mobility," especially in women. One airline advertised, "I'm Cheryl — Fly Me." Braniff International "ended the plain plane" in 1966, offering "stews" who made several flashy costume changes en route, ending with hot pants. Travellers with another airline were treated to in-flight announcements set to a perky jingle and sung by the stewardesses. A rioting planeload of drunken male football fans once forced the women to take refuge in the cockpit while the pilots made an unscheduled landing.

10   The trend was finally quashed, but only in the feminist seventies, after innumerable scandals and complaints, and a series of court rulings. Hostesses were eventually permitted to marry and have children if they chose; they could no longer be dismissed because of age; and the profession was at last opened to blacks. The change of image brought about a new official name, "flight attendants": long, colourless yet slickly modern, and unisex. For by 1972, prestige as well as respectability having been restored, males were re-entering the field.

---

1. Number the stages Visser identifies in the historical process that transformed couriers into flight attendants. Underline the words and phrases the author has used to create transitions between paragraphs.
2. This essay is more than just a history lesson. Find examples of paragraphs, sentences, or even words that convey the author's opinion about her subject.
3. Consider the descriptive details in paragraphs 3 and 4. Which senses does the author appeal to in these paragraphs?
4. What inferences can we draw from this essay about the changes that took place in our society between the 1920s and the 1970s?
5. What other professions' histories could be traced to illustrate some of the changes that have taken place in our attitudes, beliefs, and prejudices over the last 50 years?
6. Write a job advertisement on behalf of Icarus Airlines appealing for couriers in the 1920s, one for hostesses in the 1940s, one for stewardesses in the 1960s, and one for flight attendants today.

All Quiet on the Hiring Front
Michael Park

1   Put yourself in this frame. For as long as you can remember, people have been telling you to stay in school. You've heard it from parents, from teachers, from politicians and pop stars. You've heard it in church, in locker rooms, in music videos and bars. Don't be a fool, stay in school. The logic goes something like this: Do you want to be happy? they ask. Do you want to be popular, independent and respected? Do you want to be well-dressed and have nice toys? Do you want to be *cool?*

2   You say, "Well, um, yes, I think so."

3   "And what do you need to be cool?"

4   You, in your innocence, suggest that lots of cash might help.

5   "And where do you get lots of cash?"

6   "By winning Lotto 6/49."

7   "Be serious, kid. Work with me on this."

8   "OK. You can get cash from working at a job."

9   "And you can get *lots* of cash from working at a *good* job, right?"

10   "If you say so."

11   "And how do you get a good job?"

12   "Get your rich uncle Chuck to hire you."

13   "And if you don't have a rich uncle Chuck?"

14   You know what they want you to say. "Stay in school."

15   That's the mantra of received opinion that you've been asked to chant for most of your young life: to get a good job, you need a good education. Be cool, stay in school. You'll be glad when you're a grad.

16   So you stay in school for as long as you can. You finish high school and go to college or university. You dive into your studies and into debt; you work at part-time McJobs for bus fare and lunch money; you study what you're told to; you pound away at the books and your computer keyboard until that glorious day when you graduate and start looking for full-time work.

17   After a couple of months of sending out resumes and cold-calling prospective employers, you start asking yourself, "Where are all those good jobs that we were promised?" By "good jobs" you mean interesting and challenging work that pays you enough money for a nice apartment, for your own set of wheels, for a vacation trip once in a while, for a decent wardrobe, for paying down your huge student loan, for building a small nest egg for the future — enough money to be cool.

18   You can't find such a job, and you feel betrayed. You played by the rules. You studied hard and got good grades; you're literate, numerate and Microsoft-friendly. Yet the only work you can find pays peanuts, makes you wear a uniform and a badge with your first name on it, and uses none of your newfound skills and knowledge — the tools that you were told were "in demand" when you chose your major four or five years ago. What's happening here?

19   The painful truth is this: the pool of good jobs in North America is shrinking. While you were cocooned in school, single-mindedly focussed on finishing

your education, some powerful forces have been changing the very nature of work in our brave new economy, forces called automation, de-skilling, downsizing and globalization. Here's how they operate.

20   *Automation* is the application of information processing technology to production processes — using computers in making things to sell. Employers automate to increase efficiency and eliminate jobs. In the automobile industry, long an economic mainstay of Central Canada and the Midwestern United States, the use of computer-managed production lines complete with robot welders and painters has allowed big employers like General Motors and Ford to shed jobs and workers while simultaneously boosting production and profits. The use of automated tellers has allowed banks and trust companies to do the same thing. Automated information management systems have enabled employers to eliminate thousands of clerical workers in areas like payroll and accounting. This is a good thing if you own shares in these companies but a bad thing if you are a recent graduate hoping to find entry-level work with them.

21   The *de-skilling* of work is the application of technology to make jobs simpler to do. For example, when computer-controlled optical character scanners were installed in supermarkets a few years ago, the job of check-out cashier was de-skilled, or "dumbed down," significantly. In the old days, cashiers used mechanical adding machines — cash registers — to record and tally the prices of the various cans of beans, loaves of bread and heads of lettuce that customers were buying. They had to be fast and accurate with their machines, and they needed to know the prices of many unlabelled items — produce, for example. And they even bagged their customers' purchases. Nowadays, only the scanner's computer brain knows the price of everything, and the customers do the bagging. All the cashier does is swipe an item's bar code across the laser-eye of the scanner; the computer records the prices and calculates the total.

22   This sort of efficiency improvement has had two negative effects for recent grads. Because cashiers and workers in other de-skilled jobs can now work more quickly, fewer of them are needed to maintain previous levels of productivity. And because fewer skills are required to perform such jobs, more potential employees are able to do the job satisfactorily. In a free enterprise world governed by the law of supply and demand, a larger pool of available workers drives down average wages in the occupation. The more brainless the work, the lower the wage it commands. And lots of jobs are being de-skilled.

23   *Downsizing* is the sanitized buzzword used to describe the axing of jobs made redundant by automation and de-skilling. Employers downsize to increase profits and efficiency, usually at the cost of lowered morale among the remaining workers, who are required to sustain the productivity gains achieved through the termination of their former colleagues. The good jobs that such employers eliminate are, of course, no longer available for new graduates, and the workers displaced from them swell the pool of those competing for the good jobs that do occasionally come on the market. And the victims of downsizing have lots of work experience on their resumes, unlike most new grads.

24   Some good jobs aren't being eliminated or de-skilled; they're just being sent far away. *Globalization* is the practice of locating production and jobs where labour and related costs are lowest. Government deregulation initiatives and trade treaties like NAFTA have made it easier for North American employers to shift their labour-intensive operations from high-wage areas like

B.C. and Ontario to low-wage ones like the Carolinas and Mexico. Again, this trend is bad news for recent grads hoping to find well-paid work near home.

25   Jobs being eliminated, jobs being de-skilled, jobs going south: is there *no* good news on the hiring front? Of course there is; new jobs are being created every day — lots of them. But proportionately fewer of them are the sort of "good" jobs that new Boomer grads had their pick of in the 1960s and 1970s when they first started looking for work. The fact is that doing well in school is no longer a guaranteed ticket to a successful and rewarding career. The times — and the economy — have a-changed. For new grads without a rich uncle Chuck, they've changed for the worse.

Michael Park, "All Quiet on the Hiring Front," 1996. Reprinted by permission of the author.

1. What readers did the author have in mind when he wrote this piece? Is his message intended only for students, or is there another, wider audience in his sights?
2. Which paragraph contains the author's thesis statement? Identify the subject and main points of this essay.
3. Why do you think the introduction of this essay is so long? Consider the author's use of dialogue in paragraphs 2 to 14. What is its purpose? Is it effective?
4. Based on the example provided in the essay, define what the author means by a "received opinion."
5. Write a response to this essay in which you argue either that earning a "guaranteed ticket to a career" is not the only reason for staying in school, or that there *is* "good news on the hiring front."

Eat Your Hearts Out Cinephiles: The Tube Is Where It's At
John Haslett Cuff

1   Although film-festival fever is breaking out in [Canada] this [fall], moving west from Toronto and Montreal and eventually winding up in Vancouver, I could care less, because day in and day out, television is more important and more entertaining than the movies. Even watching summer reruns of *Law & Order, ER* or *The Drew Carey Show* is more appealing to me than a trip to the Cineplex to see the latest megabuck Hollywood bombast, whether it's *Independence Day, The Fan* or *Courage Under Fire*. But this has not always been the case.

2   Chronologically I am a TV baby. I was born a year after ABC became a "network" of four stations, and I was starting to take my first steps about the same time CBS abandoned its premature commitment to colour and signed the first television superstar, Jackie Gleason. But I was, at first, far more attached to movies, enthralled as a child by the big-screen spectacle of *Quo Vadis* and *War and Peace* and almost any 25-cent double bill that the local Famous Players would let me watch.

3   My passion for films grew, unabated, through the sixties and seventies as I discovered Ingmar Bergman, Akiro Kurosawa, Stanley Kubrick, Martin Scorsese

and Robert Altman. And then, somewhere around the mid-seventies when *Jaws* and *Star Wars* began establishing box office records, the movies began a nosedive into the irrelevance of special effects, even as television began maturing and offering viewers an unparalleled range of entertainments such as *I, Claudius*, and, at the other extreme, *All in the Family*.

4   With the exception of independent and foreign films, still the staple of film festivals and the diet of devoted urban cinephiles, the bloated products of mainstream Hollywood continue to run a poor second to television. The medium has grown up in my lifetime to become the most economical, varied and influential source of information and entertainment.

5   The obvious advantage television has over movies is its accessibility and the familial intimacy it has established with its audience after decades in the home of virtually every class of person. Even without TV's unquestioned rule as the primary provider of news and information, the culture of television drama and comedy is clearly superior to most of the $30-million-plus (the budget of an average studio movie) offerings available in cinemas.

6   Any five episodes of *Seinfeld*, *Frasier* or *Roseanne* are arguably funnier and more meticulously crafted than a Jim Carrey, Robin Williams or Eddie Murphy blockbuster, not to mention more sophisticated and relevant. The same comparison can be made of a top-flight TV drama such as *NYPD Blue* or *ER*. On an ongoing basis, these fine shows deliver more emotional punch and subtlety, as well as character and plot development, than almost any $100-million-grossing action flick.

7   While this is true even of some of the most commercial network shows, the quality gap is even more marked when imported and specialty television is brought into the mix. There is simply no equivalent in contemporary, mainstream moviemaking to the oeuvre of Dennis Potter or Alan Bleasdale, British TV writers who create multi-hour dramas that make most movies look like puerile drivel.

8   But these are highly subjective, qualitative comparisons and television is also superior in other significant and quantifiable ways. Most obviously, network television produces more entertainment for much less money than the Hollywood studios. Carrey's payday for a 90-minute movie would almost finance a whole season (22 hours) of prime-time TV drama.

9   Culturally, television is richer in ideas and issues and in its representation of society. Just look at the number and range of roles for women in television, and compare them with the paucity of good parts for women of any age in the movies. There are no film-actress superstars who can open a film and command the money that such muscle-bound hacks as Sly Stallone or Arnold Schwarzenegger routinely earn.

10   Yet television abounds with women stars, young and middle-aged, fat and anorexic. Many of the most enduringly popular sitcoms, such as *Roseanne*, *Murphy Brown*, *Grace Under Fire*, *Ellen* and *Caroline in the City* dominate the ratings, and TV shows employ award-winning movie actresses such as Christine Lahti, Madeline Kahn and Mercedes Ruehl in increasing numbers.

11   Television engenders loyalty and empathy with its characters in a way that movies don't, because over the course of a season viewers develop relationships with TV characters, sharing in their development in a way that is impossible in one-off movie fare. Such characters as Dr. Frasier Crane have been visiting

12 us in our homes for years, and we have watched them age through story lines that reflect changes in fashion, society and even politics.

12 While television has produced a rich mix of exceptional dramas over the past decade, movies have all but abandoned them, preferring high-octane, live-action cartoons instead. Perhaps the most important difference is that TV writers are forced to be more creative with language, plot and even sex than the creators of movies. Since TV writers are not allowed to use profanity, nudity or violence with the graphic abandon of their movie peers, the resulting drama is often more powerful, suggestive and complex.

13 In addition, due to the immediacy of television and the speed with which it is produced, it is more relevant than the movies, more rooted in the social and political news of the day and better able to explore issues that affect the audience and are a vital part of the public dialogue.

14 So, despite the volume of dreck that marks the beginning of any new TV season, I must confess I'm looking forward to the [fall] offerings. As for the few movies I really want to see, I'll probably catch them on pay-TV or video. That's a win-win situation.

John Haslett Cuff, "Eat your hearts out cinephiles, the tube is where it's at," *The Globe and Mail*, September 2, 1996, C1. Reprinted by permission of The Globe and Mail.

1. In point form, summarize the author's reasons for preferring television to film.
2. How has the author organized this essay, in "chunks" or in "slices"? (See Chapter 19.) Would the piece be equally effective if he had used the other pattern?
3. For what audience is this piece intended? Consider the author's level of language, the references to people, titles, and events, and the writer's strong preference for television over movies. What is Cuff's purpose in the article: to persuade, entertain, inform, or what?
4. While he admits that he grew up enjoying movies, the author maintains that films today aren't as good as they were in the '50s, '60s, and '70s. Is his argument convincing, or is this the opinion of an out-of-touch, middle-aged individual for whom the "good old days" were invariably better than today? In your answer, consider the evidence Cuff relies on to support his opinion. Is it sufficiently numerous, varied, and representative?
5. Write a contrast paper of your own in which you argue that movies are superior to television.

Human Hibernation

Linda Hasselstrom

1 Every winter, newspapers print stories about depression right next to advice on diet and exercise. Where several people gather together this time of year, whimpers about weight gain, exhaustion, and guilt fill the air. "I've got to get some exercise," everyone says, wandering toward the buffet table.

2   The fact is, all these folks are trying to fight nature, and it can't be done.

3   Humans are mammals, after all. It's perfectly natural for a mammal to gain weight in the late fall and winter. Fat is insulation against the cold, a food resource the body can draw on to survive when victuals are hard to find. The tendency to tuck fat under our hides originated long before supermarkets we can reach by car, and restaurants on every corner. We are a species that had to find our food while swinging through the treetops. Later we galloped, bare-foot and naked, across the hills after our lunch, carrying a rock in case it slowed down. When our mothers urge us to have another piece of pie, they aren't trying to control our psyches; they're following innate mothering instincts to cushion us against the coming cold. When we reach for another glass of eggnog, we are helplessly following dictates established before we came down out of the trees; we really can't help ourselves.

4   The genetic codes deep inside our skins don't know that manufacturers of down coats claim their products keep us warm; our bodies wouldn't believe it anyway. All they know is that the time of icicles is coming, and they must get ready. They prepare by starting suction, slurping in fat from every direction. They can sense a cheesecake or brownies three blocks away, and immediately snap into ferocious action, forcing our legs to carry us in that direction, mak-ing our hands reach for the goodie, our lips part, our throats open to swallow. Guilt about this behavior is not only unnecessary, it's against our nature too. Why should we feel guilty about behavior we couldn't possibly control?

5   Many mammals also hibernate. Only humans fight this instinctive and prop-er need for sleep. Only humans struggle to stay awake when every fiber of their being, every physical, emotional, and mental message tells them to curl up next to a warm furry body and sleep. Every time we walk past a horizontal surface or a sleeping cat, hidden muscles try to make us lie down, slowing our pace. If our pitiful, confused minds try to drive our bodies on, our bodies lurch as will battles instinct. The result is tension. When we suffer headaches, pain in our hunched shoulders, when we snap at spouses and co-workers, we say it's "stress," brought on by moods of the season, by overwork, by whatever national crisis is boiling over at the moment. Wrong. We suffer from denial of our need for naps.

6   Other habits hint at our mammal nature. Both men and women work hard to scrape hair from several body surfaces in winter, but we ought to let that pelt grow. Its historical purpose is to keep us warm, and it would do the job better than miniskirts, sheer nylons, and turned-up collars. Probably some of the stress we waste good nap time discussing is caused by frustrated little hair follicles on every inch of our bodies. Answering age-old imperatives, they try to grow enough fur to cover all that naked hide before it gets frostbitten, while we are determined to leave it nearly bare.

7   The truth about our mammalian nature is also demonstrated by what hap-pens to our muscles during the winter. After the holidays, when we return to our exercise program and realize we're gasping after half our normal routine, our mammal background is the cause. We were made for exercise; we were built to run down our food, not program it on a computer screen. Our bodies are designed to clamber up rock faces and swing from vines, not balance on a padded posterior in a padded chair. When we deny our native functions, we pay. Our bodies are meant to be used completely every single day, and they're

structured so that if we stop, everything falls apart at once. It's a principle of natural selection. When we stagger out the door of the exercise room, we're lucky it's no worse; if we had skipped a week of exercise in the early days of our tribe, a faster mammal would have eaten us.

8   But that exercise was meant to occur during warm weather; once we'd built up a good layer of fat, we reverted to our mammal nature, curled up, and slept. Winter exercise sets off age-old alarms inside our bodies, causing the fat suction to grow stronger. It's a losing battle — our bodies can pull in more fat than we can sweat off. We might as well give in and nap.

Linda Hasselstrom, "Human hibernation," as appearing in *Utne Reader* (January/February 1994), 130. First printed in *Dry Crik Review*, Lemon Cove, CA. Reprinted by permission of the author.

1. What is the purpose of this essay? Does the author really want us to stuff ourselves all fall and then sleep the winter through?
2. Paragraph 2 is only one sentence long. Why? What is the function of this paragraph? What effect does it have on the reader?
3. The impact of this piece is due, in part, to the writer's use of language, particularly her choice of specific, colourful verbs. Find at least six examples that you think are particularly effective.
4. Have you noticed that you or your friends and family become irritable or depressed during the winter months? If so, can you think of causes for this mood change other than those that Hasselstrom has proposed?
5. The author has presented an amusing case for doing what she wants to do: eat and nap. Draft a blueprint for a convincing argument in favour of something you want to do but know you shouldn't (e.g., smoke, play computer games when you should be studying, spend money on clothes you don't need, read trashy novels).

The View from Italy: Puritans R Us
Antanas Sileika

1   I'd forgotten my disposable lighter in Toronto, and so, when the taxi dropped me in the heart of Rome, I bought a new one at a tobacco shop. In the Campo di Fiori open-air market, I tried to figure out where the childproofing device was hidden. Each brand puts this safety device in a different place, and they are devilishly hard to find. An inquisitive *caribinieri* noticed my confusion, lit my cigarette and returned the lighter with a flourish. No wonder I'd been confused. There was no childproofing device.

2   Far too much has been written about cigarettes and even lighters for me to want to add to the debate. But this difference between Italy and Canada was only one of a series. Rebecca West once wrote that people in the East try to make the world a better place by adding good things to it, while we in the West try to make the world a better place by taking bad things away.

3   She must have had Canada in mind. Puritans R us.

4 I wandered around the medieval marketplace admiring the raw-milk cheeses (soon to be forbidden by law here) and admiring as well the Roman women who walked with assurance across the streets and through herds of motor scooters. No crosswalks for the pedestrians. No helmets on the drivers. All of them should have been ashamed of themselves, and probably they would have been if they lived in Canada.

5 In Toronto, speed bumps multiply faster than mushrooms after a rain, and they are joined by other related fungi, such as all-way stop signs. At several intersections where I live, conscientious drivers even stop at all corners when there are not four-way stops. Just in case. Through their windshields I can almost hear their thoughts. "You can never be too safe. No one ever got a ticket for being too careful." This high civic concern is received telepathically by the bureaucrats who live to make our lives better, saner, safer and more just.

6 This Canadian concern for safety covers linguistic dangers as well. At my first meal in Rome, I noticed that *spaghetti putanesca* was on the menu — "whore's spaghetti," a salty, even earthy mix of anchovies and olive oil. Could we have such a name in Canada? Not at all. We'd call it, "Not a Love Story Spaghetti," and add a warning that high salt intake leads to hypertension. And speaking of warning signs, I saw none that warned pregnant mothers against the dangers of drinking.

7 Are Roman women less forgetful than their Canadian counterparts? Not at all. The signs exist in Canada not to warn pregnant women against drinking so much as to proclaim publicly our commitment to public health. Somewhere in our hearts we are like the reedy farm couple with pitchfork in the painting, *American Gothic* — self-righteous and armed, albeit discreetly.

8 There seemed to be a women's club in the Roman café where I took my morning coffee. Almost 15 of them, aged from 20 to 80, chatted and laughed together. When a scruffy young man in jeans, leather jacket and Mohawk haircut stopped his scooter on the street outside, the women called out to him. He smiled back and came in to chat over a thick black coffee that I am sure was not decaffeinated. There was no disapproval on the women's faces. Similarly, there was none on the faces of the older men who stopped to chat with punks lounging in the city streets. Live and let live, their attitude seemed to say. No need to "improve" lost youth.

9 On our Vatican tour, my wife and I fell into a hot debate spurred by the massive buildings and ornate decoration, and magnified by the rain outside, which prevented us from walking off our hardened positions. In the Sistine Chapel, we and thousands of other tourists strained our necks to stare up at the intense colours of Michelangelo's restored ceiling. Was it too much? Was it too rich? Perhaps, but the world would not be a better place without it. In Toronto, we seem to have decided that we will be better off without an opera house and without any more subways.

10 Many more Italians have come to Canada than the other way around, so there must be something superior to this country. In a nutshell, I'd say we have more space and more money, yet as a society we are always crying poor and trying to eliminate the dangers in everyday life. This country feels like a child-proofed room; the safety latches are on, and all the sharp objects have been put away. Like the cuckolded husband in the trashy *Bridges of Madison County*, the best that can be said about us is that we are clean.

11   And yet, I am not immune to self-improvement. On our final evening in Rome, we had intended to go to a Pentecost festival where the Pope carries an icon across the river to St. Peter's Basilica. Yet another pair of aging boomers in a quest for a little spirituality. But as we stepped out on the Campi de Fiori, we found it crammed with tents and people. What was going on?

12   It was a festival, too, but one very different from the religious event we had planned to attend. It was a festival of spaghetti and music. High-school bands played music, the likes of which I haven't heard since seeing some of Fellini's older films. Dozens of chefs served plates heaping with spaghetti covered in a rich brown bacon and Parmesan sauce. Only three dollars a plate! I ate two. I could always worry about the fat content after I returned to Canada.

13   What about improving ourselves spiritually? The spaghetti was very good and the music was charming. We decided to stick around where the fun was. After all, heaven can wait.

———————

Antanas Sileika, "The view from Italy: Puritans R us," *The Globe and Mail*, October 15, 1996, A20. Antanas Sileika is the author of *Buying On Time*, a story collection, and *Dinner at the End of the World*, a novel. He teaches English at Humber College. This article has been reprinted by permission of the author.

1. What are the main points of contrast the author identifies between Canadian and Italian lifestyles?
2. What is the purpose of this essay? Does the author want us to overturn the motorcycle helmet law and the prohibition against raw-milk cheese, or to stop warning pregnant women about the dangers of drinking? How do you think Sileika hopes readers will respond to his essay?
3. Write a brief character sketch of the author, based on what you learn about him in this essay.
4. Canadians are renowned for their conservatism and caution, but the author of this piece suggests these are not necessarily admirable characteristics. How might his arguments in favour of the less restrictive atmosphere of Italy be challenged? Is it possible to write an equally effective essay that takes the opposite point of view — that the Canadian lifestyle is preferable because it is less risky and more sane?
5. If you have travelled outside the country or your province, write a contrast essay along the same lines as "The View from Italy." Begin, as Sileika does, with a short anecdote, and support your point of view with ample evidence.

Speak for Yourself
Amy Willard Cross

1   A single woman in the big city, Anna has dated 12 men over two-and-a-half months. She has talked her way into popularity. This Toronto professional is doing the telephone personals; she recorded a personal ad and received an overwhelming response.

2   After hearing her voice, 180 men wanted to meet her. "Most people comment that I have a mellifluous voice — it's low and they say it's sexy," she reports. It's the opposite of traditional courting, when men and women look before they bother to talk. Anna's admirers listen first, then inevitably ask what she looks like. Her legions of admirers have said other women on the system sound stilted, nervous or introverted, but Anna's message comes across as smart, articulate, with a sexy edge. "I have the sort of voice they feel they can hear for a long time." That's important when looking for long-term mates, and Anna applies the same test. She listens to a man's message for about five seconds; if one sounds like a dead body, she clicks onto the next.

3   As Anna has discovered, sounding good counts as much as looking good. Now that teledating lets singles dial the scene and voice mail guards people at the office, person-to-person calls increasingly replace face-to-face communication. Today, your voice serves as a type of calling card. Speech pathologist Elizabeth Hunt says, "We gain information by watching people's faces, by listening to their voices and listening to what they say. On the phone you've only got two of those parameters, so the voice increases in importance because you don't have the visuals."

4   "In business, the way you dress makes a difference, and the same is true for the voice — the way you use your voice is what people will judge you on," continues Hunt. Essentially, she feels that hitting the right tone and inflection is no different than brushing your hair or pressing your clothes. You need to style your voice just as you match an outfit to an occasion. Indeed, one study published in the early eighties stated that 38 per cent of a first impression comes from someone's voice — while what is actually said creates just seven per cent of that impression.

5   A person's voice reveals just two hard facts: the speaker's sex and age — within 10 years. Nevertheless, when hearing your voice for the first time, people make judgements — however inaccurate — about your integrity, education, height, weight, personality, intelligence, even hair colour.

6   Although the voice is a powerful communications tool, only actors and singers really learn to use it. The majority of us misuse our voices. For instance, you probably can't disguise your emotions in your voice — if you are nervous, chances are you sound nervous. Hunt also notes that many people sabotage themselves by not coordinating the underlying meaning with the tone of their voice. "If the sound isn't right, it doesn't matter what you say." So whimpering or shrieking endearments leaves the hearer cold. What's more, a lot of people have acquired bad habits such as speaking too fast, or too softly, or forcing the voice — which Hunt compares to slouching with the voice.

7   These bad habits undermine women's communication especially. Men talk sloppily, too — mumbling, dropping consonants or talking too loudly. But women often get judged by stricter standards: as Hunt says, "I don't know the male equivalent of shrill, strident or harsh." And as author Deborah Tannen discussed in her bestseller, *You Just Don't Understand*, bad vocal habits such as failing to break in, indirectness and adding modifiers reinforce negative stereotypes about women. For example, talking fast makes you appear nervous and lacking in self-confidence. Nasal voices sound complaining and nagging. And although some men find breathy voices sexy, they tend to conjure notions of an airhead or cinematic bimbo.

8   That bad voices hurt women in business is born out by Hunt's experiences. She has coached an insurance executive whose soft voice lost her a job, and a lawyer who was told clients lacked confidence in her.

9   Naturally, women's voices sound different from men's. Although both sexes' voices change at puberty, women's voices deepen as they age, whereas men's rise in pitch, until they equalize in the seventies. Often women make their voices artificially too soft and too high — which may be more habit than nature. Voice specialist Joan Kenley, who wrote a book called *Voice Power,* says that women often speak from their throats, rather than use their full power. "When we want to express emotions we don't feel are okay or are not accepted in the world, we actually tighten the throat which raises the tone," she says. An ex-actor who went on to earn a Ph.D. in psychology because she realized her own voice problems had psychological roots, Kenley thinks that women's voices deepen with age not only due to hormonal changes: "It's not that everything is sagging; it's just that they become less tense, less fragile, more confident."

10   Even when a woman's voice naturally hits the lower register, her gender is identifiable since women use more inflection — sort of singing with their voices. But too much or inappropriate inflection can be a problem. Witness the recent epidemic of upspeak — a rising inflection at the end of a sentence which turns statements into questions. Upspeak seemingly asks for approval and permission, rendering whatever is said less than authoritative.

11   None of this means you should try to talk like a man. "Women in the career world often get harsh in order to masculinize their voices. But the voice doesn't have to be harsher; it just has to be fuller," says Kenley.

12   So what's a good voice? You've probably never heard one — or paid attention. As with movie music, you only notice a voice when it goes off key. And like good music, a good voice contains subtleties, complexities, variation in pitch and loudness and hits the middle range since people are uncomfortable listening to very high or low voices. Working with both male and female clients, Hunt tries to help them find "a commanding strong powerful voice in the right pitch range." Joan Kenley's is probably one of North America's most listened-to voices; she records the voice mail greetings for Northern Telecom and Pacific Bell as well as dispensing 411 numbers for New York's phone company, Nynex. She says the ideal voice should join body, breath and emotion.

13   Although improving the quality of your voice without a coach is like learning to dance without an instructor, Hunt says you can work on your vocal presentation. Tape yourself during phone conversations and listen objectively to how you sound — analyzing your speed, volume, tone. Compare it to other voices and note what you would change. Listen to your outgoing message. How do you feel on hearing it? Does it convey the characteristics you want people to perceive as "you"? If you sound flat, uninteresting and insincere, people won't believe you will call them back.

14   And to avoid off-putting flatness when you're actually talking, try standing up and walking around. There's also the old radio trick of looking into the mirror and smiling to put emotion into your voice. If you tend to talk softly, hold the mouthpiece away from you and project your voice into the room to sound more alive. For practice, Hunt suggests you re-record your voice mail message every day.

15   Before making really important calls, we often plan what we are going to say, rather than how we want to say it. Hunt suggests thinking like an actor and deciding beforehand on your intent and motivation, as well as on what outcome you seek — a sale, a friendship, trust? Hunt says, "I have people call me up and they're attacking me verbally, yet the point of the call is that they want something from me." She also recommends practicing the sound of the conversation before you actually pick up the phone — loosening up your vocal chords by yawning or chewing air.

16   To communicate more expressively, you need to develop a larger and subtler repertoire of tone, just as an actor does. One way to practice is to read the editorial page aloud, trying to capture the feeling of the article. Hunt also has clients take a simple phrase — such as "Yes" or "That's it" — and say it with varying ranges of emotion from ecstatic to happy to resigned.

17   When used properly, the voice can serve as a very powerful tool in all aspects of life. "A pleasant voice will stop all the obstructions that prevent people from listening to you, listening to your ideas, doing what you want them to do," Hunt says. "It will persuade people, it will convince people, it will make people buy. It's the added touch."

18   She concludes that if you know a little about voice, "you will also observe better. You will not react vocally to what you're presented with — for example, automatically responding angrily to an angry voice. Hunt says you can diffuse intense situations and cites 911 operators who are trained to stay calm when confronted with panicked voices on the phone.

19   In our increasingly high-tech environment, developing one's voice becomes more and more important. As Joan Kenley says, "We are in a world where often we will never meet and our voices are the only things that connect us in a human way."

Amy Willard Cross, excerpts from "Speak for yourself," *Toronto Life Fashion* (August 1996), 82, 84, & 116. Reprinted by permission of the author.

1. This essay suggests that a good voice can have a profound influence on one's success, both personal and professional. Can you recall any personal experiences that would support Cross's point of view?

2. Examine the structure of this essay. Divide it into segments or "chapters," and give each part a title. Why do you think the author has arranged her main points in this order, beginning with the teledating example and ending with expert advice?

3. The author concludes her essay by saying that improving the quality of one's voice will become even more important in the future. Draft the blueprint of a paragraph in which you outline reasons to support this assertion.

4. Much of the supporting material in this essay is in the form of quotation and paraphrase. Assess the credibility of the sources Cross has used. Are they convincing? Would the essay be equally effective if the author had not relied on sources but simply presented the information and instruction herself?

Is It Wrong to Cheat on Your Income Tax If Everyone Else Does?

Thomas Hurka

1   At income tax time, people across the country cheat. Not in a big way, perhaps, but in little things: they hide some income or claim meals with their friends as business expenses. They pay less than they should by the letter of the law.

2   There's some unfairness here. Many Canadians, especially low-income Canadians, can't cheat on taxes. Their incomes come entirely in wages reported on their T4 slips, and they aren't allowed any business deductions. But let's ignore this and assume that everyone has some latitude for cheating. If they all cheat, is it wrong for you to cheat?

3   One moral reason to pay taxes is to finance government programs that benefit everyone. But this can't be the decisive moral reason. You'd do even more good if you paid more than your legal share of taxes, yet not doing that isn't the same as cheating.

4   The main reason to pay is that it's the law, and there's a general obligation to obey the law. Sometimes this obligation makes no moral difference: you ought not to murder whether there's a law against it or not. But sometimes it tips the balance, making morally required what would otherwise be optional. So it seems to be with taxes. Without a tax law, paying would be nice; with a law, it's mandatory.

5   But what *is* the law about taxes? According to a theory called "legal realism," the law isn't just words on paper, it's a complex institution involving the police, courts, and prisons. The real law is only what this whole institution enforces.

6   On a city street the posted speed limit may be 50 kilometres an hour, but the police arrest only drivers going over 55. If so, legal realists say, the real speed limit is 55. If you drive 54 you aren't breaking the law, you're obeying it.

7   Tax law seems to work like traffic law. Revenue Canada goes after the big cheaters but lets the little stuff go. So is the little stuff really illegal? In her book *Behind Closed Doors*, Linda McQuaig reports that Mickey Cohen, architect of much tax law in the 1970s, believed in giving taxpayers "breathing space," so they could feel they'd "gotten away with a bit." If you do what the lawmakers want you to, how do you violate their rules?

8   Maybe legal realism is wrong and the law is just what's written on paper. Even so, we need to know who the obligation to obey the law is owed to and where it comes from.

9   The most sensible view is that the obligation is owed not to the government, but to your fellow citizens. They've restrained their self-interest by supporting a system that benefits everyone, including you, and it would be unfair if you didn't do the same. You do your share because they've done theirs.

10   But on income tax they haven't done their share, at least not entirely. Since they're all cheating, you can't owe it to them not to cheat. In fact, if you didn't cheat it would be you who was treated unfairly.

11   It's not that all cheating is okay. If there was a time when nobody cheated, the people who started cheating acted wrongly. The same goes for people

who, when others are cheating a little, cheat a lot. But if everyone cheats a little, no one violates an obligation.

12　　　Nor is the amount of cheating in Canada something to be pleased about. For one thing, it's not universal: those whose incomes are all in wages can't participate. (Should they get a special tax credit, as compensation?) And the practice has a built-in tendency to escalate. People who've cheated a little decide other people are cheating more and cheat more themselves, which causes other people to cheat more, and so on. The system can run out of control.

13　　　This is a reason to want Revenue Canada to crack down on cheating. If more people pay the full amount, we'll feel a stronger obligation to do the same. It's also a reason to hope this essay won't be read by someone in the middle of doing [a] tax return.

Thomas Hurka, "Is It Wrong to Cheat on Your Income Tax If Everyone Else Does?" from *Principles: Short Essays on Ethics* (Toronto: Harcourt Brace & Company, Canada, 1994), 109–111. This essay first appeared in *The Globe and Mail*. Copyright © Thomas Hurka. Reprinted by permission of the author.

1. One of the reasons the paragraphs in this piece are so short is that the author is developing a complex argument. Summarize each paragraph in a single sentence, then decide whether or not Hurka believes it is all right to cheat.
2. Explain how the theory of "legal realism" operates in other aspects of our lives, such as the legal smoking, drinking, or driving age; recreational drug use; prostitution; or petty theft.
3. Write an essay along the lines of "Is It Wrong" in which you consider the morality of cheating on tests.

The Dating Game
Merrill Markoe

1　　　The next century will be a time of many informational breakthroughs. Most notably, the battle between the sexes will take on a new complexion because it will be scientifically documented that men and women are completely different species of animals (not unlike, say, hyenas and pumas, although there will be a lot of heated arguments about who gets to be the pumas).

2　　　Once everyone accepts that we're speaking different languages, a computer system will be developed that allows instantaneous intersexual communication to occur. For the first time, certain simple but formerly bewildering transactions will become clear. At the end of an evening out, when the single man of the future says to his date, "I had a nice time. I'll call you" (I predict that men will still be using this line), the woman to whom he is speaking will immediately hear in her headset: "What he means is that while he thinks you are attractive, he's concerned that you already have expectations of him that he will never be able to meet. He's associating you with his needy, castrating mother because she had the same hair color as yours."

3   By this time, sex and dating will be so dangerous (owing to the numerous rampant communicable diseases and personality disorders) that they will be attempted only by the kind of thrill seekers who now do things like bungee jumping, sky surfing and eating at Denny's. By the year 2020, in fact, "casual dating" will be a popular arena sport. People too terrified to pursue something so hazardous themselves will witness actual live human beings who, for big money stakes, will eat dinner with and then perhaps (if dinner goes well) become intimate with people they are attracted to but basically know nothing about.

4   Because the average person will be far too cautious to risk even a single totally worthless encounter, we will see the transformation of the medical clinic into a kind of after-hours meeting place where nervous but lonely people will be able to undergo a battery of health tests and, while awaiting the results, stop by the bar to enjoy a trendy snack with others who may have the same ailment. (I predict that honey-roasted songbirds will be the snack of choice by then because they will turn out to be the last remaining edible creature that is domestically plentiful, low in fat and still has not been made into a trendy snack item.)

5   All of this escalating terror will, oddly, increase the number of marriages taking place, even though we will see the divorce rate rise from 1 in 2 marriages to 2 in 2. These alarming statistics will cause the birth of a new nuptial tradition. Savvy couples will create the most intimate bond two people can share by agreeing to get married and divorced simultaneously. At that point, they will possess so much file data about each other that they will negotiate in advance the terms of every day they plan to spend together, deciding what annoying habits they are willing to tolerate and, more important, what personal details each one will permit the other to use either in court or in the eventual tell-all book. "Looking at me cross-eyed" could emerge as the most common charge of misconduct in the personal nuisance suits that will clog the legal system.

6   Playing right into that will be the amount of specific evidence people will have accumulated about each other as "compulsive video documentation" becomes the most common new addiction. By the year 2010, TV networks will decide to give all video-equipment owners a shot at their own show as long as they promise to supply footage that is extremely disturbing. Recorded evidence of violence and malicious mayhem will draw such astronomical sums that criminals contemplating an illegal activity will consult with movie developers during the important planning stages of the crime. They will thus make sure that the approach they are taking with regard to plot and details is the one that will have the best eventual effect on sales figures and marketing potential.

7   The blurring of the line between life and entertainment will culminate in a scandal when a giant underground facility is discovered in the Midwest that is being used as a breeding lab by desperate talk-show producers who have been completely out of new guests since the mid-1990s. It will be discovered that the producers have been assembling affable humanoids from the fat, tissue, bone and spare parts of celebrities who have undergone a lot of plastic surgery, training the "guests" to cultivate zany or inappropriate hobbies and schooling them in how to tell 10 different 15-minute anecdotes about themselves. This will constitute their entire life-span, after which they will be melted down and reworked for an additional booking.

8   Yes, it's going to be a bold new world, full of brand new dysfunctions, addictions and disorders: a million new things to worry about! But that's progress.

———————

Merrill Markoe, "The Dating Game," as appearing in *Departures: A Reader for Developing Writers*, eds. Randall Popken, Alice Newsome, and Lanell Gonzales (Boston: Allyn and Bacon, 1995), 109–110. This article first appeared in *Time*, Fall 1992. Copyright © Time, Inc. Reprinted by permission of Time, Inc.

1. What is the subject of this essay? Is it really about what dating will be like in the future, or does it have a wider application to the present?
2. What is the tone of this essay? Identify four or five phrases that you think are good examples of the author's attitude toward her subject.
3. Find at least six examples of transitional words and phrases the author has used to ensure coherence in this essay.
4. Do men and women really have such desperate difficulty communicating with one another as the author suggests? Do people of the same sex understand one another better than members of the opposite sex? Use your personal observations and experiences to explain your opinion.

Canajun, Eh?

John Robert Colombo

1   Is there a distinctive Canadian humour? We could argue forever about the matter, but I believe that a humour that is distinctively Canadian does exist. There are four reasons for this belief.

2   But before I give my reasons, permit me to offer definitions of "Canadian" and "humour." For our purposes, it is easy to define a Canadian. Someone who lives in Canada is a Canadian. It's as simple as that. You might object that tens of thousands of people live in Canada who are not Canadian. You are right, of course, but most of these people are immigrants and refugees who are residing in the country while awaiting citizenship. There are also men and women, like diplomats and business people, who are temporary residents of Canada. They may not be Canadian citizens, and they may have no intention of applying for more than landed immigrant status, but they are more knowledgeable than many Canadians about federal and provincial laws and also sensitive to the national and local issues. What immigrants, refugees, diplomats, and business people have in common, then, is the fact that every day is a learning experience for them. They learn more and more about this country's culture. They share this process of continuous learning with the citizens around them. The ongoing process of learning about Canada is an important consideration when discussing the country's humour because humour reflects culture and makes fun of its characteristics.

3   If it is relatively easy to define a Canadian, it is difficult to define humour. Humour is what is funny. But what is funny? Humour is what people laugh at. But what do people laugh at? Comedy, parody, farce, caricature, slapstick, wit, satire, irony, gags, jokes ... these are but a few of the words used to distinguish types of humour. What they all have in common is that they tell us a truth or

two and they make us laugh a little or a lot. In other words, humour is an interpretation of life that makes us giggle or guffaw. Tragedy makes us cry; comedy
makes us laugh. Jokes make us wince. It was Stephen Leacock, our most
famous humorist, who called humour "the mingled heritage of tears and
laughter that is our lot on earth." He had in mind the fact that great humour
is more than gags and jokes because it reveals the state of our lives to ourselves. The revelation is full of surprises, and if we wince, we sometimes want
to cry. But mainly we smile ... grin and bear it!

4   Humour in Canada begins with the storytelling of the Native Peoples. Many
of the stories of the mischievous actions of the Raven and the Trickster and
Sedna the Sea Goddess are inherently improbable and hence funny. The tradition of funny stories continues with the "tall tales" told by our pioneer ancestors, including the absurd account of how Paul Bunyan and his blue ox, Babe,
created Niagara Falls and the Great Lakes. To the tall tale, T.C. Haliburton
added satire and social criticism in his "Sam Slick" stories. These stories are
based on the travels of a fictional Yankee trader who went around Nova Scotia
hoodwinking its inhabitants. After Judge Haliburton, there are so many
Canadian writers who have made good use of humour in their stories and
novels that it is impossible even to list them.

5   Perhaps the easiest way to isolate the characteristics that make our
humour quintessentially Canadian is to examine a series of jokes. For many
years, I have been collecting Canadian jokes. For me the word "jokes" includes
"anecdotes." The distinction is minor, yet interesting. A joke is a made-up
story about ordinary people, or, if it concerns a famous person, it is obviously
untrue. An anecdote is a story that may be true or false or a mixture of the
two, but is told about people who are known to us, either family members or
public figures. Using jokes and anecdotes for examples, I will illustrate some
of the characteristics of Canadian humour.

6   *Characteristic No. 1.* Canadian humour tells us about Canadian places. There
is a tiny town in Saskatchewan called Biggar. In the 1940s, someone with both
a sense of local pride and a sense of humour erected a sign outside the town.
It read as follows:

NEW YORK IS BIG

BUT THIS IS BIGGAR

That joke turns on a place name and a pun. It is justly famous.

7   The most widely told story about a Canadian place name is the one about
two English ladies who are crossing Canada by train. At a brief stop in
Saskatoon, the older turns to the younger and says, "I wonder where we are."

8   The younger replies, "I have no idea, but I will find out."

9   She steps onto the platform and spots the dispatcher. "Excuse me, could
you tell me where we are?"

10   "Saskatoon, Saskatchewan," he replies.

11   She boards the train and the older lady asks her, "Well, where are we?"

12   The younger one replies, "I still don't know. It's obvious they don't speak
English here."

That joke has been told and retold since the 1900s.

13   *Characteristic No. 2.* Canadian humour tells us about Canadian personalities.
Most public figures in this country are hockey players (like Wayne Gretzky),
politicians (like Brian Mulroney), and entertainers (like comedian Dave

Broadfoot). Innumerable jokes and anecdotes are told about public figures, especially politicians. But in my opinion more jokes have been told about Joe Clark than about any other federal or provincial politician. The Rt. Hon. Joe Clark served as Prime Minister of Canada in 1978–80, and immediately became the object of jest and ridicule. Here are two of the anti-Joe Clark jokes:

Question: What were Joe Clark's three hardest years?

Answer: Grade 1.

Question: Is Joe Clark bilingual?

Answer: Yes, but mostly in English.

The jokes are unfair to Mr. Clark, and one of them that I am not retelling here even refers to him as "Joke Clark," but nobody ever said jokes have to be fair.

14   *Characteristic No. 3.* A Canadian joke tells us about a Canadian subject. Countless jokes and anecdotes are told about federal government policies (official bilingualism), social programs (safety net, medicare), and national institutions (the monarchy, Air Canada, the House of Commons, the beaver, the Maple Leaf).

15   Official bilingualism has been the subject of hundreds of jokes and anecdotes. Here is one of the most loved of these jokes.

16   During the 1970s, a young man was hired as the lifeguard at the pool at the Prime Minister's residence at 24 Sussex Drive. The Trudeau family was making use of the pool when one of the three boys encountered some difficulty and cried for help. The lifeguard ignored the cries, so Trudeau himself had to plunge into the pool and rescue his son.

17   Afterwards Trudeau grilled the lifeguard. "You ass! Didn't you see that my son was in trouble?"

18   "Yes, sir, but I can't swim."

19   "How the hell did you land the job of lifeguard, then?"

20   "I'm bilingual."

21   If I had more space, I would retell jokes and anecdotes about beavers and maple leafs and even about Newfoundlanders. I should note that the latter subject is a touchy one. Folklorists make a point of studying "numbskull" stories, that is, jokes that are told at the expense of stupid or ignorant people. Numbskull stories are told about minorities all around the world. For instance, in Bulgaria, numbskull stories are told about the inhabitants of the town of Gabrovo. In Canada, such stories are directed against the Newfies, and in Quebec against inhabitants of that province's Beauce region. In public, Newfoundlanders object to Newfie stories, but it is a curious fact that the best ones are told on the Great Island, and that Bob Tulk, a Newfoundlander, has published a series of best-selling collections of Newfie jokes. My feeling has always been that such stories reveal the foolishness inside each one of us, not the fools who may or may not live somewhere else.

22   *Characteristic No. 4.* Finally, a Canadian joke is a joke that is funny only to a Canadian. This is a generalization and it may not be literally true. If you tell an American or a Britisher a joke about official bilingualism, he may laugh, but he will not laugh as hard as a Canadian who knows only too well what is overstatement and what is understatement. Similarly, a joke told about Prime Minister Jean Chrétien is going to be a lot different from a joke told about President Bill Clinton or Prime Minister John Major. They may all be funny, but to a Canadian the Chrétien joke will "hit home" in a way the others will not.

23   Here is a joke about the War of 1812 that means a lot in Canada and nothing at all anywhere else.

24   The primary-school teacher was telling her pupils how Laura Secord bravely made her way through the woods at night to warn the British troops of the planned American attack. Her little charges were thrilled to learn about Mrs. Secord's bravery, as they had never before heard about this episode in the War of 1812.

25   "Now," asked the teacher, "what would have happened had Mrs. Secord not succeeded in warning the British?"

26   One little fellow shot up his hand in answer. "If she hadn't made the trek, we'd be eating Martha Washington chocolates today."
We appreciate that joke because we know that Americans buy Martha Washington chocolates (named after the wife of U.S. President George Washington), whereas we buy Laura Secord chocolates (which bear the name of the heroine of the War of 1812).

27   The four characteristics mentioned above are found in Canadian jokes but are not limited to them. They are features of Canadian humour generally, whether it is verbal or visual. The same features are found in a skit performed by the Royal Canadian Air Farce, a takeoff presented by the Second City or Codco, a monologue on Sergeant Renfrew of the Mounties delivered by Dave Broadfoot, a talk performed by Don Harron impersonating a Parry Sound hayseed named Charlie Farquharson, a concert of Nancy White's political songs, a political cartoon drawn by Aislin for the *Montreal Gazette*, a column written by Eric Nicol in the *Vancouver Province*, a motion picture set on Cape Breton Island like *Margaret's Museum*, a book of sketches like Stephen Leacock's *Sunshine Sketches of a Little Town* which is based in Orillia, or a novel like Mordecai Richler's *The Incomparable Atuk* which is set in the Arctic and in Toronto.

28   What all of these performers, artists, and writers have in common is that they make fun of Canadian places, personalities, and subjects, especially those that are known only to their fellow Canadians. Yet I have the feeling that they share something else, something that has yet to be mentioned. Indeed, there is a fifth characteristic of Canadian humour.

29   The fifth characteristic is the character and personality of the Canadian people, in the past as well as in the present. That feature is a sense of reserve that is so extreme that Canadians find themselves harbouring reservations about everything under the sun. We add "eh?" to what we say. Most Torontonians express embarrassment in the presence of tourists who show they are excited about the fact that the CN Tower is the world's tallest or that Yonge Street is the world's longest designated street. Canadians shrug their shoulders when a visitor mentions how wonderful it must be to live near Niagara Falls or the Rocky Mountains, or how satisfying it is to inhabit the world's "second-largest country." Canadians seldom boast; Canadians are uneasy in the company of boasters. We are even embarrassed by our own accomplishments.

30   This reserve, restraint, or reticence — call it what you will — is the cornerstone of the national character. It is also a characteristic of the humour of Canadians. Our national reserve caught the attention of Jan Morris, the Anglo-Welsh travel writer. Morris so enjoyed Canada that she devoted an entire book to the country. It is called *City to City*, and in it she makes the following observation about the spirit of Canada: "The genius of Canada remains essentially a deflationary genius."

31   According to Morris, not only do we belittle ourselves and our accomplishments, we have a positive genius for it! We hate to adopt extreme measures, and we avoid taking sides on issues. This characteristic is well illustrated in a popular "chicken/road" joke:
       Question: Why did the Canadian chicken cross the road?
       Answer: To get to the middle.
    Our "deflationary genius" may not be much, but it is something that we can call our own! It is an essential characteristic of our personalities and of our humour and our jokes.

32   The next time you hear a Canadian joke, listen for one or more of the four essential characteristics, not to mention the fifth characteristic, our "deflationary genius."

---

1. This essay is developed primarily according to the principles of division (see Chapter 17). What characteristics of Canadian humour does the author identify?
2. Where in the essay does the author state his thesis?
3. Find at least four definition statements in this essay. Why is the author so careful to define his terms before he offers examples of them?
4. How does the chicken/road joke exemplify the distinctive Canadian character?
5. Think of a Canadian joke that is not mentioned in the essay and analyze it in terms of the five characteristics the author has identified as being typical of Canadian humour.
6. Do you know a typical joke from some other country or region of the world? What does this joke reveal about the humour of the people who live there?

Light

Bruce Rolston

1   Much of the history of progress can be seen as the growing control of light by humanity: from the introduction of artificial illumination that pushed back the boundaries of night and made modern life possible to the development of photographic film and television and the expansion of the shared cultural experiences they allowed.

2   Today we continue to improve upon our mastery of light. Running through fibre-optic cable it provides super-efficient transmission of information; concentrated into a laser beam, it can perform delicate surgery or read information of another kind off a compact disc or a supermarket bar code.

3   But a growing number of physicists and engineers believe the potential of light is just beginning to be tapped. If they are right, we may be only decades away from being able to manipulate beams of light as easily as we now do

electric current. The 21st century could see an optically based technological revolution as breathtaking as the electronic-computer revolution of today.

4   One of the leading theorists of the new optics is Professor Sajeev John, a quantum theorist at the University of Toronto. At the remarkably young age of 39 he is already one of the big names in the growing field of quantum optics or "photonics" — the manipulation of light at the sub-microscopic level.

5   A professor's son from London, Ont., John dreamed of making substances that could store light permanently the way a battery stores electricity. "It started out fairly innocently," he says. "I wanted to create a structure to make light stand still." It was a vision that he would keep at the back of his mind through his undergraduate studies at MIT and graduate studies at Harvard. Then in 1989 he returned to Canada to U of T and his first love: light localization.

6   To understand what John is going into, one must know a little about what it could replace. In essence the entire electronic and computer revolution we are now living in is based on the development of materials known as semiconductors: substances that act like a tap on the flow of electricity, turning it on and off. Efficient semiconductors have reduced electric switches to a minuscule size: first in the transistor, next the integrated circuit and now progressively faster generations of computer chips, each one a collection of millions of tiny switches turning on and off as the chip processes information.

7   But while electricity can now be manipulated literally on the head of a pin, the manipulation of light remains largely a matter of classical optics, of mirrors and prisms — the vacuum tubes of light engineering. While an excellent medium for data storage and long-range transmission, light is still difficult to manipulate.

8   That's unfortunate because the qualities that make light attractive are equally useful on any scale. Electrons, the charged particles that make up electric current, experience resistance: the feature that makes electric current slow and fade as it runs through wire. Photons, individual particles of light, do not. As a result most long-distance cabling is being converted to photon — using fibre optics.

9   Fibre optics also takes advantage of light's other big plus: it can transmit more information in less time. Because of their electric charge, electrons tend to interfere with each other and so have to be comparatively widely separated. Photons, massless and chargeless, can run side by side and just sail by, each delivering its own information.

10   These days science is finding itself closing in on the limits of the electronic semiconductor. The interference of electrons dictates that the computer chip in its current form can only be made so small and so fast. Electrons just won't work on the scale computer theorists are now contemplating: if the chips are made much smaller the pathways would be too narrow for the electrons to stay safely away from each other. It's a limitation that threatens to bring the whole computer revolution to a crashing halt.

11   Photons don't have that problem, but there's no way now to manipulate them once they've come from the cable or off the disc. They must still be converted into electricity to be used in your phone, computer or fax

machine. It's comparable to jet travel. That 747 may get you to your destination quickly and easily but once you land at the airport, you still need to switch to some form of ground transportation to get you to your hotel or your meeting or your visit with Gran.

12   John's work goes a long way to solving that problem. He and his colleagues have developed a new class of materials called "photonic band gap" materials, made by etching submicroscopic lattice works in crystal.

13   In electronics semiconductors are basically crystals in one of two states: various versions of "on" and "off." They either conduct electricity beautifully or don't conduct it at all. There's no grey area. In semiconductive materials like silicon, electrons simply can't possess an energy level between the two extremes. This phenomenon is called a band gap. Slight influences, like heat or electric flow, can switch the crystal's electrons from one side of the band gap to the other, making it an effective electronic switch.

14   What John has done is design crystals that exhibit a band gap for photons. By sculpting the structure to his specifications, a crystal from which light will escape only in the frequencies it's designed to leave in will be created. It's the first step towards an incredibly small photonic switch. In theory switches made of such a photonic semiconductor could reach speeds hundreds of times faster than a circuit on the fastest electronic computer chip, turning on and off over a trillion times every second.

15   "There are many things optics do that electronics just can't do," he says. "Today if you want to send and receive a file of one megabyte over a computer, it takes some time. A completely optical system could send many thousands of megabytes in a matter of seconds."

16   In a computer light could be used all the way from disc to chip: it would be a 747 that could drop you off at home and do your shopping, too.

17   The technology also holds out hope for another great tool of our times: the laser. Lasers that increase the power and efficiency of light energy by releasing all their photons on the same frequency could have their efficiency increased by several orders of magnitude through the use of the new materials. Where in the past laser designers used such techniques as semipermeable mirrors to concentrate the light emitted on just one frequency, filters made from the new materials could perform the same task as efficiently as an ant-sized semiconductor now converts alternating current to direct. Making lasers a thousand times more efficient could open up a whole new sphere: lasers used for microscopic tasks, running on minuscule amounts of energy.

18   If microlasers and a computer revolution sound exciting, remember they could just be the beginning. For the new materials also offer a possible path to what is fast becoming the moon shot of computing: the quantum computer — so small that each switch is an individual atom.

19   It's an idea that has only been talked about. Make the switches atom-sized and you can make computers so powerful that tasks now considered impossible would become easy: the instant factoring of huge numbers is a commonly cited example. Problems that would take the smallest, most efficient electronic computer an unimaginable length of time could be accomplished in a matter of hours.

20   [The] trouble is, until now no one knew how to do it. Packs of lasers have been used to isolate and manipulate individual atoms, removing electrons and putting them back (turning the atom "on" and "off"), but electrically charged particles are proving not to have the permanency needed for a quantum computer to work. Electrons do the unpredictable, often changing their orbit around an atom spontaneously. On the vastly large scale of a computer chip with millions of atoms making up one switch, one electron's eccentricities don't matter. But on the phenomenally small scale theorists are dreaming of now, it would be like creating a light switch that would occasionally just turn off on its own. Not much of a building block.

21   But maybe not with John's photonic band-gap materials. In them it becomes possible to "bind" a photon to an atom, similar to an orbiting electron being bound by its electric charge, effectively preventing the photon from wandering away from its atom. A power source like a laser could then be used to bind or unbind the atom and because the photon has no mass and no charge, it would be far less likely to alter its behavior. Once on the single-atom switch would stay on. Add together a number of such atoms, each containing one piece of binary information (a "bit") and you have the beginnings of a quantum computer.

22   It's still all theoretical; but MIT physicist Seth Lloyd, who was the first to envision what a quantum computer would look like, considers the angle promising. "If they can pull it off, even to a limited extent, it would be an important result. Systems like photonic band-gap crystals [would be] revealed to be not just examples of a curious quantum effect but useful quantum logic devices."

23   It's this kind of far-reaching outlook that John shares. Part of what is driving him is the fact that nobody can fully predict where this line of inquiry is leading. To him it's the epitome of what working in science is all about.

24   "You go through all this education and you think you know a lot. And then you come up with something that totally baffles you and you realize you really don't know much after all. And then you struggle with it and after a while something clicks and then you realize you've entered some completely new territory. You're an explorer. You've come across a field or a lake that no one else has touched. That's the most exhilarating feeling. But then you're sort of like a blind man. You don't know where the paths are. Nothing is paved or anything like that."

25   Not everyone has always believed John was onto something. His theories about photons have already been pronounced dead once, by a prominent science magazine in 1989, before the first successful microwave experiments vindicated his theories. Now he refuses to countenance pessimism of any kind. "When there are people that say something can't be done, and there are a lot of them, I'm always very sceptical," he says, smiling. "They're generally proven wrong."

Bruce Rolston, excerpts from "Light," *University of Toronto Magazine*, Autumn 1996, 20–22. Reprinted by permission of the University of Toronto Magazine.

1. Using information taken from this essay, compare and contrast the electron and the photon.

2. This essay was written for a general (non-technical) audience. Does it succeed in explaining a complex technology simply enough for a general reader? What techniques does the author use to help make his subject accessible?

3. Identify five examples of the author's use of simile. How do these comparisons help the reader understand the information the author is presenting?

4. The semiconductor, which makes computer chips possible, is just over 25 years old. Given the information contained in "Light," predict what computers may look like and be able to do 25 years from now.

The Joy of Car Wrecks, or Beast-Slayer Meets Highway 401

Michael Park

1   My friend Greg from Calgary is tough. Every fall during hunting season, he hikes off by himself deep into the Rocky Mountains to shoot whatever large mammal the Alberta government has licensed him to "harvest" that year. It's cold and dangerous work. He's been caught in a blizzard high above the tree line with only the eviscerated corpse of a freshly-killed big-horn mountain sheep for company. He's shared trails — and the contents of his pack — with prime specimens of *ursus horribilis*, the fearsome grizzly bear. He's traumatized family and friends by staying out days longer than planned, in vile weather and rough country, only to show up exhausted and grinning with a dead beast on his back whose lolling head soon joins the glass-eyed menagerie hanging on the walls of the grisly mausoleum he calls his den.

2   Heights and speed don't faze Greg. He had spinal fusion surgery a few years ago (humping all that dead meat out of the wilderness did him in, I expect), yet every winter, he still flings himself down the nearly-vertical walls of snow, ice and rock that comprise the double-black-diamond ski runs of his favorite Rocky Mountain resorts. Most of us eastern Canadian lowlanders swoon with vertigo merely contemplating these suicidal drops, yet they aren't "challenging" enough for Greg. For kicks of a voltage high enough to turn his crank, he "heli-skis" and "cat-skis" in remote, avalanche-prone bowls of powder snow that are hours away from roads or hospitals or help of any kind.

3   My friend also has the courage of his convictions. During our last federal election, living as he does deep in the fed-bashing heartland of Preston Manning's neo-conservative Reform Party, Greg voted Liberal ... and told his Preston-loving friends and work colleagues what he'd done.

4   Like I said, Greg is tough. But all of his abundant physical and moral courage wasn't sufficient to armour him against the paralyzing bout of raw terror that unmanned him on his first trip east to Toronto. Life in rugged, self-reliant, friendly Alberta hadn't prepared Greg for the savagery of Toronto-area driving.

5   It was a family wedding that drew him to the Big Smoke. A distant relative picked him up at Pearson Airport and drove him via Oakville to Hamilton, the scene of the nuptials. It was this car trip — for us locals, a routine, unremarkable

excursion down our 400-series expressways and the Queen Elizabeth Way —
that left him twitching and flinching in the passenger seat, checking and
readjusting his seatbelt, his endocrine system buzzing in fight-or-flight over-
load, blood-spattered visions of every creature he'd ever killed dancing in his
head. What Greg was experiencing was a new sensation for him: physical fear.
For an hour or so, he was convinced that he was about to die in a flaming car
wreck.

6   "You guys drive like freaking idiots!" was what he told me later — only he
didn't say "freaking."

7   Months afterward, I heard him describe this trip to his buddies back in
Calgary. It wasn't an appealing portrait. According to Greg, Torontonians tail-
gate constantly on our freeways. We leave no more than a yard or two
between bumpers — less during rush hours — and we do so at appalling
rates of speed. Even vehicles in our slow lanes go 130 klicks an hour. Turn signals? We never touch the things, except for the radically-polarized minority
who leave their left- or right-turn flashers on perpetually as a symbol of their
political allegiance. And we steer with our knees: one hand is occupied holding our cell phones to our faces while the other is busy gesticulating wildly
at whomever we're talking to on the phone as we drive.

8   Greg claims that many of us Torontonians are afflicted with an uncontrol-
lable central nervous system disorder that causes us to suddenly brake or
accelerate violently and veer from lane to lane, regardless of whether the
space we're entering is occupied by another vehicle. Ontario truckers seem
to be prime carriers of the virus responsible for this condition. The afflicted
are easy to spot from a distance: they drive as if they have no brakes, flashing
high-beams and blaring horns at all who dare to impede their progress,
chugging coffee and flipping the Trudeau salute as they blast on by. The
highway police? Their cruisers were the fastest speeders he saw. According
to Greg, the fact that there aren't hundreds of commuters killed and maimed
on Toronto's highways every day proves the existence of a benevolent and
forgiving God.

9   Greg's western friends, sheltered and unworldly as they are, were skepti-
cal about the details of the apocalyptic highway culture he'd ascribed to people in my more degenerate part of the world. "Is this dork here telling the
truth?" one dubious ingenue asked me.

10   "Absolutely," I replied. I told them about the 401 drivers I'd seen on my
daily trips to work who were reading road maps or the *Toronto Sun* as they
changed lanes; the driver going 140 while eating a salad from a bowl with a
fork (another "knee-steerer," in Greg's lexicon); the drivers who suddenly and
without warning cut across three lanes of traffic, screech to a stop and back
up on the narrow shoulders of car-choked throughways because they missed
their exit; the gravel-, garbage- and tire-spewing trucks; the stop-and-go
summertime traffic jams with the horn-honkers and fist-shakers who get out
of their gridlocked cars and slug each other, unable to cope with the frustration of the endless construction bottlenecks....

11   There was a respectful silence, then someone asked, "Why do they do it,
drive like that?"

12   I had to confess that I had no idea why people from my part of the country routinely take such dreadful risks to life and property on our daily com-

mutes. Something in our Lake Ontario water, toxic seepage from Love Canal, perhaps? Too many rats in the box? The spirit of downsizing and deregulation made flesh?

13   I had no answer, so I glibly suggested that such irrational behavior was probably in our nature, just as wandering in the mountains in late fall and shooting innocent wildlife was in theirs — a genetically-programmed regional absurdity. In other words, we're all just freaking idiots.

14   I didn't have a better answer until recently, when *The Globe and Mail*, the font of all true wisdom in Canada, offered me two more intriguing explanations for our self-destructive driving habits: sex and money.

15   In a review of David Cronenberg's latest film *Crash*, I read that it is the *auteur's* thesis that for some people, car wrecks are sexually stimulating, that there are people living in our post-modern urban ruins whose lives are so devoid of pleasure and joy that they drive around looking to plow their vehicles into others so that they can achieve orgasm. That explains it: all those speeding wackos who regularly cut me off on the 401 or run red lights in Scarborough are simply lost souls in heat, wannabe rutters looking for the release that only squealing rubber, twisted metal and gushing blood can give them.

16   Another, more plausible, possibility is that vast numbers of my fellow Torontonians have cottoned on to a get-rich-quick scheme that the *Globe* exposed: pack some well-insured friends into a couple of well-insured old Pontiac 6000 beaters and stage a collision on the public roads somewhere. Find a malleable quack who'll certify that you've all suffered debilitating spinal injuries and pool the buckets of loot that the insurance companies then shower upon you. According to the experts consulted by the *Globe*, this is a widely-practiced scam that is growing in popularity. Even on our high-speed expressways, apparently.

17   So maybe that's why we Torontonians drive the way we do. And, faced with the choice between love and money, I'd bet on money.

Michael Park, "The Joy of Car Wrecks, or Beast-Slayer Meets Highway 401," 1996. Reprinted by permission of the author.

1. Look up the meanings of the words "irony" and "hyperbole." Do they apply to this essay? Where?
2. Why does the author devote the first part of this essay to his friend Greg's hunting, skiing, and voting behaviour? What function does the character Greg serve in this essay?
3. What is the purpose of this essay? To illuminate the differences between the lives of the author and his friend? To condemn Alberta's hunters and Ontario's drivers? Or does the writer have a broader purpose in mind?
4. What is the author's attitude toward hunting? What evidence can you find in the essay to support your position?
5. Does the author really believe that sex and money are the keys to understanding Torontonians' driving behaviour? Why does he suggest that they are?

A Smoky Lament for a Father
Tony Wilson

1   As my father and I sit down to lunch at a restaurant near the sea, the unmistakable odour of cigarettes begins to overpower both the aroma of my food and the smell of the ocean. I'm reminded of how he compelled me, as a 12-year-old boy desperately trying to hold back tears, not to smoke again. With a voice that often thundered in anger like a 747 in take-off mode, he threatened me with the back side of his hand if he ever caught me with another cigarette. Cigarette smoking, he claimed, led teen-agers down the slippery slope of drugs, crime, and of all things, venereal disease. Not wishing to test either his theory or his hand, I never smoked again.

2   He, however, never quit, and as we speak about the inoperable lung cancer that will soon kill him, I feel like that 12-year-old boy again, desperately trying to hold back the tears.

3   The diagnosis is only days old and carries with it an air of urgency. He will be lucky if he lives until Christmas. I have come to his town for the weekend to spend some long-overdue time with him, and to help him deal with the doctors' reports. It occurs to me that although we speak on the phone once a week, we haven't actually seen each other face to face for many months, and the telephone has hidden the swift progression of the disease. His body is frail and gaunt: his breath is short. The man who used to march around our house to the music of the Royal Scots Guards now takes cautious, gingerly steps as if the pavement or the floor were a sheet of ice. The fire in his belly is gone, replaced by ash in his lungs. The voice that used to roar like a jet engine is soft and high, like an old woman's — the result of one of the tumours. The hand that I used to fear (more in theory than in practice) is bony; the skin hanging badly like a suit a size too large. He claims to have lost 40 pounds in the last six weeks and is still not hungry.

4   He does, however, want a cigarette.

5   My father has smoked at least 20 cigarettes a day (and perhaps more) since he started the habit in 1940 at the age of 13. The first medical links between cigarettes and lung cancer published in the 1960s didn't stop him from smoking, nor did the advertising bans and the price increases of the 1970s and 1980s. Nor, for that matter, have the various and sundry death threats now engraved on each package. Nor has terminal lung cancer caused by smoking compelled him to stop smoking. For 56 years, he has been addicted to tobacco and, to my sorrow, it appears that only death will stop him. Yes, he admits (with just a touch of gallows humour), lung cancer will inevitably force him to quit, but he will smoke until his last gasp.

6   The four words embossed in black and white on the package in his hand are easy enough to read, even from across the table: "Smoking Causes Lung Cancer." But my shock and despair play tricks with my mind. Like letters moving on a Scrabble board, the prophecy on the package rearranges itself and reads, "He was warned, wasn't he?" What kind of warning would compel someone to stop smoking, I wondered. "Your grandchildren will not remember you?" "This will be your last sunny September?" "Your last days will be painful?"

7   As my mind rearranges the letters back to their original positions, smoke from his cigarette drifts toward me and takes strange shapes, like clouds moving in the sky. For an instant, I envision the emaciated figure from Edvard Munch's painting *The Scream*, screeching like a siren to everyone in the room, louder than he once did to me: "He Is Dying. Look What This Did To Him." But no one sees and no one hears, and when my father begins to speak again, the apparition is blown back into the stale air, to rest on the clothes of the other patrons, or to be inhaled by both the smokers and non-smokers in the room, oblivious to the overworking of my imagination.

8   No doubt to the tobacco industry, he has been a customer "to die for," giving his very life to the product the industry so masterfully sells; a proud tribute to his constitutional right to choose. He chose menthol. Of course, these days, the industry is more concerned with advertising cultural events and fighting lawsuits than thanking its dying customers for their lifelong patronage. And to the restaurant industry, he is one more reason why there are still smoking sections in restaurants. That is, of course, until he dies and abruptly becomes one fewer reason. To the medical establishment, he will become another death directly attributable to cigarette smoking, and for whose palliative care the taxpayer (not the tobacco industry) will pay. And to me, he is the father who, by the sheer force of his own will, prevented me from smoking, but who couldn't will himself to stop.

9   So, in the company of smouldering ash and dark beer, we must grimly discuss the reality of life's end, and plan for the next few months of my life, and the last few months of his. We speak of fortunes made and fortunes lost, the city he helped to build, the streets of London, the lakes of Switzerland, the things that made his life enjoyable. Inevitably, the topic turns to wills, executors and funerals. Yet, as words become difficult for me, he is surprisingly chatty, and speaks of his demise as if I am trimming his hair.

10   But I am thankful to have even these morbid moments with him, knowing that there will be little but memories in eight months, nothing but pain in two. Some people don't get a chance to tell their fathers or mothers how much they love them. When death unexpectedly comes, so much that could have been said can never be said. In my father's case, I am getting my chance to say it all.

11   As we leave the restaurant, the patrons at the next table, cigarettes dangling from their lips, continue to puff away, oblivious to my father's obvious illness. Their fathers probably didn't give them the tongue lashing I once received. Perhaps in years to come, their adult children will have to speak to their fathers over smouldering ash and doctors' reports as I have just spoken to mine.

12   A newspaper lies discarded nearby displaying the headline "President Declares Nicotine a Drug," and the two of us open the door into the fresh air of the afternoon, and start to cry.

Tony Wilson is a Vancouver lawyer and writer. His father, Victor Wilson, died in Victoria on November 12, 1996. This essay appeared in *The Globe and Mail*, November 18, 1996, A14. Reprinted by permission of the author.

1. This essay contains some very powerful description. Find six or seven descriptive phrases that you think are particularly effective.

2. Paragraph 3 is based on a contrast. What specific points does Wilson select to show the reader the difference between the way his father is now and the way he was when the author was growing up?

3. What sort of introductory strategy does the author use? Is it effective?

4. In paragraph 8, the author identifies some of the different roles his father has played in relation to organizations and institutions with which he has come into contact because of his smoking. For example, to the tobacco industry, he has been an excellent customer; to the medical authorities, he is a statistic. List the roles the author identifies, then identify ten additional roles his father has played and will play on his death in relation to organizations, agencies, businesses, and individuals.

5. How does the author convey to the reader the mixture of sorrow, love, and anger he feels toward his father? Identify two or three passages that you think are most effective in communicating the author's conflicting emotions. What one sentence or passage do you think hits home the hardest?

6. According to the author, health warnings cannot stop people from smoking, nor can price increases, nor even lung cancer. If you have stopped smoking or know someone who has, write a short essay explaining how the addiction to tobacco can be overcome successfully.

7. According to arts and sports organizations across Canada, if tobacco companies are prevented from sponsoring cultural and athletic events, these events will not survive. They argue that printing the brand names of cigarettes on theatre programs or race cars or sports arenas does not constitute advertising and should continue to be permitted. Do you agree? You might want to research both sides of this issue and consult the federal laws restricting tobacco sponsorships.

Index

Reader Reply Card

We are interested in your reaction to *Essay Essentials with Readings*, by Sarah Norton and Brian Green. You can help us to improve this book in future editions by completing this questionnaire.

1. What was your reason for using this book?
    - ❏ university course
    - ❏ continuing-education course
    - ❏ professional development
    - ❏ college course
    - ❏ personal interest
    - ❏ other (please specify)

2. If you are a student, please identify your school and the course in which you used this book.

3. Which chapters or parts of this book did you use? Which did you omit?

4. What did you like best about this book? What did you like least?

5. Please identify any topics you think should be added to future editions.

6. Please add any comments or suggestions.

7. Please give your reaction to the essays listed by title and author in order of their appearance in the book, rating each essay from 1 (liked least) to 5 (liked best).

Title/Author	Rating	Didn't Read
Heavenly Hostesses (Visser)	_____	_____
All Quiet on the... (Park)	_____	_____
Eat Your Hearts Out... (Cuff)	_____	_____
Human Hibernation (Hasselstrom)	_____	_____
The View from Italy... (Sileika)	_____	_____
Speak for Yourself (Cross)	_____	_____
Is it Wrong to Cheat...? (Hurka)	_____	_____
The Dating Game (Markoe)	_____	_____
Canajun, Eh? (Colombo)	_____	_____
Light (Rolston)	_____	_____
The Joy of Car Wrecks... (Park)	_____	_____
A Smoky Lament... (Wilson)	_____	_____

i

(fold here and tape shut)

MAIL ≫POSTE

Canada Post Corporation / Société canadienne des postes

Postage paid
If mailed in Canada

Port payé
si posté au Canada

**Business
Reply**

**Réponse
d'affaires**

0116870399   01

0116870399-M8Z4X6-BR01

Heather McWhinney
Director of Product Development
HARCOURT BRACE & COMPANY, CANADA
55 HORNER AVENUE
TORONTO, ONTARIO
M8Z 9Z9